WESTPORT
CONNECTICUT

The Minuteman

WESTPORT
CONNECTICUT

*The Story of a New England Town's
Rise to Prominence*

WOODY KLEIN

Foreword by Joanne Woodward

Sponsored by the
Westport Historical Society
Westport, Connecticut

GREENWOOD PRESS

Westport, Connecticut • London

Library of Congress Cataloging-in-Publication Data

Klein, Woody, 1929-
   Westport, Connecticut: the story of a New England town's rise to prominence / Woody
   Klein; foreword by Joanne Woodward.
        p. cm.
   "Sponsored by the Westport Historical Society, Westport, Connecticut."
   Includes bibliographical references and index.
   ISBN 0-313-31126-9 (alk. paper)
   1. Westport (Conn.)—History. I. Title.

   F104.W39 K58 2000
   974.6'9—dc21
                                                                              00-023143
British Library Cataloguing in Publication Data is available.

Library of Congress Catalog Card Number: 00-023143
ISBN: 0-313-31126-9

First published in 2000

Greenwood Press, 88 Post Road West, Westport, CT 06881
An imprint of Greenwood Publishing Group, Inc.
www.greenwood.com

Printed in the United States of America

The paper used in this book complies with the
Permanent Paper Standard issued by the National
Information Standards Organization (Z39.48-1984).

10 9 8 7 6 5 4 3 2 1

Cover and book design: Miggs Burroughs
Frontispiece: the Minuteman statue, illustration by Kassie Foss

Every reasonable effort has been made to trace the owners of copyright materials in this
book, but in some instances this has proven impossible. The author and publisher will be
glad to receive information leading to more complete acknowledgments in subsequent print-
ings of the book and in the meantime extend their apologies for any omissions. Photos from
the Westport Public Library came from various public domain sources and were provided as
a courtesy to the author.

To the people of Westport,
past, present and future

Town Seal:

This is a view of the village of Saugatuck named
Westport in 1835. The view looks west toward
Norwalk. On the far side of the bridge is Riverside
Avenue. Right foreground is the site of the old library.
The seal was drawn by John Warner Barber.

Jacket cover: Westport then, and now.

CONTENTS

Contents page photo: National Hall by Andrea Fine

FOREWORD

My mother loved old houses and antiques, and I inherited my appreciation for things historic from her. My earliest memories are of visiting my great-aunt in her marvelous old Victorian house in Marietta, Georgia, playing in her attic, curling up on a wicker chair, and having lemonade on the big wide porch. I guess my curiosity about history started there. It's like eating peanuts, the more you learn, the more you want to learn. Westport has struck a deep chord for me, I think, because the crosscurrents of the town's history are subtle and timeless and reverberate in the mind. Westport is as Yankee as Georgia is Southern, but both have a diverse population symbolizing deep-set values, both have a sense of being part of the river of history. The history here fascinates because its pre-Revolutionary roots and Yankee ways make you wonder just what in its past allowed it to develop into a town that is so much more "democratic" than many of its New England neighbors.

Westport's roots can be traced back to the days when a dissident group of the original Massachusetts Bay Colony, led by the Reverend Thomas Hooker, ventured south to seek freedom of expression and independence for themselves and their families. Their victory in the Swamp War in 1637 against the Pequot Indians opened up the territory for colonization. The early colonists founded Fairfield in 1639, but a group known as the Bankside Farmers continuing the tradition of independence broke away and formed their own community in Green's Farms. In those early times, the seeds of democracy were planted in the form of the church and the parish. In 1835, striking another blow for freedom, the descendants of some of the early settlers petitioned the legislature in Hartford to incorporate a new town, comprised of parts of Fairfield, Westport, and Norwalk, to be known as Westport.

Since those days, Westport has been the destination for those who want to freely express themselves, live in relative privacy, and yet be part of a vital community, as well as for those who want to work and travel elsewhere but always return to an attractive home base where they can feel safe, secure, and accepted.

The one common characteristic that Westporters from all walks of life share is love of community — a special sense of place. Westport is a place where the rich and the famous live side by side with descendants of the original Yankee farmers — a real patchwork quilt of people. It is eclectic and cosmopolitan; it has unusual beauty, but it is still a small New England town. Settled by farmers and fishermen, diversified by immigrants from many countries, developed by tradesmen and professionals in all fields, enriched by artists, actors, writers and celebrities from around the nation and the world, Westport has become a mecca for those who are traditionally untraditional.

Woody Klein has done a remarkable job of telling the story of Westport's modest beginning, of the people who have lived here, and of how it came to be an internationally celebrated town with a healthy social conscience.

Joanne Woodward
Westport, Connecticut
January, 2000

Foreword page photo: Rippe's Farm, Westport News

PREFACE

*There is no subject, perhaps, to which a mind given to
reflection, more frequently turns, than to the history of the
generations which have preceded us.*

> —The Reverend Thomas Davies,
> Congregational Society of
> Green's Farms, 1839

During the past two and a half years, I have been on a most rewarding and meaningful journey. Although Westport has been my home for only 33 years, I now feel that I have been here from the beginning, not just from the town's official birth on May 28, 1835, but from the moment our forefathers first laid eyes on this beautiful place. Indeed, as a result of my exploration of this town's event-filled past, I feel that my roots have been transplanted to Westport. The quality of life we enjoy in Westport today is a direct reflection of the actions of all those who have come before us. This personal realization has made me feel deeply connected with Westport; it is, in a word, my *home* in every sense.

There is a brief passage in Thornton Wilder's classic, the 1938 Pulitzer Prize-winning play, *Our Town*, spoken by the stage manager in the play, the guide who takes us through the journey of life in the mythical town of Grover's Corners, New Hampshire: "So—people a thousand years from now—

this is the way we were in the provinces north of New York City at the beginning of the twentieth century. This is the way we were in our growing up and our marrying and in our living and in our dying." In a similar manner, I have tried to take the reader through the journey of life in Westport and to describe the way we were at the end of the twentieth century.

I have probed deeply to find how Westport has changed and matured while, at the same time, remaining devoted to the principles and philosophy on which it was founded: self-determination, freedom of expression, and respect for individual differences.

For me, Westport, Connecticut is a one-of-a-kind town that, over the generations, has managed to retain its special identity. It is a place where the famous and not-so-famous have come together to forge a creative community, a place where one can savor privacy and live in relative peace and quiet, or, conversely, one can become totally immersed in activity.

My approach to this assignment was that of an investigative reporter searching for factual evidence on which to base observations and analysis. In the process of this research, I interviewed many people, read innumerable published accounts of the town's past, and leaned heavily on newspaper stories. Just as one might try to understand a human being by going back and tracing his or her roots and family heritage, so I portray Westport at the outset of this book as it is today at the millennium, and then offer a perspective on the historical traits that have made this New England town a place where life can be lived to the fullest.

The story I have written is not meant as a public relations document. Nor is it intended to point up Westport's shortcomings. Rather, I have tried to make it an objective composite of all the forces and subtleties of life that have gone into shaping this town; it is the story of a dynamic, ever-changing locale renowned for its extraordinary mixture of people and professions. The legacy of individual liberty and freedom of expression resonates in every aspect of life here.

I hasten to add that the views expressed in this book are those of the author and do not necessarily reflect those of the Westport Historical Society.

Woody Klein
Westport, Connecticut
January, 2000

Preface page photo: Woman in Westport 1890, Westport Historical Society

ACKNOWLEDGMENTS

In the course of my interviews and research in compiling material to write this book, I have had the privilege of meeting many gifted and generous people in Westport, all of whom have contributed to this book. It has been a most rewarding experience discovering how many hundreds of residents share a special sense of place that is Westport.

At the outset, I wish to acknowledge Joanne Woodward, a longtime supporter and friend of the Westport Historical Society, who was kind enough to write the foreword to this book. I thank her for her thoughtful observations. She is truly one of Westport's most precious assets and we are fortunate to have her among us, actively participating in the artistic, cultural, and educational life of our town.

I would like to thank formally the Book Committee of the Westport Historical Society for selecting me to write this book. It is a singular honor. I am especially indebted to Pete Wolgast, a past president and Book Committee chairman, whose unswerving support from the beginning has been an enormous source of strength to me; to Roy M. Dickinson, a past Westport Historical Society president, whose perceptive eye and appreciation of Westport history contributed greatly to the final manuscript; to Mollie Donovan and Eve Potts, both prolific Westport historians and writers, for their knowledgeable, constructive critiques of the manuscript while it was in process. I also thank Ann

Sheffer for her encouragement and insights; Howard Munce, one of the town's most celebrated illustrators, for his special knowledge of the arts community and for his editing skills; and Sheila O'Neill, who conceived the idea for this project when she first joined the Society as executive director in 1995. In addition, my thanks to the current president of the Historical Society, Darlene Letersky, for her personal support; and my compliments to Miggs Burroughs, my colleague and friend in this adventure, whose tasteful and professional design talent considerably enhanced the writer's text.

I would like to express my appreciation to Robert Hagelstein, recently retired president of the Greenwood Publishing Group, for his initial acceptance of and enthusiasm for this book. It is sufficient to say that this project occurred "on his watch." I hasten to add my thanks to members of Greenwood's editorial team: to Susan Baker, vice president, production; to my discerning editor, Betty Pessagno, whose fine editing skills helped shape the manuscript; to Penny Sippel, production supervisor, for her proofreading, advice on style and production; to Margaret Maybury, for her administrative assistance in helping bring the book to market; and to Gary Aleksiewicz, a freelance indexer.

I also want to thank Town Historian Dorothea Malm, who retired in 1998, for sharing with me her unpublished manuscript of Westport's early history and, in doing so, provided me with an accurate base of information. Her first-hand knowledge and interpretation of this town's history provided a firm base of knowledge on which to build.

My special appreciation, too, to Thelma Shiboski, whose good humor, knowledge of Westport, and natural ability as an unrelenting researcher provided me with hundreds of pages of newspaper articles, books, and other references from Westport's past, on a wide variety of topics, and whose photography research, and fact-checking were indispensable; to Town Historian Allen Raymond, Jr., whose advice and counsel at the very outset of this project was invaluable; and to his wife, Barbara Raymond, the Westport Historical Society's volunteer archivist, whose uncompromising dedication to historical detail and accuracy kept the manuscript factually afloat.

I am especially indebted to Marta Campbell, Westport Public Library reference librarian, whose patience I tried over a period of two years and whose willingness to dig out valuable historic documents was crucial to the completion of my research. She always responded to my requests in a timely and accurate manner—with a smile. She is truly one in a million. Her colleagues at the library who assisted in this project include reference librarians Kathy Breidenbach, Deborah Celia, Tilly Dutta, Margie Freilich-Den, Sylvia Schulman, and Joyce Vitali; Joanne Marshall, of Adult Services; and Claire

Quigley of Interlibrary Loan. Their efforts were supported by Assistant library Director George Wagner, and Westport Library Director Maxine Bleiweis, whose energy and innovation at the library have transformed it into a veritable information haven; also, my thanks to Grethe Shepherd, reference librarian in the Norwalk Public Library; and to Mary Witkowski, Historical Collections Librarian at the Bridgeport Public Library.

One of the main sources of Westport's recent history was the *Westport News*, from which I gleaned many facts, thanks to Kevin J. Lally, publisher of Brooks Community Newspapers, which is owned by Thomson Newspapers Corporation. I am grateful for their cooperation in giving me full access to their clipping and photo files. Thanks, too, for assistance from Jo Fox, the *News'* first editor, for her keen insights; from Dan Woog, author and *News* columnist, whose many columns about the town's history were a valuable resource; from Jim Lomuscio and Christina Hennessey, editors of the *Westport News* and from Gail Stephens and Jennifer Iacurci, *Westport News* receptionists.

In addition, my appreciation for editorial assistance goes to archaeologist Professor Ernest Wiegand of Norwalk Technical Community College; Charles Brilvitch, Bridgeport historian; Ralph Bloom, director, Norwalk Centennial Museum; Steven Young, executive director, and Barbara Austin, librarian, Fairfield Historical Society; Jane Cullinane of the Connecticut Historical Society; Ed Sarabia, Indian Affairs Coordinator, Office of Indian Affairs, state of Connecticut; and the late John Capsis, a friend and colleague, whose writings included numerous stories about Westport history. Thanks to his wife, Sandra, who provided me with his research for use in this book. Had John lived, he would have been the first to take me to task for some detail I might have missed or did not get right.

I am grateful to Martha Baldwin Ordeman, a daughter of former First Selectman Herb Baldwin, for making available to the Westport Historical Society the unpublished manuscript of her father's life story. My appreciation also goes to Joanna Foster, whose collection of *Stories from Westport* were most helpful; Gordon Joseloff, a native-born Westporter, journalist, and history buff whose knowledge of town affairs as moderator of the Representative Town Meeting helped make the book more readable; Dr. Lucinda McWeeney, Westport archaeologist, who gave the author a cram course in archaeology and helped shape the initial chapter of the book; Elizabeth Meyer, a Staples '99 graduate who spent a year interning with the Historical Society and assisted in the editorial and photo research; Judy Landa, who pitched in on photo and art research and whose knowledge of Westport's Sister City relationship with Yangzhou, China, was invaluable; Cheryl Bliss, a member of the Board of

Education and a former Historical Society president, who assisted with painstaking research of the town's public schools; Edward J. Keehan for his help in gathering information about World War II; Jim Feeney and William Vornkahl III for their advice and knowledge; Phil Woodruff, head of the Society's Oral History project; Thomas A. DeLong, who shared with me his manuscript of his new book, *Stars in Our Eyes: Luminaries of Stage and Screen at Home in Westport and Weston, Connecticut in the 20th Century*, published by the Westport Historical Society; Tom Ghianuly, owner of the Compo Barber Shop, who generously made available his collection of historical photos; Daniel Cruzon, an archaeologist; the Rev. John H. Branson, rector of the Church of Christ and Holy Trinity; the Reverend Kevin Pleas, minister of the Green's Farms Congregational Church; and Richard Foot, executive director, Westport–Weston YMCA.

My thanks to all the following people who contributed their time and expertise: Ruth Adams, Connie Anstett, Stan Atwood, Bill Balch, Dorothy Barlow, Al and Janet Beasley, Ruth Bedford, Julia Bradley, Suzanne Brainerd, B.V. Brooks, Dorothy Bryce, Fred Cantor, Ed Capasse, Richard G. Cholmeley-Jones 2d, Leo Cirino, Nancy Coley, Bernice Corday, Betty Lou Cummings, Dorothy Curran, Nancy Cuseo, Barlow Cutler-Wotten, Frank Deford, Louise Demakis, Zoe Donnell, Lucy Draves, Bob Driscoll, Jane Edmundson, Venora and Leroy Ellis, Bobbie Elmer, Susan Farewell, Janet Filling, Linda Frazier, Jo Fuchs-Luscombe, Nancy Gault, Jack Gibbons, William Gladstone, Steve Goldberg, Marty Hamer, Ted Hampe, Marty Hauhuth, Jacqueline Heneage, Pam Heydon, Nat Hentoff, Bob Hertzel, Barbara and Ray Howard, Linda Hudson, Joan Hyde, A.J. Izzo, Sue Kane, Eugenie Kantor, John Kemish, the Reverend Dana Kennedy, Sidney Kramer, Margaret LeBedis, Richard and Paula Leonard, Emanuel Margolis, Edward Meehan, William Meyer III; Ed, Bill and Jack Mitchell; Howard and Ann Morse, Lloyd Nash, Leo Nevas, Robert Orkand, Rita Papazian, Eric Passero, Harry Peabody, Tammy Pincavage, Paugussett Chief Aurelius (Big Eagle) Piper, Kenneth Powers, Florence Remlin, Bob and Yvette Rose, Len Rovins, Lou Santella, Phil Scheffler, Joy Schmitt, Ed See, Ralph Sheffer, Alice Shelton, Claude Clayton Smith, JoAnne Siebrasse, Ruth Steinkraus-Cohen, Sandy Stumberger, Tracy Sugarman, Arthur Tauck, Joyce Thompson, Audrey Thomson, Barbara Van Orden, and Wally Woods.

In addition, a number of Town of Westport public officials provided valuable information and records, including First Selectman Diane Goss Farrell and Second Selectman Carl Leaman. I would be remiss if I did not also recognize the information supplied by the first selectman's obliging office team of Pat Scully, office manager; Sue Brown, secretary; and Carol Leahy, secretary and Certified Local Government Coordinator to the Westport Historic District Commission; Town Controller Donald J. Miklus; Barbara Butler, director of the Department of Human Services; Town Clerk Patricia H. Strauss; Assistant Town Clerks Ruth Cavayero and Georgette Higgs; Director of Planning Katherine Barnard, Planning Assistant Alicia Mozian, and Secretary Pat Voris, of the Planning and Zoning Department; Westport Police Department Captain David Heinmiller; Director of Public Works Steve Edwards; Town Counsel Ira Bloom; Assistant to the Superintendent of Schools Joyce Losen; Westport Postmaster James Long; Tax Assessor Glenn Werfelman; Marcia Ball, and Shirley D'Aiuto, Town Hall information operators.

In addition, I want to recognize the help of Lois Schine, president of the Westport-Weston Chamber of Commerce, and Gale Beyea, of the Chamber staff. I also thank Lisa Shufro, co-president of the League of Women Voters.

I extend my appreciation to photographer Larry Silver for the use of his creative photos; to Andrea Fine, manager of the Memories of Westport Gift Shop at the Historical Society's Avery Place headquarters, for her photographs; to photographers Peter Barlow, John Brewster, Linda Chumilla, Seth Goltzer, Doug Healey, Mary Ellen Hendricks, Carmine Picarello, Ray Porter, Stephen Schwartz, George Silk, his daughter, Georgianna Silk, and Steve Zavatski, for contributing their photographs; to artists Lane Dupont, Naiad and Walter Einsel, Kassie Foss, Howard Munce, Walter Reddy, Katherine Ross, Tracy Sugarman, and Alfred Wilmott for contributing their works.

My thanks also to the following for recommending me to be author of this book: Colonel C. B. Hansen, John W. Kiermaier, and Professor Robert Pack.

I am enormously grateful to my wife, Audrey, for her understanding, patience, and sound editorial judgment, all of which boosted my confidence in the process of writing this book. She also served in an official capacity as Greenwood Press editor responsible for getting permissions to reprint the artwork and quoted material. I would also like to express my gratitude to my daughter, Wendy, whose constructive criticism of an early draft and substantive editing critiques helped tremendously.

Finally, to the readers of this book: Should anyone take issue with any facts, figures or reportage of events, or if there are any errors in its contents, the author takes full responsibility. On the other hand, if the reader enjoys the journey as much as I did, please credit all those above mentioned people for contributing to this record of Westport's history. It is my fondest hope that this book will contribute to the special heritage and enduring spirit that is Westport, Connecticut.

Acknowledgment page photo: Compo Beach cannons by Andrea Fine.

TOWN HALL TEAM: First Selectman Diane Goss Farrell, front center, is the elected head of Westport's local government, which consists of more than 290 men and women working in more than a dozen departments—including police, fire, parks and recreation, public works, conservation, building, controller, tax collector, highway, human services, planning and zoning, personnel, and more. Town Hall, background, was formerly Bedford Junior High School. Originally built in 1917, it was converted into Town Hall in 1979.   LARRY SILVER PHOTO

Introduction

Westport at the Millennium

*The town [Westport] is so heterogeneous that a crazy quilt
will do as a metaphor for it, provided you mean one
in which there is not even any unity of fabrics.*

— Peter DeVries, *Holiday* Magazine, 1950

As Westport moves into the twenty-first century, a composite description of the people in this town today could include such positive qualities as ambitious, leading edge, sophisticated, and education-oriented. On the other hand, there are some observers who perceive Westport as materialistic, self-centered, and status-conscious. Like the overachiever or perfectionist, Westport personifies many conflicting characteristics. But beyond the stereotypes and media sound bites, Westporters are, on balance, people who possess enormous compassion, generosity, imagination, creativity and, above all, an appreciation of their history — a past that is rooted deeply in the continuing quest for liberty, tolerance, and respect for people of all races, religions, and nationalities.

Its heritage aside, Westport attracts young families because it has a superior school system, a wide range of recreational facilities, fashionable

MAIN STREET as viewed from Oscar's Delicatessen on a quiet Sunday morning at 8 a.m. without the usual hustle and bustle of daily life.   LARRY SILVER PHOTO

stores and restaurants, and, perhaps most important, a general ambience of friendliness and a strong tradition of inclusiveness. Furthermore, it is the home of world-famous people in business, the professions, and the arts.

Westport is both a suburban bedroom community of New York City and a focal point for businesses that use the town as a base. Located a comfortable 47 miles from midtown Manhattan, it occupies 22.4 square miles. It is a place where most people can find a sense of well being from the relative privacy and peace offered here. Of course, it has changed markedly in its outward appearance compared to the post-World War II period when "The Man in the Gray Flannel Suit" began to commute to New York City. The homegrown charm of Mom and Pop stores of yesteryear has been replaced by the cachet of high-class chain stores such as Pottery Barn, Ann Taylor, J. Crew, Restoration Hardware, Williams-Sonoma, Brooks Brothers, and Banana Republic.

Although Westport is known widely as a place where celebrities reside, the town is comprised of an unlikely mixture of old Yankee families, descendants of the Italian, Irish, and other immigrant families who helped build Westport, famous artists and writers, and high-profile New Yorkers and *Fortune* 500 corporate executives, who are attracted by the ambience of the town. This mix of people brings a vitality to this town that is missing in other nearby towns along Connecticut's "Gold Coast." As a result, Westport rates in the state among the top towns to live in. In *Connecticut Magazine*'s latest annual "Rating the Towns" survey of the state's 169 municipalities, Westport, with a population of 25,000, ranks fourth overall behind Ridgefield, Simsbury, and Glastonbury as the best place to live in the 20,000 to 50,000 population categories. However, Westport ranks first in both the education and leisure/culture categories.[1]

Westport has long been known as a magnet for artists, musicians, writers, and creative people of all kinds. Today, the town is arguably the home of more people whose name appears in Who's Who than any other town of comparable size in the United States. Among its best known residents over the years are actors and show business stars Michael Bolton, Rodney Dangerfield, Bette Davis, William S. Hart, June Havoc, Francesca Lodge, John Malkovich, Paul Newman, Elizabeth Taylor, Marlo Thomas, Gene Tierney, and Joanne Woodward; artists/illustrators John Steuart Curry, Stevan Dohanos, Leonard Everett Fisher, Hardie Gramatky, John Held, Jr., Robert Lambdin, Rose O'Neill, Harold Von Schmidt, and George Hand Wright; sculptors James Earle Fraser, Laura Gardin Fraser and J. Clinton Shepherd.

Also, others are TV and radio broadcasters and hosts such as Phil Donahue, Douglas Edwards, Pauline Frederick, Don Imus, Jim McKay, Brent Musburger, Jim Nantz, Win Elliot and Harry Reasoner; and writers Frank Deford, Peter DeVries, P.D. Eastman, Zelda and F. Scott Fitzgerald, Nat Hentoff, A.E. Hotchner, Hilton Kramer, Ira Levin, Robert Ludlum, Ralph Martin, John Maxim, J.D. Salinger, Max Shulman, and Max Wilk. Other well-known names include Helen Keller, Charles and Anne Morrow Lindbergh, John Davis Lodge, and Martha Stewart; corporate moguls John F. Akers, chief executive officer of IBM; George Grune, CEO of *Reader's Digest*; U.S. Supreme Court Justice Abe Fortas; Securities and Exchange Commission Chairman Arthur Levitt, Jr.; David Roosevelt, a grandson of Franklin Delano Roosevelt, and David E. McKinney, president of the Metropolitan Museum of Art. And the list goes on, and on.

These celebrities and other opinion-makers in the worlds of business, finance, international trade, government, and academia have made Westport, Connecticut an eye-catching headline in the news business for more than half a century. Journalistic pundits have long felt that if it happens in Westport, it's news. If there is some crisis, Westport makes it a *newsworthy* crisis. This has given the town a certain amount of prestige in newspaper and network newsgathering centers around the world.

On the other hand, while Westporters enjoy the status accorded to this town, they know they do not live in a vacuum. Comments Frank Deford, author, editor and a senior contributing writer for *Sports Illustrated*: "Westport is a complete place and has more of an edge to it, and a breadth, than most other suburbs. We are part of Fairfield County, part of Connecticut and part of Greater New York and there can't ever be any real full sense of definition.

INTERNATIONAL TOUCH: The flags of every United Nations country are unfurled annually on "jUNe Day" on the bridge in downtown Westport. The town hosts UN diplomats and their families.
LARRY SILVER PHOTO

Nobody can ever say: 'Ich bin ein Westporter.' But it's a warm place and there is a very positive sense that abounds."[2]

Westport also has an international flavor, which comes, in part, from the various exchange programs with other cities abroad and from its close ties to the United Nations, whose representatives visit Westport year-round. In a message to Westporters on the thirtieth anniversary of the annual jUNe Day in 1995, United Nations Secretary General Boutros Boutros-Ghali stated: "You are a small town, but you share the global vision, which inspires us at the United Nations to achieve the goals of the Charter. Thank you for being a grass roots partner in this great challenge...my thanks for your continuing hospitality to United Nations personnel and their families for these many years."[3]

Internationalism has many faces in Westport. The town hosts more than 3,000 foreign guests annually, who are sent here by at least 15 different organizations, including the United Nations, the U.S. State Department, and the International Center in New York.[4] In addition, many immigrant families choose to make Westport their permanent home. The town also serves as headquarters for the Save the Children Federation, Inc., which operates both in the United States and in 42 countries overseas. Charles MacCormack, president of Save the Children, says: "The Westport community has been very supportive of our work. Its educated and involved members have an interest in issues impacting the global community."[5] In the public schools, the English as a Second Language program has enrolled more than 80 students, who speak 29 different languages, in the elementary grades through high school. These students are from South America, Central America, the Middle East, Asia, and Europe.

So what is the *real* Westport? First and foremost, it is a beautiful place to live, offering a fortuitous convergence of rolling farmland, wooded landscape and long stretches of Long Island Sound shoreline. Westport attracts many summer residents, welcoming them annually to all that year-round residents enjoy. Westporters take pride in the town's many attributes, among which are its excellent school system, the arts, Main Street, the beaches, the Saugatuck River, and the Longshore Club Park, the publicly owned country club to which every resident has access.

Despite its national reputation, Westport continues to be a place where its residents maintain a small-town attitude in the midst of big-town personalities. First Selectman Diane Goss Farrell expresses it this way: "In

GRAND ENTRANCE: The 191-acre Longshore Country Club off South Compo Road includes a golf course, swimming pool, tennis courts, marina, restaurant and clubhouse overlooking Long Island Sound. LARRY SILVER PHOTO

many ways we are a legendary town. I am always amazed when I visit other places that so many people are familiar with our community, and not just because of our celebrities. Our town enjoys a wonderful reputation. The town thrives on excitement. Westport people are fighters. For people to be able to live here, they have had to be successful. They have worked so hard to get here that they feel they need to protect, nurture and preserve their investment. They channel their energies in whatever direction they believe in passionately about the town. It's not that we're all Type-A personalities, but we're all very motivated, very energetic people who want to get things done. And we're not too big a community. People still have a sense that Westport is a hometown."[6]

PATRIOTIC PUPIL: A lone student waves an American flag from a Westport schoolroom. More than 4,600 students attend a public school system that encourages participation in community life.

LARRY SILVER PHOTO

Westport's youth represent its crown jewels: About 60 percent of the town's $96.9 million budget for fiscal year 1999-2000 is devoted to their education, a dramatic rise from 17 percent at the turn of the last century.[7] Westport has consistently run one of the state's most outstanding school systems: its four elementary schools, two middle schools, and one high school are part of a system that *Town and Country* magazine rated one of the finest in the nation. Westport also has a private school, Green's Farms Academy. Moreover, the children and young men and women in the schools often participate in community-wide, extra-curricula activities. In this town, community service is a widely accepted form of participation in a healthy, vibrant town in which young people are encouraged to look beyond their own needs and wants.

Westport is a lesson in grass-roots democracy, especially for the future leaders whose ideas, opinions, and personalities have been shaped by their experiences growing up here. The town is governed by its executive branch, a board of three selectmen; by its legislative branch, 36 elected, nonpartisan representatives from eight districts; and by numerous boards and commissions, some appointed, others elected. Even the politicians feel a sense of pride when they represent

Westport in the state's capital, Hartford. G. Kenneth Bernhard, State Representative from the 136th District, says this about the town: "The thrill I feel when representing Westport in Hartford comes from believing that I represent the most dynamic town in the state."[8] Adds State Senator Judith G. Freedman, who represents Westport from the 26th Senate District in the State Legislature: "I educate my colleagues in Hartford about Westport, making sure they understand Westport is a microcosm of Connecticut, not just a

FOLLOW THE RED BRICK WALK: The entrance to the Westport Public Library is beautified by a Riverwalk and Gardens. The walk consists of 11,000 bricks, about half of which are engraved with the donor's name. LARRY SILVER PHOTO

financial resource to fill the state coffers, without returning dollars back to Westport. Conversely, Westporters occasionally need a reminder that the capitol of Connecticut is Hartford and not Albany."[9]

At the same time, while it exudes affluence, Westport has its own oft-forgotten and mostly unseen minority of people who suffer in silence. They consist of a small but broad spectrum of people: adults living in shelters, senior citizens barely managing to get by as shut-ins in their homes, lower-income people living in modest, crowded quarters, many of whom must supplement their incomes with the help of welfare and food stamps. Their numbers may be few, but they are very much among us. Fortunately, the majority of well-to-do people and the extraordinary cadre of volunteers in this town find a way to look after those in need. There may well be more support groups at work in Westport than in any other suburb in America.

Westport is predominantly composed of well-read people. The public library is the second busiest in the state in terms of circulation per capita, and it averages 1,200 visitors per day. Leading to its entrance is a beautiful, brick-filled Riverwalk, with the names of those Westporters who donated bricks etched on each one. The town also has

SCENE IN WESTPORT: The Westport Country Playhouse officially opened on June 29, 1931 with Streets of New York. *Hundreds of famous actors and actresses have played here over the years in major hits headed for Broadway.*
KASSIE FOSS ILLUSTRATION

a healthy YMCA, an Arts Center, Nature Center, and Community Theatre; the Levitt, an outdoor pavilion for live summer entertainment; The Westport Country Playhouse, Toquet Hall, a teen center, and an active Historical Society. Its town-owned recreational facilities include four beaches, and the Longshore Club Park, which includes an 18-hole golf course, a marina, a sailing school, three swimming pools, and outdoor tennis courts. For seniors, there is a Senior Center, and, for kids, there are vigorous, constantly expanding programs including Little League, soccer, softball, ice skating, sailing, tennis, swimming, Pop Warner and Police Athletic League football, and a roller blading park.

There are more than 3,000 business establishments, of which 46 percent are in service industries, 26 percent in trade, and 12 percent in finance, insurance and real estate. The town's businesses occupy some 2.5 million square feet of office space and 1.5 million square feet of retail space, according to Ted Hampe, chairman of H T Hampe Associates, a leading regional, commercial real estate firm located in Westport. "There is virtually no more commercial space to be built," says Hampe. "Westport is a popular town for employees. They love to work, eat and shop here. It's also a natural attraction for shoppers from nearby towns."[10] Westport business achieves retail sales of nearly $1 billion a year. The town has 12 banks, 660 retail outlets, and 93 liquor licenses

LANDMARK: National Hall, built in 1870, has housed a bank, a newspaper, a business, and was used as a meeting and dance hall, school and theater. Listed on the Register of Historic Places, it is now a first-class inn with a nationally acclaimed restaurant.

KASSIE FOSS ILLUSTRATION

for stores and restaurants, which number more than 100.[11] Lois Schine, president of the 600-member Westport-Weston Chamber of Commerce, calls Westport the "marketing capital of the world." There are no longer any factories (they are prohibited by zoning laws). They have been replaced by offices housing a variety of service industries. Retail and restaurant businesses to support these industries have mushroomed, as well, and Westport has become a regional shopping and dining mecca.

In years past, the slogan once applied to this multi-faceted town by advertising executives in New York City was: "Let's put it on the train and see if it gets off at Westport." Westport has a plethora of specialty businesses dealing in eclectic niche markets such as those that sell space on tankers for shipping, sell sports memorabilia and collectibles, ship soda ash all over the world, provide sports medicine, arrange historical tours in Connecticut, sell worldwide freighter cruises, perform fundraising for FDA clinical trials on new medical approaches, offer psychic reading, plan sailing adventures, market hazardous materials packaging, manage an international tea firm with tea farms in Rwanda, distribute cosmetics internationally, offer wellness services, buy and sell valuable coins and stamps, offer an international translation service, provide international energy and management consulting advice, offer advice on how to entertain and create an elegant home, and, of course, there is Newman's Own, which sells food products and gives the profits for charity.

How much is Westport worth? The market value of all real estate, motor vehicles, personal property, commercial, industrial, public utilities and other miscellaneous items is an astounding $8 billion, a figure based on the state of Connecticut's 2000 update of the town's last revaluation in 1985.[12] Fortunately, in spite of its leading-edge assets, the town has maintained its New England charm and continues to be a destination for folks from all over the region. Westport ranks near the top of many surveys of wealthy communities and finished 81st on the 1999 *Worth Magazine* annual list of America's 250 richest towns. Million-dollar homes are common here; the average sale price for a home in 1998 was $672,421 and, in the first half of 1999, that figure rose to $775,584 and continues to climb. About 500 homes—or approximately 6 percent of all single-family homes—a year change ownership. The number of building permits recorded by the Planning and Zoning Commission was approximately 750 in 1999, with a forecast of some 775 for the year 2000. And the space available is going fast. In fact, Westport is 90 to 95 percent developed and open space is increasingly scarce, according to planning officials. The town's latest planning survey found that the town is between 90 and 95 per-

SAILING ON THE SOUND: *The Cedar Point and Saugatuck Yacht Clubs are two bases for those who wish to enjoy themselves on the water in Westport.* WESTPORT NEWS PHOTO

cent developed. There are just 850 vacant acres of land, or 6 percent of the town's 14,000 acres that remain available for commercial or residential development, aside from knocking down houses and rebuilding new ones.[13]

Environmentally, in January 1998, Westport was ranked number one in Connecticut in efforts to preserve Long Island Sound. Local environmental groups have recognized the town as one of two coastal communities in Connecticut and New York that show the strongest commitment to preservation of the environment of this estuary. The results of a study by Save the Sound of Stamford, the Connecticut Fund for the Environment Inc., and the New York-based Natural Resources Defense Council Inc. showed that out of 78 towns studied, Westport ties with Smithtown, New York, as one of the most pollution-free communities. "This is a wonderful pat on the back for the whole town," said Sheila O'Neill, chairman of Save the Sound's Board of Trustees. O'Neill, who is also executive director of the Westport Historical Society, attributes Westport's top rating to the commitment of its conservation professionals and to residents dedicated to protecting their community's environment.[14]

There are many ways to view Westport. Perhaps Joanne Woodward and Paul Newman explain it best when they say: "In one word, Westport is special to us because it's HOME. The old buildings and beautiful views are part of what makes Westport unique and special and, still in some ways, the sleepy town we fell in love with 36 years ago."[15]

But Westport's demographic profile (see Appendix A) and a listing of its attributes cannot hope to tell how this town rose to prominence. Only an in-depth look at its history can fully explain how and why Westport developed over the centuries into the dynamic town it is today.

HOME AWAY FROM HOME: Compo Beach, long considered one of the town's prime assets, attracts many thousands of summer and weekend visitors, in addition to year-round residents.
ANDREA FINE PHOTO

NOTES

1. *Connecticut Magazine,* November 1998, pp. 58-59.

2. Statement from Frank Deford, December 1999.

3. Statement provided by Ruth Steinkraus-Cohen, Westport's representative to the United Nations, August, 1999.

4. The *Westport News*, April 19, 1996.

5. Correspondence with Charles MacCormack, October 1999.

6. Interview with Diane Goss Farrell, October 9, 1999.

7. Westport Controller Donald J. Miklus, August 5, 1999; the proposed operating budget for 2000-2001, as of March 13, 2000, was $104,538,092 — the town's first $100 million budget, about 61 percent of which was earmarked for education.

8. Statement from State Representative G. Kenneth Bernhard, October 10, 1999.

9. Statement from State Senator Judith G. Freedman, December 10, 1999.

10. Ted Hampe, chairman of H T Hampe Associates.

11. Katherine Barnard, director, Westport Planning and Zoning Department.

12. Miklus.

13. Barnard, October 20, 1999. Based on memorandum dated April 15, 1997, from Alicia Mozian, planning assistant.

14. The *Westport News*, January 30, 1998.

15. *What Makes Westport Special?* An Album of Comments from Westport Citizens compiled by the Westport Historical Society, 1997, p. 3.

Photo, p. 1, Westport train station, Westport News.

PART I
ROOTS

This arctic photo resembles the way the Saugatuck River may have looked between 19,500 and 17,000 years ago as glacial ice melted into a spillway.
                                    DOROTHY PETEET PHOTO

CHAPTER 1

A PREHISTORIC PERSPECTIVE

While recent development projects and nearly four centuries of farming activities may have removed much of Westport's prehistoric record, we know that people were living and, perhaps hunting, in downtown Westport by 6,000 B.C.

— Dr. Lucinda McWeeney,
Westport archaeologist

In the beginning, of course, there was no Westport. No Fairfield County. No Connecticut. No North America. So when was the land we now call Westport created? In order to understand why Westport looks the way it does today, it is necessary to go back in time. Archaeologists who have studied this area's origins say that 500 million years ago there were a number of continents, unlike those existing today, separated by ocean. In the next 250 million years, land masses moved together and formed a supercontinent, only to break apart later into smaller land masses, as the beginnings of North America, Europe, and Asia emerged.

The continents formed over bedrock. Erosion of the bedrock over millions of years by flowing water, weather, and chemical changes has been the primary force in shaping Connecticut's (and Westport's) landscape, according to archaeologist Michael Bell.[1] Giant continental glaciers, similar to ice sheets, advanced over the region and then retreated, leaving in their wake silt, sand, gravel and boulders, collectively called glacial drift. In most of Connecticut, drift is what lies directly beneath our feet, burying the bedrock.

In the 200 million years after the birth of the Atlantic Ocean, streams moved the bedrock while the melting glaciers poured water into the oceans. This set off a rising sea level that inundated much of the land. The rising sea level continues today and, according to some scientists, may be accelerating due to global warming. The retreat of the glaciers over what has become

Projectile points found in Westport, from left, point from approximately 6,000 B.C.; broad-bladed point (tip broken and missing) from about 2,000 B.C.; Stark point from about 5,000 B.C. From private collection of Dr. Cindy McWeeney, Westport archaeologist.

known as Connecticut resulted in soils here that abound with rock, which any farmer who has tried to plant in this area knows all too well.[2]

It is believed that the earliest settlers in North America migrated from Siberia and moved through the various environments that developed in the glaciers' wake, entering Long Island and New England probably between 8,000 and 10,000 B.C., according to Lucinda McWeeney, a noted Westport archaeologist.[3] Small family groups and bands of nomadic hunters migrated into the area as the Ice Age glaciers melted and the land warmed and became hospitable to humans. As the northeastern woodland environment developed, these early people invented specialized tools of their own: the tools became more varied and sophisticated, and family groups coalesced into more complex community settlements that were formed to ensure survival.

The early inhabitants manufactured and used a distinctive type of projectile point called a fluted point or Clovis-like fluted point,[4] so named after the site where the first point was found in Clovis, New Mexico. These points range from three to six inches in length. Some experts believe they were used for spears, while others say the stone tools were apparently used as knives and butchering tools, as well. The fluted points have been found along the Aspetuck and Mills rivers. A Paleoindian site dating to 10,000 years ago was found in Wilton by an archaeology team from Norwalk Community Technical College. This is the largest Paleoindian site dating to this period, excavated in Fairfield County. Projectile points with bifurcated or forked bases have been found in the Green's Farms and Old Hill areas of Westport, demonstrating that people were living and, perhaps hunting, in downtown Westport by 6,000 B.C.

The most abundant signs of Native American life found in archaeological records date to the Late Archaic period (4,000-2,000 B.C.) probably owing to more stable food and water supplies, which limited the need for people to move in search of subsistence and stimulated the population increase.[5] Some of the tools found in the Westport area that date back to this period are the gouge, adze (an axe-like tool), ground slate points and knives, the semilunar knife or ulu, a knife with a broad, almost semicircular blade, bannerstones, broad-bladed, side-notched bifaces, and barbed points.[6] A broken ulu was found on the beach at Sherwood Island State Park; ground stone axes were found during dredging operations in Grey's Creek next to the Longshore Golf Club course.[7]

In addition, evidence of campsites 4,000 years old have been discovered at the Taylor site in Green's Farms, the Watts site near Hillspoint Road, and the Indian River site that extended south of the railroad station on both sides of Saugatuck Avenue. Artifacts from this prehistoric era have been found as well around the Longshore Golf Club and in the Winslow Park area. There is also archaeological evidence of life in Fairfield County for all the historical periods following the late Archaic: soapstone, an innovation of the 2,000 B.C. to 1700 A.D. period, found in the area of Cross Highway and Silent Grove; pottery from the 700 B.C. to 1,500 A.D. period, found in the Green's Farms area and near the base of Ball Mountain; rim shards (pieces from the rim of the vessel), found at the Green's Farms Congregational Church site, which appear to be from the decorative style Clearview Stamped,[8] placing it between 115 and 185 A.D.; and arrowheads from A.D. 800 to 1500, found in several Westport sites, including the Green's Farms area, Wakeman Farm, Gilbertie property, and Indian River. From the south and west, agriculture began to spread into the region about 1,000 years ago, with the people beginning to grow corn, beans, pumpkins, squash, tobacco and other products.[9]

Archaeological excavation of the Wakeman Farm site in Westport. One arrowhead discovered there dates back to 4000 B.C.   CINDY MCWEENEY PHOTO

*SIGNS OF THE TIMES: In Westport, projectile points dating back to 6,000 B.C. have been found in the **(1)** Green's Farms area and **(2)** the old Hill area; a broken knife with a blade from 2,000 B.C. was found **(3)** on the beach at Sherwood Island State Park; ground stone axes were found in **(4)** Grey's Creek near Longshore Golf Club course; evidence of campsites 4,000 years old were found **(5)** at the Taylor site in Green's Farms, **(6)** the Watts site near Hillspoint Road, and **(7)** the Indian River site; artifacts from the prehistoric era have also been found **(8)** around the Longshore Golf Club and **(9)** Winslow Park; soapstone from 2,000 B.C. was found in the area of **(10)** Cross Highway and Silent Grove; pottery from 700 B.C. to 1,500 A.D. was found in **(11)** the*

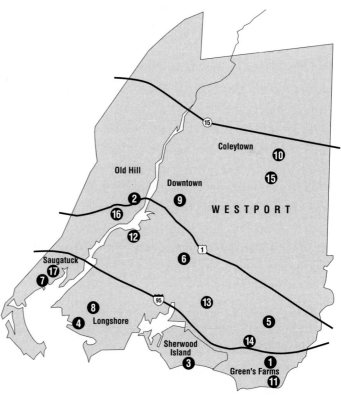

*Green's Farms area and **(12)** and near the base of Ball Mountain; rim shards from 115 to 185 A.D. were found at **(13)** the Green's Farms Congregational Church; and arrowheads from 800 to 1,500 A.D. were found at several Westport sites including **(14)** the Green's Farms area, **(15)** Wakeman Farm, **(16)** the Gilbertie Property, and **(17)** the Indian River.* MAP BY MIGGS BURROUGHS

NOTES

1. Michael Bell, *The Face of Connecticut, People, Geology and the Land*, Bulletin 110, State Geological and Natural History Survey of Connecticut, Department of Environmental Protection, 1985, pp. 10-11.

2. Daniel Cruzon, *The Prehistory of Fairfield County*, The Newtown Historical Society (Newtown, CT., 1991), p. 8.

3. Lucinda McWeeney, *Archaeological Settlement Patterns and Vegetation Dynamics in Southern New England in the Late Quaternary*, Ph.D. Dissertation, Yale University, 1994, p. 6.

4. McWeeney, p. 137.

5. Dena F. Dincauze, "A Capsule Prehistory of Southern New England, The Pequots in Southern New England" (Norman: University of Oklahoma Press, 1993), pp. 19-32.

6. J.E. Pfeiffer, *Late and Terminal Archaic Cultural Traditions of the Lower Connecticut Valley*, Ph.D. Dissertation, SUNY, Albany, NY, 1992.

7. McWeeney, personal communication, September 1998.

8. The decorative style, Clearview Stamped, was identified by Connecticut archaeologist Lucianne Lavin of Seymour, CT.

9. Alvin M. Josephy, Jr., *Now That the Buffalo Have Gone* (Norman: University of Oklahoma Press, 1982), p. 34.

Photo, p. 15, Wigwam, Lucinda McWeeney

CHAPTER 2

THE NATIVE AMERICANS

The American Indian, although savage, is not cold. He has a sensitive development of spiritual nature, of vision, born of intercourse with the vibrant moods of the world he lives in.

—Westporter Edward Coley Birge, *Westport, Connecticut, The Making of a Yankee Township*, 1926

A conservative estimate of the number of Indians in Connecticut at the time the English arrived in the early 1600s is about 12,000.[1] At this time, a total of approximately 25,000 Indians were living in Southern New England and on Long Island.[2] Today in Fairfield County, 1,226 of the total 830,000 residents are Native Americans. But only about 300 can trace their ancestry to villages in the county that now bear the English names of Stratford, Bridgeport, Shelton, Brookfield, Fairfield, New Fairfield, and Westport.[3]

The Indians did not understand the English tradition of land ownership. To them, the land—similar to the air—is something owned in common and used for the good of everyone. When the tillage around their villages was depleted, the Indians simply moved on to a new site, and the land was left to return to its natural state. They assumed that the white man would do the same, and when they "sold" the land, they thought the white man was just renting its use for a limited time period, or until the land was no longer good for growing food.

When colonists first came to this area, they were outnumbered by the Indians. It would have been relatively easy for the Indians to drive the New World explorers out. But, because of dissension and squabbling among the tribes, the white man learned to divide and conquer by turning one tribe against another. Further, the separate Indian tribes competed for the white man's fur trade, in return for precious goods the Indians had never seen before — mirrors, beads and trinkets, for example, that captured their imagination.

There were a number of distinct Indian tribes in Connecticut, located along the Sound running west from the Connecticut River: the Hammonassets, the Menunketucks, the Quinnipiacs, the Paugussetts, the Siwanogs, and the Pequots, one of the largest and most powerful. The Paugussetts, known as the Paugussett Nation, lived in villages along the coast at Pequonnock (Bridgeport), Uncoway (Fairfield), Sasco (Southport), Machamux (Green's Farms), Aspetuck (Easton), Saugatuck (Westport), and Norwalke (Norwalk).[4] The word "Paugussett" literally translated means "where the river widens out."[5]

Shaded area shows where Paugussetts settled.

Reservations were set up for the Indians soon after the colonists arrived. In 1659, the General Court in Fairfield ruled that 80 acres of land should be held for the Paugussett Indians at Golden Hill — named after the corn grown on the hill — located in Bridgeport. Over time, however, the tribe was forced to sell off its land to succeeding generations of New Englanders who inhabited the area. Today, only one log cabin on one-quarter of an acre of land remains there.

While other tribes exchanged land for goods from the colonists, the Pequot Indians — who lived near Groton — refused to surrender their land to the white man. They first clashed with the colonists in 1632 and in the ensuing five years the tribe's fate would be determined. The Pequots had been warring with other tribes as well as trying to hold off the British by delaying to conform with the colonists' demands for their land.

In the spring of 1636, at a special session of the Connecticut General Court, Roger Ludlow, then deputy governor of the Commonwealth of Massachusetts, was appointed as one of the key advisors to the Connecticut forces. When the Pequots murdered two white traders — Captain John Stone and John Oldham in 1637 off Block Island — the British launched a force of 90 men, who sailed into Pequot Harbor and demanded that the tribe turn the killers over to them. Negotiations were held with Sassacus, the Pequot chief. The renowned warrior [6] lived in his fortress at Weinshauks, the present town of Groton.[7] Eventually, negotiations broke down, and the colonists drove the Indians down the coast, moving through the towns of Mystic, Groton, New London, Saybrook, and on to Fairfield in the final battle at Sasco Swamp. Troops were gathered from Hartford, Windsor, and Wethersfield, as well as from the Massachusetts Bay colony to attack the Pequots.

Monument marking the Pequot War on the Post Road in Southport: "THE GREAT SWAMP FIGHT HERE ENDED THE PEQUOT WAR JULY 13, 1637."
MIGGS BURROUGHS PHOTO

The full-scale war, known as the Great Swamp War because of its location, erupted on May 26, 1637, led by Ludlow and Captains John Mason and John Underhill, both renowned Indian fighters. Ludlow allied his troops with the Mohegans and the Narragansetts, two tribes who hated the much-feared Pequots. The colonists struck in a predawn attack on the Pequots, killing hundreds. Although the massacre lasted less than an hour, most of the Pequots perished. Sassacus and the Pequots admitted defeat. Most of the last-ditch fighting took place near where the present Connecticut Turnpike crosses the Post Road just before Southport as one travels east from Westport to Fairfield. The Society of Colonial Wars has erected a granite monument on the Post Road to commemorate the event. The inscription, easily seen by the many thousands of people who daily pass in cars, reads: "The Great Swamp Fight Here Ended the Pequot War July 13, 1637." [8] The war was the major turning point in the history of the Indian-white relations in colonial America, marking an end to any illusion that the Indians and whites could coexist on an equal footing. Some historians consider it one of the most important wars in New England history because it set a permanent precedent for the colonists to seize land from the Indians.

Another war marked a second milestone event in the history of relations between the early colonists and the Indians in New England. The King Philip's War of 1675, named after an Indian of that name, was spurred by the controversial issue of land sales to colonists. Matacom, known in American history as King Philip, led the fight against the colonists burning Deerfield and forcing the colonists south. When he failed to enlist the few remaining Pequots and the Mohegans in his cause, he was driven back by the English military, ensuring that New England would remain in English hands. Despite these two defeats, the Indian tribes posed a continuous annoyance to the white man throughout the seventeenth century. Skirmishes between the Indians and the white man became routine, with the colonists getting the better of such confrontations. Westport historian Edward Coley Birge summed up the attitude of the early colonists who arrived in what is Westport today when he wrote: "The American Indian, although savage, is not cold. He has a sensitive development of spiritual nature, of vision, born of intercourse with the vibrant moods of the world he lives in."[9]

Only a handful of Paugussetts remained when the white man first arrived in the area now called Westport. The English came from England to the Massachusetts Bay Colony, to Fairfield and, finally, to this area in the 1600s. It was a long and difficult journey for those explorers who, in search of freedom and self-determination, persevered until they finally found what they wanted.

NOTES

1. Elsie Florence (Nicholas) Dannenburg, The *Romance of Norwalk* (New York: The State History Co., p. 3.

2. Alvin M. Josephy, "Indians of the Sound, 120 Centuries of a Noble Heritage," *On the Sound Magazine*, Seascape Publications, 1972, p. 93.

3. Delphine Red Shirt, "Native Sons and Daughters," *Fairfield County* Magazine, November 1998, p. 30.

4. Franz Laurens Wojciechowski, *Ethnohistory of the Paugussett Tribe, An Exercise in Research Methodology* (Amsterdam, The Netherlands: DeKiva, 1991), Monogram, Series 9, Ch. 4, p. 39.

5. The Paugussetts' name is variantly spelled, depending on the town clerks of the time, as Pagaset, Paugasuck, Paugusit, Pawgassutt, and Paugussett.

6. John W. DeForest, *Indians of Connecticut* (Hartford, CT: Wm. James Hammersly, 1852), p. 73.

7. Arthur L. Peale, *Uncas and the Mohegan-Pequot* (Boston: Meadow Publishing Co. 1939), p. 28.

8. Despite this defeat, the Pequots are once again a power among the political forces in Connecticut. Not only do they run the profitable Foxwoods Resort Casino in Mashantucket, Connecticut, but also they opened a museum in August 1998, built on their reservation at a cost of $135 million to tell the tribe's story.

9. Edward Coley Birge, *Westport, Connecticut, The Making of a Yankee Township* (New York: Writers Publishing Co.,1926), p. 2.

Photo, p. 19, Beadwork by Chief Big Eagle, Woody Klein

PART II
GRASS ROOTS DEMOCRACY

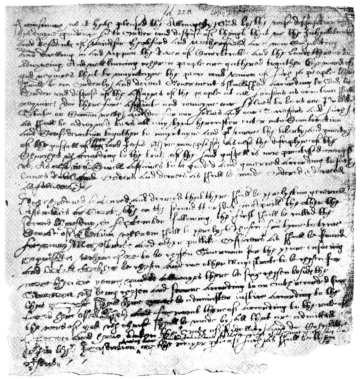

THE FUNDAMENTAL ORDERS, a set of democratic principles about self-governing and disavowing allegiance to England, were officially adopted in Hartford on January 14, 1639, marking the birth of Connecticut as a Commonwealth. Framed by Roger Ludlow, founder of the town of Fairfield, and based on the writings of the Reverend Thomas Hooker, the "father of Connecticut," they were seen as the first "Constitution" of Connecticut. They laid the groundwork for the creation of Westport's independent grass roots government almost 200 years later. The state's motto, "The Constitution State," stems from this document.

WESTPORT PUBLIC LIBRARY

CHAPTER 3

THE MOTHER TOWN

What I like most about Westport is that life is pretty much what anybody here wants to make it. It's ultimate freedom. Isn't that what Thomas Hooker was seeking for himself and for others?

— William Meyer III, Westport

The Indians were not the colonists' biggest challenge in the early days of settlement. Ironically, it was the Massachusetts Bay Colony itself that imposed the greatest constraints on the colonists' dream of freedom and liberty. The first dreamers had deserted their mother country for religious, political, and economic reasons. While some of the English colonists were members of the British middle and upper class, the majority were a disparate group of people representing a broad spectrum of English life. They united in one goal — to seek a new and better world. However, just 11 years after the pilgrims had landed at Plymouth Rock in 1620, all was not well in the Massachusetts Bay Colony. In 1631, the people began to demand more land, more opportunity, and more self-determination. Impressed by reports of the richness and potential of the verdant Connecticut River valley, some colonists began to press for resettlement there, while still retaining their identity as Englishmen.[1]

According to one historian, the Indian sachems [leaders] urged the governors of Plymouth and Massachusetts Bay to send Englishmen to begin settlements in Connecticut.[2] Other chroniclers of the time disagree, stating that the Massachusetts settlers themselves, without any prodding from the Indians, made the first move. Roger Ludlow, of Worchester, who later led the attack on the Pequots chronicled in the previous chapter, supported the idea of migrating to Connecticut. Ludlow, a sturdy, outspoken man who would become the first lawyer to practice in Connecticut, hoped to become governor of the Massachusetts Bay Colony in 1635, despite an outburst in General Court of that colony in 1632, showing him to be argumentative, ambitious, and even brutal.[3] On the other hand, a contemporary described him as "courageous, intelligent and a fine thinker. He knew what he wanted, believed he was right and didn't allow anything to stand in his way."[4] Another historian described Ludlow as "the kind of man that people trust and respect, even though they may not love."[5]

Statue of Roger Ludlow displayed in Hartford. After leading the successful war against the Pequot Indians in 1637, he founded Fairfield two years later and became the first lawyer to practice in the Commonwealth of Connecticut.
MIGGS BURROUGHS PHOTO

Ludlow, defeated in his quest for governor by John Haynes, began to concentrate on moving to Connecticut. The Connecticut colony, a large and highly desirable area, was then in danger of occupation by the Dutch, and in 1635, colonists from three Bay towns —Newtown, Dorchester, and Watertown— moved to Connecticut. That same year, Hartford, Windsor, and Wethersfield were officially settled, with Ludlow taking up residence in Windsor. Having conquered the Pequots in 1637, Ludlow, with eight or ten families, moved from Windsor to Uncoway, attracted by the land and the natural resources in the area. In 1639, Ludlow founded Fairfield by purchasing an expanse of open fields at Uncoway from the Indians. Uncoway was an Indian word meaning "looking forward." The area, was part of a larger region that eventually became the present-day

Fairfield, Green's Farms, Redding, Weston, Easton, and the western section of Bridgeport. Virtually no Indian threat remained after Fairfield was created. The only Indians in the area were members of the Pequonnock band, which was part of the Paugussett Nation. The English referred to several subdivisions of the Pequonnocks according to their place of residence: the Uncoways, who lived between Black Rock Harbor and the Mill River, as these landmarks eventually came to be known; the Sasquas, whose home stood between Mill River and Sasqua Creek, so named by the Indians because it was wet and marsh land; and the Maximus, also known as Machamux (meaning "beautiful land"), who lived between Sasqua Creek and the Saugatuck River, especially around Compaug or Compo, and at Aspetuck, located in what is now Weston.[6] The name Saugatuck comes from the Indian words "sag," meaning pouring out or outlet, and "tuck," meaning river or tidal stream.

Under Ludlow's guidance, the little Fairfield plantation grew into a town.[7] He made treaties with the Pequonnocks, the Norwalke Indians and the Sasqua Indians between 1639 and 1661. The agreement with the Norwalke Indians gave the colonists all of the land lying between the Norwalk and Saugatuck rivers, a day's walk from the sea into the country. In exchange for the land, the colonists gave wampum, coats, hatchets, knives, scissors, tobacco, kettles, looking glasses, and yards of cloth. The Indians were given fishing, hunting, and fowling rights but could not set traps that might injure the cattle.

Ludlow was active in framing the state's "Fundamental Orders" in Hartford on January 14, 1639, a date that marks the birth of Connecticut as a Commonwealth.[8] The General Court had called for an "orderly and decent government established according to God with duties and powers and restrictions put into writing for Connecticut and for the civilized world from that day."[9] The Fundamental Orders, a set of principles about self-governing, recognized no allegiance to England on the part of the colonists but in effect set up an independent government. In the sense that they were intended to be a framework of government more permanent than the usual orders adopted by the General Court, they were in essence, the first Constitution — the beginning of Connecticut as a Commonwealth.

Remarkably, the Fundamental Orders, also known as the State Constitution of 1639, were created without fanfare. As a direct result of this extraordinary contribution to American democracy, Connecticut became

29

known as "The Constitution State." The founders of Fairfield were firm believers in the Fundamental Orders. For these men of principle, righteousness and purity formed the basis of personal character.

Ludlow was always closely involved in writing and interpreting all treaties and laws pertaining to the colony. In 1646, he was given permission to codify Connecticut's laws, and in May 1650 the General Court adopted what has become known as "Ludlow's Code," a seminal work on the importance of civil liberties and the equal protection of the law. These were emphasized in the preamble to the Code.[10] For this contribution, Ludlow received plaudits from many quarters, including the French sociologist Alexis de Tocqueville, who wrote, "the code of laws promulgated by the State of Connecticut in 1650 [is] a body of laws which, though written 200 years ago, is still ahead of liberties of our age."[11] The establishment of the Code marked another milestone in the Puritans' early history — emphasis on education as a means of establishing the Puritan work ethic in children. The Code ordered that every township of 50 families or more "shall then forthwith appoint one within theire Towne to teach all children to write and read."[12] This marked the beginning of the generations-old focus on quality education Westport embraces to this day.

1654 Lawsuit saves outspoken Mary Staples from a witch trial.

Linda Frazer

Tile designed by Marian Grebow

While Ludlow spent most of his time developing Fairfield after he founded it, internal problems among the colonists began to develop. In 1651 a woman by the name of Goody Knapp of Stratford was charged with being a witch because she allegedly "entertained the Devil." She claimed there was another witch in Fairfield. Buttonholed by Ludlow and pressed for the name of the other witch, she implicated Mary Staples, wife of Thomas Staples, a prominent member of the community who had helped Ludlow found Fairfield. When Thomas Staples learned of the rumor, he brought suit against Ludlow in the New Haven court for defamation of his wife's character. Ironically, Staples used the very same Code of Laws that Ludlow had written to file the suit, which was heard on May 29, 1654. The court found for the plaintiff and awarded Staples 10 pounds in damages.[13]

In 1665, Ludlow faced a grave problem. The town of Fairfield was aroused by mounting tensions between the Dutch and the Indians. The Dutch had come from Holland via New York. Having been rebuffed by New Haven when it asked for protection from the Indians, Fairfield residents unanimously voted at a town meeting to send troops and carry out the war against the Dutch on their own. This did not sit well with New Haven Colony officials, who called the action by the Fairfield citizenry "reprehensible and seditious." Ludlow knew that the criticism was directed at him and that if he remained in Fairfield, he would be brought to task.

As a result of this setback, as well as the fallout from the earlier incident with Thomas Staples, the proud, sensitive Ludlow was certain his standing in the community would be adversely affected. Seeking above all to protect his reputation, on April 26, 1654, he and his family left for New Haven and eventually settled in Virginia, where his brother, George, was a successful planter. Later, at the request of Oliver Cromwell, he went to Ireland where he served on the first Irish Commission from 1654 to 1658. Ludlow is believed to have died in Dublin in about 1665.

Meanwhile, Fairfield had become the leading town in the western part of the colony; it was rapidly becoming the hub of navigation as well as the seat of the county courts. Had he lived in Fairfield beyond 1654, Ludlow would have been gratified that a new county — called Fairfield — was established by the government in 1666, named after the town he had founded.

Another giant in Connecticut history, Thomas Hooker, was an idealistic, nonconformist, British-born Puritan preacher who shared Ludlow's passion

ALL IN THE FAMILY: Westport resident William Meyer III poses in front of the statue of Thomas Hooker, the father of Connecticut, in front of the Old State House in Hartford. Meyer is an eleventh-generation descendant of the famous colonial minister-reformer who founded Hartford and led his congregation into Connecticut. The inscription on the base of the statue (hidden) reads: THOMAS HOOKER, 1586-1647, FOUNDER OF HARTFORD, PASTOR – STATESMAN. "THE FOUNDATION OF AUTYHORITY IS LAID FIRMLY ON THER FREE CONSENT OF THE PEOPLE."
MIGGS BURROUGHS PHOTO

for freedom and liberty.[14] Growing religious persecution in England drove him to leave his motherland in 1633, after he was silenced for nonconformity in some of his remarks. He first traveled to Holland and then moved on to the Massachusetts Bay Colony where his former congregation had already settled. It soon became apparent, however, that he could no more conform to Boston's religious and political hierarchy than he could to the English monarchy and the Anglican Church.

Hooker and his Newtown congregation soon sought to leave Massachusetts in search of complete freedom. He led his congregation — 100 strong — together with their goods and cattle, westward more than 100 miles on a historic adventure through the wilderness to the Connecticut Valley, which the Indians called Quinnehtukhut ("Beside the Long Tidal River"). With only a compass to guide them, they traveled through barely passable mountains, swamps, and rivers, living mostly on cow's milk. Mrs. Hooker, too ill to walk, was carried on a litter. At the end of an arduous fortnight, they arrived at their destination, naming their first settlement, "Hartford," honoring Hertford, England. Hooker then became the leader and first minister of the First Church of Christ in Hartford.[15]

Outgoing, warm, and friendly, Hooker often showed his affection for others. As a result of his personal integrity, his inspiring sermons, and his initial exploration of the state, Hooker is considered "the father of Connecticut." As far as can be determined, there are no written records of exactly how the state's declaration of independence — the Fundamental Orders — was drawn up. While Roger Ludlow drafted it, many historians believe Hooker conceived the idea and was, perhaps, the chief source of much of the language incorporated in the document. A year before the Orders were drawn up, he preached a sermon at the General Court titled, "Doctrine and Reasons." Speaking mainly to members of the General Court, Hooker took for his text Deuteronomy 1:13: "Take you wise men, and understanding, and known among your tribes, and I will make them rulers over you." Hooker proclaimed three doctrines: First, "the foundation of authority is laid in the free consent of the people"; second, "because by a free choice the hearts of the people will be more inclined to the love of the persons chosen, and more ready to yield obedience"; and third, "they who have the power to appoint officers and magistrates, it is in their power to set the bounds of the power."[16] Thus, Hooker planted the seeds of modern-day democracy in America.

The spirit of the Reverend Thomas Hooker lives on into the twenty-first century in Westport. Today, Westport boasts a direct eleventh-generation descendant of Hooker: William Meyer III, a semi-retired businessman who has lived here for over twenty-eight years. "What I like most about Westport," Meyer says, "is that life is pretty much what anybody here wants to make it. It's ultimate freedom. Isn't that what Thomas Hooker was seeking for himself and for others?"[17]

NOTES

1. Albert E. Van Dusen, *Connecticut* (New York: Random House, 1961), p. 7. It should be noted that a Dutch explorer, Adrian Block, sailed the coast of Connecticut in 1614 and claimed it for the Netherlands. However, according to published documents, a lack of manpower put an end to the dream of a Dutch empire in America. See also Joanna Foster, *More Stories from Westport's Past* (Westport, CT: 1985), p. 36.

2. Elias B. Sanford, *A History of Connecticut* (Hartford: S. S. Scranton and Co. 1887), p. 15.

3. John M. Taylor, *Roger Ludlow, The Colonial Lawmaker* (New York and London: Knickerbocker Press, 1900), p. 32.

4. Marcus Miner, *The Fairfield Citizen-News*, December 17, 1997, p. 25.

5. R.V. Coleman, *Roger Ludlow in Chancery* (Westport, CT: 1934), p. 8.

6. Thomas J. Farnum, *Fairfield, the Biography of a Community, 1639-1989* (West Kennebunk, ME: Phoenix Publishing 1988), p. 12. Farnum states that the best study of Fairfield area Indians is Franz L. Wojciechowski, *The Paugussett Tribes: An Ethnohistorical Study of the Tribal Relationships of the Indians of the Lower Housatonic River* (Nijmegen, The Netherlands, 1985).

7. D. Hamilton Hurd, *History of Fairfield, Connecticut* (Philadelphia: J. W. Lewis & Co., 1881, press of J.B. Lippincott & Co.), p. 278.

8. The Fundamental Orders are seen as the foundation on which the Constitution of the United States was based.

9. Frank Samuel Child, *An Old New England To*wn (New York: Charles Scribner's Sons, 1895), p. 7.

10. Eleventh Annual Report, Fairfield Historical Society, p. 16. The preamble to Ludlow's Code reads as follows: "That no mans life bee taken away, no mans honor or good name shall be stained, no mans person shall be arrested, restrained, banished, dismembered nor any way punished; no man shall bee deprived of his wife or children, no mans goods or estate shall bee taken away from him, not any wayes indamaged, vnder colour of Law or countenance of Authority, vnless it bee by the vertue or equity of some express Law of the County warranting the same, established by a General Courte, and sufficiently published, or in case of the defect of a Law in any particular case, by the word of God."

11. Alexis de Toqueville, *Democracy in America*, (New York: Harper & Row, 1966), p. 41.

12. Arthur E. Soderlind, *Colonial Connecticut* (Nashville, TN: Thomas Nelson, Inc., 1976), p. 58.

13. In 1692, another outbreak of hysteria over witchcraft occurred involving charges against four women, including Mary Staples again. Of the five women indicted that year, only one was brought to trial — Mercy Disbrow, who lived at Compo, in what was then Fairfield. The trial turned into a circus. Connecticut Governor Robert Treat and his assistants all came to the courthouse in Fairfield to attend the proceedings on September 15, 1692. After two trials — the jury failed to agree on a verdict in the first — Mercy Disbrow was found guilty. The plan was to throw the women into a deep pond, giving them a chance to sink or swim. If they were witches they would die. If they were not, they would float on the water. This test was applied with "indifferent results." The

governor subsequently ordered a death sentence, but, by the time that happened, the witchcraft contagion had abated to such an extent that the townspeople were reluctant to execute the women. The death sentence was commuted; Mercy Disbrow's life was spared because the jury which brought in her guilty verdict was not the same jury that had heard all the charges, and the accusations against Mercy did not meet the criteria for conviction of witchcraft (Child, p. 66).

14. Sanford, pp. 19-20. Hooker was born in Marfield, England on July 7, 1586. He was educated at Emanuel College, Cambridge, where for some time he was a Fellow. After leaving Cambridge, he preached for a while in London and its vicinity; in 1626, he became assistant minister at Chelmsford. Faithful to the dictates of conscience, he was silenced in 1630 for nonconformity against the protest of 47 ministers in which they certified that they "knew Mr. Hooker to be orthodox in doctrine, honest in his life and conversation, peaceable in his disposition and no wise turbulent or factious." After a brief retirement in which he was kindly provided for by his friend the Earl of Warwick, he determined to leave his native land and to seek a home in Holland. Hooker remained in Holland for three years but he is said not to have enjoyed that experience. The emigration of the Puritans from England to New England was increasing and among those who planned to go were many of Hooker's old friends. They asked him to accompany them as their spiritual guide and, after spending a short time in England, he sailed for Boston about the middle of July 1633. "Mr. Hooker's Company," as it was called, which afterwards constituted his church at Cambridge, had preceded him. On September 4, 1633, Hooker first set foot on American soil at Boston. He was ordained on October 11, 1633, and began to seek practical application of his faith. During the two years that he remained in Massachusetts Colony, his influence was marked. He became deeply interested in the plan of emigration to the beautiful valley of Connecticut. It was a combination of a desire to seek an environment in which they could preach freely as well as a desire to improve their economic situation that motivated Hooker and his followers to move to Connecticut. After 11 productive years in Hartford, early in the summer of 1647, an epidemic swept through New England and tragically claimed his life.

15. Ibid., p. 20.

16. Ibid., pp. 29-34.

17. Interview with William Meyer III in Westport, October 6, 1998.

Photo, p. 27, Thomas Hooker, Westport Public Library.

CHAPTER 4

THE BANKSIDE FARMERS

The herdsman saw that it was a goodly land for white settlement.

—George Penfield Jennings,
Green's Farms, Connecticut, 1933

The seeds of modern-day Westport were planted in the fall of 1648 when five farmers from Fairfield "with Yankee knack for a good bargain"[1] acquired a strip of land along the coast from the home of the Indians of Machamux, who occupied the area around what is now Beachside Avenue and Sherwood Island on the west bank of the Saugatuck River. One historian described it this way: "The herdsman saw that it was a goodly land for white settlement. From the crest of Clapboard Hill, the foot of which was skirted by the plateau of the red men's homes, a fair country was spread before him. Below lay a flat terrain soon to be devoted to a 'Common' and just beyond the rounded slope of Bridge Hill with its oak tree — one of our

BANKSIDE FARMER: The home of Daniel Frost, one of the original five farmers who settled in "Machamux" (the beautiful land) in 1648. Tents on the left were once occupied by the Indians under an agreement that enabled the farmers to own 20 acres of land each and pay taxes to the Town of Fairfield. The area became known as Frost Point.

JOHN B. MORRIS, JR. PAINTING, COURTESY GREEN'S FARMS CONGREGATIONAL CHURCH

first landmarks. To the right was wooded Long Hill, and then the grassy expanse long known as the Horse Pasture (so named for the grassy upland leading to Sherwood Island); beyond the salt meadows and Gallup Gap Creek (so named after Captain John Gallup, whose vessels protected the English in the Great Swamp War in 1637) the beach, and the shining waters of Long Island Sound."[2]

The first three farmers were Thomas Newton, Henry Gray, and John Green. They were soon followed by Daniel Frost, who occupied the land now called Frost Point, and Francis Andrews, who lived near what is now called Sherwood Island. These early settlers took one look at the beautiful stretch of fertile fields on the banks of the Long Island Sound and staked out their claims along the Indian path that is now Beachside Avenue.

For nearly two decades, these five proprietors — variously known as the Bankside Farmers because they were located on the banks of Long Island Sound, "the West Parish Farmers," or "the Maximus Farmers"— were the only settlers in Machamux. Their land acquisition was recognized by an agreement (see Appendix B) drafted in November 1648,[3] under which the "Town of Fairfield and Thomas Newton, Henry Gray and John Green shall have Liberty to sit down and inhabit Machamux," to each own 20 acres of upland, and to build fences around their planting fields. In return, they agreed to pay taxes and to allow cattle belonging to their Fairfield neighbors to graze along the shore and to cross the Bankside lands.[4] The farmers were the first white men to acquire land in an area that had previously been occupied by the Indians for centuries.[5] The colonists made their way toward the Saugatuck River by traveling on Compo (from the Indian word, "Compaug," meaning "the bears' fishing ground") Road,[6] which the early deeds refer to as the "Broad highway," and on Green's Farms Road, which was then called the "Country Road." At that time, all major roads from one town to another were designated "Country Road."[7]

The farmers settled in a relatively untouched location, with open fields interrupted occasionally by ponds and streams, as well as tidal salt meadows full of shellfish and wild grain. Nearby was what was then called Fox Island (named from the baying of foxes; later known as Sherwood Island). The Sherwood name can be traced to one Thomas Sherwood in 1634 who sailed from Ipswich, England, on the ship *Francis* and settled in Fairfield. A fifth-generation descendant, Daniel, a patriot and soldier in the Revolution, lived on Greenfield Hill. His son, Daniel, married Catherine Burr, and they built the first house on two acres of the 100-acre island. The island was separated from the mainland by Gallop's Creek.[8]

Soon Machamux became so successful that Fairfield's town fathers kept a wary eye on the area. When the farmers purchased more land in Machamux in June 1649, Roger Ludlow brought the matter to the General Court's attention. The wily Newton, a representative to the Assembly from Fairfield since 1645, suggested a survey of boundaries. Fairfield, not wanting this investigation of its boundaries, quickly dropped the matter. The farmers' holdings were situated side by side along the shore between Frost Point and the southeast slope of Clapboard Hill, so named for the oak timber found there which was split and wrought into clapboards. A sixth farmer, Simon Couch, purchased land in 1657.

Daring pioneers all, the farmers were God-fearing, upright Puritans with the notable exception of Newton, who had daring but was not especially upright. He was involved with lawsuits for trading liquor and gunpowder with both the Indians and the Dutch. In 1650, Goody Johnson, a woman in Fairfield, said that Newton had fathered her child. Newton was arrested and jailed.[9] Possibly with the help of Thomas Staples, he escaped and was known as a lawbreaker and bounder. In 1650, he sold out his right to the land and left to find a new life, becoming one of the founders of Newtown, Long Island.[10]

Machamux attracted many more people over time. Hearing that the Bankside Farmers were reaping valuable crops at great profits and that they owned slaves and had the benefit of cheap Indian labor, the court permitted other farmers to follow from Fairfield and join those at Bankside. Their settlement did not come without dispute with Fairfield: questions involving the land boundaries of the Bankside Farmers would go on for decades.[11] The tension between farmers and others in the new community led to a number of confrontations that were immediately taken to court. Perhaps this was the origin of the litigious nature of modern Westport.

John Green, a remarkably energetic man, was the largest landholder among the Bankside Farmers. By 1699 his neighbors already referred to his holdings as Green's Farms. But the name was not officially changed to Green's Farms until 1732, because Fairfield did not want any individual landholder to become too independent.[12] Before coming to Bankside, Green had run a gristmill in Fairfield. He is said to have lived to a ripe old age and showed his humanity, according to a document recorded in 1699, by freeing his Negro slave, Harry, "upon condition that said Harry shall choose some good man to live with, and serve two years and get 20 pounds to pay the board and education of his grandson." Green signed the document with a cross because he had become paralyzed and was no longer able to write his name.

While Machamux was being settled, a nearby town was about to be born: Norwalk in 1651. It grew so rapidly that it threatened Fairfield's growth. Thus began a series of territorial disputes that made Bankside a buffer between the towns. Around this time, too, Fairfield granted a large tract of land along the Saugatuck River to the Fairfield minister, the Reverend Samuel Wakeman, to further establish the border with Norwalk that they hoped would not be crossed. The Fairfield officials' rationale was that it would be much more difficult for Norwalk to take issue with the transaction if a minister owned the land.

The western boundary of Fairfield was extended two miles from the Sasqua River. As this still left a strip between the western Fairfield limits and the east bank of the Saugatuck, Norwalk's claim to these lands came to be recognized on May 17, 1654. The original agreement of 1648 between Fairfield and the farmers at Machamux was formally sealed in 1666, and the West Parish — the ecclesiastical name of the settlement — was recognized as an entity unto itself. The agreement was signed on behalf of the farmers by John Green, Daniel Frost, Simon Couch, and Henry F. Smith. Two years later, in 1668, Fairfield taxed its citizens in order to purchase a swath of land from the Indians, six miles in

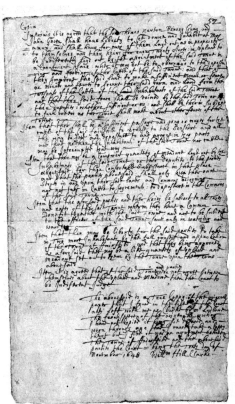

HISTORIC AGREEMENT: The document in which farmers John Green, Henry Gray, and Thomas Newton were given permission to leave the Town of Fairfield and to inhabit Machamux "forever" as farmers.
WESTPORT PUBLIC LIBRARY

width, extending north to Redding and west to the Saugatuck. North of the Bankside home lots and pasturelands, a half-mile common stretched from east to west. It was eventually determined that Fairfield should extend to the Saugatuck River, and when, in later years, the town of Westport was organized, it took portions from both sides of the Saugatuck.[13]

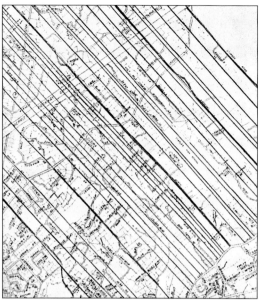

Roads have always had special meanings in Westport. The term "long lots" — ranging in breadth from 1,155 feet (or 70 rods) to 66 feet (or 4 rods), and running as long as 10 miles — came from the way the land was divided and distributed to landowners. Between 1704 and 1714, five roads were laid out across the top of Fairfield. Beginning at Long Lots Road and heading north-

LONG LOTS: Colonial map drawn up by the colonists in the early 1700s when roads were laid out across the top of the Town of Fairfield. The five main roads were Compo, Roseville, North Avenue, Bayberry Lane, and Sturges Highway; one road was even named Long Lots. Old family names appeared on the lots.

THE WESTPORT HISTORICAL SOCIETY

west into Weston, the roads were Compo Road, Roseville Road, North Avenue, Bayberry Lane, and Sturges Highway. Old family names appear on the list of those sharing the land allotments. These were the Eleven O'Clock roads, so named because officials wanted them to run true north. It was assumed that in this longitude at the time of year in question, the sun's shadow at eleven o'clock in the morning would lie true north. The width of each lot was determined by a calculation including the amount of land a Fairfield landowner already had. In other words, the rich got richer, but, presumably, landowners were taxed in proportion to their property.

Three strata of people migrated to Machamux: the professional headed by the clergy; the mainstream people who did the farming, milling, shipping, and the like; and the servants. The word *servant* applied primarily to Indians and Negroes, but also included whites who paid for their passage from England by becoming indentured servants. There were also convict indentures, called redemptioners, who were committed to four years of bound labor.[14]

The census of 1756 shows that Connecticut's Negro population totaled 3,109, which constituted 2.3 percent of the colony's total population. They were most numerous in Fairfield, which counted some 260 among its residents.[15] Although many proprietors owned slaves, even the most successful farmers did not use more than one to three slaves. Apparently, they endured a mild form of slavery, with none of them forced into hard labor. The first official mention of Negroes appears in Roger Ludlow's Code of 1650, which stipulated that Indians captured for committing crimes against white men could be sent out of the colony or exchanged for Negroes. Neither Negroes nor Indians were permitted to serve in the militia until President Lincoln put out the call in the fall of 1863 for so-called Colored volunteers.

All in all, the Code of 1650 was an enormous step forward in codifying the beliefs held by leaders of the day. It dealt with the indigent by assigning the General Court the responsibility of making each town look after its own. When families refused to provide for their poor relatives, the town took care of their needs.[16] The early settlers of pre-Westport days lived in different districts: the Compo District, first settled in 1790, the Cross Highway District, and the North District. Not much is known about the Cross Highway District farmers other than the fact that they were poor and spent much of their time at hard labor. In the North District, the long lots were laid out in 1700. Among the first inhabiting the North District were John Coley, Nathan Morehouse, Jabez Morehouse, Joseph Ogden, Joseph Gorham, as well as the Beers, Guyer and Taylor families. All of these names remain familiar to Westport as part of the town's history.

Transportation was one of the most important aspects of life in the early colonial days. Hardly a day went by when someone did not think about how troublesome it was to travel from an outlying area to Fairfield. A resident of Compo or Saugatuck, for example, faced half a day's trip to Fairfield. But, as has always been the case, it took political clout to get something done. The idea for paved roads crystallized when Governor Francis Lovelace of the nearby New York colony wrote to Connecticut Governor John Winthrop, Jr., in 1672, suggesting a plan for a "Post" system so that the two men could regularly communicate with one another. "It would be much advantageous to our designe, if in the interval you discoursed with some of the most able woodsmen, to make out the best and most facile way for a Post, which in process of tyme would be the King's best highway," wrote Governor Lovelace. Fortunately, the Indians had already forged a trail, which served as a blueprint for such a highway. But the trail was narrow and was covered with trees and bushes and there were few bridges. Therefore rivers had to be crossed where they could be forded, or waded. Nonetheless, history records that in 1673 the oldest mail route in the United States from New York to Boston along the King's Highway was established and on January 22, 1672, when the first post rider made his monthly trip, starting from New York and arriving in Boston two weeks later. Once a week service did not start until 1693.

King's Highway was improved during the 1750s and following the appointment of Benjamin Franklin as Postmaster General in 1775, the Post Road was established in 1779. It was the primary corridor connecting the northeast colonies' major urban centers. Franklin managed the setting of milestones along the newly laid-out Post Road and supervised many of the placements himself. It was not until the early eighteenth century, in fact, that anything was done about the crossing of the Saugatuck River, where King's Highway Bridge now stands.[17]

In 1715, a house that stood between Kings Highway North and the river — later identified as #1 because it was the first house on King's Highway — became the homestead of Lieutenant John Taylor, an early member of the large Taylor family, for whom the neighborhood was later called "Taylortown."[18] In 1718, Lieutenant Taylor acquired the property at #6 Old Hill Road and, in 1725, he transferred ownership of the house at #1 to his eldest son, Captain John Taylor. In 1744, Lieutenant Taylor died. He and his offspring are buried at the foot of the hill on King's Highway. Other houses nearby of historical importance are #41, the home of Daniel Nash, built by John Norris between 1727 and 1731; and on South King's Highway, #6, the house of John Platt, built around 1700 and thought to be the oldest extant house in what is now Westport.

The first sign of the Nash family in Machamux dates back to the turn of the century when two acres of land were granted to the first blacksmith in town, Thomas Nash, whose skills would become the basis for Westport's iron works industry. The earliest mention of the Nashes is in the Fairfield Town Records of November 18, 1701: "The town grants to Thos. Nash, ye smith an acre and a half of land to be laid out between Clapboard Hill and the Country Road near ye run *Hothole* Run, which grant is on condition yet he live and die in ye possession of it carrying on ye trade of a smith of Maximus."

By the early 1700s, the small original settlement of the Bankside Farmers had already developed into an independent ecclesiastical society with both religious and civil components. As was true of all of New England, the church would serve as the foundation of the modern township.

NOTES

1. George Penfield Jennings, *Greens Farms, Connecticut, The Old West Parish of Fairfield* (Green's Farms, CT: Modern Books and Crafts, 1933), p. 8. The document, dated 1848, referring to this agreement, states in part: "It is agreed that Thomas Newton, Henry Gray, and John Green shall have liberty to sit down and inhabit at Machamux; and shall have for each of them laid out as in property to themselves and their heirs, forever, twenty acres in upland."

2. Ibid., p. 7.

3. Ibid., p. 9.

4. Thomas J. Farnum, *Fairfield: The Biography of a Community* (West Kennebunk, ME: Phoenix Publishing, 1988), pp. 35-36.

5. Jennings, p. 3. In 1625, an Indian sachem variously known as Chickens, Sam Mohawk, Warrups, or Chickens Wallups was reportedly the first Native American to see a white man. Jennings refers to Chickens as "a young sachem of the Wallops tribe."

6. There was another interpretation of the word "Compo," published in the *Westporter-Herald* on November 11, 1930. According to J.W.F. Ruttenberg of New York, an authority on early Indian works and author of the book, *Indian Tribes of the Hudson Valley*, the word originated with Charley Compo, a French-Canadian who had come with the Hudson's Bay people, had married a Cayuse woman, and had learned the language of several of the tribes. Compo is said to have gone along as an interpreter.

7. According to records in files of former Town Historian Dorothea Malm.

8. From Westport Historical Society records.

9. J. Hamilton Hurd, *History of Fairfield County, Connecticut* (Philadelphia, J. W. Lewis & Co., 1881, Press of J. B. Lippincott & Co.), p. 811.

10. Elizabeth Hubbell Schenk, *The History of Fairfield, Fairfield County* (New York: Published by the author, J. K. Little & Co.1889), p. 59.

11. Charles M. Selleck, A.M., *Norwalk*, CT: Published by the author, 1896.

12. Ibid., p. 375.

13. As an outgrowth of this original concern by Fairfield's town fathers, Green's Farms has alternately been spelled with or without an apostrophe, depending on who was using it. Some people argued it should be Green's because it was Green's land. But a look at the records and signs down through the years shows no apostrophe. This weighty matter has never been officially resolved. The local newspapers prefer Green's Farms.

14. Robert Joseph Taylor, *Connecticut, A History*, KTO Press, 1979, pp. 158-159.

15. Albert E. Van Dusen, *Puritans Against the Wilderness* (Chester, CT: Pequot Press, 1975), p. 92.

16. Ibid., p. 107.

17. In 1974, the North King's Highway Area Historic District was established by the Representative Town Meeting. Many houses of note remain today: Among them: 41 Kings Highway, with its 10-foot square chimney owned originally by Noah Taylor and later Daniel F. Nash; and 40 Kings Highway, the original part of which Dennis Wright built in 1733. See Historic District records in Town Hall.

18. Westport Historical Society Archives.

Photo, p. 35, Colonial Farmhouse, Historical Picture Service, Chicago, IL.

CHAPTER 5

THE CHURCH IS THE TOWN

*The backbone of all American settlement
at the beginning was the church.*

— Edward Coley Birge, Westport historian

On the morning of June 12, 1711, the townspeople were dressed in their Sunday best to attend their first parish meeting of what became known as the Green's Farms Congregational Church. Though an unfinished structure, the square building with a pointed roof that stood on what is now called Green's Farms Road at the foot of Morningside Drive, was complete enough to be used for services. The families of the West Parish of Fairfield had been looking forward to this meeting for months, but few of the 270 residents — 88 in Compo and 182 in Machamux[1]— could have predicted its historical importance. What was then called the West Parish of Fairfield eventually became known as the Congregational Society of Green's Farms.

The foundation of modern-day Westport was being laid. The first of what would be four successive meeting houses was located at Machamux on the large open green common. The new parish was bound on the east by Sturges Highway and Sasco River, on the south by Long Island Sound, on the west by the dividing line between Fairfield and Norwalk (at the time Compo Road), and on the north by Redding.

Residents had been compelled to travel on foot or in ox-carts anywhere between two-and-a-half to eight miles from Green's Farms to attend church in Fairfield on Sundays.[2] Unhappy with this arrangement, some 24 men from the district had petitioned the General Court in 1708 to legally recognize their land area as a separate and totally self-reliant parish. Among the petitioners were Daniel Frost and Henry Gray, two of the original Bankside Farmers.[3] The others who signed the petition were Simon Couch, Joshua Jennings, Christopher Sturges, Robert Couch, Samuel Couch, Edward Jessup, Henry Gray, Jr., Thomas Nash, Thomas Disbrow, Nathan Morehouse, Benjamin Rumsey, John Andrews, William Gray, John, Peter and James Bennet, Matthew Smith, John Blackman, Thomas Morehouse, Edward Lasi, Isaac and Daniel Sherwood.

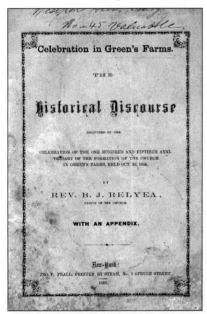

HISTORICAL DISCOURSE: Document by the Reverend B. J. Relyea, of the Green's Farms Congregational Church, October 26, 1865, celebrating the 150th anniversary of the formation of that church.
WESTPORT HISTORICAL SOCIETY

Among the families of these early settlers, in addition to the petitioners, were those of John Hyde, Joseph Hyde, Humphrey Hyde, Aaron Sherwood, Esq., James Chapman, Daniel Bradley, Aaron Jennings, Lamon Burr, Ephraim Burr, Jonathan Burr, Joseph Adams, Nathan Adams, Samuel Platt, Thomas Taylor, John Taylor, Seth Taylor, Gamaliel A. Taylor, Samuel Pearsall, and John Goodsell.

Fairfield, anxious not to lose its Green's Farms revenue, objected at first, and the petition failed to pass in the legislature. However, when the matter was brought up again in October 1710, the General Assembly in Hartford approved it, effective May 1711, unless Fairfield could show "sufficient reasons why it should not be granted."[4] The Assembly's bill also granted the parish the right to appoint a minister, and "that they shall be a distinct parish or society by and of themselves."[5] Fairfield could not mount an effective legal defense and was compelled to follow the General Assembly's directive.

The minutes of that first meeting in June 1711 are a mundane account of what transpired. They remain in print to this day because of their historic significance. They read, simply:

> At a meeting warned and accordingly held on June the
> 12-1711 at maximus Johan Drews [John Andrews] then
> being Chosen recorder for the meeting. there was then a
> cleere [clear] vote passed that thare [there] should be
> seventy pounds given to mus dannil [Daniel] Chapman for
> a years salary for preching [preaching]. Further it was voted
> that Simon Couch, John Cabel and John Andrews should be
> selectmen for this present yere. Furdere [further] it was
> voted that these men should set up notification of meetings
> in ritting [writing] one at neere the meting house in maximus
> and another at Compo sine post at lest three dayes before
> the meeting and that to be sofisunt [sufficient] warning.[6]

The church's first minister, the Reverend Daniel Chapman, had graduated from Yale in 1707; though young and untested, he soon attracted a following through his energetic, inspirational sermons.[7] In 1713, the parish members voted that a house should be built for the Reverend Chapman on six acres of land granted to the West Parish by the town of Fairfield. The church would soon become the central point of the town's religious, social, economic, and political functions.

In addition to a meetinghouse, the community needed yet another mainstay — a gristmill. In 1714, John Cable, a member of the church, built the first Tidal Mill next to what is now Old Mill Beach on Hillspoint (so named after Thomas Hill, an early English settler) Road. Cable and his family owned the mill for 76 years, selling it to the Ebenezer Sherwood family in 1790; they, in turn, worked it for more than 100 years until it burned down around 1895. The Sherwoods ground cornmeal for the West Indies trade. The story of the Mill Pond, which covers 80 acres of open water and saltwater marsh, and the Old Mill section of Westport, is filled with folklore. The pond contained clam and oyster beds, winners of blue ribbons. Tide gates to keep the level at the optimum controlled the flow of water from the pond into the Sound. The outgoing tide provided the waterpower for the Old Mill at this location. The Saugatuck and Aspetuck rivers and even Stony Brook and Muddy Brook, turned mill wheels. The mills were one of

Westport's thriving industries. Farmers from all over the countryside brought their corn to the mills, where it was ground and shipped by schooner to the West Indies.

On October 26, 1715, the church was formally organized with men named as "pillars" of the church. Among them were Joseph Lockwood, Jonathan Squire, Joshua Jennings, Henry Gray, Samuel Couch, John Andrews and Thomas Nash. That same day, the same men signed the original Covenant of the church, which stated that they pledged to deny "all ungodliness and worldly Lusts, to live Soberly, righteously, and Godly in this present world" and to follow the teachings of Jesus Christ.

The first meetinghouse rose slowly on the large, open Common or Green. It was about 36 feet on each side with 16-foot posts, the four roofs rising to a point in the center, framed of hewed oak, sides and roof covered with 4-foot clapboards cut from timber on Clapboard Hill, no fireplace, no chimney, no plaster, no paint, rough seats instead of pews, unfinished for some ten years though used steadily, and the entrance on the east side. It was not officially completed until 1720.

The church, the oldest institution in Westport, was the town. It collected taxes from the members of the parish, supervised the election of selectmen, created and ran the schools, and passed and administered the town's harsh laws. Even minor crimes or offenses meant fines or the whipping post, which was installed on the green near Green's Farms Church.[8] Although the parish church did not have a representative in the General Court in Hartford, in all other ways the church society and the local government were one.

The church's first burial place was located on the crest of the Couch family cemetery, which would become known as Burial Hill, not far from the first cabins built by the Bankside Farmers. About 1730, a beautiful rolling plot facing the probable site of a second meetinghouse across Green's Farms Road was consecrated as "God's Acre." The Old or Colonial Cemetery, as it was called, remained the burial ground for half a century, and later was returned to use, continuing to the present day. Many of the early graves in this cemetery are marked by stones in parallel rows facing due east. The idea was to be ready for Judgment Day when the faithful would rise up out of their graves facing the rising sun. Another Green's Farms graveyard was located next to the Green's Farms Church on Hillandale Road.

The membership of the church grew so rapidly that by the 1730s the first meetinghouse was drawing standing-room-only crowds. As a result, construction of the second meetinghouse began in 1738 following a great deal of discussion as to where it should be built. Disagreements between parishioners about church matters would become a tradition. But argument among parishioners and the churchmen went beyond the location of the churches; it was carried even into the sensitive issue of who should get which pews. The people were seated according to their rank in society, but that ranking in itself could be a cause of disagreement. Discussions became so heated that in one instance, the General Assembly appointed disinterested outsiders to decide on the seating.

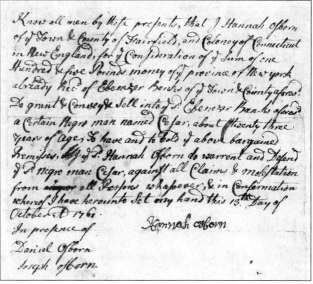

SALE OF SLAVE: Document dated "October AD 1761" affirms the sale of a slave named Caesar by Hannah Osborn to Ebenezer Banks, of Green's Farms, "for Consideration of the Sum, of one Hundred & Five Pounds money..." Caeser was paid 2 pounds 10 shillings for ringing the church bell.
WESTPORT HISTORICAL SOCIETY

The parish's second meetinghouse was located nearly opposite the present gate of the Colonial Cemetery on Green's Farms Road near the Sherwood Island connector. It was built with a long side parallel to the road, and it had a belfry, steeple, and pews. A bell was bought and hung in 1755. The congregation voted that certain people should have liberty to build their own pews around the sides of the building. The center of the church had long seats. There was a gallery where the tithing men sat in front and Negro slaves sat in the rear. There is mention that "a Negro named Caesar was paid 2 lb 10 sh for ringing the bell." A document still exists, dated "October AD 1761," that confirms the sale of Caesar to Ebenezer Banks. It reads: "Know all men by these presents, that I Hannah Osborn of the Town & County of Fairfield, and Coloney (sic) of Connecticut in New England, for the Consideration of the Sum of one Hundred & five Pounds money of the province of New York already Rec. of Ebenezer Banks of the Town & County afores Do grant & Convey & Sell into the said Ebenezer Banks afores a Certain Negro man named Cesar, against all Claims & molestation from all Persons whosoever, & in Confirmation whereof I have hereunto Set my hand this 13th Day of October ADS 1761. (signed) Hannah Osborn." [9]

The Reverend Daniel Buckingham, who graduated from Yale University in 1735, replaced the Rev. Chapman in 1742. Buckingham's pastorate, coinciding with times of economic prosperity, not surprisingly, was both peaceful and happy. From 1736 to 1757 this church served the entire West Parish from the immediate area to Redding. Reverend Buckingham served 25 years until his death in 1766. He was succeeded by the Reverend Hezekiah Ripley in 1767. Ripley would carve out a special niche for himself and the church during his tenure of more than 50 years. He came from a distinguished background: He was the grandson of an early Massachusetts settler, and his grandmother was the daughter of Governor Bradford of Plymouth. Like his predecessors, he graduated from Yale University.

The community was growing so fast that, in 1756, the northern part of the parish, Norfield, petitioned the General Assembly to become a separate parish. Ironically, as Fairfield had done when the West Parish wanted to separate itself, the West Parish now objected, but to no avail. Although Weston, which grew out of the Norfield Parish, would not officially become a town until 1787, the northern parishioners won their case in the legislature. With this change, Green's Farms lost one-third of its parishioners and the Norfield Parish itself was split because of the need for more land for the next generation of farmers.

A third meetinghouse was started in 1781, after the Revolution, on the site of the present church building and was equipped with a belfry, a steeple, and a weathervane. Once again, arbitrators had to be called in to choose the building site. Thomas Nash, a direct descendant of Thomas Nash, the town's first blacksmith, named the site "meeting-house green" which extended easterly to the church burial ground. In 1852, it burned to the ground in a fire of unknown origin, necessitating construction of a fourth meetinghouse in Green's Farms in 1853. The Nash family would become prominent in this parish for many years and would produce, as part of its indirect lineage, Daniel Nash, Jr., the man who would found Westport a half-century later.

In 1832, a group of 36 Green's Farms parishioners decided to split off and organize their own church, which would become the Saugatuck Congregational Church. The departing group wanted $1,250 of Green's Farms funds they felt that they had coming to them in overpayments. Green's Farms grudgingly agreed and handed Ebenezer Jesup a note for the "said sum payable at 60 days from the date thereof." The money given to the Saugatuck Church was raised by the Green's Farms congregation in contributions ranging from $1 to $100.

The new Saugatuck Congregational Church was built on land owned by Ebenezer Jesup located on the south side of the Post Road, some 600 yards east of and across the road from the present church site. The meetinghouse was built and dedicated on July 5, 1832, built at a cost of $6,000. The Rev. Charles Boardman became its first pastor. In 1884, Ebenezer Jesup's grandson, Morris, would donate the house Ebenezer had built in 1809, considered one of the finest in Westport, to become the parsonage for the church. In 1950, the church was moved across the Post Road to join the parsonage, a scene so unusual it was depicted in *Life* magazine.

Uriah Ambler was selected as the contractor for the Saugatuck Congregational Church in 1832. The specifications were most carefully and minutely drawn by Samuel Burr Sherwood, a distinguished lawyer. A devout Congregationalist, Sherwood was a big man, over 6 feet tall, and noted for his good humor and the hearty greeting he always gave

SAUGATUCK CONGREGATIONAL CHURCH: Formed in 1832 by parishioners from the Green's Farms Congregational Church, the new church was built on land owned by Ebenezer Jesup on the south side of the Post Road. The Reverend Charles Boardman was the first pastor.
COURTESY WESTPORT HISTORICAL SOCIETY

his friends. He became so highly respected that he was called "Squire" or "Judge" Sherwood.

From the outset, ministers played a major role in the church and the community. The Green's Farms Congregational Church's most influential ministers included Dr. Hezekiah Ripley (1767-1821), who had the longest tenure, and the Reverend Edward W. Hooker (1821-1829), a direct descendant of the legendary Reverend Thomas Hooker. All the ministers of this church encouraged the people of the West Parish to follow the church's religious, social, moral, and ethical beliefs. As a result, certain fundamental ethical and moral values have flourished down through the years and remain ingrained in members of this church today.

The ministers were the foundation of the town, but they were not alone. They were strongly supported in their basic beliefs by other educated men in the community, personified best, perhaps, by teachers and selectmen who were knowledgeable about religion and the governmental changes involved in the colonization process. Above all, they were committed to what later became known as "the work ethic."

The early colonists worked so intensely they hardly had time even for conversation. Some trace the New England Yankees' taciturn nature to their difficult beginnings. They were especially spare in their spending of money. Indeed, as one observer of the era put it: "The 'foremothers' of the West Parish of Fairfield looked well to their households. It was their pride to work and save. Thriftiness and economy were racial inheritances; conditions made them frugal. Somewhere hidden away was a stocking to hold the coin — the beginning of our mutual savings bank. Nothing was wasted; it was a case of waste not, want not. It's a Yankee, an Anglo-Saxon bit of wisdom, that still holds good. Everything was saved and put to use."[10]

Even their annual meetings took place with dispatch. The business ordinarily conducted throughout the eighteenth century started with the appointment of a moderator and a clerk. The next item on the agenda was the minister's salary and the amount of taxes that had to be levied to pay that salary. Then a tax collector was appointed "and allowed a certain compensation to collect the tax and *make it good*."[11] Firewood for the minister was at first gathered by voluntary donation, and when that did not do the trick, an annual tax of eight pounds was levied to pay it. Parishioners were also allowed to pay in wood and were credited with two shillings for half a cord of oak or walnut. Next, selectmen were appointed to make certain the parish's finances were being handled prudently. Another person was named to clean up the meetinghouse and beat the drum on Clapboard Hill to call the meeting together. Then a sheepmaster was appointed; the sheep were pastured in a common flock under the care of an appointed shepherd. This job went to the lowest bidder.[12]

Next came the appointment of a tavern-keeper. According to the minutes of the meeting of 1717, Mrs. Abigail Couch was appointed to the post, marking one of the few mentions of women in the minutes. The next mention would not come for nearly 200 years, on January 10, 1913, when it was reported in the *Westporter-Herald*, "The ladies are having electric lights installed in the church buildings."

Finally came the most important topic — education and the schools. Regulating school affairs was a part of the business of the parish meeting and was a constant source of controversy — a harbinger of many such disagreements over education that were to become part of the political fabric of the town for generations to come. The first schoolhouse was erected in

1703 on the Town Green, within the guidelines of the Code of 1650, which called upon every town of 50 households to teach all children to read and write. Towns of 100 households or more were directed to set up grammar schools, but as the population of Compo grew, its location on the Green was not considered convenient for many residents. By 1732 there were three schools: Muddy Brook, Compo, and Long Lots; the more remote districts made use of private homes. By 1747, schools had also been built at Cross Highway and at Albany (the neighborhood at the foot of the hills on the road to Weston).

GREEN'S FARMS CHURCH: Circa early 20th century, this Congregational house of worship adapted to new needs as the people and the times have changed.
WESTPORT HISTORICAL SOCIETY PHOTO

At the bicentennial anniversary ceremony of the Green's Farms Congregational Church in 1911, it was written that "The genius of Congregationalism, as of every institution to endure, lies in its ability to adapt itself to new conditions and to meet new needs as they arise." The Green's Farms Congregational Church today, under the ministry of Reverend Kevin Marshall Pleas, is proof that his church has, indeed, adapted itself to new needs. In the past half century, this parish— like all other churches across the country — has had to deal with sometimes traumatic social changes while, at the same time, upholding the traditions of the church of the past.

NOTES

1. George Penfield Jennings, *Greens Farms Connecticut, The Old West Parish of Fairfield,* (Modern Books and Crafts, 1933), p. 29.

2. Hamilton D. Hurd, *History of Fairfield County, Connecticut* (Philadelphia: J. W. Lewis & Co. 1881, press of J. B. Lippincott & Co., Philadelphia), p. 819.

3. Ford C. Slater, Slide presentation and script, "Some Bits & Pieces of Green's Farms & Church History," March 21, 1976, p. 31.

4. Reverend B. J. Relyea, *The Historical Discourse,* Green's Farms Church, October 26, 1865 (New York: P. Prall, Printed by Steam, No. 9 Spruce Street, 1865), p. 23.

5. Ibid., pp. 23-24.

6. Jennings, p. 132.

7. The Reverend Daniel Chapman, who served as pastor of the Green's Farms Congregational Church, was dismissed in 1741, having been "overtaken with too much drink." He was the son of Deacon Nathaniel Chapman, of Saybrook, and grandson of

Robert Chapman, one of the first settlers of that town. Daniel Chapman was born in 1689 and graduated from Yale College in 1707. He married Grissel Lovel, or Lovewell, of the island of Cape Breton. He inherited several tracts of land in Saybrook and 1,500 acres in Hebron. Little is known of him as a preacher. He served as pastor at the church for 26 years. He died at his home in Green's Farms in 1782, leaving seven children. He had served as a captain in the Revolutionary War and had two sons, Major Albert and Lieutenant James Chapman, who were officers in the same war. Their descendants still live in Westport; some are scattered throughout the country, and are spoken of as the "big guns" of the nation (Hurd, p. 819).

8. James T. White, "Westport, Past and Present," *The Norwalk Hour*, June 20, 1966.

9. Westport Historical Society Archives.

10. Jennings, p. 105.

11. Relyea, *The Historical Discourse*, p. 32.

12. Ibid., p. 33.

Artwork, p. 43, Saugatuck Congregational Church, 1711, courtesy of the church.

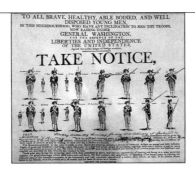

CHAPTER 6

THE REVOLUTIONARY WAR

*Westport is one of those fortunate localities which
have a clear Washingtonian tradition.*

—Julie Haggeman, Westport, writer

On Friday, April 25, 1777, a sunny and mild afternoon under a cloudless
blue sky, Green's Farms and Compo residents were astonished as they
peered off the shores of Compo Beach up the Sound and saw a fleet of
British warships approaching.[1] At first, the apprehensive observers
thought the fleet was headed further eastward, but then they saw that the
ships were rounding the eastern end of the reef off Caukeen (Cockenoe)
Island.[2] Soon, they were seen anchored off Compo Beach.

The local citizenry was taken completely by surprise. They had
heard about the battles of Lexington and Concord two years before; they
knew about Paul Revere who had spread the alarm through every village

BATTLE OF COMPO BEACH: Some 1,850 British soldiers make their way into the harbor from 26 warships on April 25, 1777. The surprise attack was met with little resistance from the "Minute Men" on the beach and the British quickly penetrated inland some 8 miles by nightfall on their way to Danbury. PAINTING BY WALTER REDDY

and farm to as many towns as possible around Boston. But they had hardly expected to see the British on their front doorstep. The strategic purpose of the British landing on Compo was to make their way to Danbury, the colonists' war supply center, and to destroy as much material as possible.

One of the first to spot the British was Mercy Disbrow, wife of Peter Disbrow. At about 4 o'clock in the afternoon she was boiling a large brass kettle of sea water on Compo Beach to make salt for her household. Her baby was asleep alone in her house. Some 100 sheep belonging to Thomas Nash were grazing in a meadow above the beach. It was an idyllic scene. "An occasional gull dove and plucked an early supper from the gentle swells, and sandpipers walked the rocky shoreline seeking small crabs and snails. Pairs of mallards swam close to the shore, and a solitary muskrat dined on sweet wild iris."[3] As Mercy Disbrow tended the fire under her cauldron, she glanced out at the water beyond the beach and, much to her astonishment, saw a fleet of 26 mainmasts, a Union Jack flying from each, carrying what appeared to be thousands of brightly uniformed, well-armed British soldiers off Compo Beach. She heard a distant volley of musketry sounding the alarm. Undaunted, she raced back to her home, snatched up her baby and boldly posted herself in the doorway in defense of her home. Meanwhile, her husband, Peter, had mounted his horse and galloped to Ebenezer Ogden's Tavern, the meeting place of the "Minute Men," on Cross Highway to spread the news. The name of the militia came, of course, from the colonists' willingness to move into battle at any time. When the British arrived at Mrs. Disbrow's house, she asked them to spare her, which they readily did.

The British landing — about 1,850 men in all — at Compo Beach and Cedar Point, led by British Major General William Tryon, had been virtually uncontested.[4] Tryon, formerly the colonial governor of New York, had visited the area after his appointment in 1771 and was now intent on dealing a blow to the Revolutionaries by destroying their food and munitions in Danbury. Two pieces of artillery were included with the first wave of soldiers, whose orders were "to occupy the advantageous Ground to cover the landing." With no opposition, this was done handily.[5] The British, guided by loyalists, proceeded up to what is now Compo Road. About two miles inland, the British troops encountered their first resistance. The local militia, armed Americans who wanted to defend their land, first confronted the enemy near the corner of Post and Compo Roads. According to one account, a group of 18 men gathered behind a stone wall on Compo Road and all agreed to fire at least one shot from their "well-aimed" muskets. They killed a major and wounded three others. The British returned the fire and, according to one storyteller, "The bullets rattled against the fence like hail against a glass window."[6]

The British penetrated as far as eight miles inland by nightfall and encamped that night in the northern part of Fairfield. Early the next morning, they headed for Redding, where they made a rest stop. They next went through Bethel without inci-

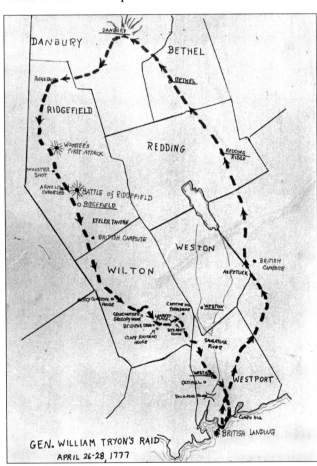

GEN. WILLIAM TRYON'S RAID
APRIL 26-28, 1777

TRYON'S RAID: British Major General William Tryon marched through Fairfield, Redding, Bethel and on to Danbury where he and his troops arrived on April 26, 1777. They destroyed an ammunition depot and burned stores and barns filled with foodstuffs and supplies. On the way back, the Redcoats met stiff resistance in Ridgefield, crossed the Saugatuck and, after a bloody fight, made their way back to their ships — but not without losing 300 of their men.

WESTPORT PUBLIC LIBRARY

dent and then on to Danbury where they arrived at 4 o'clock in the afternoon of April 26. There, the British destroyed an ammunition depot, burned 19 houses, 22 stores and barns with all their contents, including ammunition, meat, and other foodstuffs, great quantities of clothing, medical equipment, tents, tools, candles, and even a printing press. Not all of the damage inflicted at Danbury had to do with military objectives; there were reports of British soldiers getting drunk and creating havoc.

With word that American troops were approaching, General William Tryon, along with British General William Howe, departed Danbury at 10 A.M. on Sunday, April 27, heading for their ships. The British considered the entire landing a daring military operation, a raid into enemy territory to reach an objective well inland. But Tryon's escape route was by no means secure, for there were fewer Tories in the area than expected. The success or failure of the operation rested solely on the elements of surprise and speed.

On the way back, the British faced tough opposition in Ridgefield, where the still-loyal colonial officer, General Benedict Arnold rallied the local militia and had his horse shot out from under him.[7] The next day, the faithful Minute Men lay in wait for the British on the west side of the Saugatuck. There the colonial forces had a cannon in place. As the British headed toward the ambush, a Tory, Deliverance Bennett, rode north and warned the British about the ambush set at Old Hill. The British then doubled back to the Saugatuck River fording place and crossed the river. According to one account, the Redcoats came down what is now called Redcoat Road, and crossed the Saugatuck River at Ford Road. Benedict Arnold,[8] following from Ridgefield, rushed to intercept the British at a spot near the Kings Highway Bridge (which had been first constructed in 1761), and when he saw what was happening, he led a charge across the bridge so he could meet them coming down. But no one followed. He was leading about 200 militiamen and they decided this was something they really didn't want to do. Arnold lamented in his official report: "The Militia, as usual, I wish never to see another of them in action."[9] Arnold then rushed to the foot of Compo Hill where a full-scale battle was being waged, forcing the British to fight their way back to their ships in the harbor.

The British lost 300 out of 1,800 men on the way to Danbury and back. Even with reinforcements from their ships offshore, the British took a drubbing. They would later claim that the resistance they encountered was more severe than what they had faced at either Lexington or Concord. While the British were retreating, they stormed Compo Hill with their artillery and made a stand. The colonial troops, led by Colonel John Lamb tried to retake Compo Hill.[10] The American attack was so fierce that the British had to retreat from their defensive positions. After they had completely run out of ammunition, the British, fearing they would be overwhelmed, ordered a shoulder-to-shoulder charge with fixed bayonets. The ploy so demoralized the American forces that they made no further attempt to dislodge the British, allowing them to get back on board their ships and head out to sea.[11]

After the British returned to their ships and sailed away, the Minute Men burned tar barrels on a high flat-topped rock near the intersection of Compo Road and Narrow Brook Road. This unusual beacon was mistaken as a shore beacon, and one British admiral, as the story goes, crashed his vessel on the rocks. This area came to be known as Tory Reef, east of Cockenoe Island — the original name of the island off the mouth of the Saugatuck River.[12]

No one knows exactly how many people the British killed in the Danbury raid. Among the colonists who were killed were General David Wooster and Colonel Abraham Gould. Twenty-two bodies were known to have been buried in one grave on the beach, and afterward three more bodies were discovered in houses nearby. One young soldier killed was Samuel Elmer, whose gravestone can still be seen in the old cemetery at Green's Farms:

> *Lieut. Samuel Elmer,*
> *son to Col. Samuel Elmer,*
> *of Sharon,*
> *was killed at Fairfield fighting for*
> *the Liberty of his Country,*
> *April 28. 1777*
> *In the 25th Year of his age*
> *Our youthful Hero, bold in arms,*
> *His country's cause his bosom warms*
> *To save her rights, fond to engage,*
> *And guard her from Tyrant's rage,*
> *Flies to ye field of Blood and Death,*
> *And gloriously resigns his Breath.*

Two years later, on July 6, 1779, the British returned to the area, landing at Fairfield with a force of between 2,000 and 3,000 men. Tryon's forces burned 97 homes and 77 barns, 48 stores, two schoolhouses, the county house and two churches. The next day they came to Green's Farms

COMMUNION SET SAVED: *Thanks to Deacon Ebenezer Jesup and his wife, Abigail, who wrapped the Green's Farms Congregational Church's Communion silver in a bag and hid it in a well, the British were not able to steal it. They attacked Green's Farms on July 6, 1779, burning homes, barns and stores. Many Green's Farms residents lost their homes.* MIGGS BURROUGHS PHOTO

and torched everything along their way: 15 homes, including Reverend Hezekiah Ripley's home, 11 barns, several stores and the second Green's Farms meetinghouse. Before the British arrived, however, the congregation at the Green's Farms Congregational Church scampered to salvage valuables. Deacon Ebenezer Jesup and his wife, Abigail, wrapped the church's silver Communion set in a bag and lowered it down a well to keep it from the Redcoats. Jesup's home was burned but the Communion service set was saved. Others who lost their homes were Nathan Godfrey, Grummond Morehouse, Simon Couch, Widow Eunice Morehouse, Ebenezer Morehouse, George Batterson, John Davis, Abraham Adams, Widow Sarah Andrews, Jessup Wakeman, Gideon Morehouse, and Moss Kent. [13]

Over the years Westport commemorated the battle in many ways. In 1901, the community placed cannons at Compo Beach to show the exact spot where the British landed.[14] Another monument to the events of the Revolutionary War, which has long been a familiar part of Westport, is the Minute Man statue, which symbolizes the Connecticut Militia under the leadership of Colonel John Lamb. Facing north in the direction of Compo Hill, where the final battle took place, this memorial was dedicated in 1910 and was sculpted by H. Daniel Webster from a composite of descendants of colonial militia.[15]

The Revolution produced many American heroes, but none more glorious, of course, than George Washington. As a visitor to Westport on several occasions, Washington occupies a special place in Westport's history. One Westport journalist/historian wrote: "While the spirit of George Washington goes marching on in distant places where his feet never trod, we must not forget to identify and cherish the places in our own community where our records show that he once moved among us. Westport is one of those fortunate localities which have a clear Washingtonian tradition."[16]

Washington made his first visit in 1756, when he was only 24 years old and England still had relatively peaceful relations with the colonies. Summoned to Boston by General William Shirley on a military matter, he went through Norwalk and parts of Fairfield (including the area that was to become Westport), crossed the Saugatuck by ferry at the mouth of the river, and continued along Kings Highway through Fairfield on his way to Massachusetts. He is said to have traveled through "Saugatuck" (now Westport) on his way back to New York.

Many years later, on June 28, 1775, after the Continental Congress in Philadelphia had appointed Washington commander-in-chief of the Colonial Forces, he came through Green's Farms on his way to Boston on horseback. The Reverend Hezekiah Ripley, pastor of the Green's Farms Congregational Church, met him and his party near the spot where they forded the Saugatuck River. Washington is said to have stopped at the Disbrow Tavern on the east side of the river, the site where Christ and Holy Trinity Church stands today.[17] As the general and the minister continued along Green's Farms Road, they paused at Ripley's church, which stood across from the cemetery (near the modern Sherwood Island Connector). The general is said to have stopped and dismounted. He stood on the steps of the meetinghouse in Green's Farms and observed that he thought it was "a comely

GEORGE WASHINGTON RODE HERE: The drill grounds on Old Hill Road and King's Highway was along the route that General George Washington took in his 1756 visit to this area on his way to Massachusetts. He visited three more times, the last on October 16, 1789 after he had been inaugurated as the first president.

PHOTO BY MIGGS BURROUGHS.
INSET WESTPORT PUBLIC LIBRARY.

little church."[18]   When they mounted again, Washington and Ripley talked about the American rebellion. Ripley accompanied Washington as far north as Stratford and on their way they stopped at Bulkley's Inn in Fairfield. After dinner at Bulkley's, Washington continued his conversation with the reverend, a man with whom he shared a deep interest in God and religion.[19] Washington passed his fingers through the buttonhole of Reverend Ripley's coat,[20] stating that if the Americans could prolong the battle for just one year they would ultimately succeed because by that time arms and ammunition could be obtained and they would be invincible.

Washington made another visit here in September 1780 — the exact date is unclear — when he was supposed to have met the General Marquis de La Fayette and the General Count de Rochambeau at the Disbrow Inn and spent the night talking strategy.[21] When Washington returned on October 16, 1789, the Revolutionary War was over; the Constitution had been adopted, and Washington had been inaugurated as the first president in New York City on April 30, 1789. He came through Norwalk and Fairfield (Westport today) again. For this visit, which was part of his tour of inspection of the northeastern states, Washington traveled by carriage stopping between Norwalk and Fairfield. He described his trip in his diary as follows:

> At Norwalk, which is ten miles further, we made a
> halt to feed our horses. To the lower end of this Sea
> Vessels come and at the other end are Mills, Stores,
> and an Episcopal and Presbyterian Church. From
> hence to Fairfield, where we dined and lodged, is 12
> miles; and part of it a very rough road...the superb
> Landscape, however, which is to be seen from the
> meeting house... is a rich regalia. We found all the
> Farmers busily employed in gathering, grinding and
> expressing the Juice of their apples; the crop of which
> they say is rather above mediocrity. The average crop
> of Wheat they add, is about 15 bushels to the acre from
> their fallow land — often 20, and from that to 25. The
> destructive evidences of British cruelty are yet visible
> both in Norwalk and Fairfield; as there are the chimneys
> of many burnt houses standing in them yet. The principal
> export from Norwalk and Fairfield is Horses and Cattle-
> salted åBeef and Pork — Lumber and Indian Corn, to the
> West Indies, and in a small degree, Wheat and Flour.[22]

And yet again Washington stopped in Westport. A few weeks later on his return journey from Boston, the president spent the night of November 11, 1789, at the inn of Captain Ozias Marvin, who had fought in various engagements during the war. The inn then stood beyond the west bank of the Saugatuck River. When word arrived that President Washington and his party would spend the night at their inn, the owners, the Marvins, went into a flurry of preparations. Sarah Marvin and her daughters cooked up a mammoth meal for their august guest: loaves of brown bread and pies, the finest vegetables from their farm, huge roasts hanging from an open fire. They were destined to be disappointed, however: While his party took part in the banquet, the general declined the feast prepared for him, asking only for a bowl of bread and milk. Washington was not especially pleased by his visit. In his diary for that day, he wrote: "Set out [from New Haven] about sunrise, and took the upper road to Milford, it being shorter than the lower one through West Haven. Breakfasted at the former...dined and lodged at Maj. Marvin's, 9 miles further; which is not a good house, though the people of it were disposed to do all they could to accommodate me." For many years, the tavern was known as "The Washington Inn." It stood on what is now the north side of the Post Road, opposite King's Highway South.

Memories of Washington's visits delighted Westporters for many years thereafter, and those fortunate to have any memorabilia connected with Washington were ever eager to display them. For example, the blue bowl from which he ate the simple meal at the Marvins' residence was in Westport in the possession of Mrs. Ambrose Hurlbutt, "who will let a caller both see and examine." It is no longer in Westport. And Mr. and Mrs. Crauford, of Hendrick's Point, saved something that was even more impressive: a sleigh formerly owned by Mrs. Crauford's father, Alexander Lawrence, in which Washington once rode. "It might be a good idea," said an article in the *Westporter* near the turn of the century, "for Mr. and Mrs. Crauford when they visit the Congregational Church ladies' Martha Washington reception, Colonial Supper and Revolutionary relics in Toquet hall, to journey there in this sleigh, so that all the patriotic people may feast their eyes on it...[this is] as near we may ever get to the greatest of Americans." [23]

The war finally drew to a close, and the preliminary articles of peace were signed on November 30, 1782. News of England's formal acknowledgment of America's independence did not reach Connecticut until April 1783, however. In May, the Connecticut General Assembly repealed nearly all of its wartime military laws, even though the definitive Peace of Paris was not signed until September 1 of that year. And so ended one of the most challenging and proudest eras in Westport's history. As the new nation gathered its resources and began to install its governing bodies through the Founding Fathers' grand designs, the people of Green's Farms began to return to the business of daily living. With their now proverbial Yankee ingenuity, they were soon on the road to prosperity.

COMMEMORATING COMPO: These twin cannons had been deteriorating since they were placed on Compo Beach in 1901 in remembrance of the British landing in 1777. They were refurbished in 1998 by the Westport Rotary Club, which raised $75,000 in donations. One cannon was restored, one recast from the original. Here, Rick Benson, in the uniform of a Continental soldier, represents the Rotary at the official ceremony on April 24, 1999 unveiling the "new" cannons. The event was attended by Rotary members, town officials and the public. The 11-foot-long guns fired balls weighing 42 pounds each. The two muzzleloaders were known as Seacoast cannons manufactured in the United States between 1800 and 1820. They were originally dedicated on June 17, 1910. MIGGS BURROUGHS PHOTO

NOTES

1. D. Hamilton Hurd, *History of Fairfield County, Connecticut* (Philadelphia: J. P. Lippincott & Co., 1881), pp. 814-815.

2. Pronounced Ka-Keenee, stemming from Caukeen and Chachanenas, one of the Indian signers of a deed giving the island to the settlers of Norwalk, 1651. The name is also identified with an Indian named Chekanoe, an Indian of Manhansick (Shelter) Island.

3. Fairfield journalist/historian Harry Peabody, research for article for the *Westport News*, April 9, 1986.

4. William R. Stewart, "The British Are Coming, the British Are Coming, "*Profile Magazine*, October 1983, pp. 30-33.

5. Ibid.

6. Hurd, p. 814.

7. Ford C. Slater, Paper, "Some Bits & Pieces of Green's Farms Church History," March 21, 1976, p. 55.

8. Elsie N. Danenberg, *Naval History of Fairfield County Men in the Revolution* (Fairfield, CT: Fairfield Historical Society, 1997), p. 31.

9. Westport Town Historian Allen Raymond, in an address to Y's Men, March 1998.

10. William Hanford Burr, *The Invasion of Connecticut by the British and the Landing at Compo Beach* (Westport, CT: Westport Library Association, 1928), p 7.

11. Robert McDevitt, *Connecticut Attacked: A British Viewpoint, Tryon's Raid on Danbury* (Chester, CT: Pequot Press, 1974), p. 63.

12. In 1835, when Westport was incorporated as a town, Cockenoe Island became part of it. Geologists have reported that the island is a leftover from the Ice Age. When ice melted, it dropped a mound of debris called recessional moraine. Today, only the higher parts of the moraine are above water, showing themselves as islands.

13. In 1792, 500,000 acres of land as reparations in the Western Reserve were given to those from Fairfield and Norwalk who were attacked.

14. *The Minuteman*, August 13, 1998, p. 1. The Rotary Club launched a "Save the Cannons" effort in 1998 to restore the deteriorating guns. The "mystery" of where the Compo cannons came from was revealed in 1998 when Walter Nock, artillery specialist at the U.S. Military Academy at West Point Museum, addressed the Westport Rotary Club and told them his conclusions. This was believed to be the first time that Westporters heard of the cannons' origin. The 11-foot-long guns fired balls weighing 42 pounds each. The two muzzleloaders were known as Seacoast cannon, manufactured in the United States between 1800 and 1820, according to Nock. The Army gave the cannons to Westport from its obsolete ordinance in 1901 to commemorate the Revolutionary War Battle of Compo Beach in 1777. Although it has long been known that the guns were not used in the actual battle, local and state archives shed no light on their origin or history before 1901. On June 17, 1910, the Minuteman statue was dedicated with considerable ceremony. It has become part of the town flag, which was designed by Westporter Miggs Burroughs for the 1985 150th celebration of the town's founding. The inscription on the cannons reads: "To commemorate the Battle fought on and near this Point, between the British Forces and the American patriots April 28, 1777. Ordinance Presented by the United States Government and Erected July 4, 1901. Tablet presented by the Compo Beach Volunteer Life Guards."

15. The inscription on the Minute Man statue reads: "To commemorate the Heroism of Patriots who defended their country when the British invaded in this State April 25, 1777. General David Wooster, Colonel Abraham Gould and more than one hundred Continentals fell in the Engagements at Danbury, Commencing and Closing on Compo Hill. Erected by the Connecticut Sons of the American Revolution, 1910."

16. Julie Haggeman, "Westport's Washingtonian Tradition," *Westporter-Herald*, December 29, 1943.

17. Joanna Foster, "The Way Westport Was," *Westport News,* February 20, 1985.

18. Ibid.

19. Reverend Ripley's meeting with Washington in 1775 in Westport is commemorated on the Machamux memorial boulder at Green's Farms, dedicated on April 17, 1932 by the Daughters of the American Revolution, mainly to memorialize the friendly relations between the Indians and the early settlers. The boulder is inscribed: "Ye Indian Name — Machamux. Ye Bankside Farmers —1648. Ye First School House — 1703. Ye First Meeting House — 1711. Ye Name Greens Farms — 1732. Rev. Hezekiah Ripley, D.D., Chaplain of the Continental Army, escorted General George Washington along the high-

way — 1775. Ye Burning by the British — 1779."

20. This gesture of George Washington while talking to Ripley is said to be the source of the term "buttonhole," referring to someone who seeks the ear of another.

21. Haggeman.

22. John C. Fitzpatrick, *The Diaries of George Washington, 1748-1799* (Boston and New York: Published for the Mount Vernon Ladies' Association of the Union, Houghton Mifflin Company, November 1925), p. 51.

23. *Westporter,* February 19, 1898.

Photo, p. 53, Revolutionary War recruiting poster, collection of Woody Klein.

PARKIS, VINCENT & HINMAN,
SHIPBUILDERS.
Repairing done on most favorable terms.
SAUGATUCK,
Near the Westport R. R. Depot.

CHAPTER 7

THE RISE OF COMMERCE AND INDUSTRY

The hungry cities of the world were beckoning
to the fertile fields of virgin New England.

— Edward Coley Birge, Westport historian

In the immediate aftermath of the Revolutionary War, the farmers of Saugatuck, weary from battle but basking in their new nation's independence, embraced their fresh, new lives with seemingly limitless possibilities. Excitement in the Village of Saugatuck, as the town was then called, was palpable as the town began to combine its farm-based economy with a bustling, new shipping industry that would soon carry their produce to all parts of the world. As Westport historian Edward Coley Birge expressed it, "The hungry cities of the world were beckoning to the fertile fields of virgin New England." [1]

At the turn of the nineteenth century, 85 percent of the men in this

SEAFARING TOWN: In the early 1800s, market boats enabled Saugatuck entrepreneurs to use the waterways to vastly increase commerce with other towns and cities such as New York, Boston and Providence, and as far away as the West Indies. National Hall is at right. PAINTING COURTESY OF AL WILLMOTT

grain-growing village were still farmers, "sunrise-to-sunset men — robust, hard-laboring, industrious fellows, obtaining from the earth annually large quantities of rye, corn, oats, flax-seed, etc." Even as recently as the beginning of the twentieth century, Saugatuck was the largest grain and flax market in Fairfield County.[2] The almost universal feeling among these new Americans was that prosperity was at hand for the new nation.

One important route to this success was by water. By 1800, New York City had grown to a population of just under 96,000, and this giant port represented a major new market for farm products. The only way to reach the city in a timely manner was by boat. This part of the world did not yet have a railroad, and travel by coach or horseback along King's Highway was long and arduous. The market boat business soon became a booming enterprise. It was ushered in when the first market boat, *Pedler*, sailed to New York City in 1806. Built in Westport by Captain Samuel Pearsall and the company of Rowland & Barlow, it was the first of the weekly market boats out of Saugatuck bound for the city. It marked the opening of an era of rapid growth in trade and commerce by water. In 1814, two local men, L.T. and S.E. Downs, bought the sloop *Diana* for the coastwide trade. The next year the *Intrepid* was built and in 1817 the *Iris* was built by G. Bradley & Co. Cargoes.

With all its waterways, Saugatuck naturally became a seafaring town. All along the river there were warehouses and shipyards, one of which served as the site for the construction of the schooners *Sara B. Bulkley* and *Francis Burritt*. Merchants built many ships here; they were a daily sight at Old Mill and the Compo Cove. The Saugatuck River could be navigated farther up from the Sound than any other Fairfield County stream. Westport writer-historian Eve Potts observes: "The sea captains built their homes along the river where they could see their vessels in the harbor. Ships sailed from Westport to New York, Boston and Providence with grain, vegetables — especially onions — and butter, to Texas for cotton and to the West Indies for sugar, molasses and hardwood lumber."[3]

Harvests were plentiful, and the boats carried food for tens of thousands of people both in America and the West Indies. An important historian of the 1880s described a ship's cargo in detail: "If we could go back, say to 1825 or 1830, and step on board one of those boats as it was about to leave…we should see in the hold one hundred to two hundred bushels of oats, ten to twenty bags of rye flour, one hundred to one hundred and fifty tubs of butter (averaging about twelve pounds each), five to ten barrels of eggs, fifty or more boxes of hats, boxes of combs, boxes of axes, and any quantity of bundles of unknown contents. On deck we should see five to ten calves, and in the cabin or quarter-deck ten to fifteen passengers."[4]

Indeed, the Yankee spirit of free enterprise was much in evidence. There was a dramatic change in how people viewed themselves in the post-Revolutionary era. No longer were the farmers of Green's Farms simply Puritans. Nor were the working-class people satisfied to be laborers subservient to the upper-class merchants and ship captains. The metamorphosis from Puritan to Yankee was abundant and clear. A spirit of individualism and self-determination resonated throughout Saugatuck, indeed, throughout the north. A strong laissez-faire attitude took hold in a free market where the bottom line was profit and the accumulation of material wealth. A sense of freedom permeated every institution — the church, the school, government, the farm, business, even the family. The result was much stiffer competition and personal confrontation, and yet it also was a challenge for the creative-minded, in virtually every field.

Journalism was one of the first professions to bloom in this fertile new era. An early newspaper, *The Norwalk Gazette*, a family newspaper published by A. H. Byington & Co., began publishing in 1817 and covered Saugatuck. In 1829 the town launched its first newspaper, *The Saugatuck Journal,* edited by Seth W. Benedict, a local man who had a flair for writing. The first issue was published on Christmas Day. Benedict also published the *Gazette* in Norwalk. Three years later he sold the paper to Albert Hanford, another businessman who envisioned a newspaper that would serve not only Saugatuck, but also other towns in the county. Accordingly, he changed the name of the newspaper to *The Fairfield County Republican*.

Also in 1828, the Woods factory, run by William Woods, provided jobs that kept the economy going. Woods did an extensive business in cotton batting. Tanneries produced leather for harnesses, hatbands, and satchel linings. Saugatuck had a reputation for making the finest satchels in the country.

The Town of Saugatuck was attracting many of the professions, although as yet few doctors served the community. The first permanent physician in the Civil War period was David Richmond, who was soon joined in partnership by Talcott Banks. Before that, the people of Saugatuck relied on the local druggist and on those few physicians who traveled through town for medical advice. Doctors in those early days were perceived as men in whom one could confide. One observer referred to them as "a court of first resort," pointing out that many people brought their problems to a doctor seeking advice and counsel.[5] At the same time, starting a trend that would accelerate in future generations, more and more young men turned to the law, as life in the New World became more complex. Among the attorneys who practiced in Saugatuck were Samuel Burr Sherwood, Eliphalet Swift, James C. Loomis, Samuel Chamberlain, Theodore Kellogg, M. L. Mason, M. W. Wilson, Wesley Lyon, William K. Seeley, James R. Jesup, E. M. Lees, Albert Relyea, and Joseph G. Hyatt. Perhaps the best known of these is Sherwood, whose name looms large in Westport's history. A Yale graduate, Sherwood was one of the town's first lawyers and, in 1809 at age 42, he traveled to Hartford to begin his first term in the Connecticut Assembly. In 1817, he won election as a Federalist to the fifteenth United States Congress. Horace Staples, a contemporary of Sherwood's, observed that Sherwood "despised quibbling and chicanery," so Sherwood decided to leave the Congress in 1819 and resume his law practice in Saugatuck.

The new era of broader freedom of expression and economic expansion was accompanied by social progress that manifested itself through progressive legislation. The Connecticut Constitution of 1818 included a bill of rights stating that "all political power is inherent in the people" and guaranteed individual rights such as freedom of speech and press, trial by jury, and the right of habeas corpus. This guarantee had a profound effect on the slave trade. Slaves could no longer be sold at public auctions. Instead of being forced to take up new roots, however, with the exception of a few private sales between owners, slaves were permitted to remain with the families where they were born. The state constitution also disestablished the church as a quasi-government institution, as a result of which public schools would be run by the states or towns and no longer by the churches. The Negro population was permitted to form its own churches in the 1820s, as well as schools and lodges. Although a "gradual emancipation" law had been passed in 1784, the state didn't completely outlaw slavery until 1848.[6]

The townspeople of Saugatuck, in addition to showing increasing tolerance towards Negroes, slowly began to welcome people of different religions into the social fabric of the town. The first Jewish family to come to this area was the family of Michael Judah. Judah, who had arrived in 1742, was a merchant trader specializing in corn that he bought from local farmers and shipped to the West Indies. He had relatives in Savannah, Georgia, which was then known as "a cultural center of Colonial Jews."[7] The Sephardis, who for centuries had been part of the wealthy, intellectual class in Spain and Portugal, arrived in Savannah in 1734, having fled religious persecution in those countries. They also came to New York, Connecticut, and Rhode Island, where they hoped to start a new life.[8]

Judah had strong ties to the oldest Jewish congregation in America, Sherith Israel (*Remnant of Israel*), which gathered in New York City. The congregation generously helped young Michael to establish a business in Norwalk, which would later be annexed as part of Westport. He married the daughter of the Raymonds, a local Gentile family in Saugatuck. And after the war, their son, David, married into the Taylor family, one of the early settlers in Saugatuck. As this example shows, intermarriage between Jews and Gentiles was not unknown in colonial America. Today, when one sails into the Saugatuck River from the west, one passes a prominent rocky point that has become known as Judah's Rock or Cove (so named after the Judah family who lived there until about 1850) and later called Judy's Point.

One of the Judah's neighbors was the second Ebenezer Jesup, a descendant of Deacon Ebenezer Jesup of the Green's Farms Congregational Church. The Judah-Jesup relationship became closer over the years. Ebenezer's son, Edward, married Esther, one of Judah's daughters. Another of the Judah's daughters, Patty, married Lewis Raymond, whose cotton factory on the Saugatuck eventually became Lee's Mill. Judah's son, David, became a sea captain; and one of the younger sons, Henry, became an Episcopal minister. Michael Judah died in 1824, but the long relationship between the Judahs and the Jesups continued. Nonetheless, it was not until 1843 that the civil rights of Jews were, for the first time, officially protected through an act of the state legislature that guaranteed them equal privileges with Christians in forming religious societies.

Meanwhile, religion appeared to take a back seat to prosperity in business where everybody was accepted. The Saugatuck businessmen needed to expeditiously transport all their goods and produce to the ships waiting at the shore's edge. In 1803, a major problem arose impeding the free flow of products across the waters. A bridge under construction on the new Post Road (or State Street) became a major navigation hurdle. The federal government, eager to avoid any blockage of commerce, found the perfect solution: Why not adopt the medieval method, the drawbridge, that could be operated with pulley and chain? The problem would remain unsolved until 1848 when the railroad finally came to the area.[9]

In 1816, Easton Road was built, providing a thoroughfare that saved time and enabled people to travel in greater relative comfort than before when they traversed dirt roads with gaping holes in them. The new road was bitterly opposed by Fairfield, which feared that the port of Saugatuck

TIDE MILL: Erected in 1833, the famous landmark's specialty was grinding kiln-dried corn for shipment to the West Indies. It housed a cooper shop for making barrels that were put on ships at the mill, which was destroyed by fire in 1891.
THE WESTPORT HISTORICAL SOCIETY PHOTO

would take shipping business away from nearby towns. The courts, however, rejected Fairfield's legal objections. The anger of Fairfield officials was not quickly abated. Even after 1835 when Westport would be incorporated as a town, rumblings about the "infamous Saugatuck road" could be heard.

On November 3, 1810, the birth of the "Sherwood Triplets" — Francis, Franklin, and Frederick — to Daniel and Catherine Burr Sherwood, signaled the beginning of a new generation of mariners. Millers by trade for five generations, the Sherwoods built the foundation and breakwater of Compo Mill, the famous Tide Mill of Westport, erected in 1833. Inside the building was a cooper shop for making barrels that were loaded into ships docked at the mill.[10] The mill's specialty was grinding kiln-dried corn for shipments to the West Indies. The mill was destroyed by fire on November 9, 1891.

The Sherwood Triplets — the youngest of ten children — all went to sea at the age of 16 and eventually became famous sea captains. One story handed down through the years and often told by Westport Town Historian Allen Raymond concerns a trip by Frederick. On one of his many voyages, returning on his ship, *Starlight*, laden with gold, Frederick became aware that another ship was chasing him. One can imagine what it must have been like in the middle of the ocean: two of these great square-riggers, one loaded with gold, and the other trying to get the gold. This went on for three days, and at one point Frederick had all the gold put on deck; if he was caught he could dump the gold into the ocean. Fortunately, he got away and sailed into port with his cargo intact.[11] Legend has it that it took only 108 days for Frederick to make it to California and that he was rewarded by the ship's owners with a set of silver coins and a new uniform. Prior to this incident, Frederick had been in Liverpool, England, in 1861 just when the Civil War broke out in the United States. The owners of his ship directed him to register the *Starlight* under the British flag, but loyal and independent Captain Frederick responded that he would sail only under the American flag. So the order was rescinded, and, with his Stars and Stripes flag flying proudly in the wind, he sailed out to sea.

The brothers were, for the most part, engaged in the coastal trade of passengers and freight between New York and southern ports. Captain Francis Sherwood carried General Winfield Scott's messages to New Orleans announcing the capitulation of Mexico City under the command of Santa Ana in the Mexican War of 1846. From 1835 to 1839, Captain Franklin Sherwood was engaged in trading between New York and Havana, New Orleans, and Texas ports, as well as European cities such as Le Havre and Liverpool. Capt. Frederick Sherwood traded with southern ports and made six voyages to California by way of Cape Horn.

The three brothers looked very much alike and often delighted in playing jokes on the unwary. As the story goes, once when they were in Charleston, S.C., one of them went into a barbershop and asked for a shave.

THE SHERWOOD TRIPLETS: From left, Francis, Franklin and Frederick signaled a new generation of mariners. The triplets looked so much alike that they were frequently taken for one another and, blessed with a good sense of humor, all three enjoyed playing games with people who could not tell them apart.

WESTPORT HISTORICAL SOCIETY

A little while later, the second brother walked in and also asked for a shave. The barber looked at him rather curiously but somehow managed to shave the fastest growing beard he had ever seen. Finally, the third Sherwood brother entered the barbershop, with a beard, and, apparently overcome by bewilderment, the barber fled, shrieking that he was "voodooed."[12] The triplets were but a few of the many men in Saugatuck for whom the sea became a new home.

As part of the folklore of this era, we also have the tale of Captain Ned Wakeman, a strapping, broad-shouldered, six-foot sailor who also put to sea at age 16 and made it his life's journey. He was born in Saugatuck in 1813, and by the time he was 12, he taught himself how to read and write. Among his acquaintances were men like the Sherwood triplets and Ambrose Hurlbutt. Wakeman was not especially liked and had a reputation for being unreliable. For example, while men like the Sherwoods were building a reputation as accomplished seafarers, Ned Wakeman, very early in life, developed a reputation for "chance taking." On one occasion, he rode his sled down a hill right into the frozen Saugatuck River, nearly drowning. A neighbor who knew him well concluded that "A boy that's born to be hanged ain't likely to drown."[13] Another story was that once he stole a brand-new ship, *New World,* a shallow-draft side-wheeler meant for river travel, which had been impounded because the owner had gone bankrupt. He had no official papers, but with the owner's approval, he took the boat out all by himself from New York harbor and down the North and South America coasts, around Cape Horn, and then arrived in San Francisco. The storyteller adds: "When he stopped to refuel in Brazil, he had to face the problem of no ship's papers. As he was being rowed ashore in his second-best uniform, he lost his balance and fell overboard. The black box that supposedly contained the ship's papers was gone. The U.S. Consul in Brazil made out new papers for Captain Ned Wakeman and the *New World,* and they were in hand when the side-wheeler steamed into San Francisco harbor with all flags flying. As Ned assured the owner, the *New World* soon became 'the fastest boat on the Sacramento River.'"[14]

Mark Twain, an admirer of Ned Wakeman, described the sea captain as "hearty and sympathetic and loyal and loving a soul as I have found anywhere, and when his temper is up, he performed all the functions of an earthquake without the noise." An obituary in the *San Francisco Call* in 1875 reported that his name was known in every quarter of the globe and that he numbered his friends in the thousands. Ned Wakeman came back to Westport from time to time to visit his family and friends. He is said to have loved his hometown. He came from sturdy stock, sharing an ancestor with Horace Staples and Mary Wakeman Staples, the nemesis of Roger Ludlow in the era when he founded Fairfield.

Among the other sea captains of note in those days were Burr Thorp; his son, Henry Thorp; John Bulkley and Peter Bulkley; Charles Allen, Sereno Gould Allen, Charles H. Allen, Ebenezer Allen, William H. Allen; Abram Sherwood, a brother of the Sherwood triplets; John Hyde Coley; the Fairchild brothers: Samuel and Charles H. Fairchild, Francis Godfrey, Henry Pierson Burr, William S. Guyer, Edgar Wakeman, William C. Staples, John B. Elwood, Hezekiah Elwood, Charles H. Jennings, and Increase A. Parsell.[15]

The Jesup clan dominated those early post-Civil War years of transition in Saugatuck. Ebenezer Jesup was reputed to be the most successful grain dealer in the county and even in the state.[16] He and his family were among the most highly esteemed of all those in Saugatuck. The Jesups were an old colonial family from Manhattan with large holdings of land along the north shore of Long Island Sound. Four Jesups, two Edwards followed by two Ebenezers, connect the early settlement with the eventual founding of Westport. The first Edward (1663-1732) was a farmer and maintained the Green's Farms tract in good shape with buildings and stone walls. The second Edward (1697-1750) prospered in the West Indies trade and played a key role in developing the wealth of businessmen along the eastern seaboard. The first Ebenezer Jesup (1739-1812) was a country doctor in Green's Farms, served as a surgeon in the Continental Army, and was a deacon of the Green's Farms Congregational Church. He and his wife, Sarah Wright, had a son, Charles Jesup, born on March 10, 1796. Charles and Abigail Jesup raised nine children, one of whom was Morris Ketchum Jesup, born in 1830. Morris Jesup, after amassing a fortune in the railroad business, would become a philanthropist and the benefactor of the Westport Public Library, among the accomplishments for which he would become well known in later years.[17]

MARITIME MAN: Ebenezer Jesup (1767-1851), was an innovator who played a key role in the rise of business and free enterprise in Saugatuck. He made a reputation for himself in the shipping industry as well as in the field of horse-drawn carriages.
WESTPORT
HISTORICAL SOCIETY

The second Ebenezer Jesup (1767-1851) at age 23 built the first wharf and warehouse on the banks of the Saugatuck River in 1790 and initiated a major maritime development of the Saugatuck River. The Jesups joined the Saugatuck Congregational Church when it was established in 1832. The church was founded by 36 members of the Green's Farms Congregational Church who were, at their own request, as we learned earlier, dismissed to form a separate church nearer their homes. They decided they wanted to split off from the Green's Farms church, just as the Green's Farms Church in 1711 had split off from Fairfield.

With improved roads, many new modes of transportation appeared. The first stagecoach, which passed through Westport near the Three Bears Inn on Newtown Turnpike and Wilton Road, was introduced soon after the founding of Westport. Different kinds of carriages were seen; some of the fanciest were called wheeled pleasure vehicles. Ebenezer Jesup, who continued to be addressed as "Major" after the war, had one of his ship captains, Hezekiah Allen, purchase an elaborate horse-drawn carriage from Boston for $300 and bring it to Saugatuck on one of his vessels. "So startling an innovation was this in the quiet life of Saugatuck that we are told that Major Jesup kept it in his carriage-house for six months before he ventured to use it."[18]

Through his persuasive personality and his business acumen, Jesup, a dealer in wholesale grain and produce shipping, would eventually become the wealthiest resident in the village of Saugatuck. During the first 25 years of his business, his books show that he bought 500,000 to 750,000 bushels of grain a year from farmers in the area and kept three to four ships that constantly moved his produce. Ebenezer Jesup was an entrepreneur of the first order: "He was prominently identified with progress. Not only did he have interests in vessels, but in his life of activity he displayed those qualities which, were he alive now, and could be placed among the bold financial operators of the metropolis' great business center, would mark him as a king in their midst."[19]

In the spirit of the rapidly expanding enterprises, Saugatuck encouraged the formation of community-minded organizations. In 1824, the Free and Accepted Masons established Temple Lodge No. 65 in Westport. According to the records of the Most Wonderful Grand Lodge in the Masonic Temple in Hartford, the charter was signed by Ralph I. Ingersoll, Grand Master. The Order's origin can be traced back to 1717 in London.[20] This fraternal organization has played a behind-the-scenes role in helping the community in a number of ways through financial contributions to good causes.

One of the very first general stores in Saugatuck opened in 1798 near the west side of the river. It was owned and occupied by Joel Scribner, sold in 1801 to James Hurlbutt, and passed along to Henry Haydock, of New York in 1804, only to be sold to "Uncle" Daniel Nash, who ran the only grist mill in the center of town at the turn of the century. Nash sold the house to Lewis Raymond, who kept it until 1815. Much of this time, a market boat was run from it. Another early store belonged to John Warren Taylor, who combined a drug store with a book enterprise in 1834. It was one of the most successful stores in town in the early days, attracting both young and old. Taylor also had the distinction of serving as town clerk for thirty-seven years.

One of the town's most outstanding citizens, Ebenezer Coley, built a structure in 1775 on Main Street that was eventually used as a ship's store. Almost two centuries later when it was painted pink and converted into The Remarkable Book Shop,[21] it became a beloved landmark to Westporters and visitors alike. Another landmark erected in 1810 was Levi T. Downes' general store, later known as the Levi Downes homestead, was eventually used as a private school house. Today it is known as Tavern on Main, one of the most historic and attractive buildings in downtown Westport. Retired Town Historian Dorothea Malm points out that the industries that grew up in Saugatuck included the production of hats, shoes, carriages, harnesses, leather, stoves, and products of cotton and woolen mills.[22] Dan Taylor's shoe manufactory was also one of the notable businesses.

Among the entrepreneurs of that day was Daniel Platt, who bought a house at the corner of Post Road West and Riverside Avenue and had a carriage shop and plank shop on the opposite side of the street. He placed an ad in *The Saugatuck Journal* in 1829: "I have enlarged my establishment and have several first rate workmen from New York. CARRIAGES/ BLACKSMITH work."[23] In 1903, the *Westporter-Herald* published a nostalgic column, *Reminiscent Westport,* that recalled Platt's "energy and goatheadativeness" (sic). The article told of how Platt in 1832, built a 26' x 36' barn in *one* day. Builder Stephen Nash was selected; he, in turn, hired nine carpenters and sixteen farmers to do the heavy work. Before they finished the barn, including painting, and laying the floors, six shock of wheat were threshed, the grain carried to Nash's Mill, the flour returned and, finally, biscuits for all made by Mrs. Platt. "All this in only ten hours," said the article. The Platts were widely known for manufacturing fine carriages, which were shipped down south to rich landowners. The Platts also made coffins, barrels, wagon wheels, and other vehicle parts.

One of the most notable of the other young businessmen in the early nineteenth century was Horace Staples. Staples was born on January 31, 1801, in the Fairfield home that had been built by Deacon John Staples, Sr., of the Greenfield Hill Congregational Church, and occupied for 85 years by John Jr., Horace's father. Horace Staples was a direct descendant of Thomas Staples, one of the settlers who helped Roger Ludlow found the town of Fairfield in 1639. Staples' lineage can also be linked to John Banks, a wealthy barrister, who came from Windsor to Fairfield in 1651; Horace Staples' mother Patty Banks, was a descendant of John Banks. As Horace Staples gradually became a successful businessman and public-minded servant, his Yankee thriftiness became one of his hallmarks. "He was not afflicted with a champagne appetite and a beer income," is the way one historian described him.[24]

At 26, Staples entered upon a business career in Saugatuck. He married and built the house that was to be his home for the remainder of his life, and he formed a partnership with Edwin Wheeler. As Staples & Wheeler, they dealt in lumber, hardware, paint, and other building and farm supplies. The patronage of this firm was very large, coming from all sections of Fairfield County. Staples also had a canal dug across the Great Marsh to Cedar Point, which cut across the mouth of the Saugatuck River and thus reduced sailing time to and from New York.

Two other businessmen, Scudder Bradley and Alva Gray, joined the rapidly expanding business activities in the early nineteenth century. Bradley was involved in the building trade; he was an investor as well and, by 1833, owned four houses. Gray was descended from Henry Gray, one of the original Green's Farms Bankside Farmers. Gray had a wharf and general store on Main Street where he sold builder's hardware. He came to prominence when he became chief clerk to Saugatuck's first postmaster, Stephen Barlow (see Appendix C), who held that office for twenty years. The first post office in Saugatuck was established in 1815. Gray became a power in the town, serving as county surveyor and later as president of the Westport

Savings Bank. He was a citizen volunteer in a group that was formed to apprehend anyone caught stealing. An 1829 notice in the newspaper announced that he was "Secretary of the Saugatuck Society for the Apprehension of Thieves."

Other businesses of the day included William T. Woods' cotton factory, named Phoenix Mills, located near Guilder's land in the Richmondville area. The Woods factory was important to the economic health of the community. Built in 1828 and run by William Woods, it did an extensive business in cotton batting. Tanneries produced leather for harnesses, hatbands, and satchel linings. Farther up the Saugatuck River at Ford Road and Sipperley's Hill Road, on the site of Sam Coley's gristmill, the Branch Manufacturing Company erected a building and installed machinery for spinning cotton in 1829. It later converted to grinding grain. Robert Holden had a mill in Aspetuck that made cotton batting. It was located at North Avenue and Coleytown Roads. Yet another entrepreneur was Zalmon Adams who had a woolen factory at Easton Road near Bayberry Lane on the Aspetuck River.

Saugatuck had numerous merchants who were able to profit from the political circumstances of their day. In 1814, Edward Nash, the great grandson of Daniel Nash, Sr., owned a gristmill known as the Nash Mill on King's Highway. Corn was ground there for feed and flour that was shipped to the West Indies trade. In that same year, Lewis Raymond and a local doctor, David Richmond, organized the Saugatuck Manufacturing Company in response to the high price and scarcity of cotton cloth caused by the War of 1812 when the British blockaded American ports. Raymond and Richmond determined to manufacture cotton at a much lower price, but they would not have a great deal of success.

Interest in manufacturing cotton was evident. In 1815, the second Ebenezer Jesup applied to the General Assembly for a charter that would allow him to manufacture woolen and cotton fabrics. He and his numerous stockholders invested in a

FAMILY AFFAIR: Lees Manufacturing Company produced ribbons, boucle, seine, cotton twines, candlewick and cord. Four generations of Lees oversaw the manufacturing facility and Lees Mill.

WESTPORT PUBLIC LIBRARY

77

stone factory built near the King's Highway bridge. The machinery was originally run by waterpower, which is why the river was dammed, forming Lees Pond. They began to manufacture cloth in their mill at a much lower cost than the going rate, turning out large quantities of cloth that were shipped from the Jesup dock. When the War of 1812 was over, however, they couldn't compete with English textiles dumped on the American market.

In 1844, the Richmondville Manufacturing Company mill on Richmondville Avenue next to the Saugatuck River became the Lees Manufacturing Company and was run by John Lees for 28 years and by his son, Thomas R. Lees, after him. Four generations supervised Lees Mill and the manufacture of tinsel ribbon cords, fringes, ribbons, boucle, seine and cotton twines, candlewicks and cord. The work was done mostly by children and women, often at home.

Women, as they had traditionally done over the ages, stayed home but a large proportion of them engaged in loom work at home weaving thread or woolen yarns. They manufactured both men's and women's apparel as well as all bedding materials. Women may not have been valued as highly as men in the classroom, but they were much appreciated at home. The social etiquette of the time required that a lady possess enough worldly goods to make her an attractive candidate for matrimony. She needed a sizable wardrobe, and those with substantial linens and woolens were held to be akin to an heiress. Tea parties were frequent, and sewing society meetings were held weekly. Gentlemen were invited to join them.[25]

The economic boom brought with it an increase in the number of commercial and residential buildings. Since many of them were wooden structures, the new prosperity also created a new fear: fires. Since the town had no fire equipment in 1832, a number of citizens purchased a small hand-engine and concluded that they would need to purchase fire equipment. In that year, the Connecticut General Assembly granted a charter to Robert Raymond, George W. Comstack, William S. Comstack, and Edwin Bennett, to form the "Saugatuck Fire Company." It was a volunteer department and included 16 volunteers, among them men from the Wheeler, Bradley, and Platt families, as well as Horace Staples. In 1859, "Union Engine" was reorganized as "Compo Engine Company Number 2," and the town's firefighters, through the generosity of Richard Henry Winslow, succeeded in raising $420.50 to buy a new engine, a Nan Ness from Waterbury. In 1860, the firemen voted to build a firehouse. The first major fire the company was called upon to fight was that of Wakeman's candle factory, which stood on the wharf later occupied by the Starch Company. Even though it was midnight, the company saved the adjoining lumberyard and buildings.[26] In 1874, Vigilant Engine Company No. 3 was organized. That same year, Asmbrose S. Hurlbutt purchased a hook-and-ladder truck from a Norwalk company, which was turned over to a new Pioneer Hook-and-Ladder Company No. 1 in Saugatuck, which, in turn, purchased a new engine in 1887 to protect businesses downtown from any fires.[27]

All of this commercial enterprise did not deter the townspeople from continuing to emphasize the importance of education. The first schoolhouse, as already noted, had been built in Green's Farms in 1703. Until 1795 when the Connecticut General Assembly had taken control of the schools away from the ecclesiastical bodies, schools were run by the parish society of Green's Farms. In 1795, nonetheless, ministers were sometimes on local school committees mandated by the state. Until 1800, education in school meant spelling, and reading, writing, and arithmetic — later known as the 3 Rs. Not until 1812 were teachers required to pass an examination in English grammar. That year, a young man from Simsbury, Oliver Cromwell Phelps, came to Saugatuck to introduce the teaching of grammar. Soon, a brief review of history and geography was introduced. It was not until 1820, however, that an atlas was found in any common school. The town paid $9 to $12 per month for male teachers, plus board, for the winter terms; for females, in the summer, the town paid $4 to $6 a month. By 1835, the student population had grown so quickly that the town was already divided into five school districts.

The citizens of Saugatuck — women in full bloom and men pursuing dreams of making their fortunes — had reached the point where they wanted to chart their own course. The momentum was certain. Unmistakably, the surge for self-rule reached a peak in the mid-1830s. Like their ancestors, the Bankside Farmers who broke away from Fairfield to form Green's Farms, the residents of Saugatuck now sought to carry their desire for full independence to its logical conclusion. They wanted to create their own town, and to do so they needed a leader who would be willing to lead them in this most worthy cause.

NOTES

1. Edward Coley Birge, *Westport, Connecticut, The Making of a Yankee Township* (New York: Writers Publishing Co., 1926), p. 9.

2. Horace Staples, "Recollections of Saugatuck," a paper read before the Saugatuck Historical Society, April 13, 1889.

3. Eve Potts, *Westport...A Special Place* (Westport, CT: Westport Historical Society, 1985), p. 7.

4. D. Hamilton Hurd, *History of Fairfield County* (J.W. Lewis & Co., Philadelphia, 1881), p. 819.

5. Wakefield Dort, *Westport in Connecticut's History* (Westport, CT: Connecticut Tercentenary Edition, 1835-1935), p. 37.

6. David M. Roth, *Celebrate Connecticut, 1635-1985* (The Connecticut Historical Commission, Center for Connecticut Studies, Eastern State Connecticut University, 1986), p. 199. After the U.S. Constitution was adopted in 1787, Connecticut became the fifth state to ratify it on January 9, 1788.

7. Max I. Dumont, *The Jews in America* (New York: Simon and Schuster, 1978), p. 46.

8. Ibid., p. 55.

9. Birge, p. 143.

10. The Compo Tide Mill, built in 1833, was destroyed by fire on November 9, 1891.

11. From a talk by Municipal Historian Allen Raymond before the Y's Men in March, 1998. The story came from "Reminiscence of Captain Frederick Sherwood by His Granddaughter," Westport Public Library.

12. Dort, p. 36.

13. Joanna Foster, *Stories from Westport's Past* (Westport, CT: The Judahs of Judy's Point, 1985), p. 8.

14. Ibid.

15. From a Westport Historical Society paper, "Sea Captains of Westport," by Eileen Meyerson, 1976.

16. Staples.

17. Morris Jesup distinguished himself in the fields of the arts and in funding extraordinary expeditions. See Chapter 8.

18. William Adams Brown, *Morris Ketchum Jesup, A Character Sketch* (New York: Charles Scribner's Sons, 1911), p. 13.

19. The *Westporter-Herald*, June 1904.

20. Alvin J. Schmidt, "Freemasonry, Ancient Free and Accepted Masons" in *Fraternal Organizations*" (Westport, CT: Greenwood Press, 1980), p. 120.

21. Owners of this building down through time comprise an honor roll of Westport clans: Betts, Bulkley, Mitchell, Coley, Reimer, Downs, Morehouse, Jesup, Gorham, Baker, Gray, and Bradley. It drew special attention when it was transformed into The Remarkable Book Shop at 177 Main Street in 1962 and the building was painted pink. From then on, everybody who came to Westport immediately spotted the store on the corner of Main Street and Avery Place. However, as a result of chain book stores moving into Westport and the stiff competition that followed, Remarkable closed its doors in 1997 when its owner, Sidney Kramer, turned the premises over to Talbot Petites. Now the charm and lore of Remarkable [Remark is Kramer spelled backwards] Book Shop has completely disappeared, replaced by yet another Main Street clothing store. Asked in 1998 if he was disturbed by the commercialization of Main Street, Kramer — who is founder and president of Save Westport Now, an accredited minority political party that has fought for preservation of town structures — commented: "It may be that Main Street at this point is just fine. I don't know. At least we have been able to keep the building size down. New businesses in town are proof that our labors in the past have made a difference."

22. From an original manuscript by Dorothea Malm of an uncompleted book on the history of Westport. Mrs. Malm generously donated her research and draft chapters for use in this book.

23. Ibid.

24. Birge, p. 87.

25. Hurd, *History of Fairfield County*, p. 817.

26. Fire Department records from Harry Audley, retired chief, November, 1999. The Saugatuck Hose Company would be created in 1880, the Green's Farms Engine Company in 1929, and the Coleytown Engine Company in 1956.

27. *Westporter-Herald*, February 1914, p. 9.

Newspaper advertisement 1854, p. 65, collection of William Scheffler.

PART III
PRIDE IN A
COMMUNITY

*A view of downtown Westport, circa 1878,
shows the Post Road intersecting with Main
Street. Gorham Island is above, center.*

CHAPTER 8

THE BIRTH OF WESTPORT

Daniel Nash [Westport's founder] was quick, positive,
and independent in his nature and he had a fine sense
of right and wrong. His word was as sacred as his bond.
And neither were ever repudiated.

— D. Hamilton Hurd, historian

It has become a truism that leadership is most often an accident of history. At the beginning of 1835, many residents of Saugatuck and the surrounding area whose lives were centered on the thriving riverfront port sought a man with vision and vigor who would help make their dream of a new town a reality. Daniel Nash, Jr., a patient but passionate 65-year-old man who over the years had won the respect and friendship of his fellow townspeople, fit the bill. His peers — farmers, manufacturers, sea captains, and merchants — turned to him because the veteran farmer-businessman-banker had the requisite wisdom and experience. And, as is often the case when a major historical event occurs, the timing was right. As one historian put it: "The 1830s was a decade of revolution both in the national mood and in the style of government."[1]

As Saugatuck began to flourish in the early 1800s, the people began to talk seriously about creating a new town that would be made up of territory from the three surrounding towns of Fairfield, Weston, and Norwalk. Their primary objective was to establish a self-governing town of their own in which they could determine their own destiny. They also wanted to eliminate the practical day-to-day burden of having to travel to Fairfield for official records of any kind — up to six miles away from Saugatuck. In addition, the rival seaports of Fairfield and Norwalk were treating Saugatuck as their "stepchild." The older towns tried to stop Saugatuck from creating its own town, primarily because it would mean a loss of tax revenues from the prosperous businessmen of Saugatuck. To counter this opposition and to establish Saugatuck as an independent village the townspeople turned to Daniel Nash, Jr., one of the town's most prominent citizens.

Aside from his undisputed leadership qualities, his friends and neighbors knew that he neither sought nor was interested in public office. Yet, when people came to him to represent them, he always obliged. Nash was a forceful, highly respected man who exhibited much understanding and compassion for his fellow townspeople. He was the perfect choice to organize the petition for an independent Westport because he was able to bring people of different viewpoints together, and when he acted in their interests, it was not out of personal ambition. He simply enjoyed getting things done. Though not directly engaged in politics, Nash had first been a Whig and then became a Republican. One historian said of Nash: "He was noted for his skill and love of telling stories.... He was quick, positive, and independent in his nature and he had a fine sense of right and wrong. Tenacious of his rights, he wanted all his own, but never an unjustly acquired dollar. His word was as sacred as his bond, and neither were ever repudiated."[2]

A mature, experienced businessman, Nash was well prepared to carry the burdens of leadership. On April 28, 1835, armed with signatures from 145 other residents,[3] Nash formally petitioned (see Appendix D) the General Assembly in Hartford requesting the formation of a new town because the residents he represented "are subject to great inconveniences of living on the borders [of Norwalk, Weston, and Fairfield] and a majority of them must travel more than six miles to do the ordinary town business, to attend town and electors meetings, to examine records and to have deeds recorded."

Daniel Nash
1770-1865

The
Nash
Family
Lineage

Edward Hawkes Nash
1809-1900

Lloyd Nash
1865-1908

Edward Colt Nash, Sr.
1887-1971

Edward Colt Nash, Jr.
1924-1978

Lloyd Williams Nash
1948-

NASHES TO NASHES
Daniel Nash, Jr., top, was the
founder of Westport. He led a delega-
tion of local residents to Hartford
with a petition that officially incorpo-
rated Westport as a town on May 28,
1835. Lloyd Williams Nash, and his
son, Daniel Moreland Nash, are the
fifth and sixth generation Nashes and
still live in Westport today.
PHOTOGRAPH OF LLOYD WILLIAMS
AND DANIEL BY CARMINE PICARELLO

Daniel
Moreland Nash
1978-

*Westport
Town Records
A.D. 1835.*

*Charter of the town of Westport
Passed May 1835:*

*At a General Assembly of the State of Connecticut
holden at Hartford in said State on the first Wednesday
of may in the year of our Lord One Thousand Eight, hundred*

TOWN CHARTER: The General Assembly in Hartford granted Westport its official town charter on May 28, 1835. It begins: "Charter of the Town of Westport. At a General Assembly of the State of Connecticut holden at Hartford in said State on the first Wednesday of May in the year of our Lord One Thousand Eight Hundred and Thirty Five. Upon petition of Daniel Nash and others..." (see Appendix D)

Exactly one month later, on May 28, 1835, the State of Connecticut granted the petition to incorporate Westport as a town and directed the fledgling town to take care of its poor and to pay its fair share of taxes. Thirteen days after Westport received its charter (see Appendix E), a notice was nailed to the Saugatuck Congregational Church — which then stood on the south side of the Boston Post Road — informing Westport's 1,800 citizens that the first town meeting would be held on June 16, 1835. These historic events took place in the midst of a heat wave,[4] causing everyone involved to be a bit short-tempered and providing a greater sense of urgency. The general boundaries of Westport that were set covered an area of 22.4 square miles, including Green's Farms. The town would be bounded on the south by Long Island Sound, on the north by Wilton and Weston, on the east by Fairfield, and on the west by Norwalk. Green's Farms, however, did not become a part of the new town until 1842, wanting instead to retain the independence that the Green's Farms Church had instilled in its community. Green's Farms residents had been understandably reluctant to separate themselves from the town of Fairfield, which, since 1648, had provided a wide variety of public services and facilities. It was a case of leaving the security they knew for the insecurity of going it alone.

How did Westport get its name? Some maintain that it was simply because it was a port west of Fairfield. Others say that a substitute was found for Saugatuck in deference to those who did not live in Saugatuck. Still others simply wanted a new name as a symbol of a fresh, new start. Legend has it that a state representative from Saugatuck in the legislature said, "I really don't like the name Saugatuck because in Hartford they call me the legislator from Succotash!"[5]

The first Town Meeting took place in the Saugatuck Church Meetinghouse, thus continuing the close relationship between church and town. Notices of town and church meetings were posted on the old oak tree by the meetinghouse. The minutes of this meeting reflect the no-nonsense attitude that these Westport pioneers took in running their own government. Everyone who showed up could vote.[6] The minutes were written in ink in flowing longhand and can be found in the first bound volume of town meeting records in Westport Town Hall. They read as follows:

> In a Town Meeting warned and held at the Meeting
> House in Westport on the second Tuesday of the 16th
> day of June 1835. Thomas F. Rowland, Moderator;
> Voted Edwin Wheeler —Town Clerk; "Voted —
> Thomas F. Rowland, Taylor Hurlbutt, John Gray 2nd
> Select Men (see Appendix F); Voted — Lewis Raymond
> — Treasurer; Voted — David Coley, Lonson Coley,
> Ebenezer Disbrow, Sylvester Stevens, Levi T. Downs,
> Constables; Voted — Lewis Raymond, Daniel Nash,
> Alfred Taylor, Grand Jurors; Voted — Samuel Jackson,
> Davis Taylor, Josiah Raymond, William Nash, Tything
> men; Voted – Andrew Comstack, George N. Hurlbutt,
> Henry Platt, Platt Pearsol, Daniel S. Perry, Stephen Nash —
> Haywards [to look after fences and hedges]; Voted —
> Levi T. Downs, Henry Sherwood, Andrew B. Godfrey,
> Gershom B. Granger — Pound keepers [to look after
> stray cattle]; Voted — William Coley, Gershom B. Guyer,
> Abram Sherwood, Jabez Adams — Fence Viewers
> [to determine property boundaries]; Westport June 16th
> 1835, Edwin Wheeler, Recorder.

Two months later, on August 15, 1835, at the next Town Meeting, this time in the schoolhouse in the back of the church, the residents voted to regulate catching oysters in the waters within the limits of the town of Westport for one year. The residents decided that if anyone caught more than three bushels of oysters on any single day, he would forfeit a sum not exceeding $17 nor less than $1, at the discretion of the court. In 1840, the town allotted to certain individuals underwater land in Compo Mill Pond for oyster planting, marking the beginning of oyster cultiva-

CONSTABLE: David Coley was voted as one of the first three constables of Westport at its first Town Meeting on June 16, 1835. The other two constables were Lonson Coley and Ebenezer Disbrow. The Coley family was one of the best-known in town for its involvement in town matters.
WESTPORT
HISTORICAL SOCIETY

89

tion that grew in Long Island Sound. Mill Pond oysters, moreover, sold for $20 a barrel in the Fulton Street Market in New York.

At a special Town Meeting in September 1835, there were more appointments: three assessors — Seth Taylor, Ebenezer B. Sherwood, and John Gray 2nd; and a Board of Relief — Lewis Raymond, Thomas F. Rowland, H. John Gray, Lonson Coley, and Daniel Nash, Jr. In December, the first town budget was presented: $608.42. After one year of self-rule and in the best Puritan tradition of sparse spending, Westport officials in 1836 managed to find a balance of $242.31. At the same time, a wooden fire station located on Wilton Road beyond the Post Road intersection with the requisite bell in its belfry was built in 1841 as the home of the first Vigilant Engine Company. In 1874, Vigilant Engine Company No. 3 was organized on the west side of the river. Saugatuck, now Westport, was a town in transition. One citizen described it this way:

> The streets, now known as Main and State, were both
> residential and business streets. State street was known
> as the turnpike, being the thoroughfare between New
> York and New Haven. Commencing on upper Main street,
> the first house then standing on its present site was the
> house of Thomas F. Rowland (a member of the first Board
> of Selectmen). The old house formerly the home of
> Mrs. Williams, (who died at the age of 93) was, at one
> time the residence of Mr. Hooker, the pastor of the
> Green's Farms Church. The little house opposite the
> Methodist Church was also in existence. From that
> point to the house owned by the late John N. Betts,
> I can recall but one, that now owned by Mrs. Bulkley,
> whose first occupant was the Hon. James C. Loomis,
> who later moved to Bridgeport. On the East side of
> the street, where is now the residence of Capt. Sereno
> Allen, another captain, Samuel Avery, built what was
> called in those days, a very handsome dwelling...[7]

Another perspective on Westport in 1835 came nearly 60 years later from Horace Staples, who would become one of the most famous and most highly respected businessmen-educators-financial wizards in his time. He wrote a letter in 1894 to *The Westporter,* which read, in part: "At that time [1835], all of the Danbury and Bethel trade came here instead of to Norwalk.

The *Rushlight* ran from Westport leaving Sherwood's dock every other night and landing passengers and freight at Peck's Slip in New York City. She was a side-wheel steamer and was purchased by a stock company called the Westport Steamboat Association for about $5,000. Captain John Hendricks, Captain Lyman Banks, and Captain Daniel Burr were successively captains of the craft. The first board of directors were Henry Sherwood, Horace Staples, Charles Jesup, Andrew Comstack and Alva Gray."[8]

A PASSION FOR EXCELLENCE: Horace Staples was a giant in Westport history. Among his many accomplishments were earning a fortune through hardware sales, owning a fleet of sailing vessels and starting a bank; bringing the railroad to Westport, building National Hall and, finally in 1884 spending much of his fortune to build and open Staples High School. He lived to the age of 95.
WESTPORT HISTORICAL SOCIETY PHOTO

While the townspeople had been restless for their independence, it was not until Daniel Nash, Jr. agreed to lead the crusade for independence that Westport actually came to be. Nash is probably the single most important figure in the town's history. One scholar wrote: "Daniel Nash was a visionary. He organized the establishment of Westport on the foundations of community spirit and obligation to the community as the guiding principle. On a larger scale, this sort of life view fostered the conservative American ideals that played such a large role in the 1800's throughout the United States." [9] While others who came along after him indelibly fashioned their own image on the pages of Westport's past, a glimpse into Daniel Jr.'s background offers valuable insight into his character. He was born on May 12, 1770, to Daniel Nash (1746 – 1824) and Freelove Wright Nash in Patchogue, Long Island, New York, where his family lived until after the Revolutionary War because of their loyalty to the British.

The Nashes moved to Saugatuck in 1784, when Daniel Jr. was 14 years old. When Daniel Jr. grew up, he was seen by historians as a man who carefully balanced respect for his religious past — he remained an Episcopalian, which had once been a part of the Church of England — while, at the same time, sharply differing with both his grandfather, Micajah Nash, and his father, Daniel Nash, Sr., when it came to politics and loyalty to the colonies. At the time of Daniel Sr.'s death in September 1824, the mill complex he had owned expanded from the production of grist to include a sawmill and a cider mill, and an ice business, which Daniel Nash, Sr. had bought from David Judah after the Revolution. Power generated at Nash's Pond was created from a dammed brook on his property, which, in 1888, became the site of Nash's ice house.

Daniel Jr. had spent most of his young and middle adulthood years working hard. One modern-day academic writes: "Daniel Junior's life was characterized by strenuous labor and diligence as he dealt with varying tasks of building and sustaining mills. Nash also had business acumen. He invested carefully in what were to become profitable enterprises."[10] Nonetheless, when it came to settling down, he was a late bloomer. He married Rebecca Camp of Norwalk in 1809 when he was 39 years old, the same year when he began construction at #1 Kings Highway of a homestead, adjacent to the original grist mill property his father had purchased for him years earlier. Family loyalty and bloodline, despite political differences, were paramount in the Nash family. Daniel Nash, Jr. was the son and grandson of two prominent people whose ancestors included Edward Nash, born in 1592 in Lancaster, England, who immigrated to Norwalk in 1652.[11]

The area in which Nash Jr. lived has since become known as King's Highway Historic District and includes King's Highway from the Post Road to King's Cemetery at Wilton Road and all of Wright Street. It is considered the area of Westport with the greatest concentration of historic homes, including several Nash homes. The Nashes were the quintessential New England family. Alexis de Tocqueville offered this insightful description of the typical New Englander.[12] It describes Daniel Nash perfectly:

> The New Englander is attached to the township
> because it is strong and independent; he has an
> interest in it because he shares in its management;
> he loves it because he has no reason to complain
> of his lot; he invests his ambition and his future
> in it; in the restricted sphere within his scope, he
> learns to rule society; he gets to know those
> formalities without which freedom can advance
> only through revolutions, and becoming imbued
> with their spirit, develops a taste for order,
> understands the harmony of powers, and in the
> end accumulates clear, practical ideas about the
> nature of his duties and the extents of his rights.

One of Westport's most ardent boosters from the day it was created as a town was John S. Jones. The unforgettable editor of the *Westporter-Herald*. Jones, was one of Westport's all-time powerbrokers, and a vastly underrat-

EDITOR-IN-CHARGE: John S. Jones, a highly influential Westport powerbroker in the 19th century, used the newspapers he owned and edited to campaign successfully for education and many other civic reforms in Westport. Among the other positions he held, while running the newspapers, were judge of the Probate Court, president of the Board of Trade, chief of the Fire Department, and secretary of the Saugatuck Historical Society. He is shown here in his fireman's uniform. His business card, left, lists him as editor of the Westporter, *which he founded in 1868, and later became the* Westporter-Herald.
WESTPORT HISTORICAL SOCIETY PHOTO

ed hero. He exercised more influence on the town than many of his peers who held office or who had accumulated fortunes through business. As editor of the local paper he used his authority to make suggestions about what should be done in town, and to criticize in print those who did not follow his suggestions.

Born on May 10, 1835, only 18 days before the official founding of Westport, he represented all that was new and innovative about the town of Westport. He was the grandson of John Jones, a farmer from Ridgefield, of Scottish origin. He grew up learning the plumber's and tinman's trade, which he followed for nine years, after which he went into the home furnishings business for eight years. Jones launched his first newspaper, *The Advertiser,* in 1867, which lasted until 1874. The following year, he created the *Westporter,* and, in doing so, gained even more power and influence in town. The paper's motto, emblazoned on its front page was: "Independent in All Things, Neutral in Nothing." It was seen at the time as a professional newspaper. "The paper has ever been a newsy sheet, ably edited and successfully managed," according to an 1899 account in the *Commemorative Biographical Record of Fairfield County, Connecticut.* Jones, a registered Democrat, also served as postmaster from 1865 to 1869, five years as town clerk in the 1860s, and over a period of 30 years he was a clerk of the Probate Court, president of the Board of Trade, chief of the Fire Department, and secretary of the Saugatuck Historical Society.

Clearly, Jones was a well-known town character who became involved in almost everything. In 1860, as a volunteer fireman, he sounded a silver trumpet to summon fellow volunteers. According to town legend, after dousing a fire, he would fill his trumpet with beer, which the firefighters would then share to quench their thirst.[13] Everyone knew Jones by sight. An extrovert who enjoyed talking with townspeople, he used his newspaper to support the causes he deemed most important. And it was through his newspaper that he became one of the most influential men in town.

He married Mary Elwood in 1857, and had two children: Mary L., who became Mrs. Robert Gault, of Westport; and Willis S., who assisted his father in the office of the *Westporter-Herald* as local editor. While there have been many editors of many papers in Westport, there can be little doubt that John Jones was by far the most active and influential member of the Fourth Estate in the town's history.

In the first year of Westport's new existence, there were about 70 establishments on both sides of the Saugatuck River, a slight majority of them on the west side. Nearly two-thirds of these merchants and craftsmen advertised in local newspapers between 1829 and 1835. Newspaper advertisements in the 1820s and 1830s placed by Horace Staples and other merchants indicate the volume and breadth of this business community. There were about 15 general stores, 10 dry goods stores, 3 lumber and building supply stores, 3 shoe stores, 2 furniture stores, and one that dealt in damaged goods, usually salvaged ship wrecks. There were also some 75 houses in the village area, allowing many local entrepreneurs to live close to their businesses. One could also find a profusion of specialty shops, including a leather store, a harness shop, jewelry store, millinery shop and a bookstore and library specializing in Christian almanacs. In addition, there was a piano store, and other services were supplied by tailors, hatters, shoemakers, blacksmiths, and tinsmiths, carpenters, house painters, and blindmakers for the building trade.

Among the early merchants was Deacon Elnathan Wheeler, a pioneer in the tin business in this section of the country. Wheeler could be called Westport's first plumber, although the plumbing profession per se was still unknown in that period of history. The stoves and stove pipes that he made provided important heating equipment in the home, long before the invention of machinery that could make tin cups, pails, pans, and kitchenware from one sheet of tin. Wheeler employed a number of workmen as well as several apprentices and created a distribution system through colorful tin peddlers who sold tinware to housewives. The peddlers went about the countryside in four-wheeled, horse-drawn wagons. The peddler could assure his customers that since the products were made in Wheeler's tin shop he would make any repairs necessary. After Wheeler's death, his shop on State Street became Westport's first plumbing shop.

Merchants' inventories reveal much about the lifestyles of the 1830-1850 period. Following are some advertisements featured in the Saugatuck and Norwalk newspapers: "Hats! (The display featured is a top hat). Peanuts by the hogshead or bushel; 40 lbs pins, 1 bbl TAMARINDS; 3 BBL SUGAR; 1200 BUSHELS Curracoa rock salt." This ad was placed by William Allen, who had a wharf on the river and a general store at what is now Sconset Square. John W. Taylor, who had a store on Main Street just north of what today is known as Onion Alley and who later was the town druggist, advertised, "Crape shawls, instruments, cutlery, jewelry, drugs and medicine." Another ad placed by Miss C. Wood, Saugatuck, in 1824, simply announced, "Ladies dresses from New York." From Miss Jerusah Brown, millinery, in 1824: "Commenced the above business in the house of Mr. L.F. Downs (Main Street), Leghorn, Straw and Silk Hats, ribbons, band boxes, and artificial flowers." Public notices were well read. Here is an ad placed by none other than Daniel Nash, Jr. in *The Saugatuck Journal* of January 8, 1833: "Saugatuck Female Charitable Society's annual fair to be held at the house of Daniel Nash the 26th of December." No doubt this had something to do with his public position as a member of the Board of Relief.

Business was booming all over the area; everything from apples to friction matches to astronomical instruments to telescopes to furniture was being produced here. One of the largest and most important businesses launched during the town's first year, 1835, was the Kemper Tannery, which manufactured leathers for hatters' use — suitcase and satchel linings, hat bands and other products. The business was put on the map by Charles Kemper, Sr., who came to Westport from Hudson, New York, to manage a

tannery that had already been started by R. and H. Haight. He eventually bought the business from the Haights in 1866 and turned it over to his son, Charles H. Kemper.[14] Among the tanner's original customers was a Westport hatter by the name of Davis Taylor, who gained some local fame when he made a hat for Sam Houston when the Texan came through town.[15]

Yet another early successful business in Westport during this era was a button manufactory, owned by Elonzo

BOOMING BUSINESS: When Westport was created in 1835, one of the most important businesses launched was a tannery, which manufactured leathers for hatters' use, suitcase and satchel linings, hat bands and other products. WESTPORT HISTORICAL SOCIETY PHOTO

S. and Jonathan E. Wheeler, who moved their business in 1860 from Naugatuck where it had been launched in 1837. They had their own wharf for boats that brought in the raw materials — ivory nuts that came from tagua or corozo palm trees that grow in Ecuador, Colombia, and Panama. The factory, later incorporated as the Saugatuck Manufacturing Company, ran day and night, using child labor, which was still an accepted practice.

Another major figure in town during this period of growth was Ebenezer Jesup, who we already met in the previous chapter. When the town was named Westport in 1835, he was 68 years old, and he had already established himself in the center of town. It was his wharf, built in 1790, which opened water commerce here. Born in Green's Farms in 1767, this father of Westport's business became a prominent businessman after he purchased grain and produce from local farmers and shipped them to American and foreign ports. From 1807 to 1810, the Connecticut Turnpike, later called the Boston Post Road, was built at a cost of $30,000. Jesup gave land to the Turnpike Company for the approach to the bridge, which went right through his property. His wharf and warehouse were on one side of the road and his retail store on the other side — surely enviable business locations. But that was no coincidence. Jesup had cleverly played a behind-the-scenes role and, by virtue of his political and business contacts, saw to it that the new Connecticut Turnpike, on which he served as a director, would run past his riverfront facility.

For all of his success, Jesup had his share of troubles. He suffered major financial setbacks in the Panic of 1837 — the result of the speculation craze in state bank currency during the preceding boom years. Then he lost his son, Charles, who died suddenly at the age of 42, leaving his widow, Abigail, and their eight children penniless. Despite a lending hand from her father-in-law, Abigail left by steamboat for New York City with her children, feeling that life in Westport as "the poor relation" would not be tolerable.[16]

One of her sons, Morris Ketchum Jesup went to work at the age of 12 for Morris Ketchum, his godfather, who had been a close friend of his father's. Morris Jesup earned $200 a year as an errand boy. At a young age, however, he decided not to spend all of his energies on his business: "From the beginning of my business life, I made up my mind to engage in such religious and philanthropic matters as would excite my sympathy, so that my business should not entirely engross my mind and make me simply a business machine," he is said to have told a group of friends early in his career.[17] He fulfilled his dream. At the age of 12, he did office work for the firm of Rogers Locomotive Works, one of Ketchum's firms. Jesup learned the business from the bottom up. Gradually he worked his way up to managing the loading of locomotive parts that Ketchum's firms manufactured and, by saving his money, in 1852 at age 22, Morris Jesup started his own company marketing railroad supplies on commission. In 1854, with a partner, he created the firm of Clark & Jesup. This matured into the business of M.K. Jesup. For the next decade, Jesup had business relationships with all the leading railroads, including the Chicago & Alton, the Southern and the Atlantic Coast Line. He then devoted himself to banking where he made his fortune. He retired from business in 1884, as a wealthy businessman and then, as he had planned from the outset, he became a philanthropist.

In 1897, Jesup headed the American Museum of Natural History. He donated a large group of paintings to the Metropolitan. He commissioned a five-year anthropological expedition to Alaska and Siberia. A selection of photographs during the North American expedition now hangs in the Museum of Natural History, and the curators of this exhibit say that the Jesup expedition helped break conventional notions of racial superiority, according to Town Historian Allen Raymond. Morris Jesup also supported Robert Perry in his Arctic explorations. The northern tip of Greenland, the northernmost piece of land in the entire world, is named Cape Morris Jesup. Just before he died in 1908, he donated the old Jesup house as a parsonage for the Saugatuck Congregational Church. The church's green was named after him in 1939.

While the manufactories, as they were called then, grew faster than anyone could have imagined, farming continued to thrive — especially after onion growing became a craze around 1840. The market for crop onions was lucrative; first there was a great demand for onions in New York City, and then during the Civil War the army purchased thousands of barrels of pickled onions to combat scurvy. Demand continued until the end of the century, especially the white, yellow, and red varieties grown in Westport. New York wholesalers provided a ready market, paying as much as $10 a barrel for white and from $1.50 a barrel for red and yellow onions.[18] Ships carrying the onions would travel to New York weekly. The business became so important to the area that young boys would miss their spring and early fall school terms to help with the harvest. The onion industry reached its peak in 1860-1890.[19] However, at the end of the nineteenth century, the crop died a quick death because of a cutworm plague that was eating the onion just above the ground. It swept the eastern seaboard and the South, wiping out the industry because nobody knew how to deal with it.

The rapid expansion of the marketplace and the unseemly focus on money led some members of the community to long for spiritual renewal. Already, as we have seen, the area had a new church, the Saugatuck Congregational Church. Meanwhile, the population of the west bank of the Saugatuck River, many of whom attended St. Paul's Episcopal Church in Norwalk, had also been growing and began pressing for their own church in Westport. The roots of Westport's Christ and Holy Trinity Church can be traced back to 1831 when a number of Episcopalians grew weary of the long Sunday trek to Norwalk. In 1833, through the efforts of Daniel Nash, Jr., land was acquired and a building fund for Christ Church was launched. The cornerstone, laid on May 9, 1834, was located on the northeast corner of the Post Road and Ludlow Street. It took two years of hard work and Daniel Nash's talent for organizing to raise the $7,000 to build the church. Nash was asked to serve as chairman. He set an example with his own contribution of $500, a large sum of money in those days. Daniel Nash, Jr., and Taylor Hurlbutt were chosen as wardens of the new church, and Daniel's son, Edward, was selected as treasurer and chorister, along with Uriah Taylor.

Christ Church was consecrated on November 2, 1835, with a congregation comprising mostly farmers and agriculturally dependent merchants. Also among the parishioners on the church's opening day — just six months after Westport became a town — were Daniel Nash, Jr., his wife, Rebecca, their sons, Edward and Andrew, Nash's brother, Dennis, and his family; the Taylor Hurlbutts, the Lewis Patricks, and many others, all dressed in their finest clothes. It was a happy occasion. By 1860, a number of well-to-do families were living in Westport. Among them was Richard Henry Winslow, a direct descendant of one of the *Mayflower* pilgrims. Born in Albany, New York, in 1806, Richard Henry Winslow became a wealthy man through his success in banking, stocks, and money exchange. Already in 1828, at the age of 22, he had become an important figure in developing the railroad. His natural business instincts were sharpened by his travels abroad, after which he married and settled in New York. In 1838 he was elected vice president of the New York Exchange.

In 1853, Winslow built a mansion which he called Compo House on the Post Road, which served as his home for the remainder of his life, lavishing a fortune on the main quarters as well as guest houses, servants' and gardeners' quarters, and the beautiful flower gardens. The guest book of Compo House is a Who's Who of prominent people, including former President Millard Fillmore in 1859, and Louis-François Cartier, the French jeweler, who was a frequent visitor. The house was located on the northwest corner of the Post Road and Compo Road North. For years, it served as a sanitarium until the 1960s when it was purchased by Baron Walter Von Langendorf, and would become known to modern-day Westporters as "the baron's property."[20] Winslow also became interested in politics, serving as a member of the Connecticut House of Representatives in the General Assembly in 1858 and the State Senate in 1860.

Following an internal dispute about installing a new organ, Winslow and 18 other members of Christ Church established a second Episcopal Church in Westport on the east bank of the river. In May 1860, the site of the former Disbrow Tavern — the place where George Washington had stopped on June 28, 1775, we will recall — was chosen as a location for the new

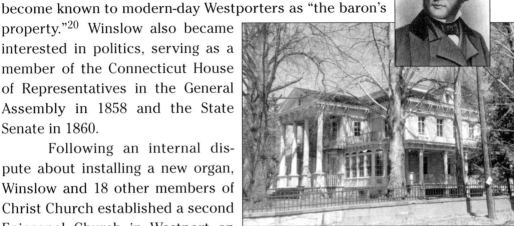

WINSLOW MANSION: This splendid estate served as Richard Henry Winslow's home for most of his life. In addition to the main house, he built guest houses, servants' and gardeners' quarters and created beautiful flower gardens. The guest book was filled with famous names from the world over. The land has since been named a park in his name.
WESTPORT HISTORICAL SOCIETY PHOTO

church. Winslow headed a committee with power to build a Gothic-style stone church edifice and chapel and to furnish it completely. He put his wealth and personal prestige behind the new project, which used the finest materials imported from abroad. The design of the church was taken from ideas that Winslow gathered in his European travels. It was the work of one architect, LeMoulinier. The windows were made for the kind of daylight that is typical in France, according to church records. The Memorial Church of The Holy Trinity was consecrated in 1863.

A number of Episcopalians formed the nucleus of The Memorial Church of The Holy Trinity. The church was organized on April 14, 1860 and the cornerstone was laid on September 19, 1860. Consecration took place on June 30, 1863. In 1868, through the efforts of Edward H. Nash and his brother Andrew C. Nash, property on Burr Street was purchased and the cornerstone for a new Christ Church building was laid on July 31, 1884 and consecrated on September 20, 1885.[21] It was not until sixty years later — February 7, 1944 — that the two Episcopal churches in Westport merged to become Christ and Holy Trinity Church.[22] There were other changes by religious groups in Westport in the mid-eighteenth century. A number of churches other than the Congregational were founded in the Westport area. The origins of the United Methodist Church can be traced back to 1789 when James Lee, a young Methodist circuit rider from Virginia, traveled on horseback to the Poplar Plains area to tell the residents about the teachings of John Wesley. It was during the presidency of George Washington that the United Methodist churchgoers had put roots down here. For some years, preaching was done in the parishioners' homes, most often at the home of James Fellow of Poplar Plains and subsequently in the ballroom of Gregory's Tavern in Poplar Plains across the road from the site now occupied by the Three Bears Inn on Wilton Road.

The tavern's owner converted and donated the land on which the United Methodist Church was built in 1790. The Saugatuck Methodist Church at the intersection of Main Street, Myrtle Avenue, and King's Highway was erected in 1851 to serve the expanding population near the center of town. The Methodist Church on Church Lane and Elm Street was founded in 1907; in1946 the Saugatuck and Westport congregations united, becoming the Community Methodist Church. In 1968, the United Methodist Church opened its doors on Weston Road.

As more immigrants arrived and Westport's population became more diverse, other religious institutions were founded. The Universalist Church was established in 1835 at 215 Main Street. With the arrival of the Irish pioneers some time between 1840 and 1847, the first group of Roman Catholics settled in Saugatuck and in Green's Farms. Some worked on the railroad, others on the farms. Some single people were hired by well-to-do families to serve in their homes. The influx of these Irish settlers into Saugatuck was so marked that, for a brief period, it was nicknamed "Little Dublin." More Irish immigrants followed in the early 1850s, many of whom found work building the railroad here. The first official record of Roman Catholic services is dated November 21, 1853, when the Reverend John Brady of St. Mary's in Norwalk came to Westport to celebrate mass for a small gathering in the Universalist Church. In 1860, a white clapboard building that would become known, as the "little white church"— the First Church of the Assumption — was erected on a site between what are now Wright and Ludlow streets. The parishioners, eager to have their own priest, received the Reverend Patrick Keating as their first resident pastor in 1877. The Rev. John H. Carroll, a longtime member of the school board, took over from 1885 to 1898. Then, Assumption parishioners and their new pastor, the Rev. James P. Ryle, made plans to build a new church to be located on the corner of Riverside Avenue and Burr Street. On April 22, 1900, the present Church of the Assumption was dedicated in a ceremony clouded by sadness and despair. The popular and well-loved Father Ryle had died just 15 days prior to the day of dedication, and the first service held was his funeral.

Catholics in Westport, as was true of Catholics everywhere in the United States during this period, did not have an easy existence. People of Irish descent were called "the Irish" and were not referred to by individual names. The popular stereotype characterized them as drunkards, quarrelsome, and lazy. The onion industry created such a great demand for labor, however, that soon the Irish, and with them another group new to Westport, the Germans, became firmly entrenched and were assimilated. Adding to the growing Catholic population in Westport who migrated to the area in large numbers in the nineteenth century were the Italians, bringing with them a distinct culture filled with rich traditions. It was the Italians, in fact, who first helped build the railroad in the 1840s and 1850s and thereafter formed the heart and soul of the Saugatuck area. The Italian families were the backbone of Westport's formative years, not only in the work they performed for the town, but also in the moral and spiritual leadership they provided to the community as a whole. It was not until the early part of the twentieth century, however, that the contributions of immigrants from European countries were recognized. Westporters began to realize the true value of the diversity they had in their town. It was that exceptional blend of cultures and religions that distinguished Westport from other more monolithic and conservative populations in nearby towns.

Westport's increasing prestige and prosperity did not attract solely the economic strivers. Homeless men, referred to as "tramps," also seemed to be drawn to the area in large numbers. The issue began to come to a head in 1878 when John S. Jones focused on the tramp problem by attacking them in a scorching editorial, warning that beggars were a "gigantic evil" that threatened residents. Instead of letting them roam at will, he called on the State Legislature to require the towns to build a "tramp house" and that charity be given those who were willing to work. In time, the town did erect a "poor house" for those in need, a forerunner, perhaps, of the shelters that would come to pass in the next century.

The population growth — Westport counted some 3,000 residents by 1850 — brought many changes in the education system. At the time of Westport's incorporation, the town already had nine school districts: Green's Farms, Compo, East Saugatuck, West Saugatuck, known as Shercrow where a school was originally built in 1812; East Long Lots, West Long Lots,

EMPHASIS ON EDUCATION: In the early days of Westport, the town already had nine school districts, including one on Kings Highway North, known as the Shercrow School.

Coleytown, Poplar Plains, and Cross Highway. A school in South Saugatuck was added in 1852. In the late 1890s, a small building in the Cross Highway area was used as a schoolhouse. It had double doors that served as separate entrances for boys and girls and Miss Catherine McCann, the teacher, would ring a hand-held bell to call the children to class. In the 1890-1902 period, there was also a wooden Bridge Street School building on Bridge Street at Compo Road. The school year was divided into two terms — the winter term, which ran from the middle of October to the first of April, followed by a vacation of one to three weeks, and the summer term, which ran from the end of that vacation to October 1. The schoolrooms had slanting desks and slab benches for the older children, and benches in the middle of the room for the younger ones. School started at 9 A.M., closed at noon for a lunch break, and ended promptly at 4 P.M. The school sessions ended so punctually every day that residents living near the schools would set their clocks by them.

Despite the proliferation of schools, just two years after the town was incorporated, in 1837, there were signs of discord in education. At the annual meeting of the Church Society on March 9, 1837, for example, the purpose of the meeting was written "for the appointing of officers...[and] reviewing the low state of our schools and the increase of the various appropriations for their benefit."[23] In their attempt to improve education, government and the church adopted two approaches: first, separate responsibility for primary education from the Church Society, an ad hoc body representing all the churches, and put it into the public realm, paying for it with taxpayer dollars; second, encourage the establishment of privately funded schools. In 1845, the town finally assumed full responsibility for the public primary education system for all of the schools through the eighth grade, replacing the Church Society. Thus ended the church's domination of the schools, which had begun in 1703 when the forerunner of the Green's Farms Congregational Church served as church, school and town. Education would soon come to play the *most* important role in the life of the town, a legacy that in the twentieth century would make Westport a magnet for those seeking academic excellence for their children.

As for private schools, the Reverend Thomas Davies of Green's Farms Congregational Church, opened a one-room schoolhouse on David Coley's land in 1830. It became the first private high school in Westport in 1837 when Ebenezer Banks Adams, a native-born Green's Farms resident, purchased it. Born in 1810 in Green's Farms, Adams was the son of Captain Joseph Adams, who had resolved to give his only son the best education he could provide.[24] Ebenezer Adams' passion for education attracted students from all over the east coast, some from as far away as New York City, Boston, and Philadelphia. They boarded in the homes of Westport families. Beginning in 1837, for 30 years Adams operated this school as a coed prep school under the name of Adams Academy. During this period, 637 students graduated from the school, and none was refused admission to college. In 1868, suffering from ill health, Adams sold his Academy and its one-plus acre of high wooded land to the Green's Farms Association, which operated the school for the next 14 years. However, their endeavors were not financially successful and the bank foreclosed their mortgage in 1882. That same year, wealthy Long Lots Road resident Robert Martin bought the Academy property and building and presented it to the West Long Lots School district, the public education organization. It was used as a public school until 1898, after which the Academy became the home of grades one through three of the consolidated West Long Lots, East Long Lots, and Green's Farms districts. In 1917, the Academy was abandoned and the Green's Farms School opened on the Post Road. It was subsequently used as an informal town park and as a home for the needy, as space for the Town School Guidance Office, and as headquarters for the Westport Historical Society. It is currently back to a one room school and is part of the historic Jennings Trail tour of the Society.

ADAMS ACADEMY: A one-room schoolhouse built on David Coley's land in 1830 became the first private high school in Westport in 1837 when Ebenezer Banks Adams bought it. For 30 years, starting in 1837, Adams ran this coed prep school.
WESTPORT HISTORICAL SOCIETY PHOTO

Ebenezer Banks Adams was the great grandfather of Ruth Adams, a former Westport reference librarian who still lives in Westport. Ruth Adams was born August 3, 1913, in the house of her maternal grandfather, Lewis P. Wakeman, on Prospect Road, and her parents were Joseph Adams and Bertha

Wakeman. When she was two-and-a-half her mother died and she went to live with her grandmother and an aunt Dorothy on a farm here. Her father, Joseph, was a farmer who became town assessor and later held a variety of other posts. Once or twice during summers Ruth would go with her father to distribute his produce and, as she recalls, "the trip always ended with an ice cream soda." It was Ruth's job to bring the cows home from pasture down the road every evening. She remembers her father as a man "who never learned to play," but he had a dry wit and was "great to be with." [25]

Education was just one of many concerns that became important to the townspeople as the population grew. In 1847, a dozen farmers under the leadership of Ambrose S. Hurlbutt began plans to establish a local cemetery; until then, burials took place on church or farm properties. The members of the original group that started the cemetery, known as Willow Brook, were Herbert Bradley, Morris Ketchum, Sr., William Edgar Nash, Charles H. Fairfield, Henry J. Morehouse, and John A. Lees. [26]

Westport, like other communities in the mid-1840s, vigorously opposed the coming of the railroad. In 1846 when the General Assembly in Hartford was petitioned to charter a railroad from New York to New Haven, a Town Meeting was held at which the town's representatives in Hartford were instructed to oppose the intrusion. After all, Westport had a bustling shipping industry in Saugatuck and it even had a turnpike; there was simply no need for a railroad. Westport, "true to the Bankside fathers," opposed the granting of the charter. There were to be "no iron horses for our fathers!"[27] The townspeople, approving a stipend not exceeding $20 for an agent, Eliphalet Swift Esq., appointed him to oppose the chartering of the "Rail-Road." The town's initial reaction to the intrusion of the railroad was, predictably, negative. This could be interpreted as the beginning of a national trend that has become fashionable in America's suburbs — a phenomenon that is popularly known as "NIMBY" (Not In My Back Yard).

The majority of the townspeople had opposed the railroad because there was good transportation to New York by boat, and no advantage could come from a noisy train racing across the town's beautiful farmlands befouling the air and frightening the livestock.[28] On the other hand, travel by stagecoach, the predominant mode by land, provided scant pleasure and certainly few comforts. Indeed, it was a test of endurance. A westbound stagecoach would stop at an inn in Westport at about five o'clock in the evening and would not reach New York until the next morning. After a bitter battle, the residents failed to block the charter, and so they sold the right-of-way for a mere $200. But they won a compromise of sorts: The route would hug the shore, cutting and grading through hills and only minimally disturbing life in town.

Trains began running from Bridgeport to New York on December 27, 1848. At that point, Morris Ketchum and Horace Staples met in Staples' lumberyard with a delegation from Danbury to discuss the building of a railroad from Westport to Danbury. "The two men offered to pay one-third of the cost. Norwalk came in and said, 'We'll pay half,' and that's why the railroad now goes from Norwalk to Danbury rather than from Westport to Danbury," relates Town Historian Allen Raymond.

The prosperity that the railroad now brought to Westport prompted Staples to propose that Westport have its own bank. So, in one of the commercial buildings which had already sprung up across from the railroad station, he occupied a large room and opened the Saugatuck Bank in 1852. With the town still two miles away, however, he moved the bank "uptown" to a new building on the west end of the Post Road bridge. That building, built by Staples, was the more impressive National Hall. In 1852 he renamed the bank the First National Bank (which, in time, would become the Westport Bank and Trust) and continued to maintain its offices on the main floor.[29] In 1853, Staples was elected president of the bank and Benjamin L. Woolworth, cashier. Staples, who lived to be 95, remained president until later years when he could no longer handle day-to-day business.

Facilitating the coming of the railroad was the wealthy Cockeroft family of New York, who owned a beautiful 21-acre estate jutting into the Saugatuck River. They would sail from the Battery where they lived in the city to their boathouse at water's edge in Westport. With the railroad all but inevitable in Westport, the Cockerofts agreed to sell some of their land to the railroad owners, providing they would build a solid brick wall 1,675 feet long around their property. This would effectively shield them from the noise and sight of the railroad.[30] This area is now known as Stony Point.

The railroad's first stockholder meeting was held on May 19, 1846, and among the board of directors chosen was Westport's Morris Ketchum, who was instrumental in bringing the new method of transportation to Westport. Hokanum, his 500-acre country estate of parks, farm lands, wheat fields, vineyards, hunting forests and flower gardens, was considered one of the nation's most beautiful estates, and was a prestigious focal point for the rich and famous. Hokanum was designed by Ketchum's friend, Frederick Law Olmstead, the preeminent landscape architect of his time who also designed

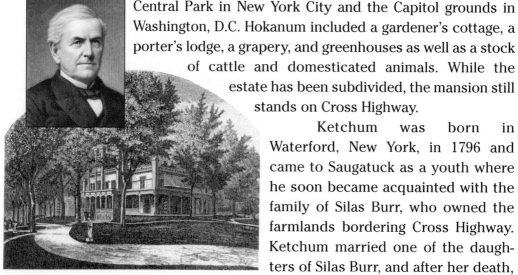

Central Park in New York City and the Capitol grounds in Washington, D.C. Hokanum included a gardener's cottage, a porter's lodge, a grapery, and greenhouses as well as a stock of cattle and domesticated animals. While the estate has been subdivided, the mansion still stands on Cross Highway.

Ketchum was born in Waterford, New York, in 1796 and came to Saugatuck as a youth where he soon became acquainted with the family of Silas Burr, who owned the farmlands bordering Cross Highway. Ketchum married one of the daughters of Silas Burr, and after her death, married another of Burr's daughters. As a young man, Ketchum visited Savannah, Georgia, where he became interested in cotton trading and in

MAGNIFICENT MANSION: Morris Ketchum, financier, investor and a locomotive manufacturer, lived in this elegant home on a 500-acre estate, called Hokanun, which was open to the public. WESTPORT HISTORICAL SOCIETY

getting Southern cotton to the cotton mills that had begun to spring up throughout New England. He founded one of the first cotton commission houses in the country, making his office in New York City. Ketchum's interest in cotton transportation led to an active association with the locomotive engine, which was then being developed in Patterson, New Jersey. When these experiments proved successful, the firm of Rogers, Ketchum, and Grosvenor was formed. Ketchum, as mentioned previously, became associated with railroads and finance, amassing a great fortune and exercising great financial power among Wall Street bankers.

So Westport enjoyed phenomenal commercial and educational growth as the year 1860 began. But all was threatened as tensions between North and South grew more intense and finally erupted in Civil War.

NOTES

1. George H. Douglas, *The Golden Age of the Newspaper* (Westport, CT: Greenwood Press, 1999), p. 2.

2. D. Hamilton Hurd, *History of Fairfield County, Connecticut* (Philadelphia: J. B. Lewis & Co., 1881), p. 840.

3. See Appendix D for full text of petition signed by Daniel Nash and 145 other residents.

4. *The Westporter*, July 15, 1876, p. 1.

5. Town Historian Allen A. Raymond in a speech to the Y's Men of Westport, March 9, 1998.

6. Lynn Winfield Wilson, *History of Fairfield County, Connecticut, 1639-1928,* Volume I

NASHES IN THE NINETIES: On the porch of the original family homestead at 1 Kings Highway North are: Top row: Daniel Moreland Nash, Timothy Allin Nash, David Engert, Lucas Colt Nash, Lloyd Williams Nash; Bottom row: Suzanne Brainerd, Leah K. Nash (pregnant with soon to be born Graham Tyler Nash), and Lloyd's wife, Kristen Moreland Nash.

CARMINE PICARELLO PHOTO

(Chicago-Hartford: S. J. Clarke Publishing Co. 1929), p. 218.

7. Paper by Mrs. E. M. Lees, read before the Westport Historical Society, October 1901, Scrapbook of Mrs. William Gray Staples, Westport, CT, 1889-1909, p. 56.

8. *The Westporter,* September 15, 1894.

9. Bernard M. Rethore, "The Nash Mills, An American Portrait," a celebration of the 150th birthday of Westport, Connecticut, in a paper for LeMoyne College, 1985.

10. Ibid.

11. Edward Nash worked as a tanner in Norwalk. His son, John, the first male of the family born in America, was born in Norwalk in 1652; grandson, John 2nd, born on December 25, 1688, remained in the area. The fourth generation was represented by Micajah Nash, born in Norwalk on March 26, 1718; he lived until 1801. There followed Daniel Sr., born on December 2, 1746 and died in 1824, fifth generation, and his son, Daniel Jr., the founder of Westport, sixth generation. Of the Nash family settlers in this country, there were between 3,000 and 4,000 until 1851, according to Hurd, p. 822. The name Nash is of Saxon origin. A genealogy of the Daniel Nash family, compiled by Margaret Robinson Carver in 1967, states:

> The English origin of our Nash family is rather obscure, and little can be told about it. The family name is derived from 'at an ash,' denoting that a man's home or place of business was beside an ash tree. There is no relationship between our ancestors and those of Thomas Nash of Lancaster, England, who landed in Boston on July 26, 1637, and was one of the founders of New Haven Colony in 1638, or of James Nash, who settled in Weymouth, Mass. quite early. Extensive genealogical studies of both the Thomas Nash and James Nash families have been made, but little has been written about the descendants of Edward Nash, our English progenitor.

12. Paperback edition of *Democracy in America* edited by J. P. Mayer (New York: Harper and Row, 1969), p. 70.

13. Eve Potts, *Westport...A Special Place*, Westport Historical Society, 1985, p. 128.

14. Kemper eventually took up three buildings on Riverside Avenue. In 1917, the company — which employed 100 men and women — was the chief supplier of leather sweatbands for the millions of hats manufactured in Norwalk and Danbury. The original building today is part of another big business enterprise, Marketing Corporation of America. It is part of the MCA headquarters that stands flush with Riverside Avenue. Inside the building, the original beams can still be seen. Kemper's business was moved

in 1893 into a brick factory on Riverside Avenue that had formerly been a foundry and then enlarged in 1913. It later became Nash's warehouse and was subsequently bought by MCA. The Westport Playhouse once was a Kemper plant as was the Italiante house, which stood where the Playhouse Square is now.

15. From Joanna Foster's "Westport Grit Plus Westport Brains," Book III, *Stories from Westport's Past*, 1988, p. 17.

16. Joanna Foster, "Jesup Makes His Mark," the *Westport News*, March 13, 1985.

17. Ibid.

18. Leslie Shaw, W.P.A., unpublished manuscript, Connecticut State Library, 1936, p. 8.

19. Wakefield Dort, *Westport in Connecticut's History, 1835-1935*, Connecticut Tercentenary, p. 27.

20. In the 1960s, it was used for a time as a nursing home—health care institute, but it was abandoned and badly vandalized. Finally, in 1973, the Winslows' beautiful Compo House was torn down and the estate is known as Winslow Park.

21. Historical records provided to the author by Suzanne Brainerd, a parishioner and mother of Lloyd W. Nash, a current Westport resident and a direct descendant of Daniel Nash.

22. After a near-disastrous fire in 1951, the church was fully restored. In 1965, Christ and Holy Trinity Church purchased the Community Methodist fieldstone building and used it for classroom space and the self-supporting Seabury Nursery School. Recently, it became the home of the Westport-Weston Arts Council.

23. Fairfield School Records, Fairfield, CT.

24. George Penfield Jennings, *Green's Farms, Connecticut* (Green's Farms, CT: Modern Books and Crafts, 1933), p. 142.

25. Interview with Ruth Adams, July 1998.

26. According to records kept by the cemetery's administrator, William Carey. The cemetery was officially opened in July 1878 and down through the years, various neighbors donated land to it. It was managed by a number of firms, and in 1985, Willowbrook underwent a restoration and beautification, including a restoration of the Victorian residence on the site that was originally built in 1887. The Loewen Group, second largest cemetery management firm in the world with 600 cemeteries and 1,200 funeral homes under its care, took over its management in 1996.

27. Jennings, p. 81.

28. The *Westport News*, March 20, 1985, p. 9.

29. Joanna Foster, *Westport News*, March 13, 1985.

30. Eve Potts, *Westport...A Special Place* (Westport, CT: Westport Historical Society, 1985), p. 174.

Artwork, p. 83, Daniel Nash, Collection of Nash Family.

NASH'S BUCKLES: These knee buckles worn by Daniel Nash, Jr. to fasten his britches below the knee were passed down through the generations and are now owned by another Daniel Nash, born in 1978, who is the great, great, great, great grandson of Westport's founder.
MIGGS BURROUGHS PHOTO

CHAPTER 9

CIVIL WAR: WESTPORT RESPONDS

*The continuing [Civil] war kept the prices of farm produce
up to a high level. The farmers prospered and one after
another bought carriages. Civilization hitched up a notch.*

— George Penfield Jennings,
Green's Farms, Connecticut, 1933

On a chilly Saturday, March 10, 1860, in Bridgeport, Westporters of all stripes joined a throng of well-wishers from nearby towns to listen to a tall, gangly, 51-year-old stranger from the prairies of Illinois deliver a speech in the city's famed Washington Hall. It was "packed to suffocation, beyond all limits of safety, and crowds milled around the entrances, vainly trying to push in"[1] and most anxious to meet the man known as "Honest Abe." The aspiring presidential candidate had generated enormous interest and excitement in Westport even though the town was strongly Democratic and some — called Copperheads — even sympathized with the South. Nonetheless, town Republicans wholeheartedly supported their candidate at the historic rally.

"They mingled…[and] shook hands with Lincoln, heard him make an inspiring address and recalled his honest countenance, his vigorous defense of his stand on the slavery question, and looked at his great personality…the hospitality and cordial greeting tended to Lincoln made a deep impression on him so that he, in later years, spoke of the friendliness and the warmth and entertainment accorded him in Bridgeport, then a city of about 10,000 residents."[2] The *Daily Standard*, a Bridgeport newspaper, published the following account on Monday evening, March 12, 1860, under the front-page headline, "Great Meeting." It read, in part:

> A great crowd attended at Washington Hall, on Saturday evening, to listen to Hon. Mr. Lincoln of Illinois. No special means had been used to insure a large attendance and no posters, even, were got out. The arrangements at the hall were changed, the platform being to the State street side. The effect was to give more audience room. We suppose that the hall never before contained as many people on any occasion, and we are told that some hundreds of persons were unable to find admission. The hall filled up rapidly and some time before the appointed hour, the gathering was called to order…. Mr. Lincoln was introduced and received with great demonstration of applause. He spoke about two hours to the most attentive audience that we ever saw at any political meeting…. Mr. L's remarks were wholly confined to the Slavery question. The manner in which he showed the progress of Pro-Slavery sentiment in the Democratic party; the manifest change of position — the sharp analysis of Mr. [Stephen A.] Douglas' views, the striking illustration…the cutting sarcasm which he bestowed upon others — are these things to be likely forgotten by his hearers? We think not.

In the course of his speech, Lincoln said he realized that he was talking to an audience made up of persons from both major parties. "Let us consider ourselves as American citizens together," he said. The issues, he observed, should be considered intelligently, and every man should vote conscientiously. He said that some issues were more important than others and that it so happened that slavery in the territories was the main issue. In 1860, there were some 3.9 million slaves in the U.S. total population of 31.4

million. In Connecticut, the gradual emancipation law passed in 1784 had not been fully enforced until 1848. With the support of many New England political leaders — including Connecticut Republican Governor William A. Buckingham — Lincoln was elected in November of 1860 in a four-way race.[3]

Lincoln had been comparatively unknown to the voters in the Northeast until his Illinois debates with Stephen A. Douglas in 1858, in a Senate race in which he was defeated by Douglas. By the spring of 1860 when Westporters caught their first glimpse of him, Lincoln was gaining name recognition and stature because of his unequivocal opposition to slavery and his appeal as a man of the people. By the time he reached Bridgeport, the man known as the prairie lawyer had already become familiar with the New England country-side, and the New England conscience.

Prior to meeting residents from Bridgeport and neighboring towns such as Westport, Lincoln had traveled all over New England, listening to what they had to say. Their message was clear and loud: Slavery was evil and intolerable. In conservative Connecticut — the "Land of Steady Habits" — the animosity towards the South because of slavery was not new; it had been developing for years.

The contingent from Westport undoubtedly included First Selectman William J. Finch. Elected in 1854, Finch served on the Board of Selectmen for 16 years, later making an additional contribution as town clerk (see Appendix G).[4] The townspeople who went to Bridgeport to hear Lincoln included a host of church, civic, business, farming, and education leaders and, of course, scores of everyday citizens who had heard so much about the plainspoken man from Illinois. But only when they saw him in person could they experience his magnetic public appeal.

Connecticut's Governor Buckingham was considered "a man of keen vision, well-balanced mind, and mature judgment."[5] On January 17, 1861, he issued a proclamation in which he declared that "when reason gives way to passion, and order yields to anarchy, the civil power must fall back upon that arm of national defence." He ordered the purchase of equipment for five thousand men and urged the militia companies to fill their ranks and get ready "to render such service as any exigency might require." Local volunteer units in the immediate Fairfield County area formed in Bridgeport and marched over the old Westport drawbridge on their way to New York before being shipped south. At the same time, Westport made available an open space — the Kings Highway green — for drills. One unit passed through town when Edward Coley Birge was a youngster. In 1926, he recalled in his

HISTORIAN: Edward Coley Birge, during the Civl War, closely inspected an artillery regiment as it came through Westport.
THE WESTPORT HISTORICAL SOCIETY PHOTO

book: "The Drill Ground at the foot of Old Hill [Kings Highway] was the West Point of Westport.... It was the military practice of peaceful and industrious people who sensed in an instinctive way the dangers ahead. It was preparedness as they understood it...." [6]

Birge got a first-hand look at an artillery regiment that came through Westport during the Civil War. The Second Connecticut Light Battery, which had been formed at Camp Buckingham in Seaside Park, Bridgeport, took his breath away. "We were all agog. Glorious war. Exhilaration...we had seen a fine cavalcade. But we did not know the fullness of what we had seen. We had been let in on a glint of enduring history.... No classic Lincoln memorial yet stood in Washington with immortal words of consecration graven on it that were first spoken by the martyred President from a platform within earshot of where stands a monument to our battery....To these important events was the cavalcade headed that we saw go down the Boston Post Road that day."[7]

Like the Revolutionary War, the Civil War touched the hearts and souls of the townspeople. The draft did not start until March 1863. The first two Westport men to enlist in the Connecticut Volunteers, James Barres and Charles King, participated in the first battle of Bull Run. Any glamor the war had for the townspeople no doubt vanished when news of casualties began to trickle in. Westport's first Civil War battle death was Elijah Leggett, who had been in the service for 208 days before he died on February 14, 1862. George Smith died after only 19 days' service; James Glynn had served the longest time of any of his Westport peers — 1,016 days before his death at Petersburg.

The question of paying volunteers to serve was regularly addressed in the town meetings. The July 25, 1862 meeting passed a resolution stating that since a large portion of the people of the southern states were in open rebellion against the United States, and since the president and the governor had asked those states that were loyal to the Union for volunteers, the Westport Board of Selectmen should be authorized to draw $2,000 from the town to pay volunteers to enter the Army.

Men could avoid serving by paying others the sum of $300 to take their places in the Army. This widely accepted procedure, known as paying "substitutes," was a common practice in the northern states. On July 26, 1864, the Westport selectmen agreed to appropriate an additional $20,000 to be used in filling the quota of the town and to pay substitutes to go to war. As a result of the informal class structure that evolved in Westport, the men of the old Irish families were in such financial need that some of them took the money and served in what they called "the rich man's war." However, it was specifically noted that only Negroes could serve in place of Negroes.

According to the 1860 census, 36 Negroes were living in Westport at the start of the Civil War, but none of them included the 14 who served in the war. This apparent mystery is easily explained: Since Westport was a station on the Underground Railroad, the 14 may have arrived through the Underground Railroad. Once they were here and the town took note that they had no visible means of support, they were probably encouraged to enlist in the Army, enabling the town at once to solve its welfare problem and meet its enlistment quota.[8]

The 29th Regiment was an all-Negro outfit except for its officers, one of whom was Second Lieutenant Louis R. McDonough, a Westport resident who would be captured by the Confederates and raised to local hero status upon his release.[9] McDonough had joined the 7th New York National Guard Regiment in April 1861 and was a captain in the 28th Connecticut. After his term of service, he joined the 29th Regiment Connecticut Volunteer Infantry (Colored). Connecticut was one of just three states that allowed black soldiers to enlist and fight under its state banner.

The 29th Regiment was led by Colonel Samuel P. Ferris. After brief duty at Jacksonville, Florida, it joined the army of General Banks in Louisiana and participated in the second assault on Port Hudson. Some 59 men were killed. After the surrender, the regiment formed part of the garrison, until it was ordered home.

The 17th Regiment, which included Westport men, left Bridgeport under the command of Colonel William H. Noble, and was assigned to the Army of the Potomac. In May 1863, the regiment was in the battle of Chancellorsville, where it lost 122 men. Captain Burr was captured and sent to Libby Prison. In August 1863, his company was transferred to Folly Island, South Carolina, where the company took part in the sieges of Fort Sumpter and Fort Wagner. On July 1, 1863, the 17th Regiment was thrown into the thick of the battle at Gettysburg. Overall, some 1,300 Connecticut Yankees fought at Gettysburg, and the casualties were high: 68 men killed or mortally wounded, and 291 wounded, captured, or missing. Among the Westporters were Private Francis Nash who was killed on July 1 at Gettysburg and Private Francis Foot, who was listed as dead or mortally wounded in action in a desperate nighttime fight to hold a position. His body was never found.[10]

Other Westport soldiers who were killed or mortally wounded in action at Gettysburg included Private James Flynn, and Private George H. Guernsey, 17th Regiment. Officially listed among the wounded in the Gettysburg conflict were Private John H. Denis, 2d Lieutenant Edward M. Lees, Sergeant Henry McDonough, and Private Eugene Warren. Among the captured listed were Private Theodore Allen, Corporal Roscoe Perry, and Corporal John Robinson.[11] Early in 1864, the 17th Regiment was ordered to Florida, where it remained on duty until the close of the war; it was mustered out July 9, 1865. One company of the 17th Regiment was largely recruited from Westport, with Henry P. Burr and James E. Hubbell serving as successive captains. There were also many Westport men in the 28th Regiment, including Second Lieutenant J. Chapman Taylor. The last survivor of the Union Army in Westport was Thomas Glynn.

One of the best-known and most highly regarded participants in the war from Westport was Benjamin N. Toquet, born in Paris in 1834 and emigrated to America in 1845. As a young man, he served on board the vessel, *Planter*. A series of letters during the time he served in the Civil War, starting in February 1863, painted a poignant portrait of the life of an ordinary soldier. In one letter to his wife, Toquet wrote:[12]

Dear Annie, We came on board the ship *Planter* yesterday, about 40 men detailed to take care of 275 horses. We are down below on the 3rd deck the horses having the best of space, we would be well enough if we had a little fresh air, but I can see no possibility of airing our dark pit. The hay and water won't last very long and besides I anticipate considerable sickness so that there will be work enough for those that can stand up. How they ever got the horses in I can't imagine they are so close as to touch each other. Also as to how they can get out the dead ones every day unless they cut them to pieces. I don't know. We understood at first that we were to go with a sergeant, and I did not like to go as we knew what to expect from the ships officers if we were on board without anyone to stand up for us. Kiss the baby for me, Your affectionate husband, Benj. H. Toquet.

Toquet was one of the lucky ones who returned safely to Westport after the war. Many years later, toward the end of the century, this now-respected businessman built Toquet Opera House on Post Road property, which had been inherited by his wife, Nellie Bradley. The second floor of the building, now known as Toquet Hall, once the setting for operas, silent movies, town meetings, is a center for the town's teenagers. The first town meeting was held there on April 2, 1892. For the next 17 years, all town meetings and assemblies were held at Toquet Hall. It was not until 1908 that a new Town Hall was built at a cost of $21,500, including land acquisition. Until the time of his death in 1913, he was a successful entrepreneur, heading up the Toquet Motor Company, which developed a variety of mechanical devices including the carburetors used in Ford motor cars.[13]

The toll for all those who participated in the Civil War was high: Connecticut sent into the Army 1 regiment of cavalry, 2 of heavy artillery, 3 battalions of light artillery, and 30 regiments of infantry, 2 of which were Negro. Westport itself contributed men to 21 regiments, most of whom fought in either the 17th or 28th Volunteer Infantry Regiments, both representing Fairfield County. Of the 219 Westport men, 27 died in the war either from battle wounds or disease, especially malaria. Another 23 were wounded, 6 men were captured and died in prison, and 52 deserted from the ranks.[14] More than 3,500 military units from the North and South fought in the Civil War, to which Connecticut contributed 36.[15]

By the time the Civil War was over Daniel Nash, Jr. — then viewed by the youth of Westport as a wise and most venerable "town father" — was well over 90. He was a staunch Republican and thus a great supporter of Lincoln, as well of Governor Buckingham. He was happy that his son, Edward, was investing some of the family's money in gold-bearing U.S. bonds to fight the "Southern Rebellion." It proved to be a profitable investment for them.

Daniel Nash, Jr. would remain attached to his land and mill until his death at the ripe old age of 95 on August 2, 1865, leaving behind his wife, Rebecca, and children, Edward H., Andrew C., Julia Ann (Mrs. J.W. Wood), and Hannah (Mrs. Ezra Morgan). But the pond on his property continued to produce top grade ice at a substantial profit. He left his farm and several orchards from which apples were collected for their cider mill press. Daniel Jr. had seen the birth and rise of Westport for which he had petitioned and, with great fortitude, he had carved out a prosperous place for himself and his family in farming, in banking and industry. Indeed, he made his mark on a town that would be embraced by many people from all parts of the world for generations to come.

Just months following Lincoln's re-election victory in 1864, General Robert E. Lee surrendered 27,800 Confederate troops to General Ulysses S. Grant, finally bringing the war between the states to an end. Tragically, within a week of the peace, John Wilkes Booth shot Lincoln in Ford's Theater in Washington, D.C. on Friday night, April 14, 1865. Though the nation was still deeply divided, Americans in all sections were profoundly shocked and dismayed by this violent act. Writes Carl Sandburg: "The tolling of the bells began in Washington, likewise in New York, Boston, Chicago, Springfield, Peoria, metropolitan centers and crossroads villages, the day had tolling bells hour on hour, flags at half-mast, the gay bunting, red, white, and blue festoons brought down and crape or any fold of black put out and hung up for sign of sorrow."[16]

In Westport, church bells tolled from Christ Episcopal Church up the hill on Ludlow Street and nearby Assumption Church. Across the river the Universalist Church and the Methodist Church bells joined in as did Holy Trinity on Myrtle Avenue with its new bell along Myrtle Avenue, Saugatuck Congregational Church on the Post Road, and, further east, the town's oldest church, the Green's Farms Congregational Church.[17] At the Green's Farms Church, the Reverend B. J. Relyea delivered a memorable sermon entitled "The Nation's Mourning," June 1, 1865. Though written in haste with no thought of ever publishing it, through the efforts of several of his parishioners it was released in pamphlet form and preserved for posterity. Relyea wrote, in part:

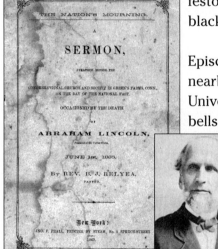

LINCOLN'S LEGACY: Reverend B. J. Relyea, of the Green's Farms Congregational Church, gave a sermon on June 1, 1865 praising the nation's fallen president. It was published as a pamphlet called "The Nation's Mourning."
SERMON/WESTPORT PUBLIC LIBRARY
GREEN'S FARMS CONGREGATIONAL CHURCH PHOTO

> What was Abraham Lincoln more than others, that a whole nation should mourn his death? I answer, simply in himself, in his own person as a citizen of our common country, he was no more than thousands of others; but in his official capacity he was more than others.... As we look back upon his finished career, it will not be denied that he possessed many of the qualifications of a wise and good ruler. His intellectual abilities, certainly, were

not of that showy and brilliant order which is apt to
captivate the imaginations of men. He was not
learned, perhaps, in all the intricacies of diplomacy
nor in all the refinements of Statecraft. It will be
doubted, however, that he possessed in good degree
that wisdom which goes by the more homely and less
imposing name of good practical common sense,
which, accompanied as it was in him, with honesty
of heart and singleness of purposes, is certainly of
infinitely the just ends of government. If it is
any proof of ability for a man to accomplish what
one-half of the civilized world for four years
strenuously affirmed never could be done — if this
is any proof of ability, then certainly he has given
us some proof of ability.[18]

Westport, like many other Connecticut towns, benefited economically
from the conflict, though it did not profit as much as larger towns such as
Hartford, New Haven, Winchester, and Middletown, all of which were
involved in shipbuilding and manufacturing arsenals of weapons such as
guns and cannons. The war brought boom times for the state's woolen and
shipping industries, some of them in Westport. Family fortunes were created during the Civil War, a period when onion raising reached its peak. It was
during the 1860s that Westport settled down to the most productive farming in its history. As one historian expressed it: "The continuing war kept
the prices of farm produce up to a high level.... Civilization hitched up a
notch."[19]

Westport served as the backdrop against which some key financial
political players reached some understandings that kept the North on firm
financial ground. During the war, Lincoln's Secretary of the Treasury,
Salmon P. Chase, was frequently entertained at Hokanum, the lush country
estate of Morris Ketchum. Chase is said to have sought advice from
Ketchum, who, in turn, is reported to have exerted considerable influence
on Wall Street to support the government's war efforts.

A few years after Lincoln was assassinated, Westport named a street
after him between the Post Road and what is now Riverside Avenue. When
the war was finally over, as the nation took up the task of binding its
wounds, everyday life in Westport resumed. The citizens took up the challenge of shaping a new future.

NOTES

1. Nelson R. Burr, "Abraham Lincoln: Western Star over Connecticut," *The Lincoln Herald*, 1983-1984, Harrogate, Tennessee, p. 1.

2. The [Bridgeport] *Daily Standard,* February 12, 1909, p. 1 story headlined "BRIDGEPORT HONORS MEMORY OF LINCOLN. Many Recall Visit of Great American and the City's Mourning When He Was Assassinated."

3. Republican presidential candidate Abraham Lincoln won election easily, receiving 180 electoral votes to 72 for John C. Breckinridge, of the Southern Democratic Party; 39 for John Bell, of the Constitutional Union Party; and12 for Stephen A. Douglas, of the Northern Democratic Party.

4. Finch served on the Board of Selectmen from 1856 to 1874 and as Town Clerk from 1882-1885.

5. Elias B. Sanford, *A History of Connecticut* (S.S. Scranton and Company, 1887), pp. 254-57.

6. Edward Coley Birge, *Westport, Connecticut, The Making of a Yankee Township* (New York: Writers Publishing Co., 1985), pp. 60-62.

7. From a Westport Historical Society paper written by Edward Coley Birge, dated June 27, 1950.

8. John Capsis, *Westport News*, January 25, 1989, p. 19, in an interview with William Gladstone, a Civil War scholar who was then a resident here. Gladstone is author of *United States Colored Troops, 1863-1867* (Gettysburg, PA: Thomas Publications, 1990).

9. Ibid.

10. *Westport News*, May 29, 1985.

11. Charles P. Hamblen, *Connecticut Yankees at Gettysburg* (Kent, Ohio and London, England, 1993), pp. 124-31.

12. From the Westport Historical Society Archives.

13. Ibid.

14. Author's interview with William Gladstone, March 30, 1999.

15. Lynn Winfield Wilson, *History of Fairfield County, Connecticut, 1639-1928* (Chicago-Hartford: S. J. Clarke Publishing Co., 1929), p. 220.

16. Carl Sandburg, *Abraham Lincoln, The Prairie Years and the War Years* (New York: Harcourt, Brace & World, 1954), p. 717.

17. *Westport News*, February 13, 1985.

18. Reverend B. J. Relyea, "A Sermon Preached before the Congregational Church and Society in Green's Farms, Conn., On the Day of The National Fast, Occasioned by the Death of Abraham Lincoln, June 1st, 1865" (New York: JNO. P. Prall, Printer by Steam, No. 9 Spruce Street, 1865).

19. George Penfield Jennings, *Greens Farms, Connecticut: The Old West Parish of Fairfield* (Green's Farms, CT: Modern Books and Crafts, 1933), p. 115.

Mural, p. 109, by Robert Lambdin, courtesy of Hudson United Bank.

CHAPTER 10

THE CHALLENGE OF CHANGE

*Westport, unlike more remote towns,
had the advantage of a broad variety of citizens.*

—Eve Potts, Westport author and historian

In the immediate aftermath of the Civil War, Westporters, like millions of other Americans across the land, were caught in a complex web of emotions as North and South struggled to re-unite and again find common ground. At the same time, Westport was facing a more localized crisis of identity as it began to grapple with absorbing a wave of immigrants, who would soon play a key role in the development of the town. The quickening pace of progress brought with it new modes of transportation and communication that would produce changes in everyday life.

Putting the post-Civil War decades in Westport's history in perspective, author/historian Eve Potts aptly describes the metamorphosis this way: "As in any community, daily life took on numerous guises depending on the fortunes of the participants. It could mean farming the land, or it could mean supervising a household of servants. It could mean work from dawn to dusk, or it could mean a life of indulgence in all the pleasures available to those with the means to enjoy them. Though we think of them as simpler days, they appear to have been more difficult days for those who had to live them without the conveniences we take for granted. Westport, unlike more remote towns, had the advantage of a broad variety of citizens — from farmers to New York millionaires. The 1800s and early 1900s were days when leisure as an end in itself was joyously discovered and the citizenry, belying its puritanical past, set out to enjoy life and all its pleasures."[1]

For an insight into daily life in Westport in the post-Civil War era, one need only read the incisive comment by John S. Jones in the December 14, 1867, issue of his newspaper, the *Westporter-Herald*: "The people, and especially the business portion of them, are looking anxiously towards Congress for solution and final adjustment of the reconstruction question: They expect them to devise some means whereby the country may be placed on a more safe and enduring basis, and until this is done, the country must, of necessity, remain in a very precarious and unsettled state."

And the writings of Myron L. Mason, attorney for William H. Jesup, Westport's state representative immediately after the war, tell us that Saturday was the big market day in town when the village was filled with people from "the back country" who brought their produce and money to buy supplies, including liquor. The mails were delivered twice a day, except Sundays, and people received their New York morning newspapers by 9 A.M. There were five clergymen and five physicians, and at least two lawyers. Most of the people of that time were what he called "practical agriculturists."[2]

But even farming was changing. Agriculture began to shift away from patterns that had prevailed since the 1630s. In the 1800s, the Industrial Revolution began to impact life and, when the farmer was faced with hard times, there were no government subsidies to shore him up. Family fortunes had been created from farming during the Civil War. Onion farming reached its peak and many young Westporters, who would later become the town leaders, launched their careers on all fours in onion fields. One such man was Edward T. Bedford, who would contribute to the town in major ways.

After the onion crop setback, raising turkeys became very much in vogue. "On Thanksgiving around 1860," [historian] Edward Coley Birge remembers, "there were five generations [of Coleys] all at the Thanksgiving table together...All were born in Westport and all would live out their lives here...." Birge remembered that in the 1860s, when he was a young boy, his grandmother Mary Ann Coley had "a fine flock of turkeys."[3] Farmers began to plant orchards, especially pears, apples, and peaches as well as vegetables, including potatoes, corn, rye, and timothy. Soon all of these crops thrived where the onions had begun to fail. But the future of farming was in doubt. Farm property began to be valued not according to what it could produce in crops, but according to what the city dweller was willing to pay. In the 1880s land was worth as much as $150 an acre,[4] the equivalent of $15,000 in the year 2000.

Farming generally was very important during America's early years, and probably the most notable farms in Westport belonged to Talcott B. and Henry B. Wakeman. In December 1881, T.B. Wakeman reported a gross income of $13,061 — the equivalent of $130,000 in the year 2000. Of the $13,061, some $8,500 came from the sale of onions of all varieties; the remainder came from sales of radishes, spinach, currants, strawberries, grapes, peas, potatoes, and nursery stock. After expenses, he showed a "paper profit" of $6,206, which included $2,000 in 1881 currency for the owner's time.[5]

Success brought with it another problem, however: the degradation of the environment. The city streets, thanks to the carelessness of storeowners and merchants, were strewn with filth. A newspaper editorial chided the merchants for their apparent indifference to health hazards. John Jones wrote in an editorial in 1868: "It is a pity that some of the proprietors of stores, especially grocery stores in the town, should be so careless as to the condition of that portion of the street that is in front of them. The throwing of decayed cabbages and potatoes, putrid meat, offensive brine and almost every conceivable rotten vegetable and animal substance into the center of the street, to be traveled over by footmen and carriages, and to render the atmosphere deadly with their fetid exhalations, is an outrage which ought not

EDITOR/FAMILY MAN: Journalist John S. Jones, a man of many talents, pictured in the 1880s with his three sons, from right, Louis, on his lap; Bill, standing; and Curtis, hand on chair. Louis would carry on the newspaper after Jones died in 1906. Jones' great, great grandson, Jeff Northrop, lives in Westport today.
PHOTO COURTESY OF JEFF NORTHROP

121

OLDEST FAMILY BUSINESS IN WESTPORT:
Founded in 1863, L.H. Gault & Son has had
five generations of leadership. From top down:
Robert Gault, Leonard H. Gault, Howard Gault,
William Gault, Samuel Gault.
COURTESY OF THE GAULT FAMILY

to be tolerated. A merchant having any regard for decency or propriety would not allow it."[6] Though well intentioned, the editorial then went on to urge the storeowners to throw their debris into the river. So much for awareness of environmental pollution in that era!

Even as agriculture turned to diversification in order to survive, an entirely new business — supplying coal, gravel, and other construction products — was launched during the war and began to flourish in the 1860s. One of these businesses whose beginnings can be traced to this period is Gault, the oldest business in Westport, founded in 1863 by Robert Gault (1833 – 1921). Robert came to America in 1847 from a little town, Claudy, in Londonderry County in northern Ireland, when he was 14 years old. His widowed mother, Elizabeth Perry Gault, boarded a sailing vessel bound for America with her four children, Robert, John, Ellen, and a son, name unknown, who died during the stormy journey.

Once in America, Robert began working as a farmhand at Marvin's dairy at Calf Pasture, Norwalk. However, adventure soon beckoned, and Robert took a job as a boy driving mules towing barges on the Erie Canal. Robert returned to Westport in about 1860, settling on Compo Street (the present-day South Compo Road) with his wife, Katherine Kirk. They had three sons, Leonard Hamilton, Robert Samuel, and John Kirk (who would become second selectman of Westport). In the summer of 1863, Robert started a freight-hauling business, which prospered immediately. In time, his sons joined him and the business became known as Gault Brothers, ultimately expanding to include such services as plowing, cutting hay, digging cellars, and threshing grain for the farms and estates in the area.

In 1897, Leonard Gault married Julia May Wheeler, the daughter of a local grocer and a director of the Westport Bank and Trust, and settled on Compo Street and a year later, Howard Wheeler Gault was born. Just before 1900, he bought a local lumber business from Hubbell Hull in conjunction with Gault Brothers and named it Leonard H. Gault. He then purchased 10 mules and 60 horses that were used for hauling goods, and also hired out for funeral coach services. In addition, he bought a 75-head dairy that was kept in the barn that still stands on South Compo Road.

In 1919, Leonard Gault purchased Taylor and Richard's feed grain and coal business located on the banks of the Saugatuck River on Main Street, and soon coal became the primary product sold. In addition, mason supplies, sand and gravel, fertilizers and hay were sold. The name of the business was changed to L.H. Gault & Son and was incorporated in 1932. After Leonard became president of the company in the late 1930s, the company finally began to sell the fuel oil for which it is primarily known today, although it also sells masonry and gravel, among other products. In 1933, Howard, Leonard and Julia's only child, married Georgiana Richards Taylor — coincidentally, one of the daughters of William Taylor, one of the few farmer-owners of the Taylor & Richards feed, grain, and coal store. A storage tank at 563 Riverside Avenue was acquired in 1929 to provide deep-water docking for larger coal and sand barges and then oil tankers, which began supplying the new growing oil business.

William L. Gault, Howard and Georgiana's only son, joined the firm in 1952 to carry on the Gault tradition. He married Nancy Marsh in 1959 and they had two children, Ginger and Samuel; the latter joined the business in 1985 and became the fifth generation of Gaults actively involved in the company. Sam is currently president. Ginger's husband, James Donaher, joined the business in 1983 and is currently vice president.[7]

Westport's accelerating business and industrial sector drove the local economy, taking on a life of its own and branching out to all parts of the country, even overseas. A map of the local township published immediately after the Civil War offers a glimpse of the products and services then important to the town: "E.S. and J.E. Wheeler, Manuf's Cloth and Metal Buttons; Dalton Knitting Machines Co., Hubbell & Wakeman, dealers in Dry Goods, Groceries and Provision; Jesse Bradley, dealer in Groceries and Provisions; A. Brear, Manuf'r of Patent Water Ejector; F.L. Hedenberg,

Manuf'r of Patent Furnace Range and Heater, and N.W. Bradley, Proprietor of Summer Board-House."

Another important business concern in the second half of the nineteenth century was the Lees Company, which sold its mattress company to Rufus Wakeman in 1862. It was the first such company in the state. First located on Canal Street and run by waterpower, the business was moved to Riverside Avenue at the Bridge Street corner so that it could be closer to the shipping facilities. Wakeman continued to run the business until his death, when his son, Austin Wakeman, took over. He would eventually be elected as the town's first selectman in 1913. The Wakeman family, one of the many original Westport families, dated back to 1626 when Francis John Wakeman arrived here from England. Eleven ensuing generations of Wakemans have earned their livelihoods, mostly as farmers, since then, the most recent being Isaac Banks Wakeman, a farmer who was born in 1912 and who still lives, with his wife, Pearl, in their 112-year-old house on Cross Highway.[8]

RIDING HIGH: Two well-known businessmen, Robert T. Lees, and son, John A., are pictured in their horseless carriage in the 1890s in front of the Lees Manufacturing Company in the old Richmondville Avenue section of town.
WESTPORT HISTORICAL SOCIETY PHOTO

Other businesses of that day were the Embalmers' Supply Co., largest of its kind in the United States in that era, launched by C.B. Dolge, of Brooklyn, in 1887 and moved to Westport in 1891; the Spool Factory set up south of the railroad near the river, later used to manufacture rubber reinforcements used in railway car springs and, in the late 1870s, housing the Willimantic Thread Company; the Westport Paper Company, founded in 1890 and run by Robert W. Post; the button factory started by Elonzo S. Wheeler in 1860 next to the railroad on the Saugatuck River; and the Atlantic Starch Works which moved to Westport from Brooklyn in 1891.[9] Many of these businesses as well as the town itself hired children, an accepted practice at the time.

Business expansion, as always, brought fears of fire downtown. Accordingly, as mentioned earlier, Vigilante Engine Co. No. 3 was formed in 1874 on the west side of the Saugatuck River, a little north of the Post Road on Wilton Road. A rivalry soon developed between the No. 2 all-volunteer company led by John Jones and the No. 3 Engine Company led by Frederick Sherwood, each of which tried to be the first at a fire. By 1879, the town had three fire companies: Pioneer Hook & Ladder Co. No. 1, Compo Engine Co. No. 2, and Vigilant Engine Co. No. 3. The Westport Fire Department was formally organized in 1884, and all 40 members were volunteers.

The town, as noted earlier, assumed control of the public school system in 1845. When it was run by individual school committees, inadequate funding had been a problem, and perhaps there were suspicions that instruction was colored by religious convictions despite the 1795 Connec-

VIGILANT ENGINE COMPANY No. 3: One of three fire companies in Westport in 1879. The Fire Department was not formally organized until 1884.
WESTPORT HISTORICAL SOCIETY PHOTO

ticut edict separating the church from school administration. Education was one of newspaper editor John S. Jones' favorite subjects, and he may well have been the first person to set off Westport's perennial disagreements over the school budget. He was among the first to call for a high school in Westport. In a column in his newspaper, he criticized the town's short-sighted attitude toward education: "Westport, whatever her other faults may be, is an *economical* town. She does not squander her money upon schools to any alarming extent.... There are 23 towns in Fairfield County...[comparing] the percentage of property [taxes] expended for schools, Westport stands 22d in the list of towns of the County! And yet there are men in Westport who advocate reducing the school-expenses! Moral. A third-rate price buys a third-rate article. From the amount of money raised for school-purposes, you can always determine, 1st, the value the citizens set upon education; 2d, the condition of the schools; and 3d, the intellectual, moral, and social status of the town."[10]

Following the Civil War, there were plenty of jobs to fill. The Nash Mills business was booming, with orders for materials coming in from as far away as New York. When the volume of orders was greater than the old sawmill could process, a new sawmill was built in 1869. That same year, Edward Hawkes Nash installed a steam engine at the sawmill to propel the newly acquired circular saw, a technology that would soon replace the traditional water-based mill.

The Nashes also produced apple cider. By 1869, Edward Nash was selling a gallon of cider for 50 cents or a barrel for $5, bringing in a handsome profit. Yearly production rose from only a few dozen gallons for family and friends in 1828 to 224 barrels for retail sale by 1870. In keeping with the tastes of that time, Nash tried to perfect the mill's own unique blend. Indeed, the tasting of cider became almost a national pastime as various mills vied for the best tasting. "There is joy in watching a few drops of the amber juice fall into the pan and some satisfaction that you have squeezed your own apples into a jug of additiveless 'country cider,' with a velvety hiss, a pure white stream plunged into the pitcher. Then it went silent and foam built up like cotton. A mellow fruity aroma floated out," is how one expert on cider described the process.[11] Edward Colt Nash sometimes worked as much as 18 hours a day to keep up with the needs of his customers.

In addition, the Nashes continued to run the profitable ice business originally built by Lloyd Nash in 1888. Filling the Ice House proved to be a time-consuming process. As a young boy, Lloyd Nash's son, Edward, would rise at 5 A.M., go out on the ice, and map out a field to be harvested that day. The six ice houses on the Nash property held 25,000 tons of ice. In a good year, the pond could be harvested twice, filling the houses as early as the beginning of February. The Ice House was insulated with walls that were 16 inches thick; the ice itself was preserved by packing it in sawdust from the Nash mill nearby. After the turn of the century, Edward Nash started a motor trucking and storage company, E.C. Nash, Inc., taking over the site of Kemper's Tannery, which had been established in 1835 on Riverside Avenue.

STAPLES' LEGACY: Horace Staples, one of Westport's most distinguished men, was a business-educator-philanthropist. He built the first Staples High School in 1884, located on Riverside Avenue.
PHOTO COURTESY OF
BILL SCHEFFLER

The man who supplied the lumber to the Nash Mills, Horace Staples, had earned his fortune through hardware sales, a fleet of sailing vessels and banking. His most memorable legacy is the high school that still bears his name. The dedication of the high school on April 26, 1884, was a most special day in Westport. All places of business closed at one o'clock. "The town turned out in force, and sirens, bells and whistles sounded in celebration. Horace Staples used his personal fortune to establish this first high school in Westport."[12] The original school was a three-story, red brick building on Riverside Avenue. At the ceremony, attended by Connecticut Governor Thomas M. Waller, the Reverend Alonzo Nodon

Lewis of the Memorial Church of the Holy Trinity read a poem of 22 stanzas, which concludes with the following verse:

> There may be men in Westport
> Who'll leave more to their heirs
> There may be men more prominent
> In church and state affairs
> There may be men, whom more renowned
> The multitude will call,
> But the name of Horace Staples
> Will outlive them one and all.[13]

The school opened with 60 students who paid an annual tuition of $16 to $20 a year. It contained 11 rooms — 2 general classrooms, 1 music room, 4 rooms for commercial studies, 2 basement rooms for shop work, one mechanical drawing room, one study hall seating 100 pupils, with classroom sizes averaged 21 by 30 feet. School was in session from 9 A.M. to 4 P.M. and the students studied a wide variety of subjects, including English, German, Latin, Greek, and algebra, which was part of the traditional curriculum for that era. The total student population for all Westport schools for that year was 807, comprising youths between the ages of 4 and 16, and the education budget was $5,219.89.

There is a fascinating little-known caveat attached to the story of Staples High School's founding. Had it not been for the town's lack of progress in education, Horace Staples' dream of a high school would not have been realized until *after* he died. Staples, at 93, disclosed his secret in 1895 in a talk to the Westport Historical Society titled: "Westport, As I Have Known It for the Past Fifty Years." He explained why he changed his will to build the school while he was alive. "In 1880," he recalled, "our town had become so low in educational advantages, that many families had removed to other towns, and many of our citizens were sending their children to Norwalk and other places, so that every morning on five days of the week, we could count a large number of scholars on the platform at the depot, with their tickets to Norwalk, by railroad. This led me to think of carrying out what I had provided by will, several years previous to be done after my decease, and by some unknown means, one or two persons had learned of that provision, and so wrought upon my weakness that in the spring of 1884, the corner stone was laid to the High School, and the first and greatest and most united meeting ever assembled in the town came to witness it."[14] The school opened in the fall of the same year. Staples was getting on in age at 78, but he continued to focus his attention on the town's educational affairs.

In 1885, Wilbur Cross, an enterprising and bright young man who had just graduated from Yale, heard that Staples was looking for a principal. He called on Staples who, in turn, told him he was looking for an "Amherst man." But Cross persevered and ultimately, with the backing of some clergymen in town, he won the appointment. Cross was given a modest salary, but he was told that he would be responsible for funding the heating and hiring a janitor. So he went to Staples to talk the matter over. "At this point," he recalled, "we began to dicker, a young Yankee against an old Yankee who, in the end, promised to pay for the janitor."[15] This job was the start of a distinguished career for Cross, who would eventually be elected governor of Connecticut in 1931 and serve until 1939. On June 24, 1887, the first graduating class of six young women was handed the Staples' diplomas made of genuine sheepskin with a picture of Horace Staples on them. For many years, the school celebrated his birthday, January 31, annually on Founder's Day. Staples died on March 7, 1897, at the age of 95.

Staples' had a passion for excellence. He directed that funds from his estate be used to maintain the school which, he said, should be run by teachers "of the best character and qualifications," and maintained in the tradition of excellence and efficiency. In 1898, following his death, the tuition was dropped, and anyone who passed the school's entrance examination was permitted to attend. Two-thirds of the school's funding would come from Staples' estate and one-third from the town. Control of Staples High School would not be transferred from Staples' estate to the Town of Westport until 1909. Other education-related activities of the era were the new requirement (1894) that all children be vaccinated before attending school, the founding of the Westport School of Music (1892), and the formation of a local Parents and Teachers Association (1897).

MODEST MAIDENS: In the early 1900s, women came to Compo Beach, changed into their bathing suits in portable bathhouses, and then were wheeled down to the water to preserve their privacy in public.
WESTPORT HISTORICAL SOCIETY PHOTO

Education was not Westport's sole concern in the area of community services. Recreational resources, especially Compo Beach, were favorite topics of discussion in the post-Civil War period as townspeople began to clamor for an easy way to travel to the beach for recreation. In mid-1879, the town began to operate an omnibus from the middle of town for 25 cents a rider. A proposal to build a bathhouse for patrons was also advanced and eventually completed. Water at the beach, however, was not as much a concern as the town's water supply. Population expansion and economic progress inevitably led to supply problems. In 1878, town officials had proposed a plan for a city water system that would go along with the wells used by inhabitants. Shortly after the July 4 holiday weekend that year, the *Westporter-Herald* urged the town to adopt a water supply system, particularly in view of the new fire hazards, which the area's economic development on Main Street now posed. The town finally built a water system in 1892 when the Westport Water Company installed a standpipe and pumping stations. In 1925, the Westport Water Company bought water from the Bridgeport Hydraulic Company so that it could give better service and more pressure. In August 1927, the Bridgeport Hydraulic Company acquired the local plant.

In the 1860s to 1890, the town also improved its roads and bridges. After the turn of the century, Edward Coley Birge commented that the most important bridge preceding the Civil War was the new Post Road Bridge completed in 1857. In 1865, Saugatuck had no carriage bridge across the river so that people who lived on Compo Street and wanted to go to the railroad station had to come up to Westport village, cross the river at State Street, and drive on the west side. In 1869, a carriage bridge was finally built at Saugatuck at the "narrows" where the Disbrow Ferry had been, but not without much acrimonious debate. In the 1860s, the prospect of a new bridge for what Edward Coley Birge called a "degraded highway" had not been good. In 1866, an $8,000 bond issue was floated. Later, at a town meeting on June 4, 1868, a charter was granted to the Saugatuck Bridge Company to build the bridge, and the town approved an appropriation of $8,000. Soon after the meeting was adjourned, however, opponents of the bridge petitioned the selectmen to call another meeting to rescind the vote. A special town meeting was held, and the vote was rescinded. At that crowded town meeting, George L. Cable, the moderator, was unable to have the vote on adjournment counted, so he sent everyone outside to line up on either side of a rope to be counted. The motion to adjourn was lost, leaving the way clear for the "uptowners" to vote against the bridge.

That was not the end of this squabble. By February of the following year, the price shot up to $21,000 and the selectmen appointed a committee to purchase the franchise of the Saugatuck Bridge Company. Ten days later, after a rowdy meeting, an injunction was served on the selectmen restraining them from paying any of the money voted by the town to build the bridge. Meanwhile the bridge contractor had started operations, and the people in favor of the bridge had raised over $3,000 to pay any expense that the Bridge Company might incur. After a letter-writing campaign in *The Westport Advertiser* supporting the bridge, the selectmen again refused to advance the money. Finally, in 1869, the bridge was built and subsequently a court order directed the town to pay $27,532.17.

In 1884, less than 15 years later, the bridge was almost impassable as a result of a seaworm, which chewed the wooden piles. Many people believed that the original bridge had been improperly constructed. After yet another acrimonious town meeting, the voters decided in favor of calling in another contractor, Cornelius Kitteridge, whose company had built the famous cantilever bridge over the Niagara River. It was to be an iron structure, 286 feet long, costing $26,000 and to be completed on October 1, 1884. Town officials promised that it would be a bridge that would "endure for generations,"[16] and indeed it has. It was widened in 1994 and completely rebuilt following yet another stormy controversy over whether it should be replaced by a new bridge. Meanwhile, the Post Road Bridge, originally built in 1807, was replaced by the town with another wooden bridge, which, over the years, has been completely replaced. Trolley tracks, which had been laid down in the early twentieth century, were removed when Parker-Harding Plaza was constructed in 1954. The bridge was widened, and extensive structural changes were made between 1990-1992. Today this bridge is used to honor the 1945 founding of the United Nations. The flags of every country in the United Nations are unfurled on "jUNe Day" every summer on the Post Road Bridge. There are five vehicle bridges over the Saugatuck River in Westport, in addition to the railroad bridge.[17]

Bridges are not the only way we measure progress; a civilization is historically evaluated on the basis of how well informed it is. Through both its newspaper and public library, Westport demonstrated the level of its civilization. In the early 1800s few Westport families had the opportunity to read a weekly newspaper. In some residential areas, a single newspaper left at a local shop, tavern, or grocery store served as the only source of news for the entire town. It did not publish much "news" in the modern sense because things simply did not change much from week to week. The first newspaper in Saugatuck was published in 1828, when the village of

Saugatuck was still part of Fairfield. A paper published in Bridgeport announced it was going out of business for lack of funds. The press and type were advertised for sale for $500 cash.

Daniel Nash, Jr., who only seven years later would lead the way in gaining independent status for Westport, loaned the money to a group of men whom he considered civic-minded and responsible: Alva Gray, Charles Jesup, Samuel Avery, Levi T. Downs, Henry Sherwood, William H. Jesup, Walter Thorp and Stephen Morehouse. Cautious lender that he was, Nash made the money available only because he had confidence in his colleagues and in the new enterprise. They moved quickly. The first issue of the paper, *The Saugatuck Journal*, was published the day after Christmas in 1828, but the newspaper lasted for only two years.

*Vol. I
Number 1
March 25, 1876*
WESTPORT
HISTORICAL
SOCIETY

During the ensuing years, more newspapers published the news about Westport, although some of them were short-lived. *The Saugatuck Journal* was merged with the *Fairfield County Republican*, but the combined newspaper folded in July, 1830 after only four months of publication. *The Westport Advertiser,* a weekly newspaper, started in 1867, as we have noted. In 1871, Westporter B.W. Maples, having boarded a train for New York one day, soon discovered that he had forgotten his commutation ticket. The conductor, not amused and unyielding, made him get off at the next stop. Angered by the action, Maples sued the railroad. He became even angrier over press coverage of the dispute, which he felt did not show him in a favorable light. Believing that the newspapers were beholden to the railroad for distribution and thus would not give his case unbiased coverage, he responded by starting his own biweekly paper, the *Westport Hour*. Two years later, he moved the newspaper to Norwalk and consolidated it with *The Westport Advertiser*. At the end of 1874, Maples won his lawsuit and was about to suspend publication when he realized that the new weekly paper was making money. He continued to publish it every Saturday until *The Hour* became a daily in 1895. Maples continued as editor and publisher until his death in 1900. The paper continues to publish to this day. One more newspaper, *The Westporter*, was founded in 1876 by John S. Jones.

SURE BET: Edward T. Bedford loved to ride his horse, Diplomat, over the half-mile track on the spacious grounds of his home on Beachside Avenue. He rode until the age of 78.   BEDFORD FAMILY COLLECTION

Westport's increasingly sophisticated and educated citizenry began to agitate for a public library. In 1877 the Westport Reading Room and Library Association was organized and in 1886 the state finally granted a charter formally establishing the Westport Library Association. Townspeople contributed books, magazines, newspapers, and some money to the original reading room on the second floor of the Hurlbutt building on State Street. Because of a shortage of volumes and an overwhelming demand for books, the public could check books out only on Tuesdays and Fridays. Mrs. Frances A. Gray served as the first librarian on a volunteer basis and 82 members came to the first meeting and contributed $1 each. At the close of its first year, the library had a budget of $150, and it had compiled 962 books that had been loaned to 146 members. A decade later, in 1896, circulation had increased to 1,513 and the total number of books had reached 1,748; by 1897, the budget was $1,389.

Many advances were also made in transportation at the end of the nineteenth century. In 1892, the town approved a new railroad station at Green's Farms at a cost of $1,325.80. This project was undertaken largely to accommodate Edward T. Bedford, whose home was near the new station. Meanwhile, the railroad tracks were being laid and the trains modernized with gleaming brass oil lamps, maps, oak floors, and plush seats. The horse-drawn trolley car replaced the omnibus in 1877. It carried passengers down the dirt road that is now Riverside Avenue to the railroad depot. A jingling bell around the horses' necks would alert the people that their ride was approaching. The fare was 8 cents. The railroad fare to New York City was 85 cents and monthly commutation cost $9.

In 1879, a group of civic leaders established a scheduled route for the horsecar that would take people from the cen-

HOTEL SQUARE: The Westport Hotel was located in a central place at Main Street and the Post Road, where the horsecars and later, the trolleys, converged. It was one of the most popular locales in town.
ROBERT LAMBDIN PAINTING/ WESTPORT PUBLIC LIBRARY

ter of Westport to the railroad station along Riverside Avenue. Listings for trips on the "Westport & Saugatuck Horse Rail-Road" leaving the Westport Hotel downtown for the railroad depot were published regularly in the newspaper. The center of activity was in Hotel Square in front of the hotel. A typical schedule in 1879, for example, offered a train running west seven times a day starting at 6:37 A.M. and running up to 6:22 P.M. From 7:14 A.M. to 6: 22 P.M. six trips were offered to the depot for trains running east. On Saturdays trips to the station were scheduled from 9:05 A.M. to 9:37 P.M. No trains were scheduled on Sundays.

In 1896, the trolley car — powered by electricity — made its debut. "It wasn't long," according to one newspaper account, "before Westport became one of the few communities of its size to have trolley service and the previously used horse drawn trolley became passe."[18] Edward Coley Birge was among those who made the maiden voyage of the electric trolley:

> The gathering around the doors to the National Hall
> and those above at the windows awaited alertly
> the arrival from up Riverside Avenue of the load
> from the train in the new resplendent trolley
> car. The writer well remembers Horace Staples,
> then nearly 95 years old, near the door of his bank,
> his hand cupped to his ear, for he was very deaf,
> talking to those around him. The moments became
> minutes crystallized into quarter hours but the new
> trolley car came not. An hour was well nigh
> exhausted when the familiar rattle of the old horse
> car could be distinguished mingled with ribald
> laughter as around the corner appeared George
> Mills slapping the reins on the back of a grizzled
> dobbin who was dragging our Toonerville loaded
> to both platforms with passengers from the station.
> The power plant at Post's Mill had experienced
> one of its breakdowns in those early days of
> generating electricity. [19]

As it turned out, power was restored later the same day. The trolleys continued running for some time, connecting the neighboring coastal towns, and, at one point, including a special route to take bathers to Compo Beach.

In 1898, the Westport trolley found itself in the red. The trolley line had been losing as much as $1,000 a month and so was sold to a New York businessman.[20] No sooner had Westporters become accustomed to the electric trolley than, to the general wonderment of the citizenry in 1899, the first automobile was seen chugging up the Post Road. Soon the gas buggies were competing with these early Stanley Steamers, named for the brothers who invented them. And, for a brief period, a third alternative was made available — an electric car, which, however, proved to be impractical. The appearance of the automobile was a stunning event. One townsman said: "Driving home from Southport one forenoon in the early summer of 1899, when near the Indian monument in Pequot swamp, just east of the 'Roundhouse,' a self-propelled open buggy carrying two men passed me going westward. Although my business took me twice daily over this section of the Turnpike, it was my first sight of an automobile, then a contrivance beginning to figure in the newspapers. At first this new invention was called a motor wagon or a horseless carriage."[21]

LASTING LANDMARK: Veteran seaman Captain Walter Allen built the now-famous Allen's Clam House in 1890. It soon became a major gathering place for residents who rented in the vicinity during the summer and used the Old Mill Beach for swimming.
PHOTO COURTESY OF
JEFF NORTHROP

The late nineteenth century also brought Westport a new landmark: Allen's Clam and Lobster House was built in 1890 by Captain Walter Allen, a veteran seaman, on the edge of Sherwood Mill Pond[22] on Hillspoint Road on an 80-acre area of water and salt marshes which had long provided Westporters and others with clam and oyster beds. The Clam House soon became a mecca for many, especially New Yorkers who rented in the vicinity during the summer. Residents of Westport had a fine bathing beach — Old Mill Beach — just on the sound side of the tide gates which were key to the productivity of the shellfish.

Westport's Longshore Country Club, another famous landmark, was also created during this period. This site, then known as Compo Farm, was owned by the Francis Cutting family of Brooklyn, who used it as a farm. Charles Francis Godfrey and his family worked for the Cuttings and oversaw the farm when the Cuttings were in New York. He subsequently operated the farm for many years. In 1868, Alexander M. Lawrence, a New York business tycoon, purchased this 180-acre farm and house, which an associate of John D. Rockefeller built, as a seasonal residence. His son, George P. Lawrence, maintained the family estate until

LONGSHORE CLUB: On July 4, 1898 flags and bunting were flying. The country club was privately owned.
WESTPORT HISTORICAL SOCIETY PHOTO

shortly after the turn of the century. In 1910, the Lawrence heirs, the Craufords, sold the property to Frederick E. Lewis for $15,000. Lewis, a Texas oil man who had made a fortune, completely remodeled the house in the Colonial Revival style, as it appears today, and he added several other buildings and more acreage. In 1929, Patrick Powers bought the estate and developed it as the fashionable Longshore Beach and Country Club, a private club with elite membership. The Powers' heirs sold the property in 1952. In 1960, the town acquired it and made it public to all residents.[23]

Another gem in Westport's crown, National Hall, as previously noted, was built in 1870. During much of the nineteenth century, business centered on the west bank of the Saugatuck River rather than on the east bank. National Hall housed the First National Bank of Westport on the first floor, the local newspaper, the *Westporter Herald*, on the second floor, and the town's meeting hall on the third. In 1884, the space on the third floor was used as classrooms, for a brief time, and so it can be said that National Hall served as Westport's first high school until Staples High School was completed that same year. Also on the third floor, with panoramic views of the Saugatuck River, Westporters regularly met for many years to attend high school graduations, dances, theatrical productions, concerts, and even basketball games.

Continuing Westport's tradition of sailing and boating, the Cedar Point Yacht Club was founded on April 30, 1887, when a group of nine men met under a tree on the banks of the Saugatuck River. The new club's first officers were: Francis Burrett, commodore; J.H. Jennings, vice-commodore; E.S. Wheeler, Jr., secretary; S. S. Dayton, treasurer; and Francis Burrett, J.H. Jennings, and P.G. Sanford, regatta committee. According to Paul Iffland, Centennial Year

Commodore, the club's founders had at least two things in common: they owned sailboats and they were confident they could sail their sailboats just a little bit faster than anyone else. Down through the years, the club has had nationally known boat races under numerous names with celebrity or superstar status in this widely acclaimed competition on water. The club established itself as one of the best in the nation with a number of celebrity status boats. During World War II the club's facilities were turned over to the U.S. Coast Guard auxiliary and many Cedar Point members actively served in their yachts under loan to the Coast Guard. After the war, the Club flotilla consisted of various types of sail and powerboats. In the early 1950s, the popular Atlantic class was introduced, soon followed by a fleet of Lightnings and Blue Jays and then the Thistle class. The club has a Junior instruction program and sailing classes. Today it is located at Bluff Point and holds 116 boats.

In 1893 Westport had its eye on national happenings, so when the first World's Fair was held in Chicago in 1893, Westport did not fail to contribute its talents. One such contribution was a "historical chair" owned by the Rev. H. N. Wayne, rector of Christ Church; it was brought to this country in 1787 and had been used by every president of the United States from Andrew Jackson to Ulysses S. Grant. The Fair, which nearly 39 million visitors attended, also featured an exhibit of Arthur S. Hoyt, a Westport inventor-businessman, at the Leather and Shoe Trade Building. The machine he invented made various kinds of glue used by shoe manufacturers.

Meanwhile, railroad competition became keener in the state after the Civil War. The increase of passenger travel in Connecticut by 1880 was notable. The New York, New Haven, and Hartford Railroad carried 4,609,537 passengers in 1880, compared to just 3,587,909 a decade before. This was an increase of more than one million passengers, or a 25-percent jump. As a result, sailing ships with their uncertain schedules became less profitable. Few boats had a regular schedule before 1880 because of the uncertainty of the amount of commercial and passenger business, as well as the unpredictable weather. Soon, the big working ships began to disappear from the docks on the water's edge. By 1880, only three sloops were used on a regular schedule for commerce and passengers between Westport and New York: the *C.H. Philips* with Captain Isaac Sherwood at the helm; the *James J. Polk*, under Captain Peter Bulkley; and *Lizzie Tolles* under Captain Sereno Allen.

With the railway in full gear, many wealthy New York families, some in railroad-related industries, came to Westport to build summer residences, many of them mansions. They expanded the residential area east from the river up to Compo Road and west from the river along Kings Highway. New York families also began to build in the Green's Farms area and along the beaches. By that time, Main Street had grown to some 35 buildings — including a tailor shop, 4 tenements, a hotel, 2 harness shops, a fish store, 3 groceries, a meat market, a firehouse, a bank, a coal shed, a barber, a dentist, a jeweler, 3 drugstores, a blacksmith, and a cabinet shop.

The last few years of the nineteenth century were not without their share of natural disasters. Perhaps the greatest single one in the Northeast occurred on a Sunday late in the winter of 1887-1888. As reported by *The Westporter,* a blizzard began on the morning of Sunday, March 11, 1888, and by the time it was over, between three and four feet of snow had fallen, with drifts in many places, including snowdrifts in the front of *The Westporter* office in the bank building reaching as high as 20 feet. No travel was possible for at least four days. The only activities revolved around keeping warm. Westport streets had never before been clogged like this. Business was entirely suspended. For three long days and nights, it snowed and rained sleet, with the temperature falling to zero.

Five years later, another disaster — this one man-made — occurred in December 1893, when hundreds of gallons of oil spilled off Cockenoe Island when the schooner *John Bonnell*, bound for New Zealand, burned offshore. Unfortunately, the spillage came at a time when Westporters were in desperate need of heating oil during a freezing cold winter. Although the ship also carried sewing machines and stoves, only the kerosene stowed deep in the hold was of any concern to those in charge of the salvaging operation. One local resident, then a child, Landon K. Allen, never forgot the sight of the blazing ship and the long efforts to save something from it. He offered this account nearly 80 years later: "When the water in and around the schooner put out the fire, I got an old pump and some of us pumped her out enough to get at the kerosene. I had a boat and took my load home. I got about 40 cans but that was nothing. All night long I could hear horses clomping by my place and I could hear the cans rattling in the wagons. There was enough oil for everyone." [24]

Had the telephone been in common use during the blizzard of 1888 and the oil spill of 1893, the townspeople might have had an easier time of it. But this technology was still too new and was little in evidence. After all, Alexander Graham Bell had only recently invented the telephone, having demonstrated it successfully at the Philadelphia Centennial Exposition in

1876, an event that 50 Westporters, including the Lee and the Chapman families, attended. It was not until 1882 that W. E. Osborn purchased a telephone from the newly formed Bell Telephone Company for his general store in Westport opposite the old hotel. "There were no phones this side of Norwalk," Osborn's son, Frank, recalled in an interview he gave in 1971 when he was 95 years old, "so my father was approached by the telephone manager, Elmer Lee, who asked us to install a pay station in the store. We put it on the side wall at the rear of the store, next to the pork and molasses barrels, to keep it out of the way." [25]

Osborn explained that the phone was made of black walnut, with two bells above and six dry cells in a boxlike desk below the speaking and hearing machinery. The user had to turn the crank to ring the bell, which then attracted the operator's attention in Norwalk, the closest outlet. In the early days, there were very few telephone poles and so telephone wires were strung over the rooftops and attached to trees and fence posts. According to one newspaper account, public acceptance of the new invention in Westport as elsewhere was slow. It was used mostly by doctors, morticians, and the sanitarium, which sums up the general public's reluctance to adopt it. The telephone cost $40 per year for businesses and $30 for residences. In 1999 dollars, that would amount to about $550 for residences. Even in 1900, Westport had only about 100 telephones and one permanent switchboard at 40 Myrtle Avenue.

Change was the watchword of the late nineteenth century. In these years, America made gigantic strides in technology, scored amazing medical breakthroughs, gave birth to a newly emerging leisure class, and experienced immense shifts in population. The end of the century witnessed the successful assimilation of an enormous number of immigrants from Europe. Between 1820 and 1900, some 3.9 million Irish and more than one million Italians arrived. In 1887, when work began on double tracking the New York, New Haven, and Hartford Railroad, jobs became available for the many Italian immigrants. In Westport as in America generally, the steady flow of immigrants offered an answer to the country's never-ending need for manpower.

Farming continued to be hard work, and Irish, Polish, Hungarian, and German immigrants helped the farmers till and weed the fields. From 1901 to 1910, another 2 million Italians arrived in America; and from 1911 to 1920, still another 1 million came. Italians formed the backbone of the town's economic growth, with most of the newly arrived families settling in

Saugatuck, the oldest part of town on the early road to South Norwalk. Many of the railroad workers settled permanently in the community, which, by then, was nicknamed "Little Italy."

The people of Saugatuck came from Naples, Calabria, Compobasso and other parts of southern Italy to work on the railroad, on the farms, and in the factories. The Italian women worked, too, finding employment in the button shop, the shirt factory, and farms. Saugatuck at that time was bounded by the Saugatuck River, the railroad, and the Bradley farm on Saugatuck Avenue where Franklin Street and Saugatuck Avenue meet. This area was inherited by the Capasses, the Carreras, the Chappas, the Lucianos, and the Valiantes, to name just a few families. As the Italian community grew, many became prosperous by establishing their own businesses, especially fruit and vegetable stands, groceries, boot and shoe shops, with a few located on Main Street. By 1918, the city directory was listing Italians in a multitude of different occupations, including gardeners, farmers, tailors, chauffeurs, barbers, masons, trackmen, florists, hatters, and carpenters.

NOTICE.

My wife Caroline, having left my bed and board, without just cause or provocation, this is to forbid all persons trusting her on my account, as I will pay no such debts from this date.
GEO. H. SLOVER.
Westport. Mar. 13, 1879

Editor John S. Jones undoubtedly touched off some gossip when he allowed one man to run the following ad on page 1 of The Westporter, March 22, 1879 issue: "NOTICE. My wife Caroline left my bed and board, without just cause or provocation, this is to forbid all persons trusting her on my account, as I will pay no such debts from this date. Geo. H. Slover, Westport, Mar. 13, 1879."

"The Italians are a versatile people. In addition to being hard workers with a desire to better their plight, as businessmen they were intuitive, perceptive and shrewd. Close to the soil, they purchased land whenever money and opportunity were at hand; not to mention how perspicacious their investments would later prove to be," observes Peter J. D'Amico, a descendant of an early immigrant and presently Westport's dog warden, who has made a study of Italian immigration to Westport.[26] The large Italian community soon began to organize fraternal and social clubs, and activities such as St. Anthony of Padua feast, which was celebrated every June 13 for two days and was held as recently as the mid-1970s. The Sons of Italy, an organization formed in the early years of the Italian immigration, sponsored social events. In recent decades, the Italian Festival has supplanted previous events and many Westporters annually attend with great enthusiasm.

As was true of most settlers, the church was the central factor in the social and spiritual lives of the Italian immigrants. The Catholic Church of the Assumption, established by the Irish only a few decades before the Italians first arrived, met the needs of the new immigrants. As their ranks

SPIRITUAL HAVEN: The Church of the Assumption on Riverside Avenue, dedicated in 1900, was preceded by the first Church of the Assumption located at the present-day Wright and Ludlow streets. The first Catholic church was built in the 1880s to meet the spiritual needs of Italian and Irish immigrants who worked on the onion farms, the railroads and in the orchards during an era of anti-immigrant, anti-Catholic prejudice.

PHOTO BY RAY PORTER

swelled, however, the need for a larger church became apparent, and in 1898 the present Church of the Assumption on Riverside Avenue was built. The Italians, like most immigrants, sometimes were subjected to prejudice. Saugatuck, in a very real sense, was seen as an Italian ghetto. Eventually, many Italians began to move from Saugatuck for a variety of reasons: to find a better home with more land, to escape the stigma of living in an ethnic community, and because what had been an almost entirely residential community became more commercial after Interstate 95 was built. But some old Italian names remain in Saugatuck — Anastasia, Arcudi, Caruso, Gilbertie, Luciano, Nistico, Santella, Sarno, among others — and, to some sentimental oldtimers, the area is still thought of as Westport's "Little Italy." [27]

There was a great sense of community in Saugatuck during the last decades of the nineteenth century and continuing into the twentieth century. Many Italian families in modern Westport trace the formative years of their lives and that of their relatives to that era. Art Reale recalls some of the names that come to his mind when thinking about old Saugatuck: Anthony Arciola, Carmello Arcudi, Ed Capasse, Sr., Joe Caprio, Frank Cribari, Anthony Cutrone, Anthony D'Amico, Frank DeMace, Carmine DeMattio, Luco DeMeo, Frank Esposito, Pasquale Gilbertie, Salvatore Gilbertie, Bruno and John Giunta, Joe Melillo, John Nazzaro, Frank Nistico, Thomas Pelicone, Salvatore Reale, Joe Reitano, Doc Renzulli, John Renzulli, Peter J. Romano,

John Saviano, Louis Stroffilino, John Tedesco, the Tremonte family, John Valiante, and many more. By 1918, the city directory was listing Italians in a multitude of different occupations, including were storeowners, laborers, chauffeurs, insurance agents, tailors, barbers, firemen, policemen, masons, trackmen, florists, hatters, carpenters, farmers, construction workers, tradesmen, landscapers, and town employees. The sense of close family ties was reflected beyond the family into the village. Italians themselves intermarried and gathered together on every possible occasion — holidays, weddings, and wakes. They socialized in St. Anthony's Hall on Franklin Street, which was the heart of "Little Italy." Westport for those early immigrants was, quite simply, for people who loved their country, their family, and their God.

One of the community's most admired leaders, Lou Santella, ran the Riverside Barbershop on Riverside Avenue until his retirement in November 1999 at age 68. Lou Santella recalls when his father, John Santella, arrived from Italy and opened a barbershop in the 1920s. Santella's mother, Elizabeth Capasse, was born in Westport in 1907. Lou and his wife, Marge, remember when families relied on one another, when there were no cars roaring above Saugatuck on I-95. "Saugatuck was a special place," he said. "It was truly a neighborhood. I remember as far back as the 1930s, at the end of the Depression, when people needed each other. Families helped each other survive. Saugatuck is still a town people want to come home to." Marge Santella added: "There was a lot of sharing. People brought each other vegetables from their garden when someone in the family was sick. It was a community; it still is. That's what the Italian Festival really celebrates."[28] While Italians provided services in those early days, they have gone on to contribute to Westport as teachers, lawyers, doctors and other professionals. "The Italians' biggest contribution to Westport," Lou Santella says, is that "they carried on tradition and provided the soul of the whole town."

Not all of the Italian-American families lived in Saugatuck, of course. Ed Capasse, a Westport attorney still in practice, grew up in the Green's Farms section of town. He remembers people "working very hard to raise their crops." He also recalls Westport in the 1920s and 1930s as a town of neighborhoods with small grocery stores and taverns. "After a hard day's work and a home-cooked meal, fathers and husbands would gather at these establishments to talk about their work and families." He said they were in bed by 10 P.M. "ready for a good night's sleep and another hard day of hard work."[29]

Westport already had a long, colorful history, but it was only in 1889 that the town finally established its Historical Society. At its first meeting on February 2 of that year, it elected its first slate of officers with Horace Staples voted as president; W. J. Jennings was named first vice president; the Reverend J.E. Coley, second vice president; L.T. Day, treasurer; and the Reverend A. N. Lewis, secretary. The Society was formed to preserve local history, collect relics and "curiosities," and erect a monument to the memory of Westport soldiers and sailors who had gone off to war. The Society quickly succeeded in expanding its membership to include more than 100 people, including some of the community's most prestigious families: Adams, Backus, Bradley, Chapman, Coley, Dolge, Gorham, Gray, Hamilton, Hazleton, Hurlbutt, Jones, Kemper, King, Lees, Mackenzie, Newton, Ogden, Osborn, Post, Purdy, Raymond, Salmon, Sanford, Saxton, Sherwood, Staples, Stearns, Taylor, Thomas, Toquet, Wakeman, Wheeler, Woodworth, Willcox, and Williams (see Appendix H.)

These New England Yankees were perhaps as sophisticated and as worldly as many of their descendants. The titles of the lectures presented by their guest speakers suggest the breadth of their interests: "Scientific Research and Eminent Names," "The Life and Works of Michelangelo," "The Excavation of Pompei," "Eminent American Novelists," "A Paper Upon Cremation," "Ancient and Modern Embalming," "New York's Real East Side," "China's Land, Customs, and Manners," to name but a few.[30] The Historical Society would flower in the next century and become one of the town's most popular attractions.

As the century neared an end, still another important structure was erected in Westport — Hall-Brooke Hospital. The Italianate country home, originally built in the 1850s as a private estate on 55 acres, housed the hospital. It remained a private estate until 1900 when it was leased to Dr. David W. McFarland, who transformed it in 1902 into a sanitarium for the care of the emotionally ill and alcoholics. He and Mrs. McFarland reportedly resided in the main house, which was enlarged to accommodate patients until the main building or Central Hall was constructed in 1918 as a residential building. In the early days, care at the institution was predominantly custodial, serving wealthy clients who often spent their entire adult lives there. Some even brought their own servants. It could accommodate 60 patients — referred to as "guests" — and the main house was furnished in the style of a country inn. The name Hall-Brooke was adopted in the early 1950s, midway through a period of major change in psychiatric care and corresponding change at the hospital. It evolved into a "therapeutic community," aiding more seriously disturbed patients and more middle-class patients. In 1999, it filed application for an assisted living facility in Westport. The hospital announced plans to tear down five existing buildings on its 25-acre Long Lots Road property and construct a replacement building.[31]

The century closed with yet another war. After the Spanish-American War was declared in 1898, some Westporters joined nearby units or volunteered for the regulars. Westport and state officials had more than a passing concern with the war. Connecticut Governor Lorrin A. Cooke gave a speech to the Sons of the American Revolution in March 1898, in which he urged the federal government to strengthen the state's coast defenses, including Compo Beach. The *Westporter-Herald* on March 5, 1898, published a headline: "PROTECTION AT COMPO POINT." In the story, the governor reminded the public that 121 years ago at Cedar Point, English soldiers had landed because there was nothing to prevent them from doing so and that, in 1898, the Point and all its vicinity was powerless as it was in 1777. "Let us have what would be done with due preparation," he declared, urging that a battery of soldiers be posted on Compo Hill, "should an enemy be foolhardy enough to get within range." He also urged that at least 150 men with repeating rifles be called up for duty on or near Compo Beach.

Westport's possible involvement in the Spanish-American War became a reality — but in an embarrassing way — when, three weeks after the *Westporter-Herald* had published a story about the governor's call to defend Compo, the newspaper carried another front-page story with this headline: "SPAIN'S CARTRIDGES MADE HERE." An employee of the local Union Metallic Cartridge Company told the newspaper that the company had received an order for 2,000,000 cartridges. The employee admitted that Union Metallic had supplied Spain with nearly all, if not all, of her ammunition for rifles and small arms. "The bullets Spanish soldiers are murdering defenceless (sic) people in Cuba with, are made by this company. We are now working on an additional order of 2,000,000 of these," said the employee. After a major controversy, the plant was shut down. Although there was no direct connection, talk of war indirectly brought about the establishment in 1899 of a local chapter of the Veterans of Foreign Wars, setting the stage for veterans of future wars to have a gathering place in Westport.

At the turn of the century, Westport was primarily a suburban residential and cultural center and was becoming a resort community. The town's population in 1900 was 4,017. So many people were arriving that the naming of its roads, which until then were known only by street numbers — 1st, 2nd, 3rd and so on — now became a topic of animated discussion at civic meetings. Soon they were given the names that are so familiar to contemporary Westporters: Bulkley, Maple, Jennings, Prospect, Turkey Hill, Green's Farms, Adams, Cemetery, Burr, Ripley, Long Lots, Square, and Roseville.

The new century was celebrated at midnight 1900. Peace, prosperity and progress were clearly evident across the nation. Westport was no exception. The townspeople recognized that, with hard work and perseverance, their best years could very well lay ahead of them. It was, Westporters felt, a splendid time to be alive. They were about to enter what historians would later label "the Cocksure Era."

COLEY'S COLLECTION: Nancy Richmond Coley, right, and her brother, James Edward Coley III, of Clinton, Connecticut, display a colonial rifle and other antiques on the hearth of the Coley homestead at 125 Riverside Avenue. She is holding a cannonball found on her property that originally came from the Battle of Compo Beach in 1777. Her mother, Kathleen A. Coley, bought the house in 1928. These Coleys are descendants of the Reverend James Edward Coley, who ran a school for boys during the Civil War.

MIGGS BURROUGHS PHOTO

NOTES

1. Eve Potts, *Westport...A Special Place* (Westport, CT: Westport Historical Society, 1985), p. 68.

2. Mason's writings were discovered recently by Barbara Van Orden and edited for publication by Larry Aasen, both members of the Saugatuck Congregational Church.

3. Joanna Foster, *More Stories from Westport's Past*, 1986, p. 23.

4. Burton Davis, the *Westporter-Herald*, May 18, 1934.

5. Wakefield Dort, *Westport in Connecticut's History, 1835-1935*, Connecticut Tercentenary, p. 28.

6. *The Westport-Advertiser*, October 17, 1868.

7. The Gault family is the source.

8. Isaac Banks Wakeman, born in 1912, comes from a long line of Wakemans as follows: Francis Wakeman, died in 1626; John Wakeman, 1635-1692; Joseph Wakeman, 1670-1726; Stephen Wakeman 1716-1760; Jessup Wakeman, 1748-1780; Banks Wakeman, 1767-1835; Stephen Burritt Wakeman, 1804-1857; Stephen Banks Wakeman, 1835-1930; John Staples Wakeman, 1874-1938; Isaac Banks Wakeman. Source: Wakeman family historian Florence Remlin.

9. Foster, *Stories from Westport's Past,* Book III, 1988, p. 24.

10. The *Westporter-Herald*, June 8, 1878.

11. Vrest Orton, *The American Cider Book* (Toronto: Noonday, 1973), p. 29, in an interview with Robert L. Cabelle, a professor of food service at Cornell University.

12. Potts, *Westport…A Special Place*, p. 61.

13. The *Westport News*, January 27, 1971.

14. Scrapbook of Mrs. William Gray Staples, Westport, Connecticut, 1889-1909, p. 22A.

15. Wilbur Cross, *Connecticut Yankee, An Autobiography* (New Haven: Yale University Press, 1943), p. 89.

16. Foster, *More Stories from Westport's Past*, pp. 5-6.

17. The first bridge, Kings Highway, was built around 1761 as a section of the first road between New York and Boston. It was replaced in 1893, and then modernized as a concrete bridge in 1965; the second bridge, a drawbridge, was built by the Connecticut Turnpike Company and completed in 1807; the third bridge, built in 1871, was at the "Narrows," the Bridge Street Bridge in Saugatuck, a ferry crossing for 100 years; the fourth was part of the Merritt Parkway, built in the 1930s; the fifth is Interstate 95, the John Davis Lodge Highway, better known as the Connecticut Turnpike. The Railway Bridge, now on the National Register of Historic Properties, was in place by 1848, affording a footpath for pedestrians.

18. *The Westporter-Herald*, March 9, 1917.

19. Edward Coley Birge, *Westport, Connecticut, The Making of a Yankee Township*, (Westport, CT: Westport Historical Society, 1855), pp. 58-59.

20. *The Westporter*, February 5, 1898.

21. Edward Coley Birge, p. 73.

22. Kevin Mayhood, "Mill Pond Had Bounty of Oysters," *Westport News*, November 25, 1988, p. 3.

23. Marie Saxonmeyer Gagg, *Marie, Autobiography of a Westport Native* (Westport, CT: 1979), pp. 5-6. The main house was used as an inn and the swimming pool, originally salt water, was added. Powers built a number of rustic log cabins and enclosed the porch and terrace of the main house. The main house was still operated as an inn and leased by the town to a private concessionaire. Second source: Connecticut State Historical Commission, Historic Resources Inventory Form, Longshore, Item 19, May, 1988, Mary E. McCahon, Architectural Historian.

24. *Westport News*, December 6, 1972, based on Westport Historical Society records.

25. "Osborn Recalls Early Telephone," *The Bridgeport Post*, February 4, 1971.

26. *Italians in Westport, A Personal Account for an Ethnohistory of the Westport-Norwalk Area From 1900 to Today,* a project of the Westport-Weston Arts Council, funded by the Connecticut Humanities Council, the state of Committee of the National Endowment for the Humanities, 1978-1979.

27. The *Westport News*, July 8, 1987.

28. Interview with Lou Santella, November 1, 1999.

29. Statement from Ed Capasse to the author, November 1999.

30. The Reverend James E. Coley, paper written for the Historical Society, March 2, 1889, Scrapbook of Mrs. William Gray Staples, Westport, Connecticut, 1889-1909, p. 1.

31. Elisabeth S. Solomon purchased the hospital in 1964 and changed it to a non-profit foundation in 1966. Between 1950 and 1970, long-term patient care was phased out and replaced by short and intermediate programs. Hall-Brooke was accredited in 1962 and provided treatment for psychiatric care and for substance abuse. Hall-Brooke was acquired by St. Vincent's Health Services Corporation in 1998 and under the aegis of the new owners, made plans in the spring of 1999 to consolidate services in one state-of-the art building and to add an assisted living facility. Source: *Report to the Community*, Hall-Brooke Foundation, 1967.

Photo, p. 119, Horse car on Riverside Avenue, 1880s, Westport Historical Society

PART IV
'THE BEGINNING OF SOMETHING GREAT'

WESTPORT. CON

GREAT SUCCESS

The Celebration of the Passing of the Old Century

TWENTIETH CENTURY WELL RECEIVED

Display of Fireworks Something Elaborate Exercises in the Hall

The celebration of the passing of the nineteenth century and the coming of the twentieth, at National Hall, Monday evening was a grand success in every particular.

The exercises began promptly at 10:45 and were opened with singing that familiar hymn "O God, Our

The January 4, 1901 issue of The Westporter *published this headline reporting on the town's celebration of the new century in 1901 – not 1900.*

WESTPORT PUBLIC LIBRARY

147

CHAPTER 11

A LEAP OF FAITH

*I honestly believe that the town of Westport is about to take
a step that means the beginning of something great in the future.*

— John S. Jones, editor,
the *Westporter-Herald*, October 16, 1900

Westporters began the twentieth century filled with pride in their past and optimism about their future. On January 4, 1901, the headline in the *Westporter-Herald* reflected the townspeople's feelings: "GREAT SUCCESS." The story began: "The celebration of the passing of the nineteenth century and the coming of the twentieth, at National Hall Monday evening, was a grand success in every particular." For Westport residents, the exciting transition from one century to the next represented a leap of faith. The ceremonies in town began promptly at 10:45 P.M., December 31, 1900 with the singing of the hymn, "Oh God, Our Help in Ages Past." The newspaper reported: "Never before did the hall ever hear such music by so many voices." The Reverend James Robinson, pastor of the Saugatuck Methodist Church, read the 100th Psalm and the Reverend Kenneth Mackenzie, Jr., rector of the Church of the Holy Trinity, read prayers. Then, the 600 people who had jammed the hall sang "All Hail the Power of Jesus' Name."

William H. Burr, president of the Board of Trade as well as the Westport Historical Society, read a paper recalling the nation's accomplishments in the nineteenth century, after which the Reverend Jabez Backus of Christ Church reminisced about Westport's past. "We have come to the last minutes of a dying century. Sufficient it is if we remember that it has been a period of incredible activity and glorious results not only in the material side of our life, but also in the social, political, physical, intellectual, moral and religious." Following the ceremonies, the townspeople left the hall and gathered on the bridge downtown at midnight to witness a fabulous display of fireworks ushering in the New Year and the new century.

Westporters wanted to start the new century with a clean slate. Among the reforms launched in the new century was a revival of the Puritan perception of alcohol as a vice. Although the dialogue on prohibition did not reach a national crescendo until the World War I period, there were early signs indicating just how important this issue would become in Westport. For example, on May 20, 1900, the *Westporter-Herald* reported on the Women's Christian Temperance Union's discussion of some "alarming statements" made by a New York doctor, Dr. M. Stewart. The doctor, an expert on heredity, had stated that drinking was becoming more widespread and that the largest increase was occurring among women. This habit, he said, was a "symptom of degeneracy." Talk like this undoubtedly was what led people in Westport to hold a temperance rally. Another activity which some Westporters disdained was gambling. In March 1901, the police raided two saloons and seized the slot machines owned by Joseph Carroll and Thomas Geoghan on the west side of the river. Westport's businessmen

BREAD AND BREAKFAST: Proprietor Edward Lehn, Jr., his wife Caroline, daughters Dorothy and Louisa, lived in one of six flats in this four-story building located on the west side of Main Street near the Post Road. The family freshly baked all that was needed for breakfast on a daily basis.
WESTPORT HISTORICAL SOCIETY PHOTO

joined in the cleanup and improvement drive, and held a meeting to drum up publicity to "bring new people to Westport, to sing its praise far and wide, always telling of its good qualities, never of its bad which are very few," said the paper.

The "look" of Westport as the new century began was still rustic and simple. Many of the merchants lived in flats above the stores. Proprietor Edward Lehn, Jr., his wife Caroline, and daughters Dorothy and Louisa, lived in one of six flats in the four-story building located on the west side of Main Street near the Post Road. The Lehns owned a bakery shop; he was also a hard-working farmer and a longtime sexton of Trinity Church, and his hobby was photography. His photo negatives of local scenes were glass plates, which have been preserved at the Westport Historical Society. Dorothy Lehn Warren, who died in 1999 at the age of 103, described the town at the turn of the century. She said in 1900 the town's population was approximately 4,100, Main Street was filled with the sounds of horses' hooves and trolleys and an occasional tugboat whistle. Over the years, Mrs. Warren saw her father's bakery and other buildings on Main Street change hands.[1]

Mrs. Warren, who was born on August 8, 1896, remembered the turn of the century, although she was only four. She distinctly recalled her older sister, Louisa, and her friends laughing and talking about how "funny" it was to write "1900." The Lehn Bakery on Main Street was located between Cannon's Drug Store and the plumbing shop. The building, as Dorothy Warren remembered it from her childhood, had ovens in the back room heated by a coal fire. Her mother sold bread and cake, doughnuts and cream puffs in the front of the bakery. "My father baked white bread and black rye in two different sizes," she said. "The smaller loaf sold for five cents and the larger for ten cents. Our cookies sold for ten cents a dozen and they were large cookies. Coffeecakes were ten cents each and if you bought three, they were three for a quarter." One of her friends was Bill Petrie, whose father had the ice cream parlor. In 1989, at the age of 93, when she was still working as a volunteer at Town Hall, she told an interviewer:

> Bill Petri was a good person to know. When his father was
> making a fresh batch of ice cream, Bill would alert his friends.
> They would gather around Mr. Petrie and when the churning
> stopped and he pulled out the dasher, the children were
> allowed to lick off the ice cream that stuck to it. People used
> to spend Saturday nights listening to the concert band play

at the Westport Hotel. There were large elm trees
in front of the hotel and the tree on the corner had
boards built around it. This is where all the town notices
as well as any legal notices were posted. It was a common
sight to see men standing around, reading and discussing
all the items.... On Main Street in back of the Hotel, just about
across the street from our bakery, was Beers Brothers, a
meat and grocery store. Further up the street on our side
was another meat market, Crossman's...[It] usually had
sawdust on the floor. One of my early childhood memories
is Mr. Crossman scolding my sister and me for mussing up
his sawdust, which he had just finished raking into a neat
pattern. I also remember particularly well Taylor and
Richards Grocery Store. My mother often sent me there on
errands. I remember that sugar was five pounds for a quarter and coffee was only twenty-five cents a pound. As you
came into the front door there was an open barrel of dill
pickles and customers selected the ones they wanted.
Usually people charged what they bought and paid at the
end of the month. When we came in and paid the bill, we
were rewarded with a small bag of penny candy. The
Taylors also sold coal for homes. The river came right up to
the back of the stores. So the coal barge could come right
up to the Taylor's coal yard and unload. We always hurried
over the bridge when the coal barge came. It was towed by
a tugboat which, when it passed through the turning bridge
at Saugatuck, would sound its whistle.... I used to love
to watch the tug. A family lived aboard. I'd see the woman
hanging out her wash. And they had a dog, which I always
looked for. [2]

Westport in those days was a small, rural town where just about
everyone knew everyone else. By the turn of the century, the 1896 "horse
railroad" had been electrified and the trolley was running regularly.
Westport had become popular with New Yorkers, who found it a friendly
place to spend the summers and weekends. They stayed in hotels and
boarding houses along the heavily traversed Post Road.

Parking on Main Street was problematic even before people had
cars. In front of each of the stores, Dorothy Warren remembered, there was

a hitching post with eight hitches. "But on Saturday afternoon or evening when it might be hard to find a place to tie up a horse and buggy, drivers would bring their own hitching post — in the form of a heavy iron block with a chain on it, which they located wherever there was room to hitch a horse to it," said Mrs. Warren. "The stores remained open on Saturday evening for people coming in from farms to do their weekly shopping. After a week of work, it was also the night to relax at one of the saloons on Main Street, such as the one in the Westport Hotel, or Manners' Saloon which was farther up Main Street. To spruce up for Saturday evening, many a young man would go the barbershop on Main Street for a haircut and a bath. Haircuts were 15 cents. An additional 10 cents would buy a towel and a turn in the bathtub in the back room. The saloons did a lively business, but luckily the horses knew the way home. So, at least in those days, we didn't have to worry about drunk driving."

The movement to improve life in Westport spread, even as the population continued to change with the arrival of new immigrants. The 1900-1910 period marked the years of the heaviest immigration in American history, and Connecticut, being close to the principal entry port, New York, received more than its share of newcomers. By 1910 the foreign-born in the state numbered 329,574, or about 30 percent of the state's 1,114,756 people. The largest flow into Connecticut came from Ireland, followed by Italy, Russia, Germany, Austria-Hungary, and England.[3]

Westport now found itself having to cope with more poor people than in the past. An effort to provide shelter for some of the new arrivals was made in 1901 when the town bought what was known as the Westport Poor Farm, or "Poorhouse," for $2,750 from Charles H. Kemper, Jr. The house, built around 1830, was located on Main Street. Westport also had larger numbers of indigenous poor — mostly blacks, or "colored" people as they were called then. Race relations were just beginning to emerge as a socioeconomic issue after a long hiatus following the Civil War. It would be another 13 years before there were any real signs of discontent among those few blacks living in Westport. In 1923 it was reported that the "Negroes went on wild revel in Saugatuck, knocking on doors and frightening women." According to the *Westporter-Herald*, the men had been brought up from Virginia to build the new Saugatuck Road and lived temporarily in shacks in the Green's Farms area.

Blacks were not the only unwelcome element in Westport; Jews, too, were discouraged from settling in the area. On November 23, 1923, hooded members of the Norwalk Ku Klux Klan met on the shore road in

Saugatuck threatening to tar and feather two Norwalk Jews unless they left town immediately. Two Klansmen wrote the KKK letters on the road, one to the north entrance to William P. Eno's estate, the other toward the Great Marsh section of Westport. On December 17, 1923, several hundred Westporters gathered in amazement to watch a cross about 15-feet-high and 8-feet-wide being burned on the west side of town at night lighting up the area, as one newspaper account reported, "in a most brilliant manner." The episode made big headlines the next morning in the *Westporter-Herald*: "Did Burning of Cross in Westport Last Evening Mean the Beginning of Activities of Ku Klux Klan in This Town?" The article reported that it had been rumored Westport had Klan members in town and the demonstration had alarmed some of the townspeople. Klan officials elsewhere in the state denied the charge. It was not until 1932 that the Klan came out publicly in Westport. According to one newspaper report, the Ku Klux Klan held special services in the Little White Church on the Hill in Saugatuck; there were about 400 people attending, 100 of whom were in the traditional white robes of the order.[4] The church had extended an invitation to the Klan and, in reciprocation, the Klan presented the church an American flag. Although Saugatuck was the site of the KKK meeting, that was hardly a reflection of the sentiments of its population, which was mostly Italian.

Landmarks are always important in a town's history. In July 1901, two cannons arrived in Westport to commemorate the Revolutionary War Battle of Compo Beach on April 25, 1777, as a gift from the U.S. Army from its obsolete ordnance. They were muzzle-loading guns known as "old style" (pre-1840) cannons, 11 feet long, weighing about 5 tons each, and capable of hurling 7-inch, 42-pound cannon balls. They were made of forged iron; their barrels were reinforced at the base and the muzzle with iron rings. They reportedly were the only guns in their class still in existence.[5] The cannons were situated on Compo Beach and through the years they have become an attraction for the town's youngsters to climb and straddle for fun and picture taking.

Another landmark, the Minute Man statue dedicated in 1910, symbolizes the heroism of the patriots who defended their country when the British troops under General Tryon invaded Compo Beach. General David Wooster and Colonel Abraham Gould, together with more than 100 men, lost their lives in the battle, which began on Compo Road. The town fathers, William H. Burr among them, decided that a memorial should be erected to mark the spot where the battle took place. H. Daniel Webster, a Westport sculptor, was commissioned to create the memorial from a composite of descendants of colonial militia, as well as former First Selectman Lewis P. Wakeman, who reportedly sat as a model. The Minute Man in colonial knee britches and tunic, a powder horn slung over his back, is Westport's best known sculpture.[6]

Compo Beach has been held by generations of Westporters as a major asset, although David Bradley challenged public use of the beach in 1902. A long and bitter legal battle — *David Bradley vs. Town of Westport*— over who owned Compo Beach, was decided in favor of the town on November 21, 1902. The *Westporter-Herald* ran the story with a huge three-column headline: "WESTPORT OWNS COMPO BEACH. Bradleys Gave up the Fight of Years at Bridgeport Yesterday and the Town Now Has a Legal Right to Do What It Pleases with the Beach, Without Asking Anyone. Many Witnesses for Town, but Few for Bradley." This episode started when First Selectman Lewis P. Wakeman, angered by Bradley's refusal to allow a town road built on what he considered private property, took matters into his own hands. Bradley had erected a fence in the middle of the night that Wakeman ordered workmen to demolish. This setback for Bradley, a home-owner who also owned bathhouses and a pavilion on the beach, is considered a milestone in Westport history. Before 1900, Bradley had for years contended that Compo Beach was part of his extensive farm near the foot of Compo Hill. However, based on this court decision, the beach became forever a free and public domain. As a residential area, it is listed in the Connecticut Register of Historic Places.

Within the next decade, however, there was another controversy about the beach. The *Westporter-Herald* front-page headline on August 6, 1909, shocked many readers: It read: "SELECTMEN CHOP DOWN BATH HOUSES." The story told of how Selectmen Lewis B. Wakeman, Robert H. Coley and Merrick H. Coley issued an order to tear down every bath house standing on Compo Beach. Coley hired employees of the Atlantic Starch Works. The workmen tore down houses that had for years been the comfort of their owners and friends. It was estimated that at least $2,000 worth of property was destroyed. The reason given by the selectmen for the action was that the selectmen had learned that the Norwalk owners of the bathhouses on Compo Beach were about to serve an injunction on the selectmen to prevent them from taking such drastic action. The town's lawyer had cited the November 1902 court decision, described above, that the town owned the beach.

Education continued to get top priority in the new century. On October 16, 1900, the town voted *not* to rescind the vote taken at the annual meeting appropriating $6,000 for a school in Saugatuck. In 1901, *Westporter* Editor John S. Jones proclaimed: "The voters of Westport did themselves proud. I honestly believe that the town of Westport is about to take a step that

means the beginning of something great in the future."[7] He was gratified to see the Town in 1901 purchase textbooks and supplies required by children in public schools; they were to be loaned to pupils and remain the property of the town. Jones remained active until the age of 71, when he died on November 23, 1906, in the town to which he had devoted his life.

PAYING RESPECT: Honoring John S. Jones at his tombstone in the Green's Farms Cemetery is his great, great grandson, Jeffrey Northrop, with his two sons, Jeffrey, left, and Tuck. The picture was taken in 1990.
WESTPORT NEWS PHOTO

At the turn of the century, there were 853 students in the schools. By 1912, the student population rose to 1,052. In 1914, the town of Westport voted the consolidation of the district schools and, in 1916, it decided to add a new wing to the Bridge Street School in Saugatuck, which had become seriously overcrowded. In 1917, the town voted to build a new school on Myrtle Avenue, thus providing for the children of East and West Saugatuck, Cross Highway, Poplar Plains and Coleytown. Edward T. Bedford gave a major contribution toward the building of this school built in 1917, which was appropriately named the Bedford Elementary School. [8] In 1925, E.T. Bedford would once again show his generosity by helping to build the new Green's Farms School, which was designed by architect Charles Cutler. The school consolidated East and West Long Lots and the lower Green's Farms four-room school. Ebenezer Beers and Maurice B. Wakeman were best remembered for their teaching in the old Green's Farms School.[9]

In the fall of 1919, an evening school was opened at the suggestion of the federal and state educational departments to promote the "Americanization" of all adults who were of foreign extraction. It was a class for adult aliens to aid them in learning to speak and write the English language, and to give such instructions as might be necessary for all aliens who planned to take out citizenship papers.

A town's library is a measure of townspeople's thirst for knowledge and

Westport was thirsty. Some 300 townspeople turned out on April 8, 1908 to attend the dedication of the Morris K. Jesup Memorial Library. Jesup, who died only four months earlier, had donated the land and $5,000 to build the library. A special trolley car brought the Jesup family from the railroad station after they arrived on the 1:22 P.M. train. Mrs. Jesup enthusiastically inspected the library and then signed the deeds conveying it to the Library Association. She was escorted to the hall where the ceremony was led by William L. Taylor, president of the Library Association, William Burr, the public-spirited official who served as president of the board of trustees, told the gathering: "The structure is ornate, symmetrical, and beautiful, in all its lines and massive grace, and bears over its portals the cordial welcome, 'Open to All.'...[The library]

BENEFACTOR: The sign over the building "OPEN TO ALL" reflects the philosophy of Morris K. Jesup, who built the Public Library on State Street. It is now being used for business purposes.
LIBRARY PHOTO BY MIGGS BURROUGHS
JESUP PHOTO COURTESY
WESTPORT HISTORICAL SOCIETY

comes from the grand spirit of our ancestors who believed in looking out for the generations to come after them." Connecticut Governor Rollin P. Woodruff then said a few words of greeting and pumped a few hands. By 1917, the Westport library was described in the local newspaper as one of the most beautiful in the county, if not in the state. It was one of 436 built in New England at the time. The librarian was Edith Very Sherwood, and the assistant librarian, Ernestine Punzelt. The same year as the library dedication, 1908, Westport built its first Town Hall, constructed of native stone, near Toquet Hall on State Street.

Even as the town made steady progress in public education and other public improvements, it took great satisfaction in its new public transportation system. The horse car line, as mentioned earlier, had been electrified and transformed into a trolley line on State Street in 1896 and therefore eased the transition into the twentieth century for local residents. The large jumbo cars were about 50 feet long and had seats for about 60 passengers, and there was standing room at each end of each car. And progress continued on the railroad, which by 1914, had modernized from steam-powered locomotives to electric engines. By then it was running from New York to Boston.

Westport's profile in 1919, according to the town's Annual Report for that year, showed a population of 5,500; an annual budget of $130,000, including $38,000 to operate the school system; a budget of $3,750 to take care of "the poor." The report also told of an outbreak of influenza that struck more than one out of 10 people and resulted in 58 deaths; of "piece work" by some 35 children in Saugatuck on sewing machines in their homes after school; and of some 905 children in school but only 28 of them 16 or older.

A key figure in improving transportation in the United States and abroad was Westporter William Phelps Eno, who would become known as a world pioneer in traffic control. He devised a plan to erect traffic lights that would later enable him to help ease traffic in Westport and in other towns and cities worldwide. According to one report, "Congestion at the turn of

TRAFFIC PIONEER: Westporter William Phelps Eno became world-famous for his breakthrough in traffic control. He devised a plan to erect traffic lights that would later enable him to help ease traffic in Westport.

WESTPORT
PUBLIC LIBRARY

the century inspired a variety of panaceas, and some fantastic proposals were suggested by otherwise practical men."[10] Eno built a home in Westport near "Judah Rock" in 1921 and used it as his company's headquarters until 1938, when he built a university-like headquarters in Saugatuck. Eno, who became known as "the Father of Traffic Regulation," wrote the seminal work, *Rules of the Road,* which were adopted by New York City and other towns and cities. Eno had a vision in the 1930s of a national network of super highways, an insight all the more remarkable because he never learned to drive.[11]

Many Westporters worked to make the town a better community. One of these was State Senator Lloyd Nash, Sr., a tall, rotund man who weighed more than 300 pounds and was a descendant of Westport founder Daniel Nash. Following the Nash family tradition, he contributed to the town's growth through both his public life and business life. In addition to his public duty in Hartford, he actively ran his own extensive ice business. During the winter of 1903, as previously mentioned, Nash's Pond harvested tons of ice. The technology involved in his ice-making business, though primitive compared to today's, helped stimulate a burgeoning economy which, in turn, contributed to a desire by the local residents for more advanced machines and inventions of all kinds that were fast coming into use.

One invention that elicited the greatest interest was the telephone. It was the rage to own one and people in Green's Farms, the wealthiest section of town, began to demand them. On February 10, 1903, the *Westporter-Herald* carried this headline: "WESTPORTERS' ARROGANCE. THEY WANT THE TELEPHONE." It read: "The residents of Green's Farms are desirous of having the telephone installed in their section of town. 'We want it' said a resident from that section while in the *Westporter-Herald* office yesterday, 'and what is more we are going to have it.'" At the time, there were a half dozen phones in operation. Shortly thereafter, a new telephone "Central" was built on the east side of the river, and a Mrs. William H. Smith was asked to run it from Norwalk. The new telephone exchange was put into operation with only three or four subscribers on one party line, as compared to 10 or 12 families who previously shared one party line. The number of telephones in town in 1903 increased to 98. Another breakthrough for the town in 1903 came when it leased the Saugatuck River for shellfish cultivation. The town announced that the selectmen were laying out part of the waterfront for the cultivation and growth of shellfish with lots of suitable size, in order to allow residents to grow shellfish. The results were a mixed bag. Shellfish lots were leased, but the town eventually withdrew the offer when it became clear far too many people were interested in shell fishing.

Meanwhile, the one new technology that undoubtedly had the greatest impact on daily living was the automobile. In 1899, J. Nelson Bulkley, a blacksmith, displayed his "self-propelled buggy," run by a steam engine and, therefore, named the Stanley Steamer by its manufacturer, the Stanley Brothers. The Stanleys competed with electric and gas buggies until it became apparent that gas-run automobiles were more popular. Others followed Bulkley. Robert and Laurance Crauford sported a Locomotive steamer. Then Bulkley bought a second car, an Oldsmobile. The Craufords retaliated by buying a Knoxmobile. E.N. Sipperly trumped everyone with a two-cylinder Stevens Duryea in 1903. And so it went. By 1908, some 41 automobiles were cruising the streets of Westport. In 1908, incidentally, Henry Ford introduced his Model T, an inexpensive, assembly-line car that rapidly became the auto of its time.[12]

Tile design by Marian Grebow

With the advent of the automobile came the need to improve the roads. The State Street trolley was still the principal means of transportation, but neither local government nor local business addressed the issue of improving the roads. What better time to create an association dedicated to the social and material betterment of the town? The Woman's Town

Improvement Association (WTIA) organized on August 12, 1907 to fill the void. This 20-member organization, which issued a statement calling for the improvement of local roads, set an annual membership fee of one dollar and elected Mrs. William G. (Mary Coley) Staples as its first president; she served for the next 10 years. Josephine Godillot was the other prime mover in launching the new organization. It eventually evolved into the Westport Woman's Club, a dynamic group of volunteer women who have done so much to improve the town over the years.[13]

The objectives of the WTIA were initially directed toward improving and developing the physical facilities of the town — cleaning streets, erecting street signs, planting trees, initiating concrete sidewalks, promoting safety at Compo Beach, improving children's health, providing hot lunches in the schools, and the like — a policy that continued until World War I when the focus changed to providing social services. The association initiated many services that were later recognized as government's responsibility. One problem they tackled immediately was the need for sidewalks. They said the town should pay for one-fourth, the property-holder one-half, and the WTIA one-fourth. It seemed like a reasonable proposal to WTIA, but the selectmen — now dealing with the women's group for the first time — were not ready to give ground. Their chauvinism was apparent. However, after a year and a lot of lobbying the WTIA prevailed and, in 1908, the first paved sidewalks were laid. At another meeting soon after the group was formed, they resoundingly voted down a motion to allow men to join the WTIA, 28-1. The association's message in this age of male supremacy was clear. Within a short time, the WTIA signed up 81 women to raise $600 earmarked for building sidewalks, planting trees in public areas, seeding small triangular areas, upgrading the condition of the beach and lifesaving equipment, landscaping and sprucing up the railroad station and the cemetery, and collecting garbage and ashes. By 1913, the group had settled on a motto: "By their works shall ye know them."

During World War I, the association launched what its history book calls "patriotic measures"— demonstrating how to use substitutes for vital foodstuffs, sending jelly to Westport soldiers, promoting Children's War Gardens, and encouraging youngsters 10 to 14 years of age to grow their own food. It organized an event on June 30, 1917, in Saugatuck at which the magician Houdini was the star performer, raising nearly $10,000. By 1919, the town had grown to 5,500 in population. The WTIA became involved in public health projects in the 1920s and it organized county fairs and circuses. Health was a growing concern as the WTIA became involved in securing nurses, which eventually led to the creation of the Visiting Nurse Service in 1925. In 1919, Westport had two diphtheria cases and five scarlet fever victims and an epidemic of mumps. Health authorities throughout the state as well as those of Westport waged an active campaign to prevent the spread of diseases, most of which was the result of ignorance about their causes.[14]

Meanwhile, as business continued to boom, taxes increased as land values — both residential and commercial — increased. In 1917, the newspaper carried a Grand List based on the assessments made by the Board of Assessors. It added up to $6.9 million, or the equivalent of $89.7 million in the year 2000. By far the biggest taxpayer in town was E. T. Bedford, who owned a magnificent estate in Green's Farms. His property was assessed at $537,138. He was followed by F. E. Lewis, $201,666; Annette Schlaet, $147,791; Frederick T. Bedford (Edward T. Bedford's son), $139,138; Westport Water Company, $132,245; Josephine Dolge, $81,700; Lees Manufacturing, $43,431; Marie McFarland, $69,775; C. H. Kemper Co., $51,653; Edward C. Nash, $37,775; and Fannie Eldwood, $30,350.

In the 1920s, the WTIA gave a boost to some newly arrived artists in town by arranging exhibitions, co-sponsored with the YMCA, of their work in an art gallery in Bedford House, named after its donor, Edward T. Bedford.[15] As previously noted, the Bedfords were "one of the families who has made a lasting impact on life in Westport…[a family that] for more than three generations has quietly donated to Westport's well-being."[16] E. T. Bedford's donations to Westport life in the early 1900s were almost always of the matching fund variety — given with the intent to encourage the community to become involved. His foresight was responsible for the building of Bedford Junior High in 1924 (now King's Highway), Bedford Elementary School (now Town Hall), Green's Farms School, and much more. Bedford, a colleague of John D. Rockefeller, was a shrewd businessman who invested in a variety of businesses, including oil, from which he made a great deal of money.

In the fall of 1919, E. T. Bedford bought the Westport Hotel and announced that he planned to build a tudor-style YMCA in its place. The initial cost was $150,000.[17] The building would occupy a large portion of the hotel property, and inside it would be reading and writing rooms, pool tables, bowling alleys and just about everything that was up-to-date. Bedford said he would endow this building so that the maintenance would not cost the town anything. In order to do this, however, the Bedford Corporation would be formed to conduct the YMCA's business. Bedford also approved building a brand-new fire station in the area formerly occupied by the Westport Hotel's stables. Bedford beamed with pride at the YMCA dedication in 1923, a year in which steak was selling for 42 cents a pound, movies were still silent, and women were bobbing their hair.

Westport's current town historian, Allen Raymond, tells this story about E. T. Bedford's ambition:

> As a young boy, Bedford worked very hard picking
> strawberries on the farms around here and he was
> setting all kinds of records. He held the local record,
> 80 quarts of strawberries in one day. Somebody
> asked him what he wanted to do when he grew up.
> He said he wanted to be successful. He became a
> New York City broker of lubricating oils for the railroads.
> Soon he was a partner in the Thompson and Bedford
> Company, and he became a sales agent for John D.
> Rockefeller's Standard Oil. In 1901, he organized the
> New York Glucose Company, and he merged it with
> Corn Products Refining where he was president until
> he died in 1931. He was a major force in Standard Oil's
> overseas business and he became a director of Standard
> Oil in 1911. Bedford liked to play pool and he would
> stand outside of the Westport Hotel where he couldn't
> get a chance to play because it was a saloon and they
> didn't allow little kids into the saloon. So, he bought
> the place and built a YMCA so he could play pool.
> Whether he really bought it because he couldn't get
> into the hotel when he was a boy, I don't know.

The extensive Bedford gardens on Beachside Avenue were the site of many Sunday afternoon walks and rides for local people and became so popular that postcards depicting the gardens sold well. The garages, two cottages and icehouse, as well as two large greenhouses that produced nectarines and other exotic fruits, stood across the street from the main house and were all part of the estate. Bedford enjoyed his garden, but it was his horses that captivated him and at age 78, he was still riding his horse, "Diplomat," over the half-mile track on his grounds.

E. T. Bedford was an aristocratic, statuesque man with white mutton chop sideburns on a round face with twinkling eyes. He had a strong hand

and a booming voice. Everyone in Westport knew when he was nearby. A *Fortune* magazine article said of him in April 1923: "Neither nicotine nor alcohol has ever touched his lips, not so much as a glass of beer. He weighs in the neighborhood of 200 pounds and, as he proudly says, eats moderately. Fundamentally, the thing he does and always has done is make money."[18] It was E.T. Bedford's son, Frederick T. Bedford, who, upon returning from a safari in Africa, gave the 52-acre Bedford farm the name Nyala Farms because of the beautiful nyala, or antelope, he had seen in Africa. The farm, owned since 1910 by his father, was the home of generations of award-winning Guernsey milk cows. E. T. Bedford established the farm as an experiment in increasing milk production through improved breeding.[19]

E.T. Bedford's legacy is still fresh in the mind of his granddaughter, Ruth Bedford, who is in her 80s and lives alone in a house that is a converted barn on her father's (Frederick T. Bedford) property. She recalled that when she came to Westport on the weekends, her grandfather let her drive his trotting racehorses. "He loved them," she said. "I drove them around the half-mile track every Wednesday and Saturday morning." She said she hardly knew her grandfather, but that she was in awe of him. She and her sisters did not see him except when they went to call on their grandmother every Sunday and he was there.[20]

When E. T. Bedford purchased the Westport Hotel, he promised to provide a place for men but he disregarded women's needs. The Town Improvement Association was quick to react. Its Civic Committee was directed to meet with Bedford to demonstrate that women had needs too and should share in the privileges already extended to men. The meeting had results: Bedford added several beautiful rooms for the use of women and girls. Subsequently, the WTIA established a Thrift Shop and a Woman's Exchange, and in 1931 started to help Westport families augment their incomes by selling goods and articles made in the homes.

Mrs. Sarah B. Crawford took over as president of the WTIA in 1931, and in 1938, the club's name was officially changed to the Westport Woman's Club. Mrs. Crawford went on to serve six two-year terms (from 1925 to 1938) as Westport's representative in the General Assembly in the state legislature, and subsequently from 1939 to 1941 as Connecticut's first woman secretary of state. The WTIA was responsible for another "first" in 1939 when, after considerable lobbying, it succeeded in getting the town to create the first Beach Commission. In 1940, as the nation edged toward war, the WTIA held the first Yankee Doodle Fair. The growth of the Fair, which is still held every June has become a Westport tradition.

Although founded long before the women's suffrage movement, the club was one of many women's organizations that helped launch other social reforms for women. The three stepping stones to passage of the Nineteenth Amendment to the Constitution in 1920 were the organization of the Women's Equal Franchise League in 1912, the founding of the Girl Scouts of America in 1912 (two years after the Boy Scouts of America was formed), and the establishment of the Women's International League for Peace and Freedom in 1915. Adelaide Nichols Baker was a lifetime member and the League's official representative to the United Nations from 1956-1962. She was involved in antiwar activities in the area for many years. On August 26, 1920, the Nineteenth Amendment to the Constitution, providing women suffrage, was declared ratified across the nation.

KEWPIE DOLL CREATOR: Rose O'Neill, one of the most flamboyant personalities in Westport's art community, was also a poet, writer, prolific illustrator, painter and sculptor before she created her famous Kewpie doll in 1909. She arrived in Westport in 1922, and purchased a 10-acre estate overlooking the Saugatuck River.

WESTPORT HISTORICAL SOCIETY

Artists and writers began coming to Westport just before the turn of the century, many buying farmhouses and converting them into offices and studios. Among them were artist Neil Mitchell, who had a feeling for the sea and lived on the Mill Pond; Edmund M. Ashe, a journalistic illustrator, in 1905; John N. Marchand, an illustrator who specialized in western scenes, in 1906; and George Hand Wright, known as founder of the Westport art colony and dean of the artists, in 1907. One of the many "name" writers in Westport was Hugh Lofting, whose book, *The Voyages of Dr. Doolittle*, won the Newbery Medal in 1923,[21] an award given each year to a book representing an outstanding contribution to children's literature.

One of the first women to achieve major status as an artist here was Rose O'Neill, known best for her famous Kewpie doll. O'Neill, one of the most flamboyant personalities in Westport's art community, was born in Wilkes Barre, Pennsylvania, in 1874. She became a nationally known poet, writer, prolific illustrator, painter and sculptor before she created the Kewpie doll in 1909. By 1913, some 5 million Kewpies — in china, chalk, celluloid, chocolate, wood, and rubber — had been sold. She did not arrive in Westport until 1922, but with the money she had made from the sale of the

Kewpie doll, she purchased a 10-acre estate overlooking the Saugatuck River. She named it Carabus Castle, inspired by the Marquis and his castle in "Puss in Boots." Between 1904 and 1930 she wrote eight books including *Lady in the White Veil, Garda,* and *The Goblin Woman* and a volume of poems entitled *The Master-Mistress.* Her writings, illustrated with her cherubs, appeared in *Good Housekeeping, Woman's Home Companion,* and *Ladies Home Journal.* The *New York Times* obituary in 1944 estimated her wealth at $4.1 million. She had several other homes and was the inspiration for the song, "Rose of Washington Square," popularized by Fanny Brice in the Ziegfeld Follies. One of the most memorable people in Westport's distinguished art community, O'Neill was said to live by the philosophy she had invented for her cherubs: *Do good deeds in a funny way. The world needs to laugh — or at least smile more than it does.*

WALD HOSTS WORLD FIGURES: Lillian Wald, left, entertains British Prime Minister James Ramsay MacDonald and his daughter, Ishbel, right, at Wald's "House on the Pond" on Compo Road South on October 15, 1929. Wald also was visited by other famous people, such as Albert Einstein, inset, who would be named "Man of the Century" by Time *Magazine in 1999.*
WALD PHOTO/
WESTPORT HISTORICAL SOCIETY
EINSTEIN PHOTO/
WESTPORT PUBLIC LIBRARY

Another famous Westporter in this period who achieved wide recognition in her field was Lillian D. Wald. She lived on Compo Road in the "House on the Pond" and spent much time there. Her sweeping social reforms in the poverty-stricken Lower East Side resulted in her election to the Hall of Fame for Great Americans at New York University. Born in Cincinnati on March 10, 1867, of German-Jewish descent, she had a legendary ancestor who was said to have been the king of Poland. She was the organizer of the first nonsectarian public health nursing system in the world. In 1895, friends helped Miss Wald establish the Henry Street Settlement House. Wald was among the first to advocate special training for nurses entering the public health nursing field. She was instrumental in diverting a large gift intended for the Henry Street Settlement to Teachers College, Columbia University, to establish the first university program for training public health nurses. She also conceived the idea of the Federal Children's Bureau, which Congress finally authorized in 1912. She enjoyed lasting friendships with thousands of people, some poor and obscure, some rich and famous. Among the notable names in her guest book at her home in Westport were those of Ramsay McDonald, who visited Henry Street on his wedding trip and later visited Miss Wald in Connecticut as former British Prime Minister; New York Mayor Fiorello H. LaGuardia, Theodore Roosevelt (who spent his boyhood summers in Westport), Cardinal Hayes; Jacob Riis, the crusading Dutch newspaperman whose writings and photographs exposed the squalor of New York City's slums; Woodrow Wilson, Alfred E. Smith, Justice Louis D. Brandeis, Chief Justice Charles Evans Hughes, President and Mrs. Franklin D. Roosevelt, and Professor Albert Einstein,[22] who would be named by *Time* magazine as "Man of the Century" in December 1999.

Another one of her friends, Aaron Rabinowitz, was key in helping Wald realize one of her life-long dreams: good, inexpensive housing for the poor. On her 70th birthday on March 10, 1937, she was honored at a public gathering in New York at which congratulatory messages were read from President Franklin D. Roosevelt, Governor Herbert Lehman, and Mayor Fiorello LaGuardia, who awarded her the Distinguished Service Certificate of the City of New York. She died on September 1, 1940, at the age of 73.

Despite its growing reputation as a haven for artists, writers, and other celebrities, Westport has had its share of setbacks. One disaster that occurred was the train wreck in Westport on October 3, 1912, in which 7 people were killed on the Springfield Express and 10 people were badly injured and sent to the Norwalk Hospital. It was described as a "death train," a misshapen mass of bent and twisted iron mixed in with splintered and charred wood. The wrecked New York – Boston express presented a gruesome appearance. The cause of the wreck was the engineer's failure to observe the standing order of the road to slow his train in taking a cross over: He had instead driven his engine at more than 60 miles an hour. Seventy-seven years later,

TRAIN WRECK: In 1912, the worst train disaster in the town's history killed seven people and badly injured 10 more when the Springfield Express, dubbed the "death train" by the media, failed to slow down in Westport, crashing off the tracks at 60 miles per hour. WESTPORT HISTORICAL SOCIETY PHOTO

in 1989, a remarkable eyewitness account from an 85-year-old Westporter, Patrick Sarno, who was seven years old at the time of the wreck, was published in the *Westport News*.[23] The article reported that Sarno was playing hide and seek in front of his house on Davenport Avenue. When it was his turn to be "it," he leaned up against a streetlight and closed his eyes and counted to one hundred. The article continued:

> He started to look for his friends and had only gone a
> short way when he suddenly heard the terrifying shriek
> of escaping steam, the whistle of the brakes, and the
> grinding of the steel and wood. Looking toward the New
> Haven tracks, he saw the Springfield Express — a
> locomotive, followed by a baggage car, a mail car, four
> parlor cars, three coaches, and a smoking car — hurtling
> toward his home. As he watched in horror, the massive
> steam locomotive lurched with the crash and derailed.
> After the cars halted with the sound of splintering wood
> and smashing glass, there was a moment of silence. Then
> came the shrieks and cries of the passengers who began
> a wild scramble to escape from the train. "God must have
> been watching over me," Pat Sarno says. "I was frightened
> and ran home to my mother. If I hadn't left the spot where
> I was standing, I would have been killed."

By 1914, Westport was becoming "the place to be" in New England.[24] The *Westporter-Herald* stated that the town "has become famed for its fine residences, its people and the goods that are manufactured in its midst." Among its people were an increasing number of celebrities, including the famous actor, William S. Hart, who strengthened Westport's fledgling image as a theatre and art colony. The movie and stage actor/director came here in 1914 and lived on King's Highway.[25] Born on December 6, 1862, in Newburgh, New York, the son of British parents, he was arguably the most important Western movie star of his era. In his films, it was reported, he tried to recreate the authentic flavor of what he called "the unbroken West."[26] "He became the quintessential cowboy of the American stage," said one theatre critic of the time. Hart's last film was *Tumbleweeds* in 1925. Hart made a fortune and became wealthy from his movie work. In addition to his home in Westport, he maintained a large estate in West Hollywood and an eight-acre ranch north of Los Angeles. In his prime, he was reported to have made as much as $3,000 per week, the equivalent of $30,000 a week in the year 2000. Hart was not just the tough guy cowboy; he donated $100,000 in honor of his sister in August 1945 to establish the Connecticut Humane Society on the Post Road as headquarters for an animal shelter.

At the same time, Westport opened its first "moving picture" theatre. In 1915, Robert Joseloff, a Norwalk grocery storeowner and real estate developer, along with his partner, Morris Epstein, purchased land next to Westport Town Hall from Edward C. Nash. They opened the Fine Arts Theatre in the early 1920s on the site. Westporters had their very own show palace complete with a hardworking piano player plunking out a musical accompaniment to the silent and foreign films, the latter a first in Connecticut. Not that Westport had been without entertainment. Toquet Hall and National Hall both had stages where theatrical productions were given.

FINE ARTS THEATRE: Opening in the early 1920s, it provided Westporters with their own show palace complete with a piano player accompanying the silent and foreign films — a first in Connecticut.
PHOTO COURTESY OF HARRY AUDLEY

The Fine Arts Theatre played an important role in Westport's social life. It was the first theatre in Connecticut to show foreign films. It also allowed teachers to issue passes to the movies to children who could not afford to attend. In later years, benefits were held there for the unemployed during the depression, and war bonds were sold during World War II.[27] When the "talkies" arrived in the late 1920s, the movies became even more popular.[28]

In 1914 Germany declared war on Russia and France, and invaded Belgium on August 1. Britain declared war against Germany. At that point President Woodrow Wilson issued a proclamation of neutrality, and he appealed to Americans to be "impartial in thought as well as in action." It wasn't until April 6, 1917 that President Woodrow Wilson signed a joint Congressional resolution declaring a state of war between the U.S. and Germany.[29] Two years earlier, in 1915, the American Red Cross had come to Westport. A committee was formed and membership gradually increased until, finally, on May 1917, the charter authorizing the formation of the Westport Chapter of the American Red Cross was granted. It has, of course, become an organization that reaches those at home and those afar and it has played an important part in the history of the town. In July 1996, the Westport and Weston chapters of the American Red Cross merged to form the Mid-Fairfield County Chapter, under the leadership of Executive Director Janet Filling.

World War I began to hit home in February 1917 when Westport's selectmen received orders from Connecticut Governor Marcus H. Holcomb to appoint 20 enrollment officers for the town who would supervise a census to determine the available "war force." Two local men — Winthrop Merrill and James H. Keyser — had already shown their desire to enlist by sending their names to the town clerk as soon as they heard of the governor's call for volunteers.[30] A few days later, the *Westporter-Herald* published a remarkably frank and, perhaps pacifist, editorial headlined: "WHAT'S THE USE OF FRIGHTENING PEOPLE?" The editorial astounded readers by scolding the press for "frightening people to death" and leading them to fear that Germany was coming over to capture America. In the main, although Westporters were willing to prepare themselves for war, they never really expected to be called upon to send men overseas to die. Nonetheless, the town began to take the census that Governor Holcomb had requested, and soon the sober mood of war began to translate into concrete actions. Anxious to avoid a repetition of the British invasion of 1777, the Coast Guard Artillery Corps of Connecticut was assigned to the defenses of the eastern entrance to Long Island Sound.

By March 1917, some 1,300 men had registered for the draft in Westport, with the grand total expected to be about 1,500. In addition to the volunteers, an aviation school located at Green's Farms on land owned by the state at Burying Hill Beach was announced by state lawmakers, who appropriated $5,000 to acquire the land. In addition, 12 Army cots were set up by members of the 13th Company, Coast Artillery, at the Saugatuck railroad station, and guards were placed underneath the Post Road bridge on both sides of the river. The bridge was seen as a strategic connecting transportation link between New York and Boston on the main line, over which ammunition and supplies for war passed daily. The government felt that this bridge should not be left unguarded because there was danger of being sabotaged. Still another request came from the federal government directed to Frank B. Dayton, head of the Compo Life Guards, asking for a list of their equipment and what the members knew about motor boats, life saving, and the like. There was speculation that the government was planning to place a coast patrol on the Westport side of the Sound and that the lifeguards would be pressed into service. That did not happen, but everyone was ready, just in case. One Westport man, Arnold Schlaet, gave up his 65-foot yacht to the government to be used as a submarine chaser.[31] An early sign of wartime mentality came in 1918, when a local "Crumb Savings Campaign to Conserve Food" was announced, as well as a crackdown on automobile travel. Cars were to be used only for business.

Meanwhile, the town enlisted men age 17 to 60 for what was known as the Home Guard. Under the watchful eye of Captain Edward C. Nash, the men met regularly and became so well trained that they held a mock war drill in Westport in October 1917. By the end of 1917, many Westport men had been sent to France to fight. Also in October 1917, Congress passed a military draft under which an army would be raised by conscription of men between the ages of 21 and 31. Registration Day nationwide was set for the first Tuesday in June 1917 for every male citizen, 21-30. And at the close of 1918, Westport had registered 561 men between the ages of 18 and 45.[32]

In the business community, small companies, having lost men to war, had to scramble to remain competitive. In one instance, in 1918, the Atlantic Starch Works, established in 1896 by Carl B. Dolge, closed its doors owing to the shortage of wheat starch used to manufacture the company's main product, throwing scores of local people out of work. It would remain

SPORTING A NEW CAR: Members of the J.V.N. Dorr Co., a worldwide engineering organization. The new company opened in 1919 to test gold, silver, and copper ores.
WESTPORT HISTORICAL SOCIETY PHOTO

closed for the duration of the war. It was replaced in 1923 by Louis B. Sametz, Inc., manufacturer of a great variety of celluloid products, including top-grade table tennis (ping pong) balls. Other firms that opened were Edward L. Greenberg's department store on August 17, 1917, in a modest 16 x 40-foot shop; J.V.N. Dorr Co., a worldwide engineering organization that tested gold, silver, and copper ores from all parts of the world; and A.F.K. Lindwall's Grindstone Hill Forge, in 1925, producers of hinges, lamps, fire screens, and other ironwork products. Some businesses started here, whereas others began in Bridgeport and then gradually moved to Westport. One example of the latter was Silver of Westport. In 1904, Samuel Silver established a store that would become a permanent fixture in Westport. He opened first in Bridgeport as an umbrella, canes, and trunk shop, which soon diversified to include luggage and handbags.[33]

The farming community also did its part in the war, answering the calls to "Do Your Bit with the Hoe." Arrangements were announced for carrying on farming extensively in Westport by asking the school children to work land donated by Edward C. Nash and others. In this way, Westport was responding to Washington's call urging every town in the nation to increase its food supply because, "*We face one of the most critical food shortages in the history of the world*" [italics the author's]. Local officials appealed in 1917: "Once this town produced not only its own food, but was famous for its exports. Now a great proportion of our food is imported. We must do our part in the national crisis by working our gardens and farms to the utmost; not a tract of land should remain unproductive this season."[34] Households, as well as hotels and eating places, were voluntarily cutting back on certain foods. They had "wheatless, meatless and porkless days." Everybody was getting into the act. The women formed a War Relief Unit and Rifle Corps, with each member pledging to do relief work that was most urgent — including learning how to handle firearms. By the fall of 1918, many Westport women had voluntarily gone to work in local factories to aid the war effort.

There was no official news about what was going on inside of Germany, but one Westport woman received a fascinating letter from a relative in Germany. The relative reported that she and her family were in the best of health and everyone was happy. Business was great, and was prospering. The letter writer then stated that the two stamps on the envelope that contained the Kaiser's picture could be steamed off as a memento of "this Great War." When the Westport woman steamed off the stamps, she was astonished by the words underneath them: "WE ARE STARVING." Only in this way did the message escape the German censor.

The war effort galvanized the whole town. By the time the war ended in 1918, everyone had become involved in one way or another. When, finally, at 11 A.M. on November 11, 1918, the end of the war came, the signing of the U.S.-Allied armistice caused an impromptu parade in town. The bells of Christ Church started tolling and within a half hour all the church bells in town, the fire bells, the fire whistle, and the factory whistles had joined in the celebration. "Some of the early birds who were upon the streets almost as soon as the news reached here quickly made an effigy of the Kaiser and hung it on a telegraph pole in Hotel Square," according to one account. "By six o'clock an informal parade had started in Saugatuck and made its way to Westport where the marchers were joined by scores more." In all, 238 Westport men and women were sent abroad. Seven were killed in action and many others wounded.[35] One of the casualties, Joseph J. Clinton of Westport, was killed on the firing line on November 9, two days before the cessation of hostilities. He had married before leaving for France and a grieving wife and family survived him. Veterans of Foreign Wars (VFW) Post 399 in Westport was subsequently named after him. In the entire state, some

WORLD WAR I HERO: John Gilbertie, of Clinton Avenue, received the Distinguished Service Cross. He had the distinction of being the only enlisted man from Westport to receive this award.
PHOTO COURTESY OF ANTHONY GILBERTIE

67,000 Connecticut men and women served in World War I.

In February 1919, John Gilbertie, son of Mr. and Mrs. Antonio Gilbertie, of Clinton Avenue, received the Distinguished Service Cross "for bravery and extraordinary heroism under fire." Gilbertie, a corporal of the 82nd Division, had been in battle for many months. He was the first enlisted man in his regiment to receive the medal. The citation from the Commander in Chief, in the name of the President, read: "During the entire (combat) action...Corporal Gilbertie carried messages from the front line to the battalion and regimental headquarters, although suffering from the effects of gas and sickness. On two occasions, he volunteered and led patrols into enemy territory, obtaining and returning with information of the utmost importance. [This] is a fine example of courage and self-sacrifice. Such deeds are evidence of the spirit and heroism which is innate in the highest type of the American soldier and responds unfailingly to the call of duty, whenever and wherever it may come. By Command of MAJOR GENERAL DUNCAN." Gilbertie had the distinction of being the only enlisted man from Westport to be awarded the Distinguished Service Cross.[36]

General John J. Pershing decorated Gilbertie at a ceremony in France. Standing beside him and also a recipient of the DSC was Sergeant Alvin York, who was later memorialized by a movie starring Gary Cooper playing the sergeant. Gilbertie also received the Italian War Cross, Italy's highest award, from King Victor Emanuel III. News of this medal reached Corporal Gilbertie on the day after Christmas, his birthday. He was awarded a third medal from the French government for fighting Germans on French soil. Gilbertie's father, Antonio, started Gilbertie's Gardens, then known as A. Gilbertie, Florist, in 1922 in Westport. The other DSC recipient was Herman William Steinkraus, an officer, from Westport, who went on to become a noted community leader and president of Bridgeport Brass, one of the largest brass producers during and after World War II.

In August 1919, at the urging of Donald H. Crawford, who had served in France during the war, American Legion Post 63 was formed in Westport.[37] The Legion Post was officially chartered on November 6, 1919, and recorded in December. It met in uniform in Town Hall and elected a slate of officers:

Morris Burr, post commander; William Coley, vice commander; Edward Lehn, secretary; and Donald Crawford, finance officer. Private Charles August Matthias of Green's Farms had been the first soldier from Westport to be killed in France in World War I. Post 63 was named after him. Ironically, the medals given to the Westport men who returned from service were designed by James Earle Frazer, a noted Westport sculptor who had designed the "Buffalo Nickel" for the U.S. Treasury and did the "End of the Trail" sculpture depicting an Indian slumped over a tired horse. He and his wife, Laura Gardin Fraser, both independently recognized sculptors, were married in 1913 and moved to Westport where they built a large studio.

POETIC PICTURE: In 1887, a photographer, posing the aged and infirm poet, Walt Whitman, with 4-year-old Nigel Cholmeley-Jones, left, and his younger sister, Catherine Jeanette, right, on the famous poet's lap. The photograph was published in the Westport News on December 22, 1972, commemorating Cholmeley-Jones' upcoming 90th birthday in March 1973. Whitman was a protégé of Cholmeley-Jones' uncle, Richard Watson Gilder, editor of The Century Magazine, an important literary publication of the time. The photographer was George Collins Cox and the picture was taken in his New York City studio. WORLD WAR I HERO: Captain Edward Owen Nigel Cholmeley-Jones, below right, with his wife, Henrietta Sturgis, and son, Richard G. Cholmeley-Jones 2d, at a Memorial Day Parade in the 1950s.
COURTESY OF RICHARD G. CHOLMELEY-JONES

One of Westport's most outstanding military officers in World War I, Captain Edward Owen Nigel Cholmeley-Jones, would lead or participate in Memorial Day parades here for many decades to come after World War I, serving as grand marshal four times. He served in the war as aide to Brigadier General A.W. Bjornstad, after having been on the staff of Major General Robert Lee Bullard in the Third Corps. In a battery of 197 men, he landed in France on Christmas Day, 1917. After attending Command and General Staff School at Langres in France as a first lieutenant, he was under fire in the trenches. He fought in France at Oise-Aisne, on the Meuse-Argonne, and at Metz, Germany, in 1918. After the war, he joined *Current Opinion* magazine and then *McClure's*, and later he became vice president and director of Paul Block & Associates, magazine and newspaper advertising representatives. In 1936, until his retirement in 1957, he was an advertising representative with the *National Geographic Magazine*. He was once a gold miner and a deputy sheriff in Goldfield, Nevada. Cholmeley-Jones died in December 1978, at the age of 95, having lived in Westport for 47 years. His wife, Henrietta Sturgis, known as "Rita," was a successful writer, artist, and poet. She died in December 1985 at the age of 89.[38]

For Westport, as for the rest of America, it was pretty much business as usual after the war ended. A minor scandal of sorts occurred in town government when it ran out of money for the first time in the history of the town. It was only a temporary setback, but in the long run would prove to be a valuable experience for the taxpayers. It served as a wakeup call that the public monies needed to be better safeguarded. Accordingly, in 1917, the voters decided they wanted a municipal arm of government that would serve as a form of "checks and balances" against spending by town agencies. Accordingly, they created an independent Board of Finance, with its members elected by the voters.

One of the major issues confronting every town in America in this period was prohibition. After much discussion, in September 1917, the controversial topic was put to the test in Westport. By a solid vote of 355 to 256, the voters rejected prohibition. Nonetheless, nationally the Eighteenth Amendment was ratified on January 29, 1919. Despite the law — and perhaps *because* of it — parties galore were held in Westport. The artist, Robert Lambdin, was quoted in a local newspaper saying that, as a result of prohibition, there was more drinking in Westport than ever before. It was no secret that prohibition challenged people and produced a lot of bootlegging.

One place that never became dry, according to some accounts, was the Penguin Hotel on Hillspoint Road, which was then known as the Miramar nightclub and was reportedly a famous speakeasy in the 1920s. Chroniclers of the time described it as "attracting affluent people from the larger metropolitan area." It had a marine motif— it was shaped like a boat, with life preservers, portholes, and other boating decor, white tablecloths, and a crystal chandelier in the upstairs dining room. Hollywood stars such as George Raft and James Cagney were said to have frequented it. It later served as an apartment building, until it was eventually torn down and replaced by a condominium development.

By 1923 the townspeople were benefiting from unprecedented advances in technology: The automobile, radio, and telephone were becoming almost commonplace. It was the decade of the flapper and the Charleston. "Talking movies" with Buster Keaton and the Marx Brothers were becoming popular. Following Charles Lindbergh's historic flight to Paris, it also became the decade of aviation. America's great flight hero maintained a residence in Westport during his glory years. In those seemingly endless days of fun, the atmosphere in the town was electric. Property valuation in 1920 totaled $14,709,222, or a $1.7 million increase over the previous year. The greatest increase was in the number of residences — more than 100 new houses were built, and there were more than 1,200 cars, or one-third more than the previous year. There were big changes downtown, too. The new YMCA had been built.[39] In 1924, Westport Bank and Trust across from the YMCA opened its new $100,000 building, designed by Charles E. Cutler. The two institutions shared many officers, including Fred Salmon, who was YMCA president and the bank's president, too, until his death in 1936. Also in 1924, the State Police Barracks were erected on the Post Road on land donated by E.T. Bedford and the Fairfield County Hunt Club was founded. In 1929, just two years before he died, E. T. Bedford donated an indoor swimming pool to the YMCA. During this time the Day Camp opened in 1848 (now known as Mahackeno), and numerous clubs sprouted up.

The Twenties also saw a new church in Westport. In 1921 St. Paul Lutheran Church opened at 98 Riverside Avenue. Many local and out-of-town friends attended dedication exercises on December 11, 1921. This was the Lutheran Church location until overcrowded conditions forced the

ENDURES: The YMCA, left, and the former Westport Bank and Trust Bank building as seen in 1928, virtually unchanged at the start of the new millennium. WESTPORT HISTORICAL SOCIETY PHOTO

congregation to switch its services to Bedford Elementary School. A new church, built on Easton Road, was dedicated on June 18, 1961. With an ever-burgeoning congregation yet another new church had to be built in 1972, with the original building on Easton Road now serving as the parish hall.[40]

There were other "firsts" during this period. In 1924, the Old Drill Ground was dedicated and marked with an emblem on King's Highway. Also in 1924, on February 13, after discussing the idea of a police department for years, the selectmen called a special town meeting to formally organize a police department and to adopt a police ordinance.[41] The selectmen were authorized to appoint and organize a police force consisting of five members, with Charles J. Quigley, an ex-serviceman and constable, named as captain in charge of the department and John A. Dolan named as Special Constable of the town.

The new department's members were the first to be paid regularly. While the need for systemized police protection had been recognized for a long time — citizens volunteered to protect the peace, but at their own risk — the selectmen's action was unexpected.[42] Actually, this was the result of a major incident. A week before a young girl had been assaulted on Cross Highway, stirring up a clamor among the townspeople for official protection. Following the adoption of the ordinance, First Selectman Edward C. Nash recommended that the Board of Finance appropriate $5,485.85 for establishment of the police force. The police department was expanded in 1930 to as many members as the selectmen deemed necessary to protect the peace. In 1938, John Dolan was named the town's first chief of police, followed by Samuel J. Luciano in 1957. Succeeding chiefs have been Louis Rosenau, William Stefan, Ronald Malone, and William Chiarenzelli.

Another significant event of 1924 was the founding of the Westport Rotary Club on March 26 by Anson Leary, then executive director of the YMCA, with 17 business and professional men who were interested in establishing a men's organization. The Rotary Club raises funds for numerous causes, at home and abroad, and has had a profound influence on progress for the public good far out of proportion to the number of its members. According to the club's official history, the Rotary Club has put a high priority on helping children and on health care in general. In the early 1960s, the Westport Rotary Trust Fund was established as a not-for-profit educational and scientific project. The Annual Roast Beef Dinner was initiated by Ed Mitchell in 1958.

Westporters have long taken great pride in the town's beautiful gardens, which reflect the efforts of the Westport Garden Club, founded on April 11, 1924, by eight women and two men.[43] The club was the inspiration of Nevada Hitchcock, a New York journalist in the 1890s and a home economics editor of the *Philadelphia Record* during World War I, who came to live on Cross Highway in Westport in 1920. Her column, "Your Own Garden," was one of the *Bridgeport Sunday Post*'s most popular features. Gardening was her passionate hobby. After her death, the town — under the auspices of the Westport Garden Club — rendered a tribute to her in the form of a memorial plaque in the center of the little triangle park at the corner of Weston Road and Cross Highway. It reads: "Nevada Hitchcock, 1863-1937.... Friend, Gardener, Civic Worker." Sara Crawford was one of the Garden Club's charter members, and Anne Arnold, Westport's state representative from 1939 through 1943, served as civic chairman. The club carried out Helen Warnock Mackie's statewide mosquito control campaign when she, too, was Westport's representative during the late 1940s. Its members also included Katherine Ordway, the heiress of the Minnesota Mining and Manufacturing Company. The club has maintained and enhanced the beauty of Westport in many parts of town, starting with its first project in 1927, which was to improve the grounds at the Saugatuck Firehouse. This project was followed by a three-year drive to beautify Town Hall on the Post Road. The concept of "Triangles," typically pocket parks, came into vogue in 1935. Trees were planted at the Old Drill Ground on Kings Highway in commemoration of the state's Bicentennial. In 1950 the club received the prestigious Kellogg Award from the National Council of State Garden Clubs for its work at King's Highway Cemetery. That award led to the town's asking the club to supervise care of the Poplar Plains Cemetery as well.

Grace King Salmon, who died in 1939, was a founding member of the Westport Woman's Club. She was the wife of Frederick M. Salmon, who was once Connecticut state comptroller and president of Westport Bank and Trust, and she left a trust in her own name to benefit the town. Virginia Sherwood, Garden Club civic chairman at the time, applied for grants from the trust and other agencies to design a park on three acres of Saugatuck River landfill opposite where the Salmons had lived, now Assumption Church Rectory. It took several years to solve the site's environmental problems, but the club developed Connecticut's first park built on a former landfill and won an award for its efforts. Today Grace K. Salmon Park, located on Imperial Avenue, is a model of civic reclamation and a delightful refuge that is one of Westport's best kept secrets.

In the 1980s, Garden Club members rescued Platt Cemetery on the Post Road from possible desecration when a shopping center owner attempted to turn it into a parking lot. An out-of-court battle by the town and the Historic District Commission led to repair of the damaged stone wall, restoration of tombstones and renewal of planting inside the cemetery. For this project, the Garden Club received the Cornelia Williamson Watson Award for Historic Preservation. The early 1990s were devoted to the beautification of Adams Academy, the nineteenth-century schoolhouse where Ebenezer Adams taught. It was restored and was made a way stop on the historic Jennings Trail, a self-guided tour of historic landmarks throughout Westport. Club members have removed the weeds and vines surrounding the building, planted bulbs, shrubbery, and dogwoods on the grounds and opened a brook-walk running alongside the property. The club also supports the Sound Waters program, informing elementary schoolchildren about the fragile environment of Long Island Sound. The club's annual Plant Sale, which began as a member plant exchange in 1925, is its principal source of income, the product of plants donated from members' gardens or nurtured in the Nature Center Greenhouse. The club shares the limelight with the Westport Historical Society during its Annual Garden Tour. In celebration of the Garden Club's seventy-fifth anniversary, a Winter Garden was established at the Westport library as a gift to the town and dedicated on April 11, 1999, the club's actual anniversary. A seventy-fifth anniversary dinner was held at the Westport Woman's Club on September 11, 1999, Mary Baumann replacing Eugenie Hamm as president.

A generous outpouring of community spirit, the promise of many good things to come, and the growth of the town in general marked the period from the turn of the century to 1925. Expansion and economic success loomed ahead. A few prescient people could see distant clouds on the horizon; everyone else could feel only optimism for the future.

NOTES

1. Joanna Foster, "Recollections, Westport 90 Years Ago," *Carousel,* July, 1989.

2. Ibid.

3. Albert E. Van Dusen, *Connecticut History* (New York: Random House, 1925), p. 264.

4. The *Westporter-Herald,* May 31, 1932.

5. The inscription on the plaque of the cannons reads: "To commemorate the Battle fought on and near this point, between British Forces and the American patriots April 28, 1777. Ordnance. Presented by the United States government and erected July 4, 1901. Tablet presented by the Compo Beach Volunteer Life Guards." Over time, the cannons deteriorated and in 1998-99 the Westport Rotary Club restored them.

6. The inscription on the statue reads: "To Commemorate the Heroism of the Patriots who defended their country when the British invaded this State on April 25, 1777. General David Wooster, Colonel Abraham Gould and more than one hundred Continentals fell in the Engagements at Danbury, Commencing and Closing in Compo Hill. Erected by the Connecticut Sons of the American Revolution, 1910."

7. The *Westporter-Herald*, October 16, 1900.

8. Bedford Elementary School was converted into the present Town Hall in 1979.

9. George Penfield Jennings, *Greens Farms, Connecticut*, The Congregational Society of Green's Farms (Westport, CT. 1933), p. 145.

10. John A. Montgomery, *Eno — The Man and the Foundation, A Chronicle of Transportation* (Westport, CT: 1988), p. 1.

11. Ibid., p. 69.

12. Joanna Foster, "Gas Buggies on the Post Road," *More Stories from Westport's Past* (Westport: Westport Historical Society, 1986), p. 7.

13. *A History of the Woman's Club,* compiled by C.X. Panish, April 1972.

14. The *Westporter-Herald*, November 7, 1919.

15. Dorothy Tarrant and Jack Tarrant, *A Community of Artists*, Westport-Weston Arts Council, 1985, p. 46.

16. Eve Potts, *Westport...A Special Place*, p. 94.

17. Westport-Weston YMCA, *Our Community Treasure: A Vision for Tomorrow*, 1988.

18. *Fortune* magazine, April, 1923.

19. By 1963, Nyala Farm was the fourth in the nation for herd production. In 1969, Stauffer Chemical, which described itself as the largest purely chemical company in the United States employing 10,000 people in a $500 million business, announced its intention to retire 60 prize Guernseys from Nyala Farm and replace them with 700 executives and their staffs. The farm was the last remaining producer of commercial milk in Westport. At the time of the announcement, the local paper carried this headline: "Udderly evaporated Westport milk industry."

20. Interview with Ruth Bedford in 1998 in Westport.

21. Joanna Foster, "Dr. Doolittle and the Newbery Medal," *Stories from Westport's Past*, Book II, p. 37.

22. The *Westporter-Herald*, December 17, 1920, p. 1.

23. John Capsis, The *Westport News*, June 15, 1987.

24. The *Westport-Herald's* special tabloid, February 1914, "The Story of Westport, Connecticut," p. 4.

25. *Dictionary of American Biography*, p. 362.

26. As a young man in New York, Hart decided he wanted to be an actor. Ironically, he made his stage debut in Newburgh. Thus began a phase of Hart's career that was to last until 1914. He made his first tour with star billing in *The Man in the Iron Mask*, and two years later in the New York production, *Ben Hur,* in which he drove a chariot across the stage. In 1905, he appeared in Edwin Milton's Royale Western, *The Squaw Man.*

27. Eve Potts, author/historian.

28. Many years later, in 1968, Stanley Joseloff, who had taken over managing the property after his father died, added a second theatre on Jesup Road just behind the original one. They became known as Fine Arts 1 and 2. The original Fine Arts was divided in half with two screens, and the Jesup Road theatre was renamed Fine Arts 3. Fine Arts 4 opened nearby on the Post Road East. In the late 1990s, attendance dwindled at all Westport theatres as multi-screen complexes opened on the Fairfield-Bridgeport line and then in Norwalk. Loews/Sony, which operated the theatres, confirmed in the summer of 1998 that it was closing them down. But co-owners Gordon Joseloff and Dr. Mal Beinfield, grandsons of the original developer, thought Westport deserved more than just locking the doors and turning off the lights. So, on a cold January evening, they threw a "Farewell to Fine Arts" party and invited everyone in town. Despite a snowstorm, more than 200 Westporters showed up for the occasion, which marked the end of movies in downtown Westport. For the first time since 1917, Westport was left without a single movie theatre.

29. When war was declared there were some 200,000 men in the U.S. Army — a figure that would be expanded to more than 4.8 million during the war. The number of American soldiers who eventually would be sent to France was a little more than 2 million. In all, 42 infantry divisions were sent to France and took part in combat. General John J. Pershing commanded the American Expeditionary Forces from June 1917, to November 11, 1918.

30. The *Westporter-Herald*, February 9, 1917, p. 1.

31. The *Westporter-Herald*, June 8, 1917.

32. The *Westporter-Herald*, September 20, 1918.

33. Philip Silver, son of Samuel, opened the Westport store in 1951. Phil Silver's son, Steve, joined the business, followed by Phil's daughter, Susan Silver. In 1993, the store moved to its present location on the Post Road across from Compo Center.

34. The *Westporter-Herald*, April 30, 1917.

35. Wakefield Dort, *Westport in Connecticut's History*, Connecticut's Tercentenary, p. 60.

36. The source is Michael Gilbertie, November, 1999.

37. Westporter William Vornkahl III, member, VFW. The idea of the American Legion was conceived and brought about by Major Archibald Roosevelt, son of the world-famous Teddy Roosevelt, who took office as president of the United States on September 14, 1901, after the assassination of President McKinley. The Westport American Legion Post was chartered on November 6, 1919.

38. Source is Richard G. Cholmeley Jones, 2d.

39. Camp Mahackeno was purchased in 1948 and the Rotarian Pavilion was constructed at the outdoor site. Women and girls were accepted at the Y as members in 1949. In 1956, a report was issued recommending that the building be sold or expanded. New locker rooms, a health center, an exercise room, and a gymnasium were renovated in 1963 and, in 1968, the Y established a branch in nearby Weston's schools. A new wing was dedicated at Westport's Y in 1965. In recent years, the Westport Senior Center started a drop-in center, and an organization called the Y's Men membership grew to more than 400 and the Y's Women were organized with a membership now close to 400. In 1984, the firehouse was converted to a new fitness center. In 1986, the Senior Center moved to the Green's Farms School building. And, in 1995, the Y established the first annual "Faces of Achievement" Tribute Dinner as its main fundraising event, honoring men and women in the community who "embody the elements of humanity — Spirit, Mind, and Body." Near the Millennium, the YMCA's membership had grown to more than 8,000 people participating in more than 100 programs under the watchful eye of its executive director, Richard Foot.

40. *And There Was Light*...The Story of religious communities in Westport and Weston, published by The Church Women United, The Ecumenical Education Committee, Westport and Weston, Connecticut, 1976.

41. The authority to organize a police department was Chapter 284 of the Public Acts of 1923 to make by-laws and ordinances to provide for police protection.

42. "History of the Westport Police Department," by Captain David Heinmiller, provided to the author in 1999.

43. Louise Demakis, the *Minuteman*; and telephone interview, May 1999.

Photo, p. 149, State Street Bridge, collection of Tom Ghianuly, Compo Barber Shop.

CHAPTER 12

ARTISTS AND THE NEW WESTPORT

Westport, which had no entrenched society — it had farmers, a smattering of millionaires with shore estates, the art community, and bootleggers — was a perfect setting for this cross-cultural fusion of Wasps and Jews.

— Barbara Probst Solomon, Westport writer

During the period from 1920s to the precipice of World War II, the bustling little town of Westport expanded and rapidly became a mecca for illustrators, artists, cartoonists, designers, writers, and innovative people of all stripes. It was a time when Westport underwent a cultural renaissance, a time when the town first appeared on the national scene as a beehive of achievement and creativity. It was the new — and eye-catching — Westport, as jazzy and as party-prone as any other developing suburb. Along with the cultural elite came the flappers, the Age of Dixieland, and, of course, the speakeasies that openly defied prohibition while town officials turned a blind eye.

THE FAMOUS FITZGERALDS: F. Scott and Zelda Fitzgerald lived in Wakeman Cottage on South Compo Road during the summer of 1920. The couple hosted memorable parties at the outset of the Roaring Twenties and attracted many of their contemporary literati to Westport.

PRINCETON UNIVERSITY LIBRARY PHOTO

In this new age, Westport even could lay claim to a writer who has come to epitomize the Roaring Twenties: F. Scott Fitzgerald, who lived in a house on South Compo Road with his wife, Zelda, in the summer of 1920. The arrival of this literary couple on their honeymoon in Westport, a town already filled with celebrities, drew little attention in the local paper. An item in the *Westporter-Herald* on June 4, 1920, read simply: "F. Scott Fitzgerald, a writer, has leased the Wakeman cottage near Compo Beach." The house, originally the home of Wakeman Couch, was later known as the "Switch House"[1] (because it was located near where the trolley tracks led to Compo Beach). Everything Fitzgerald did showed up in his writing, including the honeymoon summer months in the Wakeman Cottage, which he describes in his second novel, *The Beautiful and the Damned.* F. Scott and Zelda Fitzgerald attracted other literary figures to their infamous wild parties. Critic Edmund Wilson, who attended at least one party, said later that "he was amused that while the Fitzgeralds were reveling nude in the orgies of Westport, in another part of the village, Van Wyck Brooks was writing about 'the sterile sobriety of the country.'"[2]

Westport writer Barbara Probst Solomon grew up in a house not far from the Fitzgeralds' house. Writing in *The New Yorker,* she said Fitzgerald's presence in Westport was "mythic." The year they came to Westport was, in her words, "a dynamite year." She added that Fitzgerarld's view that a new society in 1920 was created by a fusion between Christians and Jews was right. "Westport, which had no entrenched society — it had farmers, a smattering of millionaires with shore estates, the art community, and bootleggers — was a perfect setting for this cross-cultural fusion of Wasps and Jews [the artists and businesspeople]," she wrote. During the prohibition era in Westport, she observed, "work was an effort made between parties". Solomon pointed out that it was Fitzgerald himself who pinpointed 1920, his Westport year, "as the crucial year of social change in America, and as the moment when he lost his young self."[3]

Paradoxically, the first quarter of the new century was also a time when Westport faced unprecedented economic strains during the abyss of the Great Depression; and, it was a time when the town grimly but realistically prepared to send men and women into war. In short, it was a time of serious challenges unparalleled in Westport's history. It would test both the character and commitment of all the townspeople.

Westport would rapidly become known as an art colony that attracted extraordinary talent. But even as Westport was becoming a conclave for people in the arts, there were signs that all was not well among other less-glamorous citizens, that the "Roaring Twenties" could not sustain the fast-spending pace indefinitely. As early as 1920, only three years after the Board of Finance had been created to serve as a watchdog over the town's tax monies, it approved the sum of $2,000 for the care of 15 needy families who were in desperate need of food and shelter. "The unemployment situation in Westport, while not so acute as in other communities, is such, nevertheless, as to necessitate some remedial measure," the local paper reported.[4] The Board of Selectmen put men to work building gravel sidewalks, on the roads, and constructing a sea wall on the town's now legally acquired property at Compo Beach. A few men were put to work maintaining the schools. In 1925, Green's Farms school, designed by architect Charles Cutler, opened its doors. When Bedford Junior High School opened in 1926, it relieved Staples High School of some 246 pupils.

It was, indeed, the best of times, but the worst of times were on the horizon.[5] Many New Yorkers, attracted to the rural tranquillity of Westport, continued to come from the city, forming the ranks of what can now be called the first suburbanites — a tagword that no Westporter wanted to hear at the time. With this influx, in 1926 the town's first mail carriers hit the streets at 8:15 A.M. and 3 P.M. to deliver and pick up mail from all the townspeople who had erected mailboxes with street numbers on them. The carriers were paid a salary of $1,350 a year. Mailboxes appeared all over town as a result of the new service. Also, in 1925, Tauck Tours was launched by 24-year-old Arthur Tauck behind the wheel of a seven-passenger Studebaker touring car that covered some 1,000 miles, 900 of which were over dirt roads.

In 1927, Damman Insurance and Achorn's Pharmacy were established. Before the stock market crash in 1929, interest in Westport had developed far and wide. That same year, when Westport's automatic traffic signal operation got underway, there were some naysayers. They were worried that the rate of progress was so fast that Westport would become a city. First Selectman King W. Mansfield, a politician with great aesthetic sensitivities, suggested that a local artist design original street signs. He commissioned

Garret Thew, who worked in cast aluminum to fashion large silhouette safety signs for school areas. These proved popular and practical. Said Mansfield at the time: "We want to keep Westport, as nearly as we can, a residential community. In fact, several of our more prominent men have asked that we keep it that way. Their homes were established here in the first place because Westport was rural, and it is their desire that it remain that way."

THE DOUGHBOY:This statue in bronze relief symbolizing the World War I soldier was created by sculptor J. Clinton Shepherd, who had been a pilot. It stands in front of Town Hall.
TRACY SUGARMAN PAINTING

Although World War I ended in 1918, the town did not vote to erect a monument to Westport veterans of that war until 1925. The commission was first offered to Laura Gardin Fraser, but her design, a bronze relief figure of Victory, did not meet with the approval of the town committee. Three years later, the American Legion and Veterans of Foreign Wars succeeded in raising $10,000 and this time J. Clinton Shepherd, an illustrator and sculptor who had been a pilot, fashioned the Doughboy statue, with a pensive expression, to memorialize the personal side of that "war to end all wars." Following the first Memorial Day parade down Main Street in May 1930, the Doughboy was dedicated on November 9, 1930, and placed where the Post Road and Long Lots Road meet. A formal ceremony was attended by 3,000 townspeople who turned out to watch the dedication of the 20-ton bronze soldier. Connecticut Governor John H. Trumbull came to town for the occasion; onlookers were thrilled by the seven bands, the natty uniforms, and the profusion of national colors among the marchers, which included more than hundreds of delegates of veterans' organizations. When the children pulled the ropes unveiling the memorial, the armed veterans bearing rifles stood at "present arms" and there was a sustained burst of applause. It was a touching testimonial to the beautifully simple, artistic dignity of the bronze figure, and a fitting tribute to its designer. The statue was moved to the Town Common in 1986 and rededicated on Monday, May 30, 1988 with Bob Hartsig, a retired Air Force lieutenant colonel, as the main speaker.[6]

Westport continued to be the destination for more and more talented New Yorkers who enjoyed night life. As the New York *Journal American* commented in 1926: "New York's Real Latin Quarter is now in Connecticut." It said Westport was within easy commuting distance from Greenwich Village and described the town as "the cradle of genius." The article said Westport's growing population was "chiefly artists, writers, sculptors, editors, and painters. Along Main Street one may bump into William McFee, Richard Connell, Lucian Casey, Simeon Strunsky, Ruth Hawthorne, Webb Walron, Samuel McCoy, and a hundred others of equal fame," the article continued. "The art invasion began about six years ago and came from the Village," said the *Journal American*. One of the most striking of the artists was Karl Anderson, an impressionist, who was the older brother of writer Sherwood Anderson, and who settled in Westport in 1912. Anderson had achieved success as an illustrator by the time he moved his young family out of New York City to the Westport countryside.

In 1931, a Westport magazine writer, Donald Wilhelm, interviewed by the *Westporter-Herald*, offered this description of the town he loved. "It may be said of Westport that it is the home of more well established and distinctive artists and writers than any other city or town in the world. The best argument for Westport is that there is no sound argument against it." He estimated the number of artists and writers and other creative people at about 500 to 600. This included motion picture people as well as musicians and architects. One of the most respected was Robert Lambdin, noted for his murals of life in the town in the early nineteenth century that decorate the wall of the main office and Saugatuck branch of the former Westport Bank and Trust Company. His depictions of the early stages of life in Green's Farms and Westport serve as a valuable reminder of that era.

The theatre was another example of Westport's creativity. In 1930, Lawrence Langner, the distinguished director of the New York Theatre Guild, and his wife, Armina, bought the 100-year-old Kemper Tannery buildings and turned them into the Westport Country Playhouse. The building was designed by Cleon Throckmorton to match the dimensions of the Times Square Theatre in Manhattan, with room for 500 seats. Langner conceived the idea of bringing a Broadway-caliber acting company to Westport.

The Playhouse officially opened on June 29, 1931 with *Streets of New York*. It was a major hit, an event heralded in show business across the country. Said The *Westporter-Herald* in a review: "The opening of his [Langner's] Country Playhouse fulfilled his ambition

FOUNDED PLAYHOUSE: Lawrence Langner and his wife, Armina Marshall, bought the Kemper Tannery in 1930 and turned it into the Westport Country Playhouse, one of Westport's prize attractions. The 500-seat theater was filled to capacity on opening night and has since attracted the most famous actors and actresses. The playhouse, above, as it looks today.
WESTPORT HISTORICAL SOCIETY PHOTOS

of many years, to establish a repertory company of fine New York actors in Westport."[7] The play starred Lillian Gish, Armina Marshall [Langner's wife], Moffat Johnson, actor and director Rollor Peters, Romney Brent and Frank Conlon. Local observers saw it at the time as one of the most significant days in Westport's theatrical history. Opening night drew more than 500 prominent citizens and celebrities. The Playhouse and the White Barn Theatre have since brought hundreds of well-known actors to Westport in the intervening years, including: [8]

Bette Davis

Sandy Dennis

Mason Adams	Oliva De Haviland
Dana Andrews	Sandy Dennis
Tallulah Bankhead	Donal Donnelly
John and Ethel	Diana Douglas
Barrymore	Kirk Douglas
Barbara Baxley	Michael Douglas
Theodore Bikel	Keir Dullea
Linda Blair	Rex Eberhart
Joan Blondell	Teresa Eldh
Shirley Booth	Robert Emhardt
Dorothy and Ed Bryce	Patricia Englund
Stewart Chancy	Mia Farrow
Ilka Chase	Henry Fonda
Montgomery Clift	Joan Fontaine
Whitfield Connor	Arlene Francis
Hans Conreid	Eva Gabor
Rodney Dangerfield	Zsa Zsa Gabor
Bette Davis	Cynthia Gibb

Dorothy Gish	Eva LeGallienne	Robert Redford
Lillian Gish	Armina Marshall Langner	Ann Richards
Ruth Gordon	Abby Lewis	Lee Richardson
Frank Gorshin	Christopher Lloyd	Jason Robards
David Marshall Grant	John Lodge	Amanda Rogers
David Groh	Francesca Braggiotti Lodge	David Rogers
Ellen Hanley	Lucille Lortel	Dulcy Rogers
Ann Harding	Tina Louise	June Walker Rogers
William S. Hart	Darren McGavin	Carol Schweid
Mariette Hartley	Danny Mann	Zachary Scott
June Havoc	E.G. Marshall	John D. Seymour
Michael Hayden	Pamela Sue Martin	Carole Shelley
Verna Hillie	Ruth Matteson	Cornelia Otis Skinner
Linda Hunt	George Mitchell	Otis Skinner
Jane Hyatt	Marilyn Monroe	Elizabeth Taylor
Moffat Johnson	Mary Munger	Laurette Taylor
Van Johnson	Patricia Neal	Marlo Thomas
Brad Jones	Paul Newman	Gene Tierney
Bernard Kates	Maureen O'Sullivan	Franchot Tone
Gene Kelly	Geraldine Page	David Wayne
Arthur Kennedy	Dodie Pettit	Larry Williams
Jack Klugman	Tyrone Power	Joanne Woodward
Shirley Knight	Martha Raye	Jane Wyatt

More recently, Dorothy and Ed Bryce, a well-known acting couple in Westport, collaborated in dozens of shows, from acting and directing to writing and coaching. Ed Bryce's forte was TV serials and soap operas. He was best known in the theatre for his one-man show, *Good Night, Mr. Lincoln,* which Dorothy produced and son Scott Bryce directed. Dorothy acted in comedy, drama, and musicals. Her screen credits include *A Face in the Crowd, Other People's Money,* and industrial films. The Bryces have been in Westport for 31 years and were deeply involved in the community's Interfaith Council of Westport-Weston, which promotes a climate of understanding between various religious faiths. By far the best-known contemporary acting couple, of course, is Paul Newman and Joanne Woodward, both of whom have lived in Westport since 1961. They have been the recipients of many honors, including the Westport Arts Award in 1994. The actors listed above and many other stars of stage and screen were celebrated at an exhibit in 1998 at the Westport Historical Society entitled, "Stars in Their Eyes," curated by Tom DeLong and

ACTING COUPLE: Dorothy and Ed Bryce collaborated in dozens of shows, and made their mark in the movies, directing, writing and coaching. They were also involved in interfaith education, theatre workshops, and youth projects.

COURTESY OF DOROTHY BRYCE

Wally Woods. A book by DeLong with the same title was published in early 2000.

Among the playwrights, producers, and critics who have been here are John Chapman, Cecil Holm, Hal James, Hilton Kramer, Lawrence Langner, Elliot and Margie Martin, Frank Perry, and Mike Todd. Dancers and choreographers included George Balanchine, Bambi Lyn, Ruth St. Denis, Ted Shawn, and F. George Volodine. Musicians, singers and composers include John Corigliano, George Gershwin, Alexander Kipnis, Oscar Levant, Brenda Lewis, Johnny Marks, James Melton, Andrew Metens, Richard Rodgers, Neil Sedaka. Nicholas Sokolof, and Tossy Spivakovsky, and Ruth Steinkraus-Cohen.[9]

Another artist who made a huge impact on Westport and beyond was Hilla Rebay. Rebay's importance was not just in her own art — she did portraits of American jazz scenes and she constructed paper cutouts—but she also played what was described as a "catalytic role in promoting the acceptance of abstract artists in America." She established the Museum of Non-Objective Art Painting in New York, which subsequently became the Solomon R. Guggenheim Museum in New York. She also provided refuge to foreign artists during World War II. The arts community continued to grow and be recognized in many important quarters throughout the nation. Sculptress Laura Gardin Fraser designed the Congressional Medal of Honor featuring Charles Lindbergh's likeness. Her husband and Westport sculptor, James Earl Fraser, would later create, among other works, the Theodore Roosevelt statue that was unveiled in 1940 at the Museum of Natural History.

Artist John Steuart Curry was picked to execute the decoration of the $1.3 million Interior Department building in Washington, D.C. Since the Works Progress Administration (WPA) was not created until 1935, there were no federal programs to help artists during the early years of the Depression. Accordingly, they did what so many other people in other professions did to survive: They came together as an informal group hoping to work for their common good among businesspeople in New York City. They hired a representative and, while still remaining free to pursue their individual work, these artists together with writers, typographers, and the other multi-faceted talents that existed in this community, made themselves available as a group for any commercial company in New York that might need their services.

The list of names reads like a Who's Who of Westport talent of the day:[10] Karl Anderson, Lowell L. Balcom, Leslie Benson, Samuel Brown,

Edward Boyd, Ralph Boyer, James Daugherty, Henry Bressmer Davis, Kerr Eby, Nancy Fay, Ernest Fuhr, Arthur Fuller, John Hamilton Fyfe, George Glisbee, Leland Gustavson, Charles Hardy, Alice Harvey, Howard Heath, Oscar Frederic Howard, Louis Koster, Robert Lambdin, Robert Lawson, Marie Lawson, Norman Mason, Herbert Mathieu, Neely McCoy, Eugene McNerney, Norman Neely, Rose O'Neill, Marion Patton, William Meade Prince, Leah Ramsey, J. Clinton Shepherd, Everett Shinn, Ray O. Strang, Hilton C. Swain, Harry Townsend, George Hand Wright, Harold Von Schmidt, and E.N. Young.

Despite this group of distinguished names, many did not find New York as good a market as they had hoped, at least not under the concept of a collective group of artists. Accordingly, 23 artists launched an outlet of their own in Westport "for those creations not within the scope of illustrating," as they put it in an advertisement. Those 23 members sold some 150 pieces of work in the first summer alone. But, it was not until the New Deal's Works Progress Administration got started that many artists gained financial aid for their work.

Franklin D. Roosevelt's overwhelming victory in the election of 1932 was read as a mandate for change. During Roosevelt's first one hundred days in office, George Biddle, artist and a close friend of the President — and a man familiar with the mural program sponsored by the Mexican government in the 1920s — proposed that American artists be employed to create artworks for public buildings. His suggestion was accepted immediately and the Public Works of Art Project (PWAP) was created.

In 1934, First Selectman King W. Mansfield formed the Westport Arts Committee under the Public Works of Art Program. Its members included Mrs. Nigel Cholmeley-Jones, Mrs. John A. Church, Jr., Mrs. Douglas Hadden, Mrs. Brook B. Church and Sanford Evans. The town appropriated a total of $3,000 for the project and artworks were commissioned for 15 Westport WPA artists for all of the town's public buildings. Some 32 artists joined up for the first batch of work, but only 10 were selected: Ralph Boyer, Samuel Brown, Eugene Elmer Hannan, Colcord Heurlin, Robert L. Lambdin, Gregory McLaughlin, William Schomberger, Arba Skidmore, Ray Strang and Garret Thew.

WPA ART COMMITTEE: From left, to right: Sanford Evans, architect; Brooke Peters Church, writer; Henrietta Cholmeley-Jones, supervisor; King W. Mansfield, first selectman.
RALPH BOYER PAINTING 1939/
G.W. ADAMS, FILE PHOTO

By the time the committee was dissolved in 1938, 34 pieces of art and an archive of 120 photographs of Westport as it looked at the time had been completed. The project was considered so successful by the General Services Administration in Washington that it suggested that one final painting be commissioned — a portrait of Westport's committee — which was painted by Ralph Boyer. It can be viewed today in the Selectman's Conference Room at Westport Town Hall.

INNOVATOR: Artist Bert Chernow launched The Westport Schools Permanent Art Collection in 1964, with the goal in mind that all Westport children should be surrounded by artwork. The collection includes Works Progress Administration (WPA) paintings from the 1930s.
WESTPORT NEWS PHOTO

Not a part of the WPA collection, but created during that era, are two frescoes, entitled *Comedy* and *Tragedy,* by John Steuart Curry. Curry was not selected as a WPA artist as he was better off financially than some of the other Westport artists, so interested Westporters donated $1,000 for materials and a helper, James Daugherty — and Curry — supplied his talent and time to create these priceless artworks as a gift to the town he loved. In 1964, Burt Chernow, then an art teacher at Green's Farms School, started The Westport Schools Permanent Art Collection (WSPAC) — his philosophy being that all Westport school children should be surrounded daily by original artwork. When Eve Potts and Mollie Donovan became co-curators of this collection in 1974, it was decided that the WPA paintings, some long since relegated to basements and attics, should become a part of the WSPAC. Using Henrietta Cholmeley-Jones' original WPA list, the women scoured the basements and attics of all town buildings and succeeded in locating 21 of them. As funding has become available, these have been restored and rehung — a fitting reminder that something important for art happened during those dark Depression days and that Westport was an integral part of that scene.

Today, the Westport Schools Permanent Art Collection numbers over 450 artworks, which are rotated throughout the town's school and public buildings by a volunteer committee. The work serves as a testament to Westport's continuing commitment to the arts. The committee published a book, edited by Mollie Donovan, *Westport Schools Permanent Art Collection — Our Art Heritage, a Gift for the Future*, as the basis for integrating art as part of the school curriculum.[11]

Moreover, the town's tradition of honoring the arts was high on the Westport Historical Society's agenda at the outset of 2000 with the opening of an exhibit, "A Community's Creative Heritage." Commented *Westport News* Editor Christina Hennessey: "By embracing artists and their talents, Westport has influenced generations of young people not only to honor creativity, but also to pursue it. Art is tightly woven into the history of the town and provides the vibrant colors that attract creative individuals to work [here] and new residents who want to be immersed in that culture."[12] An example of the community's fervent dedication to the arts was the formation of an informal "artistic committee" early in 2000 that announced its intention to reorganize the Westport Country Playhouse. The group is led by Joanne Woodward and includes star power (Jayne Atkinson, Maureen Anderman, James Naughton, Jane Powell, Christopher Plummer, Gene Wilder and Paul Newman). Said Ms. Woodward: "When we heard that some builder might come along and put up a mall, that was enough to terrify everybody." She said the Playhouse needed renovations, especially if the theatre is to operate on a year-round basis. It has been a summer theatre only.[13]

A landmark breakthrough took place in 1947 when the Famous Artists School (FAS) was conceived by Albert Dorne, the immensely charismatic and successful illustrator. He has been called a rare combination of entrepreneur, artist, dreamer, and doer. He was the main principal in creating and operating the school. Illustrator Fred Ludekens was a co-organizer, but Dorne was the decision-maker. The school grew out of the Institute of Commercial Art, in which artists developed a method to teach individuals how to create pictures. The 12 original faculty artists/instructors, known as the *Twelve Famous*, were Albert Dorne, Norman Rockwell, Stevan Dohanos, Jon Whitcomb, Al Parker, Ben Stahl, Fred Ludekens, Robert Fawcett, Harold Von Schmidt, John Atherton, Peter Helck, and Austin Briggs. When Atherton died he was replaced by George Giusti. Scores of other talented but less well-known artists worked behind the scenes correcting lessons and updating the courses and the beautifully printed instruction books. Ed Eberman, an illustrator and one of

FAMOUS ARTISTS SCHOOL: Conceived by Albert Dorne, a highly successful illustrator, in 1947, the FAS was launched by 12 well-known artists. As it grew, it located its headquarters on Wilton Road. At its peak, it had 800 salesmen across the country, and 55 full-time faculty teaching more than 1,100 students ranging in age from 16 to 94. WESTPORT HISTORICAL SOCIETY

the founders, ran the operation on a day to day basis and supervised and hired instructors, according to Gil Maurer, former senior vice president and chief operating officer of Famous Artists from 1971 to 1973.

Correspondence school art courses had existed for years; everyone can recall the "Draw Me" ads. However, none ever approached the original material and the thinking that went into the Famous Artist School courses. The individual talents of the 12 main illustrators who were all tops in their profession made the product unique and marvelously helpful for anyone from beginners to other illustration hopefuls of all stages. Later, the school made use of television in addition to their national print ads. Televised "shorts" of staff artists at work appeared in late nightspots, and the word "Westport" was heard on all of them across the country.

FAS headquarters were first located in the Old Sasco Mill building, 1869 Post Road East, but as the company grew it moved to a vacant building on Wilton Road and then built its headquarters, which are now occupied by Save the Children Foundation, which was established in 1932. Eventually, FAS boasted a fulltime staff of artists with students ranging in age from 16 to 94 enrolled from every one of the United States as well as from a dozen countries around the world. Gordon Carroll, onetime editor of *Coronet* and *Reader's Digest*, headed the Famous Writers School, and there was also a school for photographers headed by Victor Keppler.

The Famous Artists School continued to grow and to prosper and, for a while, had a spectacular record on the New York Stock Exchange. But a series of bad acquisitions and the sudden death of Albert Dorne began a downward spiral from which it never recovered. At its peak, it had 800 salesmen deployed across the country, 55 on the teaching faculty with a ratio of 1,181 students per instructor and an extraordinary enrollment of 65,000 after World War II because veterans could use the GI Bill. Unfortunately the FAS expanded so rapidly that in the 1960s it had to begin cutting back its staff and selling subsidiaries that it had acquired. One newspaper reported in 1971 that the FAS was in "deep trouble." Finally, after all avenues of solvency were explored, it closed its doors. The problem was that the school had been crediting each course it sold for the full tuition of hundreds of dollars on the books when, in fact, many times it never got paid more than the $20 entrance fee. The school was able to borrow money on the basis of the full amount figures but when it expanded rapidly, it could not come up with the necessary cash. Fortunately, however, the school is remembered for its success rather than its financial troubles.

As Maurer recalls the situation, "Two flash points toppled the scheme. The broader cause was the recession of 1971 when the stock market tanked and unemployment rose. The higher profile cause of the demise was a 1970 article in *Harper's* Magazine that dissected the Famous Schools business. It was widely picked up by the press. The school's reputation, formerly sterling, was tarnished just as the recession hit, and the lenders ran for the exits. The result was a Chapter 11 bankruptcy filing in May 1971. The banks formed a consortium that underwrote the instruction for those students still staying and paying. Ultimately, the business was sold in 1973 for the value of its very large tax loss to a plumbing company in Philadelphia. The creditors probably recovered 10 to 20 cents on the dollar. The shareholders got zip. The purchasers ultimately sold the materials and the courses to Cortina Schools which operates the business as Cortina Famous Schools on a much reduced basis in Wilton." [14]

The best-known Westport-based writers, some of whom aligned themselves with FAS, were Franklin P. Adams, Joan Walsh Anglund, Peter DeVries, Phil Dunning, P.D. Eastman Mignon Eberhart, Clifton Fadiman, Edna Ferber, Leonard Everett Fisher, F. Scott Fitzgerald, Hardie Gramatky, John Gunther, A.E. Hotchner, Erica Jong, Hugh Kahle, Robert Lawson, winner of the Newbery Medal in 1944 for "Rabbit Hill;" Hugh Lofting, Robert Ludlum, John McDermott, Robin Moore, Paul Osborn, Rod Serling, Max Shulman, J.D. Salinger, James Thurber, Amelia Walden, and Max Wilk.

All of these talented people set the stage for others who would be recognized by the Westport Arts Advisory Committee, formed in recent years with artist Burt Chernow serving as a guiding light and made official by the RTM in 1997. The present committee is comprised of Ann Chernow, who was elected in 1999 to the National Academy of Design, chairman; Ruth Steinkraus-Cohen, Kim Cooper, Mollie Donovan, Alfred Eiseman, Natalie Maynard, Joan S. Miller, David Rogers, David Rubinstein, John Simon, and Ann Sheffer, ex officio. The purpose of the committee is to produce and promote Westport's arts heritage, and it has recently commissioned a film entitled, "A Community's Creative Heritage: The Arts in Westport, Connecticut," by filmmaker Martin West.

In addition, the Committee's "Lifetime Achievement Award" medallion, designed and cast by Stanley Bleifeld, has gone to the following people in four categories: Music/Dance: George Balanchine, Paul Bernard, Brenda Lewis Cooper, John Corigliano, Don Elliott, Fred Hellerman, Elizabeth Lennox Hughes, Alexander Kipnis, Jeanne Kimball, Vivian Perlis, Fritz Reiner, Ruth St. Denis and Ted Shawn, Dorothy Straub. Visual Arts: Perry Miller Adato, Paul Cadmus, John Steuart Curry, James Daugherty, Stevan Dohanos,

SUPERSTARS: Paul Newman and Joanne Woodward at an informal Westport event in the 1990s. The couple has been active in many community activities, including the Westport Historical Society, since they moved here in 1961. In the 1950s, they co-starred in "Rally Round the Flag Boys!", a movie based on a book by Westport author Max Shulman. The story was a takeoff on Westport's controversy over the U.S. Army building a Nike site here.

WESTPORT NEWS PHOTO

Arthur Dove, Herzl Emanuel, James E. and Laura G. Fraser, Berthold Nebel, Hilla Rebay, Tracy Sugarman, Harold Von Schmidt, Jean Woodham. Theatre: Mason Adams, Ralph Alswang, Marcella Cisney, Hume Cronyn, Bette Davis, Sandy Dennis, Eva LeGallienne, Lawrence and Armina Marshall Langner, Elliot Martin, James McKenzie, Paul Newman, Theatre Artists Workshop, Gene Tierney, Joanne Woodward. Literature: Sherwood Anderson, Van Wyck Brooks, Peter DeVries, R.L. Duffus, Howard Fast, F. Scott Fitzgerald, John Hersey, Erica Jong, Hilton Kramer, Ralph Martin, William Meredith, Rose O'Neill, Robert Stone.

The year 1947 was a good one for the arts in Westport. It was then that Lucille Lortel, known as "the Queen of Off-Broadway," launched Westport's now-famous White Barn Theatre and Museum. One of the premier producers of her time, Lortel sponsored a number of playwrights. She had made her debut on Broadway in George Bernard Shaw's *Caesar and Cleopatra*, in 1925, met and married Louis Schweitzer, a wealthy chemical engineer in 1931, and in 1938 the couple purchased an estate in Westport.

In 1956, the Westport Community Theatre was founded and the actors were known as the Westport Players. For a long time it had no home of its own until it acquired its present locale at Town Hall in 1978; it was often referred to as "the oldest floating theatre in Fairfield County." Its purpose was to provide a mix of classical and modern theatre. Over the years, it trained any number of acting, directing, lighting, sound, set design, and technically inclined students. It has five main stage productions each year, a year-round experimental theatre company that serves as a training ground for directors, actors, and playwrights; workshops in voice production, costume, lighting, properties, and make-up; and it participates at the Levitt Pavilion and in First Night.

One of the town's best-known artists, Howard Munce, came to the Westport art scene in 1935. He got off on the right foot, having called upon Harold Von Schmidt to find out from him what to show for his entrance exam to Pratt Institute. "Von," as he was known by his friends, was everyone's mentor, including such established pros as Tom Lovell, John Clymer, Amos

Sewell, Bob Lougheed, and anyone else who sought his counsel. In those days it was common for illustrators to stop people downtown and ask them to pose if they happened to be the type needed at the moment. Neighbors and relatives were continually pressed into service. Munce was close to Steve Dohanos, noted especially for his *Saturday Evening Post* covers. When Munce, who was a Marine, wrote from the Pacific, he always included small detailed drawings of how things looked. In the beginning of the war, illustrators were desperate to get authentic research. Dohanos saved these sketches for him until he returned three years later. They are now part of the Military Art Collection in the New Britain Museum of American Art.

Munce in 1999, at age 84, has been an art director, cartoonist, painter, and teacher since. He continues to be involved in most art-related events and projects in town. He says: "Artists tend to flock together. Over the years they all manage to find each other for social and professional reasons. Many groups have come together, shared one another's company until time and tide separated them. Of all the disorganized artist organizations that ever happened here, the so-called Westport Artists — which was started by Ben Stahl and Bob Harris after the war — was the biggest and the best there ever was. They met once a month at places like the Cobb's Mill Inn, The Red Barn, and Longshore. They were merciless to guest speakers, often art directors and editors. The self-made entertainment was often wild. They also held the best costume balls in memory. But the tide came in and the tide went out, and 'Westport Artists' went with it. There are few original survivors now."

Munce continues: "On the chance that one might think that Westport's art history has mostly to do with the past, however memorable that past surely is, have no fear: this is how things stand now. At the beginning of the new century, the glory days of illustration as we've known them have passed. However, people of visual talent still abound here though many hands now guide a mechanical mouse rather than a pencil. Westport women artists are here in great numbers, the best of them doing admirable work. And look at the legacy list [of arts awards recipients] to reassure yourself that we remain a unique community in the appreciation of images of the mind and of the hand. There are permanent collections of the past and present in schools and other local buildings available to

MULTI-TALENTED MASTER: Howard Munce has been an active member of the arts community and a leader in preserving the town's artistic heritage. JOHN BREWSTER PHOTO

every one of our townspeople at all times."[15]

In the preface to *A Community of Artists*, Jack Tarrant states: "Communities, like families, have roots. The painters, sculptors and illustrators who flourished in Westport and Weston form part of our communal roots." The book was published in time to celebrate the town's 150th birthday in 1985. Among the illustrators and cartoonists who rose to fame in Westport in the 1940s and later (whose works were displayed in a 1999 exhibit at the Westport Historical Society) are the following:

Tom Armstrong	Harold Gray	Donald Reilly
Perry Barlow	Chad Grothkopf	Mischa Richter
Erik Blegvad	Eric H. Gurney	Bud Sagendorf
J.R. Bray	John Held	Richard Scarry
Austin Briggs	Jud Hurd	Noel Sickles
Dick Brooks	Crockett Johnson	Blanche Sims
W.F. Brown	Hank Ketchum	Leonard Starr
Mel Casson	John LaPick	Curt Swan
Stan Drake	Robert Lawson	Norm Tate
John Dykes	Lee Lorenz	James Thurber
P.D. Eastman	Hank McIver	Jack Tippit
Edna Eicke	Jerry McLaughlin	Bob Weber, Sr.
Randy Enos	Howard Munce	Elmer E. Wexler
Ham Fisher	John Norment	Hans Wilhelm
Jim Flora	Rose O'Neill	Dick Wingert
Tom Funk	John Prentice	Bill Yates
Tom Garcia	Garret Price	
Hardie Gramatky	Alice Harvey Ramsey	

Prior to the Depression, there were some symptoms of obsolescence in Westport. In 1926, for example, the Kemper Leather Tannery, which had been in business manufacturing skin leather hat bands and bag linings, could no longer compete with companies using substitutes or synthetic leather. Kemper could be converted, but only at a tremendous cost and none of its personnel was experienced in the manufacture of substitutes.[16] At the same time, businesses of a different kind — the small, family-owned farmstand —

CHRISTIE'S COUNTRY STORE: *This famous landmark was opened in 1927 by Christie Masiello on Cross Highway across the street from a speakeasy. She died in 1989 at the age of 88 and the store took on new ownership.*   WESTPORT HISTORICAL SOCIETY PHOTO

were starting up. Christie Masiello's Country Store on Cross Highway, across the street from a speakeasy, was one example. In that store, which she owned from 1927 for more than 60 years until her death at the age of 88 in 1989, she sold much of the produce raised on the Masiello's 45-acre farm in the Coleytown area of town. "You name it, we raise it," she said. She was assisted in her later years by her nephew, Donald Masiello. Christie's remains a landmark. She became a fixture in her popular store. "People come back to visit, even if they've moved away to California or Europe. They come in and ask me if I remember them. I surprise them when I do. It's fun to watch them grow up," she told a reporter. "It was a real neighborhood store. Sometimes people would sit and visit for hours. There was a pot-bellied stove, and they'd sit around and chat. Or else I'd be open real late, and we'd sit out on the porch and talk. Either way, nobody was rushing to get home. Living was hard but good then. People were pleased with what they had, even if it wasn't much, and they enjoyed it. When you're in farming, I would help you and you would help me. Now everything is so businesslike."[17]

The town continued to try to attract new business. In 1927, the businessmen — sensing there was change in the offing — banded together to form the Westport Chamber of Commerce, with its first president, Charles Hendricks, and secretary, Anson Leary, who were both Rotarians. It was officially incorporated on June 12, 1931 "to promote and encourage the development of the Town of Westport and the best interests of its citizens; to advertise the Town and aid in procuring new industries and business enterprises; to aid and encourage the members in their respective businesses, trades, or professions…[and] to foster the general welfare and civic betterment of the Town of Westport."[18]

Meanwhile, the town expanded its capital investments, voting to build 150 bathhouses at a cost of $7,000 at Compo Beach. With the Depression, of course, came a slowdown in all business. Nonetheless, the townspeople had the foresight to make a major effort to protect and preserve Compo Beach. Homeowners near or facing the beach formed the Compo Beach Improvement Association in 1924. Much of the land was salt marsh and susceptible to flooding. In 1919, Samuel Roodner, a South Norwalk grain and food merchant, had bought a large tract of land from the Bradley family. Roodner built a number of small homes on speculation and, along with others, wanted to make certain the beach area would be well looked after. Indeed, Westporters were not the only people using the beach. Compo Beach in the summer was a popular place, where townspeople and

GOLD'S DRAGOONS: A corps of horsemen from the Fairfield County Hunt Club in 1932 stemmed from the National Guard cavalry called Gold's Dragoons, named after Major Nathan Gold, a famous resident in the area in 1660. He organized the first Connecticut cavalry troop to protect the colonists against the Indians.

PHOTO COURTESY OF KENNETH POWERS

visitors alike went nearly fully clad to take their turn in the water. The town's population was growing — it stood at approximately 5,800 in 1928, up from 5,100 in 1920 and the people who owned land or homes on the shore wanted to be certain their homes would rise in value with the real estate market.

Adding to the hope that Westport would continue to include a wide spectrum of activities was the creation in the spring of 1932 of an elite corps of horsemen from the upscale Fairfield County Hunt Club. It was an organization stemming from the National Guard cavalry called Gold's Dragoons, named after Major Nathan Gold, a famous resident in the area in 1660, who formed the first Connecticut cavalry troop for protection of the colonists of Fairfield County against the remaining Indian tribes. Most of the members of Gold's Dragoons were recruited in Fairfield County. They included crack poloists and former cavalrymen and they drilled on Mondays at the Hunt Club, starting in 1957.[19]

During the Depression, the Board of Selectmen appropriated $3,500 to help support those who needed jobs: men who had wives and three or more children were paid $4 a day for clean-up and maintenance chores; others supporting smaller families would work for the town on a sliding scale down to three days a week. Single men were allowed to work only one day a week. The situation was desperate for some families. At the outset of 1932, at a meeting of the Westport Unemployment Relief Committee, everyone realized something must be done. Frederick T. Bedford stepped forward and offered to contribute one-quarter of every $10,000 raised by the townspeople to pay those who were unemployed. Responding to this appeal, Westport could raise only $12,000 in 15 months. Accordingly a special town meeting was held and $12,000 more was put aside to provide help to needy Westport families. Other worries in the depression era included an infantile paralysis scare that started in mid-summer of 1931 when a 9-year-old child, one of 75 New York City boys attending a summer camp, came down with the dreaded disease. Town officials immediately closed Compo to all outsiders on weekends, and swimming was severely curtailed.

In the midst of the challenges of the Depression, there was a heartwarming episode involving one of America's — and Westport's — most famous women. The *Westporter-Herald* ran a banner headline: "WESTPORT BOY GIVES FAMOUS HELEN KELLER HER FIRST REAL RIDE IN AIRPLANE ON NY—WASHINGTON TRIP." It seems that the "boy" was S.T. Jacobs, pilot of a Condor plane of the Eastern Transport Company, who took the world-famous Keller on her first extended airplane trip in 1932. After she landed, Keller told her interpreter/companion, Polly Thomson: "It's marvelous, heavenly, to be soaring like a bird under the soft, azure sky with green fields and budding trees below me. I can not tell you how much I enjoyed it." She explained that she could "hear" the roar of the engines in terms of vibrations she got throughout her body and she could "see" the sky and the land through the images that her companion described to her. Helen Keller died on June 1, 1968, in her Westport home a few weeks before her 88th birthday.

There was another bright moment in 1932 when Westporter Louis Stair Ritter built the first railroad breakfast car in the United States, hooking it up to the 7:30 A.M. commuter train.[20] Never before in the history of the American railway had anything like the breakfast car been attempted. Train innovations were not all that made the news. Westport seemed to be far out in front in terms of women's styles, especially bathing suits. Town officials announced that women would be allowed to wear abbreviated bathing suits on Compo Beach, provided straps were not dropped from the shoulders. Officials contrasted this major step forward with the early 1900s when some of the more daring women appeared on the beach with bathing suit skirts four inches above their knees, creating a local scandal at the time. Also in 1932, despite the Depression, there were a few signs that business was still alive. Taylor's Florist, for example, opened that year.

Meanwhile, as the Depression caught hold in Westport, more than 100 black families crowded into a tenement at 22½ Main Street, resulting in health and safety problems. The town was embarrassed at one point when a Yale University public health official surveyed housing conditions and described the Main Street tenement as "entirely inadequate provisions, a disgrace for any community, yet tolerated in the center of Westport." In the 1930s, at least, this issue of what to do with the "colored section" of town remained unresolved and, as time passed, would eventually haunt town officials again.

The Depression did not stop Westport from honoring its past. The town celebrated its Centenary birthday and the state's Tercentenary in 1935 in a big way featuring a multifaceted pageant on Jesup Green. Thousands of townspeople turned out to take part in the so-called "The Pageant of

Westport." Arranged in three parts of 10 episodes, it portrayed the important events in the history of Westport from the early Indian days to 1935. Gladys Mansir, a teacher at Staples High School, worked for months to arrange for the presentations. First Selectman King Mansfield was the official chairman; Edith Very Sherwood, the town librarian, vice chairman; Stewart Hemson, secretary, and David Sachs, treasurer. Special events planned by 22 committees combined with the State of Connecticut Tercentenary made it a double celebration with parades, daily exhibitions, luncheons, a series of historic speeches, and the publication of a small book, Wakefield Dort's *Westport in Connecticut's History, 1835-1935*, written expressly for the occasion. The event opened with a dedication of a plaque by the Daughters of the American Revolution at the entrance of the Old Burying Ground; the story of education in Westport was told by a group of volunteers, followed by a discussion of Westport's early houses, and recital of "Italian Street Songs in Costume."

Other activities included a symphony orchestra concert and a ball at Longshore. "The Pageant of Westport" was meant to "truly and picturesquely portray the history and symbolize the spirit of Westport — ever restless, diversified, independent and creative."[21] The pageant was presented on three consecutive nights and the cast was made up of members of the community, rehearsed and costumed, beginning with the purchase of "Machamux" as the Indians first called Westport, the founding of the Green's Farms Congregational Church as well as the landing at Compo. Many townspeople wore costumes and played the roles of onions, cutworms, bees or farmers for the "Onion Ballet." During Tercentenary week in Westport, Tercentenary medals were also given out. The medals showed a group of men, the founders of the state, dominated by the commanding figure of Thomas Hooker holding the Fundamental Orders. The legend on the medal was "1635-1935 Connecticut 300 Years."

One of the most significant historic events of the 1930s in Westport was the visit by president Franklin Delano Roosevelt on October 22, 1936. He was making a brief campaign stop on his way back from a tour of upstate Connecticut. He was the only sitting President of the United States to visit Westport since George Washington. Huge crowds gathered, including school children who had been let out of class so they could catch a glimpse of the President. In his typical patrician manner, Roosevelt waved his hat at the crowd and said: "I am honored by the wonderful reception the people of Connecticut have given me. But even more than that, I think that this

PRES. ROSEVELT TO
TALK HERE THURS.
BETWEEN 2:45 - 3:30

FDR IN WESTPORT: Franklin Delano Roosevelt was greeted by a huge crowd in front of the YMCA on October 22, 1936, on a campaign stop. Children were dismissed from school early in order to catch a glimpse of him. He was the first sitting president to visit Westport since George Washington.
WESTPORT HISTORICAL SOCIETY PHOTO

year, men and women are taking more interest in the future of their nation than ever before, and reading and thinking for themselves above all."[22]

Also in 1936 the Post Office went into full swing and more and more homes had numbers assigned to them so people could have mail delivered. It was derisively dubbed "Jim Farley's Cheesebox," since he was the Postmaster General named by Roosevelt. In 1936, the Fable Funeral Home was dedicated. By 1937, Westport appeared to be coming out of the Depression that had caused many businesses on Main Street to close their doors. One local entrepreneur, Henry Klein, a Hungarian-born immigrant and a shrewd businessman, in 1937 launched what would become one of the most successful family-owned businesses in Westport. Klein, who was joined by his son, Stanley, in later years, worked at Klein's at 44 Main Street until he died at the age of 90 in 1990.

In 1939 the Westport School of Music was founded. It was an immediate success and within a few decades accommodated nearly 200 students from Westport as well as from nearby towns like Ridgefield, Easton, Monroe, Stratford, Fairfield, Weston, Wilton and Greenwich. That same year, the town took an important step when it voted to name the town green after Morris K. Jesup. Jesup, of course, donated the library to the town.

An event in the 1930s that gave the town a sizable economic boost was the beginning of the construction of the Merritt Parkway. Westport's Assemblyman J. Kenneth Bradley, a Republican, said that since the highway would be built with a federal subsidy, it would ensure construction jobs for 2,000 workers on relief. "This infusion of good old-fashioned federal

FROM PRINCIPAL TO GOVERNOR: Wilbur Cross, selected by Horace Staples to be the first principal of Staples High School in 1884, later become governor of Connecticut. In the 1930s, he signed a bill paving the way for the Merritt Parkway. The tastefully designed overpasses were described as "beautiful" and "graceful." Westport's Exit 42, above. NEW HAVEN REGISTER PHOTOS

money," he declared, "will cause the state's rights idealism to vanish faster than the legislators could say 'creeping socialism.'" The measure authorizing Fairfield County to sell $15 million in state bonds passed quickly and unanimously in both houses and was signed by Governor Wilbur Cross. The bill offered something for everyone — workers and construction companies — and the governor could claim credit. At the bill signing, Cross seemed pleased that the federal government would pay for 45 percent of the cost. He presented the pen he used to sign the bill to Bradley. Even though magazine and newspaper editors were using terms like "beautiful" and "graceful" to define the parkway, it caused a temporary paralysis of traffic in and around Westport.[23] For a period of time the parkway ended at the Red Barn while work went on farther east. At last, when the gap was filled, Westport merchants breathed a sigh of relief. Prior to construction of the parkway all traffic had barreled through the streets of Westport. While this construction got under way, the state in 1937 purchased Sherwood Island and made it a state park, the first in Connecticut. Anticipating the inevitable traffic that would eventually flow through Westport, the town installed its first traffic light in 1938 at the intersection of Wilton Road and Kings Highway. The parkway was opened in 1940 and completed in 1943.

By 1940, there was a wide spectrum of opinion in town about the all-but-certain war ahead. The isolationist camp was strong, but a majority of people advocated helping the British fight the Nazis. The people of Westport wanted to help those in need in Europe. On June 20, 1940, a charitable Westport organization, Allied Civilian Relief, was formed to provide clothes for civilians in war-torn Europe. And, readying the town for the draft that would soon come, a voluntary Home Guard Unit was formed. It was headed by Herman Steinkraus, who had served as a captain during World War I, and made news by favoring universal military training in order to be prepared. As the war worsened for the English, tension was palpable all across America, and in Westport. Late in 1940, a Selective Service program was set up in Washington and on October 31, 1940, the first name picked in the national lottery was Hugh Maddox, a black man who was a cook at the residence of Sherman A. Manchester, of Old Hill Road. Westport thus had the dubious distinction of sending the first American soldier of World War II into the Army. Preparations for war had actually begun in the middle of 1940 when a local Allied Civilian Relief organization had been formed to provide clothes for civilians in a besieged Europe. Numerous families had held benefits to raise money for the British and the French. For those who wanted to help at home, a huge community thermometer was erected by Leland Gustavson at the corner of Main and State streets to indicate the number of people registered at the end of each week for volunteer civilian defense work. Among those volunteers were members of the newly formed Kiwanis Club of Westport. William E. Stone, assistant treasurer at the Westport Bank and Trust Co., was elected president of the club, which started out with a membership of 27 men and grew rapidly.

In addition to the isolationists, there were many in town who were fervently against the war. The Westport Citizens Against War circulated a petition in May 1941, signed by more than 400 people. At the same time, however, in September 1941, there were also those who wanted President Roosevelt to declare war on Germany. Sidney Homer, a bonds and securities expert, served as acting chairman of the Associated Leagues for a Declared War. At the outset, 200 towns — including Westport — in 36 states sent a telegram, signed by 1,000 people, to Roosevelt asking him to ask Congress to declare that a state of war with Germany now existed.

In 1941, the Westport Defense Unit was formed and it drilled every Tuesday night at the Bedford Elementary School. It was led by an instructor who was a regular Army officer. The purpose was to prepare young men who would soon be drafted, in close order drill and other fundamentals. Howard Pell, a local man, taught compass and map reading as a volunteer training in the same unit.[24] Westporters, like millions of others across the nation, were ambivalent about the possibility of the United States becoming involved in what many saw as a European war. Nonetheless, with Selective Service gearing up, a Defense Unit drilling at home, and the first Westporter already selected for active duty, the townspeople approached each day with caution and deep concern about what might lie ahead. They had good reason to be anxious.

NOTES

1. Eve Potts, *Westport...A Special Place* (Westport, CT: Westport Historical Society, 1985), p. 112.

2. Joanna Foster, "Zelda and Scott: The summer of 1920," *More Stories from Westport's Past*, 1986.

3. Barbara Probst Solomon, *The New Yorker*, September 1996. It was during this period that Fitzgerald is said to have written *The Great Gatsby*, his famous novel about life in an affluent suburb.

4. The *Westporter-Herald*, November 25, 1920.

5. *The New York Journal*, November 27, 1925.

6. As traffic on the Post Road increased vehicular exhaust took its toll on the bronze figure and in 1987 the town approved $9,000 to move it to its present site on the Town Hall Green. The veterans wanted it moved where it could be seen and appreciated in front of Town Hall.

7. The *Westporter-Herald*, June 26, 1931.

8. Potts, p. 117.

9. Dorothy and Jack Tarrant, *A Community of Artists* (Westport-Weston, Arts Council, Inc., 1900-1985), pp. 77,79

10. Article by Eve Potts, Connecticut Historic Commission, written for the book, *Westport Schools Permanent Art Collection — Our Art Heritage, a Gift for the Future*.

11. In addition to the artworks that hang in Westport's public schools, there are several smaller collections in other locations: the *Bicentennial Collection* and several WPA paintings at the Westport Town Hall, a group of paintings and cartoons at the Parks and Recreation Building in Longshore Park, *The History of Fire* at the Fire Department Headquarters, the WPA Pageant of Literature by Robert Lambdin and a collection of black and white paintings in the McManus Room at the Westport Public Library, and smaller collections at the Westport Historical Society, Westport Nature Center for Environmental Studies, Veterans of Foreign Wars Post 399, Westport YMCA, and the Hudson United Bank (formerly Westport Bank and Trust). The newest addition is a restored mural by Westport artist Ed Ashe Jr. located at the Banana Republic (formerly Kleins) at 44 Main Street. (The source is Mollie Donovan, Westport Art Historian.)

12. Christina Hennessey, editor, the *Westport News*, January 26, 2000, p. 10.

13. The *New York Times*, January 20, 2000, Connecticut section, p. 6.

14. Statement from Maurer, January, 2000.

15. Howard Munce, January, 2000.

16. The *Westporter-Herald*, May 26, 1926.

17. Dan Woog, "It's a Westport Landmark," the *Westport News*, February 20, 1987.

18. The source is the Westport Chamber of Commerce, 1999.

19. The source is Kenneth Powers.

20. The *Westporter-Herald*, October 28, 1932.

21. Deborah B. Donnelly, the *Westport News*, October 28, 1981.

22. *The Westporter*, October 25, 1936.

23. Bruce Radde, *The Merritt Parkway* (New Haven: Yale University Press, 1993), pp. 19-21.

24. The source is Howard Munce.

Photo, p. 181: Lillian and Dorothy Gish, Westport Historical Society

CHAPTER 13

THE IMPACT OF WORLD WAR II

Good schools, swimming, and boats nearby...I think
this community is going to be good for the children.

—Anne Morrow Lindbergh, of Westport, 1944

When the Japanese bombed Pearl Harbor on Sunday, December 7, 1941, the war finally became a stark reality to Westporters. They were tested immediately with a local air raid drill on Monday, December 8. Local guards, armed day and night, were stationed over the Saugatuck River bridge to prevent sabotage. One citizen almost got a bayonet in his ribs when he tried to navigate the crosswalk on the bridge. The guards demanded identification and let him go. Air raid wardens were everywhere; ambulance, fire and police gathered in front of the YMCA before dispersing all over town; people remained indoors; merchants put out the lights over their stores. Westporters listened to their radios broadcasting reports of planes reportedly approaching New York. Citizens were told of the mock "air raid" ahead of time, but it was so realistic that even many people who had been forewarned became frightened by the prospect of a real air raid.

The town manned two local aircraft spotting posts at the top of Ledgemore Road between Whitney Street and Roseville Road, and at the Compo Yacht Basin. The *Westporter-Herald* published a story calling for volunteers "to spot planes." One person would be in charge of the volunteers at the town's air raid observation posts for a 24-hour period each day of the week. Accompanying the story was a box, in which the following was published: "NOTE: A pair of night binoculars is needed at the local air raid observation post." If anybody had any doubts as to how seriously Westport was taking the threat of war, this little news item confirmed the gravity of the situation. The Red Cross readied itself to be on call at all hours. The town's defense activities became almost frenetic.

Pearl Harbor had made the possibility of an air attack real. While their mainland country had never been bombed, many Westporters now believed it could happen here. The drill went off without a hitch. Local merchants were commended by the State Defense Council for their immediate response to the request that they turn off display signs and lights. In fact, all houses had to have blankets hanging inside to cover every window.

At the same time, Schools Superintendent Heath White announced a program of strict economy in the public school system because, he said, it was an important part of the children's education. He ordered the purchase of advance supplies before acute shortages occurred and he directed teachers to instruct students in the basics of conservation — to save paper and to avoid turning on lights unless absolutely necessary. In addition, a program to teach the town's 1,713 school children first aid was initiated and Donald Tracey, industrial arts director at Bedford Junior High School, came up with an imaginative plan for boys to construct scale models of 50 different types of American and foreign planes of both Allied and Axis forces to enable them to identify such aircraft in the event of an invasion of the United States. Also emphasizing the need to conserve, the Boy Scouts from five Westport and Weston troops were given incentives to collect at least 1,000 pounds of scrap paper: They would be awarded the Eisenhower Medal for outstanding scrap collections.

It was not a very merry Christmas, but the New Year at least held out the hope that the country and this community would somehow meet the enormous challenge ahead. Westport's initial contribution to the defense industry was modest. A metal substitute for steel — called

Seybolite — was manufactured by the Westport Products Company, a new firm that had purchased the Westport Paper Company in 1940. Developed by inventor Hermann G. Seybold of New York, its first commercial production took place in a local plant in Westport owned by Alva B. See, president, who had previously manufactured elevators.

Filled with a new spirit of patriotism, hundreds of men in Westport signed up for military duty. The Volunteer Service and Registration Bureau at Bedford House on State Street downtown was swamped with applications from men of all ages who joined up to fight the Nazis. In an effort to keep townspeople calm, the Westport Police Department announced it was taking steps to ensure a safe and secure coastline. It organized the Auxiliary Emergency Police Unit, approved at a town meeting; some 50 men under the command of the chief of police manned the "spotter platforms," and patrols were beefed up along the coastline. In all, the police played an extraordinarily valuable role in ensuring calm among the townspeople throughout the war.

In the early 1940s, the Woman's Club participated vigorously in the war effort. On June 11, 1941, the club formed a Home Defense Committee, which immediately set up a civilian motor corps; nutrition, "canteen," and first-aid courses to ensure balanced diets; a telephone squad of women and a bicycle squadron to handle emergency calls; and a women's marksmanship course under police tutelage, as well as a women's ski patrol; and a cavalry. The club opened a Westport branch of "Bundles for America." The programs operated largely in response to requests by the Armed services for specific items. More than 400 women gave their time to knitting garments for the Army, Navy, and Merchant Marine. The club also published *The New Connecticut Cook Book*, which was illustrated by a group of well-known Westport artists and became a national best-seller. In addition, the club initiated a Clothing Relief Committee, which was featured in the August 11, 1947 issue of *Life* Magazine.

EVERGREEN: Evan Harding explains a landscaping concept to the Planning and Zoning Commission at a hearing in 1995.
WESTPORT NEWS PHOTO

One Westporter who showed little fear was Evan Harding, who opened Daybreak Nurseries as planned on December 7, 1941, despite the cataclysmic event of that day. Born in Wales in 1906, Harding had arrived in America on the *RMS Acquitania* only three months

207

before Pearl Harbor. His father, who had come with him, was hired to oversee the Marion Estate on Prospect Road. Harding worked on farms, including Rippe's Farms, which grew onions, strawberries and vegetables. He would develop a reputation for saving trees in town, and would serve on the town's Planning and Zoning Commission for two decades, and work with many town officials over the years. Harding later spearheaded a parking lot behind the Main Street stores because the area was so prone to flooding, with the river rising up to the store levels. Harding was also involved with landscaping the Saugatuck Yacht Club and in many other prize-winning projects. He would grow everything at his Westport nursery and then truck it into Madison Square Garden or to wherever a show happened to be taking place.[1]

On the night of Tuesday, February 24, 1942, Westport residents heard the staccato blasts of the town's fire horns sounding an air-raid warning. Every town along the Connecticut coast from the Westchester, New York state line to Milford simultaneously shut down for a major blackout test, simulating as closely as possible actual air-raid conditions. Westport looked like a ghost town as the state police working out of the barracks here stopped traffic, including trucks on all state highways and roads. Every commercial establishment was closed and darkened, all the streetlights were extinguished, all homes went dark. Some residents quietly got down on their knees in their homes and prayed.

In the spring of 1942, postal workers in Westport, responding to a request from Westport Postmaster Edward McElwee, took on the additional role of observers for paratroops, gliders, or landings. The order had come from Brigadier General A.G. Campbell, of the U.S. Army.[2] Next, a committee of local residents formed a branch of Russian War Relief, Inc., seeking volunteers to raise money for sulfa drugs, anesthetics, antiseptics, surgical supplies, and food concentrates to supplement U.S. government and Red Cross aid to the Russian soldiers battling the Germans in Europe. It was billed as a nonpartisan drive, and the sponsors invited the townspeople to view a film from the Russian front at the Fine Arts Theatre as part of a large-scale fundraising effort. Meanwhile, Westport merchants, led by businessman Nat H. Greenberg, head of the Merchants' Committee of the Westport Chamber of Commerce, met to draw up a plan for cooperative delivery of goods downtown. Greenberg's father, Edward L. Greenberg, had opened a department store on Main Street in 1917 and its 25th anniversary was marked with a small party in September 1942.

Westport's men went off to war in 1942. The first casualty from Westport was Army Lieutenant Eugene Sheridan McKenna, Jr., the only son of Mr. and Mrs. Eugene S. McKenna. Their son died in Australia of pneumonia following an attack of tropic fever while with the 208th Coast Artillery unit. A 1936 graduate of Staples High School, McKenna was a brilliant student who took an active interest in sports, especially as skipper of Star boats at the Cedar Point Yacht Club. News of his death was splashed across the front page of the *Westporter-Herald,* resulting in an outpouring of sympathy for the McKenna family, which included an aging grandfather and the soldier's cocker spaniel, Topsy. Sheridan's uncle, Edward J. McKenna, told the newspaper: "It's grandpa who's hit the hardest. He just sits there with a snapshot of Sheridan in uniform, and doesn't say a word. He looks sad and sick. Grandpa is about the only living man in Westport who once met Abraham Lincoln. He loved Lincoln. But I guess he loved Sheridan a heap sight more."

In September, Ensign Victor Malins was the second Westporter to lose his life in the war. He was killed on a training flight in Minnesota. Others who gave their lives included three brothers — all pilots — from the Wassell family, for whom a Lane was named in Westport. The brothers were Frank Lloyd Wassell, Jr., a lieutenant and flight commander in the Army Air Corps, killed on February 28, 1943, in an air collision over the field at Avon Park, Florida, while instructing another pilot; Harry B. Wassell, a second lieutenant in the U.S. Army Air Corps, killed when his plane exploded in midair over an Air Force base in Iceland; and Charles Parkin Wassell, killed in action when his plane was hit by anti-aircraft fire from a Japanese cruiser in the China Sea in the early summer of 1944. A fourth brother, George, also a pilot, was given an honorable discharge after news of the third brother's death. They were sons of Frank Lloyd Wassell, a successful Westport businessman, and his wife, Georgene Parkin Wassell. Before the war, his sons, Harry and Frank, had joined him as management engineering consultants.

The pace of readiness quickened. In July1942, defense preparations in Westport were in high gear. Members of the Westport Defense Training unit, the Westport Motor Corps, the Penguin Girls (from the Penguin Club), and the August Matthias Post American Legion Drum and Bugle Corps joined in a drill, after which regular classes of the unit, including a new Aviation Cadets class, were held. The Westport War Emergency Radio Service Corps began training people for their class radio operator's licenses, an aide, William Vornkahl, Jr., announced. In November, the Red Cross put out a call for more blood donors while, at the same time, reporting that more than 160 local men and women had volunteered to donate one pint of blood each at the organization's mobile Blood Bank.

In August 1942, Gold's Dragoons, that small group of former cavalrymen who had organized in 1932, announced that they were learning tactics in guerrilla warfare, including map-making, map-reading, and hurling deadly "Molotov Cocktails," as part of a strenuous program that would wind up with maneuvers and a sham battle in October. The formula for this deadly weapon was published on page 1 of the *Westporter-Herald* on August 6, 1942. There were few members of the Dragoons involved, however. The balance of the troop had left for active duty.[3]

At the same time, plans were drawn up for the complete evacuation of Westport under the stewardship of Howell Fuller, director of the Department of Public Welfare and chairman of evacuation for the Westport Defense Council. Everyone in town, including children, had to register and receive an identification tag. And in November, the state National Guard Reserve announced that it was forming a guerrilla or commando squad to attack enemy parachute troops who might infiltrate through the "back county." The announcement stated: "Since enemy assaults by small groups of soldiers deployed in strategic places to harass civilians have been common on all the battlefields abroad, the type of warfare the men will be taught is much like the stealthy fighting of the Indians."

In October 1942, First Selectman Albert T. Scully announced that the State Highway Commission would remove the abandoned trolley tracks in Westport in a drive to salvage scrap steel. The idea had been suggested two months earlier by the *Town Crier* newspaper. Officials estimated that the drive would net 135 tons of metal as the town's contribution to the salvage drive. Adding to the patriotic spirit, Fourth Congressional District candidate Clare Boothe Luce told a rally of Republicans in Westport in October that, if elected, she would let the public know what was going on and would vote consistently for any measures that would help the war effort. "I don't give a hang about the election," she said. "I care only about the next generation. I am a good reporter and I will get the facts for you and will have no need to distort them for political purposes," pledged the wife of Henry Luce, publisher of *Time* and *Life* magazines. Among those present were State Senator Herbert E. Baldwin, Probate Judge and Republican Town Committee Chairman Austin Wakeman, Richard R. Hohaus, chairman of the Green's Farms Republican Club, and Florence Renzulli, chairman of the Republican Women's Club. Luce would be elected to the 78th and 79th Congress from 1943 to 1947, the first woman in Connecticut elected to

Congress. Before her death in 1987, she would become ambassador to Italy, author, and a world statesman.[4]

In this same month, news reached Westport of the death of Westporter Byron Darnton, a *New York Times* war correspondent who was covering the war in New Guinea. The veteran newspaperman had worked for the Associated Press before joining the *Times* in 1934, where he was credited with establishing the *Review of the Week* section of the Sunday edition. He was one of 14 correspondents who had left with a big convoy for Australia in February 1942.

Change became a way of life after Pearl Harbor. Even the *Westporter-Herald* changed hands. In June 1943 Willis S. Jones,[5] who had taken over the paper upon the death of his father, John S. Jones, in 1906, sold the paper to two outsiders, John M. Peterson of Watertown, Connecticut, and L. Parker Likely of New York City, thus marking the end of an era.[6] Just one year later, S. Turner Blanchard of Norwalk, an attorney, a former newspaperman and holder of a master's degree from Columbia University's Graduate School of Journalism, purchased the paper from Likely. Under his leadership, circulation grew from 800 to 4,000 in 1955 when it was sold and merged with the *Town Crier*.

By February 1943, Westport's list of war dead reached 29, and another 14 were missing in action. Surely no one in Westport worried more about casualties than Mrs. Lucy Cuseo, an independent, strong-minded mother of 13 children, whose eight sons had all enlisted. The war claimed just one son, James V. Cuseo, and fortunately she never lived to know about it: She died one week after her eighth son went off to war. The headline in the *Town Crier* announcing news of her death on July 24, 1943, was: "BROKEN HEART ENDS LIFE OF MRS. CUSEO, WHO HAD SEVEN SONS IN UNIFORM." The account of her death read: "The medical examiner recorded her death as due to a heart attack, but her other children in Westport refuse to believe that. They are convinced the load she carried grew to be too much." The 55-year-old mother was given a funeral with military honors, with members of the American Legion, in full uniform, acting as pallbearers. The *Crier's* story included this unusual passage: "When her last son was called to service, she told a representative of this newspaper that she was afraid. She had never told her own family that. And when she talked to a stranger, she could not keep the telling tremolo from her voice. She was sad — the sign of the break that finally stifled that faithful heart."

Lucy Cuseo had been born in a little village about 10 miles from Rome. There she met and married her husband, James. They arrived in New York in 1905, penniless but with the same hopes and aspirations of millions

Broken Heart Ends Life Of Mrs. Cuseo, Who Had Seven Sons In Uniform

HUNT IS STILL ON FOR SPOTTERS WHO WILL DO TWO HOURS

Legion and Police Will Act As Escorts At Saturday Funeral.

OVERCOME: The headline in the July 24, 1943 Town Crier *says it all. Lucy Cuseo died just after her eighth son went off to war — the most one family contributed in the entire nation. Altogether, some 19 men and women from the Cuseo family served in World War II.*

WESTPORT PUBLIC LIBRARY

GROWN UP: Top row, in 1940s: Nicholas, Frank, Anthony, William, Joseph, Michael. Middle row: Angelo, father James; mother, Lucia, Albert; bottom row: Charles, Robert, James, George. Not in picture: Mildred.

NANCY CUSEO PHOTO

DOWN ON THE FARM: The Cuseo family as children in 1923 working on the family grape farm. From left, mother Lucy Cuseo, holding baby James; Michael, Joseph, Mildred, William, Anthony, Nicholas, Frank, Albert, Angelo, George. At right, father James Vincent Cuseo, Sr., under grape arbor.

NANCY CUSEO PHOTO

of other immigrants who had come to America. After living in New York for a while, during which time James worked as a shoemaker, they moved to the "country," because one of their sons was sickly and needed fresh air. In Westport they bought a farm and raised grapes. They lost the farm during the Depression, however, and James left for the West Coast in search of employment, leaving her to raise the family. "She kept the family together," says one of her sons, Joseph Cuseo, Jr. who, with his wife, Nancy, has kept the family history. Her first-born, Michael Cuseo, had been a popular constable and policeman in town. Known as the "Terror of the Post Road," he once arrested a dozen speeders in one day, presenting each of them with a ticket. The speed limit on the local thoroughfares was 35 miles an hour, and he allowed little room for error.

The Cuseos' contribution to World War II would later receive a great deal of recognition. In 1954, the *New York Journal American* sponsored a contest in conjunction with the Veterans' Association in Washington for anyone in the nation to match a family they had found whose six sons had gone off to war. They asked for any family that had as many or more sons in the war to come forward. The Westport *Town Crier* informed the *Journal American* of the Cuseo family's eight sons, and their story was published in the *Journal American*. With the advantage of hindsight today, the Cuseo

212

family's contribution to America's wars is nothing short of remarkable.[7] Overall, the Cuseos and their immediate relatives have had 19 men and two women serve their country in uniform.

"TERROR OF THE POST ROAD": This was the nick-name for Police Officer Michael Cuseo, a motorcycle cop in town. He once arrest-ed 12 speeders in one day. He was Lucy Cuseo's youngest son.
NANCY CUSEO PHOTO

Asked to comment about his family's contribution to Westport, Joseph Cuseo, Jr., who works as a heavy- duty truck mechanic in Milford, says: "Our family was into everything. There wasn't a time when there wasn't a Cuseo mentioned somewhere. I don't care what happened in Westport, there was a Cuseo either on it, in it or doing it." He remembers his grandparents, James and Lucy Cuseo, fondly. His uncle, Nick Restaino, ran the Penguin Inn, which he describes as a place "where famous people from New York came to drink booze during Prohibition." As for the Italian community in Westport, Cuseo says: "They did a lot. I don't think there is enough emphasis on what Italian people did in this community. When the Thruway came in it cut Saugatuck in half. Saugatuck was a community in itself. You went down to Saugatuck and it was like going to another country. People standing around on their porches speaking Italian. My grandfather James was a farmer and a shoemaker. At one time all of the Cuseos lived in Westport with their offspring. Today there isn't much left of us except what we have in photographs." Nancy Cuseo adds: "The Cuseos had the first fleet of school buses. They had landscaping, garage and then gasoline and truck and car repairs. They were firemen, policemen, school bus drivers and janitors. I am in awe of the family, into which I married," she says with a smile. "I come from a large family, too. The Christoforos of North Haven. My Dad raised 15 of us. So I know something about large families." [8]

The war's presence was felt by many families as the months and years passed. In mid-1943, the federal government, in desperate need of apartments for war workers, leased Nick Restaino's once-glamorous Penguin Inn on Hillspoint Road for seven years, obviously thinking the war would go on for some time. Selling war bonds became a high priority in every town in America. In Westport, this activity made national news in 1943. Every newspaper in the country reported that Westport, Connecticut, had held an unusual event at its Fine Arts Theatre to raise money for war bonds. It was national news because of the star-studded cast involved in the event, as well as Westport's reputation for glitz and glamour. The

Westporter-Herald published a story headlined: "RALLY HERE IS DESCRIBED FOR NATION TO READ." The paper published a press release on September 24, 1943 that was sent out nationwide by the U.S. Treasury Department, announcing that for the duration of the "Third War Loan" campaign, Westport, Connecticut would be the "vacation capital of Broadway" with a celebrity night scheduled at the Fine Arts Theatre. The event brought war bond pledges with an auction of rare first editions, original art works, steaks, a goat, and the voice of James Melton. The most piquant of various items disposed of was a copy of the much-discussed book of inside revelations, *Under Cover*, which had topped the best-seller list. Clifton Fadiman, noted literary reviewer who presided, said the author of the book, who had used the pen name of John Roy Carlson, signed his real name on the flyleaf of the copy to be auctioned. This made the bidding brisk and the volume finally went for $5,000 to Aaron Rabinowitz. He left without letting anyone else in on this deep secret. He also bought a portrait of himself, painted by Karl Anderson.

Books of another kind had made the news earlier in 1943 when Henrietta Cholmeley-Jones, chairman of the 1943 Victory Book Campaign, called for Westport residents to collect books for men in the service. The campaign ended successfully with 4,686 books contributed by the townspeople. The town's well-known artists capitalized on their own fame to raise money for war bonds by selling $32,000 worth of paintings, which were hung inside the Fine Arts Theatre at a bond rally. They also staged an "Art Attack on the Axis" in the Public Library, featuring a large illustration by Westport Second Selectman Harold Von Schmidt published in the summer of 1938 in the *Saturday Evening Post* with a story about the Javanese in Bali. The exhibit raised $151,000, far exceeding the goal of $35,000. In the first months of 1943, 3,179 individual purchases of bonds were made. Westport raised $1,010,465 — exceeding its quota by $356,465. To recognize the Westporters who offered their time and money to the war effort, the *Town Crier* published a "Citizens' Honor Roll – Westport at War." Henrietta Cholmeley-Jones had two sons who served in World War II. Edward S., a captain in the field artillery in the European theatre, had combat experience with the 9th Division in the Huertgen Forest and then in the Battle of the Bulge. He received both the Silver Star and the Bronze Star medals for bravery under fire. His brother, Richard G. Cholmeley-Jones, 2d, then a Westport resident, served as a sergeant in the South Pacific. In January 1945, in the Lingayen Gulf invasion of Luzon, he was a chief radio operator with the XIV Artillery, 6th Army.

Part of the change for the better in Westport during the war was the town's open door practice towards anyone who wanted to move here. While other towns on Connecticut's Gold Coast in the 1940s maintained an unwritten wall of de facto discrimination, Westport was far more willing to accept all newcomers, including Jews. In the mid-1930s, Westport — like so many other towns in Fairfield County — was not open to minorities, although there were a number of well-known Jewish celebrities who lived here. In that era there was one summer-gathering place where Jewish families came to enjoy summertime amenities. It was known as the Stony Brook Association, located on Easton Road. Leo Nevas, a highly respected Westport attorney who was born and brought up in Norwalk and moved to Westport in 1936, recalls that Westport was a "restricted" community until the artists and writers from New York began to move in. Nevas moved to Westport in 1936, a time when the Jewish families were few in town — notably the Greenbergs, who owned a department store on Main Street; the Shilepsky family, who ran a garage on the corner of Main and Canal streets; and real estate developer and philanthropist Aaron Rabinowitz, a Russian-born immigrant who came to America with his parents in 1884, grew up on the Lower East Side, and lived in Westport for 43 years until he died in 1973. Members of all of these families (including Aaron Rabinowitz's granddaughter, Ann Sheffer) are active in the community today.

Nevas is quick to point out that the anti-Semitism in Westport was not overt. Prejudice was shown not by the established Westport families but largely by the new Westporters who had left New York in part to get away from the Jews, he says. The Real Estate Board's word-of-mouth policy was not to rent or sell to Jews or blacks. Things began to change, Nevas states, during the war when several brokers decided to open up a real estate office. Instead of joining the Westport Real Estate Board, they formed their own Westport Real Estate Associates and they were wide open. Nevas directed a lot of people to them. At this point, Jews started moving into town. The Real Estate Board, feeling the pressure of the times and aware that this competing group was going to abrogate the unspoken rule against Jews, merged with the Associates in the late 1940s. "That," says Nevas, "was when the community really began to open up." At the outset of 2000, about 15 to 20 percent of Westport home owners are Jewish,[9] according to estimates from leading Jewish spokesmen in the community.

Julia Bradley, a retired real estate broker here who spent 50 years in the business, also remembers that there were very few Jewish families in town until after the war. She too agrees that the Real Estate Board was large-

ly responsible for keeping them out. Ms. Bradley, who was born in Long Branch, New Jersey, came to nearby Easton in the 1930s with her family. "One day I stopped in Westport and asked a man at the stationery store if he had cards to celebrate the Jewish holidays. I wanted to send one to a friend in New York. He said, 'Who would I sell them to?'"[10]

Once the Jewish families became residents, they began to think of the lack of opportunity for a religious education for their children. And when occasional incidents of anti-Semitism took place, the need for Jewish union and identity was made even more acute. In addition to forming the Birchwood Country Club in 1946, families in the Stamford, Westport, and Fairfield area met in the spring of 1948 and began laying the groundwork for a Reform Jewish congregation. Within a year, 30 families went to services in Norwalk. By 1954 there were 100 children in religious school, and, in May 1959, the new Temple Israel building was dedicated, with Connecticut Governor Abraham Ribicoff as the main speaker and the guest of Westport Rabbi Byron T. Rubenstein. In 1982, Rabbi Rubenstein retired and Robert J. Orkand became the new spiritual leader. Those who sought an Orthodox house of worship went to Beth Israel Synagogue in Norwalk, a temple that had formally been incorporated in 1899. That synagogue still serves the communities of Westport, Norwalk, Weston, and Wilton. In 1999, under the leadership of Rabbi Joshua Hecht, it celebrated its 100th anniversary. The Conservative Synagogue was founded in 1987 by a handful of families, serving lower Fairfield County, and it draws members not only from Westport but also from nearby towns. It is under the leadership of Rabbi Gabriel Mazer. The synagogue, after some controversy as to where it should be located, opened a new facility on Hillspoint Road in Westport in 1998.

While the defense effort commanded the largest share of public interest, life went on. It was in the war years that the idea of a public recreation center was first debated seriously. Two of the town's outstanding leaders, Harry R. Sherwood and Leo Nevas, in a magnanimous gesture, offered to sell the taxpayers the beautiful 80-acre stretch of land on the Saugatuck River (now known as Birchwood Country Club) for what they had paid for it — $78,000. Said an editorial in the *Town Crier* in 1943: "Never again will there be such an opportunity, for never again will such land be available."[11] First Selectman Al Scully and businessman Herman Steinkraus, then chairman of the Board of Finance, were given six months to weigh the offer. Finally, Scully and Steinkraus turned it down because, they said, the town needed to limit its expenditures during a time of war.

In 1945-46, Sherwood wanted to rezone the property for housing, business, and roads. Then, several people went to Nevas, including businessman Nat Greenberg, and talked about starting a nonsectarian country club. They formed a committee and talked to people in town about joining it. There was not much interest. So they formed it as a Jewish club, even though it had a few non-Jews. The Birchwood Country Club bought the property for the same $78,000 in 1946.

The local war effort continued, with drives and fairs being held almost weekly. On April 24, 1944, at Ipswich, Massachusetts, Norma Edna Boos, a representative of Westport school children, who raised $36,000 in war bonds to build a Navy landing craft, christened *The Westport*. The craft wound up in New Guinea. The idea of buying a landing barge originated with Westporter John Cecil Holm, who suggested that in this way the school children could assist in the rescue of children of other countries. The War Finance Board wanted the event publicized to inspire other school systems around the country to do the same.

Meanwhile, the ongoing drive to buy savings bonds had gone so well in Westport that by mid-1944, following the D-Day landing on the beaches of Normandy, Leo Nevas, chairman of the bond drive, announced that all E Bonds purchased through the Westport Bank and Trust Company through June 14 would be dated June 6, 1944, the day of the invasion. Following that, the town held a star-studded event in July to raise enough money by selling bonds to build a B-29 Super-Fortress, as the local paper described it, "of the type that darkened Japanese skies early this month."[12] Those who purchased $25 bonds comprised a throng of 3,000 people who came to see and hear noted writers and stars of stage, screen, and radio such as Clifton Fadiman of "Information Please," Mary Margaret McBride, Alexander Kipnis, Richard Rodgers and Oscar Hammerstein II, Franklin P. Adams, singing with Sigmund Spaeth at the piano; "Colonel Stoopnagle," Eddie

WORLD WAR II FLYING ACE: Lt. (j.g.) Daniel B. Driscoll downed five Japanese Zeroes flying an American "Hell-Cat" in a fighter group that shot down 148 Japanese planes in the air and sank 48,000 tons of enemy shipping. Driscoll received the Distinguished Flying Cross, the only officer from Westport to be so honored, as well as the Air Medal and the Gold Star. Driscoll was the son of Mr. and Mrs. Daniel J. Driscoll, of Westport. After the war, he returned to Westport to serve on the Board of Selectmen and with the town's Housing Authority. He is retired in Maine.
DRISCOLL FAMILY PHOTO

Mayehoff, Joan Brooks, Zero Mostel, and John LaTouche, author of "Ballad for Americans." The event raised more than enough money to pay for an airplane. It was the most successful of a series of seven bond drives in Westport, which netted a total of $7.5 million.

Westport had its war heroes. One, Lieutenant (j.g.) Daniel B. Driscoll, downed five Japanese Zeroes flying an American "Hell-Cat" in a fighter group that downed 148 Japanese planes in the air and sank 48,000 tons of enemy shipping. Driscoll received the Distinguished Flying Cross, the only officer from Westport to be so honored, as well as the Air Medal and the Gold Star. Driscoll was a Naval aviation cadet, son of Mr. and Mrs. Daniel J. Driscoll, of Main Street. The Driscolls' other two sons also served in the military, Robert

Driscoll, of Westport, was an officer in the Corps of Engineers in Korea, and Edward Driscoll, of Novato, California, was a radar officer in the Air Force in the 1950s. Their sister, Ruth Warner, was married to the late Stanley Warner, an Air Force sergeant during World War II. When Daniel Driscoll came home on leave in November 1944, he had just turned 24. A modest, soft-spoken young man, he told a local reporter on November 22, 1944 when asked about the war in the Pacific: "We don't know how long it's going to take. We know there's a job to be done and we mean to get it over as quickly as possible."

Another World War II flyer, who moved to Long Lots Road in Westport in 1944, was Charles H. Lindbergh and his wife, author and writer Anne Morrow

THE LINDBERGHS: Charles and Anne Morrow Lindbergh just before their 1931 flight to Tokyo, Japan by way of the northernmost reaches of the Pacific in a land plane modified into a seaplane. Then they flew on to China and met with Generalissimo Chiang Kai-shek, who awarded them the National Medal for being the first aviators to fly from the New World to China.
CHARLES A. AND ANN MORRROW LINDBERGH FOUNDATION PHOTO

Lindbergh. The Lindberghs had been living in Bloomfield, New Jersey, but, as a result of his consulting work in the South Pacific in connection with United Aircraft's fighter program, Lindbergh wrote his wife that when he returned, "there is nothing I would rather do than spend a few months studying and writing in a beautiful quiet place." According to a recent published account of the life of Charles Lindbergh, Anne Morrow Lindbergh "found such a place in Westport, Connecticut.... Anne felt 'it looks rather like us — settled down among trees and a field and a brook, with good schools, swimming, and boats nearby."[13] In her diary of October 8, 1944, she wrote: "Two more months gone by without writing....August spent in moving, packing, good-byes, finding a new home. September: a week in Maine and three in Englewood, New Jersey, New York and Westport, moving, shopping, collecting furniture, unpacking, looking at schools, for cooks. Feverishly.... I must let my soul catch up with me. And that I can only do by long, quiet hours in the trailer writing." Elsewhere in her diaries, which appear in her book, *War Within and Without*,[14] she writes: "I think this community is going to be good for the children." Lindbergh, who had gained worldwide attention by flying the monoplane, *Spirit of St. Louis*, from New York to Paris non-stop in 1927 in 33.5 hours, was serving in the South Pacific with the Air Force. He flew 50 missions against the enemy. The Lindberghs lived in Westport until 1946.

The stories of those Westport men who served in World War II are legion. Raymond J. Orr, a signalman 2/C, may have been the first Westporter to enter the service before war actually broke out. He joined the U.S. Navy in August 1940, "because I had an appetite for adventure." Assigned to the destroyer, *U.S.S. Bagley*, as a first class seaman, he wound up in Pearl Harbor in December 1941. "One morning," he recalls, "I was on the deck about 8 A.M. walking to the washroom to shave when I saw a plane coming down towards us. It was so close I could see the pilot with his goggles covering his face. I waved to him because I thought it was the Army fliers practicing in a drill." Seconds later, he heard an explosion and saw smoke rising near the battleship *Oklahoma*, which was berthed parallel to his ship about 1,000 yards away. "From my position I couldn't see the 'red meatball' markings [Rising Sun] on the plane. But then another came and all Hell broke loose. The *Oklahoma* took a torpedo from the plane and capsized almost immediately, trapping 450 of its crew. I was stunned. It was a complete surprise. General Quarters were sounded on the bridge. It was devastating. I was told later that one torpedo had been aimed at our ship but had missed it and it tore

into a piling near us. We were the second ship out of the harbor. We moved as quickly as we could and escaped being sunk. It's an experience I will never forget," says the 77-year-old veteran who is a retired business executive and has lived in Westport for the past 35 years.[15]

Another Westporter, Henry (Bob) Loomis, was a gun sergeant with Company D of the 87th Chemical Mortar Battalion, the heavy weapons platoon of the infantry. On D-Day, June 6, 1944, Loomis was on the *H.M.S. Gauntlet*, a British transport ship that landed on Utah Beach. "The artillery was zeroing in on the ships around us. Some of the forces were getting direct hits. The combat engineers had gone in ahead of us to blow up the fortifications that were under water. When we got to the beach, it was clear, but there were dead Americans everywhere. It was the first time we had become involved in combat. We had been in training, but when you start doing it, it is a different story. I remember being shot at. I hid behind a German tank. Whenever I would come out again, I would get shot at again. It was a sorry sight. The worst memory I have was the sight of the 82nd Airborne Division, which came in on parachutes and gliders. There were dead paratroopers everywhere. They were all young kids. It was a terrible, terrible sight." Loomis, whose father was American and mother French, wound up in the town of Marigny, some 25 miles from Utah Beach. The Germans had occupied it so the Americans shelled it. "We left that town in pretty bad shape," he said.[16]

On June 23, 1944 Clay Chalfant, a heavy-machine gunner with the 3rd Armored Division moved through Marigny and encircled the Germans in the "Falaise Pocket." "Like all the other guys, I was scared stiff. We soon got over that. We had a job to do. The officer said, 'You go this way.' So we went that way. You do what you're told. Then, we moved into our positions. We were the anti-aircraft protection to the field artillery guys. Wherever they went, we went. Wherever the field artillery moved we moved. We gave them protection. They called us the 'Anti-Anything Battalion.' I was fortunate to be with the field artillery; it was the infantry that took the main brunt of the war." He and his men fought their way to Marigny and then on to Belgium. On the way, his company captured a whole division of Germans. "How the Hell we did it, I don't know."[17] Marigny was only one of many towns devastated by both the Germans and the Americans. Following the war, Charlotte MacClear, the head of the French Department at Staples High School, sparked a successful campaign to officially adopt Marigny and assist in its recovery. Westporters sent clothes and money and raised funds with sales of toys and buckets with designs painted by Westport artists, and Christmas gifts. Some 3,000 Americans are buried in the American Military Cemetery in Marigny. In order to express their gratitude, Marigny created the "Westport School Canteen" and named the town's largest square "Place Westport."[18] The French village has remained on the minds of Westporters for the past half century. On June 12, 1994, Westport was once again represented on French soil in Marigny. As part of the fiftieth anniversary of the invasion of Normandy, Marigny invited three Westport students from Bedford Middle School and Coleytown Middle School and two Westport veterans to visit the village and stay in the homes of residents. They rode down a street called Westport Square and came across roadside businesses that included the Westport Pharmacy and the Westport Gift Shop. The veterans invited were the aforementioned Loomis and Chalfant, both of whom took part in the battle that freed Marigny from the Germans.[19]

Anticipating peace in 1945, Walter H. Crager, a World War I veteran, was named director of the Westport Service Men's Center, which provided aid for enlisted men and women from Westport as they returned to civilian life. Within the next six months, a steady increase in returning servicemen stretched the resources of the Center, which was directed by Mrs. Alice B. Atwood. A drive to raise $26,000 to keep the Center going had fallen short. Housing, insurance, and jobs were the top priorities of the veterans.

Westport was beginning to enjoy one of the greatest real estate booms in its history. Brokers were mobbed with requests for homes, and there was a long waiting list. The demand far exceeded the supply, especially for the popular $10,000 homes — or the equivalent of $92,500 in the year 2000. Housing was needed for employees of the Westport War Products Company, where women assembled goggles for all branches of the armed services. The company, owned by Earl Zinn, had manufactured and shipped more than one million goggles to troops overseas. Zinn, a professor at Yale University, had started the assembly plant because his wife, in the course of her Red Cross work, had met many women who were anxious to contribute something tangible to the war effort. Westporter Esther Shirey recalls working at the company in the 1940s. "My husband, Richard, was in the Navy in the Pacific," she said, "so I wanted to do something to help the war effort. I worked part-time for $17 a week and I took care of our six-year-old daughter, Lee. It was a great experience."[20] In point of fact, there were not very many industrial companies in existence in largely residential Westport during the war. Aside from Hermann Seybold's plant, which produced a metal substitute for steel, and Zinn's goggle manufacturing plant, there was only the Wassell Organization of Westport, founded by F. Lloyd Wassell who invented a visual control system that was installed in over 4,000 war factories to assist those plants in increasing their productivity. The device was manufactured at an old papermill, once a cow pasture on Horace Staples' farm.

Nonetheless, the townspeople spent an enormous amount of money, energy, and time in ways other than assembly-line jobs manufacturing war-related products. They saved paper, glass, rubber, silk stockings to make gunpowder bags, shovels and old radiators that were made into guns, and steel; they bought war bonds; they joined any number of local agencies that were providing instructions in how to cope with an air raid; and, perhaps most important, they sent clothing, food, and letters — many thousands of letters — to Westport men and women overseas. And they heeded the gas-rationing program that had been in effect since the war started, with only those vehicles with a "C" rating qualified for defense-industry gasoline exemptions. The other two categories were "A" for the average citizen and "B" for those who were involved part-time in defense-related businesses. In Westport, law enforcement officers took the driving stickers very seriously. In one incident, a woman who violated the Office of Price Administration (OPA) campaign against pleasure driving when she drove her two children and three youngsters from her neighborhood to Compo Beach was punished by losing all of her "A" coupons. Residents were expected to take buses to the beach, rather than use their cars. The problem was there were neither buses nor gasoline to accommodate all those who wanted to go to the beach on weekends. This became a problem for Westporters on the hot and hazy summer weekends when they normally relaxed at the beach. It was a burden that most townspeople grudgingly assumed. Rationing coupons were also issued for meat, butter, sugar, and various other food items. The rationing was done under the supervision of the Westport Rationing Board, which was staffed by community volunteer workers. Ration books with sheets of perforated stamps organized into various categories, such as gas, sugar, coffee, and meat, were allotted to individual citizens who were required to register with the local board.[21]

An example of how wartime rationing affected small things in everyday life was this small article in the June 18, 1944, *Westporter-Herald*: "WANT A BOARDER? The ladies [from the Woman's Club] who are running the Yankee Doodle Fair are looking for a big-hearted citizen who could put up some of the attractive workers at the big show over night to conserve gasoline and, thereby, the services of the fair workers who live miles from Jesup Green.... It is understood that all ladies so accommodated will bring their own coffee for breakfast." Coffee was one of the items rationed during the war. Food rationing led to the creation of Victory Gardens of homegrown vegetables in Westport and elsewhere. In addition, the Woman's Club was busy with "Bundles for America," a program later known as Clothing Relief Committee, which collected clothes for servicemen and needy families. In addition, an ad hoc welcoming committee was on hand to greet every returning soldier who came home on leave. There was a bedrock spirit and determination among the townspeople that although they could not do anything themselves about the outcome of the war, they certainly could make those who were serving from Westport aware of their gratitude. Even the youth got involved, with young boys helping out wherever they could and girls babysitting for parents who were both out working.

Meanwhile, Westporters went about their business preserving and protecting their town not only from the possibility of air raids and foreign invasion, but from the addition of liquor stores. In April 1944, a hearing was held in Town Hall by the State Liquor Control Commission on an application from Dorain's Drug Store for a liquor permit. The objections were vociferous — everyone from the Child Welfare Council to the Westport Woman's Club to the Reverend Frederick L.C. Lorentzen, president of the Ministers' Association, opposed the application. Even the Package Store Association, a statewide group, said there were more package stores per capita in Westport than in 90 percent of the towns in Connecticut. Dorain's did not get its license to sell liquor.

By 1945, Americans felt a rising sense of optimism that the United States would prevail. Then came an enormous blow: Like millions of people around the world, Westporters were shocked to learn of the death of Franklin Delano Roosevelt on April 12, 1945. Stores were closed, and community residents gathered on Jesup Green on April 18 to participate in a short memorial service. They sang "America," "The Battle Hymn of the Republic," and "Abide with Me," and war veterans fired a military salute before taps were sounded. In the public schools, young people who had known only one president met around the flagpole at each school to pay tribute to him. And, of course, all of the churches in town paid homage.

Just two short months after Roosevelt's death, the day of victory came — V-E Day, May 8, 1945. Westporters received momentous and welcome news of Germany's official surrender. President Truman delivered a radio message, and a formal proclamation of the enemy's collapse in Europe. Diverse signs of emotion were displayed, one of thankfulness and relief that bloodshed on that battle front had ended, the other sadness that so many brave men had fallen and the war in the Far East was still to be won. The fire siren proclaimed victory as soon as the president began to talk and many local church bells rang out triumphantly. But on the whole, Westport was unusually quiet throughout the day of gratitude and solemn determination to finish the war against Japan. Schools and the town offices and places of business were all closed. Later that month, the townspeople gathered on Memorial Day to pay tribute to its war dead — which numbered 30 at that time — and to their fallen president.

Looking back on V-E Day, many Westport veterans recall that in comparison to the wild, emotional celebration at Times Square in New York, the residents of Westport took it in stride. They were obviously happy, but they knew that the war was far from over. As the *Westport Town Crier* reported on May 11, 1945: "There were more tears than celebration....There was no great jubilation.... Some who might have wanted to make a carnival time of the surrender were curbed by those whose solemn faces reflected deep thoughts."

Several World War II veterans from Westport remembered V-E Day. Harold Ayers was a bombardier in a B-17 that flew missions over Vienna, the Rhineland, the North Appenines, Italy, and the Balkans. His plane was hit by anti-aircraft fire over Austria, and he remained semi-conscious for 34 days in an Army hospital in Italy. "I saw soldiers coming in from the Battle of the Bulge all shot up. I saw the real part of the war. It was terrible." Robert MacLachlan was an artillery officer in France and later served in the Indian Army fighting in the Middle East and Burma. (Some British officers were drafted after serving in Europe to help lead the Indian Army.) MacLachlan commanded a mortar battery a few miles north of Rangoon when V-E Day was declared. "We heard it on the radio, but the news meant nothing to us. There remained a strong Japanese force to be driven out of Burma and then Malaysia. We listened with indifference to the celebrations in Europe." Jim Feeney was a field artillery aerial observer in France and Germany, directing fire on enemy targets. He helped liberate the concentration camp at Dachau. He was flying over Munich, dodging enemy fire, when he heard word of the official German surrender. "We were as scared as Hell most of the time. We landed on a road next to the Dachau concentration camp and what I saw made me so sick. What has been printed about concentration camps cannot convey the horror of what went on."[22]

Just three short months after V-E Day, the war against Japan was also over. In anticipation of an announcement about the war's end, Police Chief John Dolan had encouraged his men to be "as lenient as possible, for this should be a real celebration." First Selectman Albert Scully announced that local churches would be open and that special ceremonies would be held in town, depending on what day the news arrived. With the dropping of the atomic bombs on Hiroshima, the Japanese surrendered unconditionally on August 14, 1945. On August 16, at about 7:30 P.M., word finally came via a radio broadcast from President Harry S Truman. Westporters took to the streets — some bewildered by the news, others jubilant over the victory. In restaurants, people started shaking hands; some walked around hugging total strangers. In one eating place, a woman bowed her head and made the sign of the cross as she murmured a prayer. "Times Square, let's go to New York," she said through tears of happiness.[23]

At the intersection of Main and State streets, a crowd gathered and began to cheer. Homemade confetti of newspapers showered the paraders who snake-danced through the streets, as firecrackers and skyrockets and Roman candles provided a circus-like atmosphere. Men in uniform were kissed and patted on the back (55 members of the armed forces were home on furlough when news of the war's end came), and a town fire engine swung around the square "time after time laden with ecstatic youngsters." Cow bells, Halloween noisemakers and other impromptu devices added to the general excitement. Businesses quickly closed, and although no liquor was being sold, many people brought their own bottles and toasted the moment. Still others turned first to their churches. Christ and Holy Trinity Church nearby was packed with its own parishioners as well as many strangers who simply wanted to pray. The full choir sang the "Hallelujah Chorus" during a special service, and nearby at the Saugatuck Congregational Church another service was held at 8 P.M. Emmanuel Church in Weston remained open until 11 P.M. for prayer, and special rites of thanksgiving were held at the Church of the Assumption and the Westport Methodist Church, among others. It was a day in Westport — and across the nation — when everyone was happy and thankful.

The cost in terms of human lives in Westport had been enormous. Of the 1,380 Westport men and women in service during the war, 43 had been killed (see Appendix I) or listed as missing in action.[24] The town has made certain they will never be forgotten. In 1999, Edward J. Keehan, 75, a

HONORING THOSE WHO DIED: Edward J. Keehan, a native Westporter, led the fundraising drive for a new World War II Honor Roll monument in front of Town Hall listing 1,380 names on bronze plaques. Inset: Keehan, who served in the Navy, in 1945 at age 20.   ABOVE, THE HOUR PHOTO ABOVE LEFT, COURTESY E. KEEHAN

lifelong Westport resident, was instrumental in raising funds for a new World War II monument listing 1,380 names on bronze plaques representing Westporters who served their country during WWII. It replaced the original Honor Roll, a wooden structure with 600 nameplates on it, which was depicted by artist Stevan Dohanos on the cover of the December 15, 1943 issue of the *Saturday Evening Post*. Keehan served as an Aviation Machinist Mate aboard the *U.S.S. Savannah* from 1942 to 1944 and the *U.S.S. Saint Paul* from 1944 to 1946. He managed to raise nearly $30,000 in private funds, and a number of businessmen in town donated their firms' goods and services.[25]

Many Westport men served in the Pacific. Among them were Jim Andrian, an Army infantry sergeant. He fought in the battles of Guadalcanal and Luzon, and also saw action in the North Solomon Islands and New Guinea. He was wounded by shrapnel while on patrol. "World War II ended with the bombing of Hiroshima and Nagasaki. I say thank God. The friends I left on Luzon [in the Philippines] didn't have to go and invade Japan." Joel Green was an Army technical sergeant who worked as an electrical engineer on the A-bomb project at Los Alamos, New Mexico. He was present at the first nuclear blast on the morning of July 16, 1945, at Alamogordo, where he made subsequent radiation measurements around that area. The blast was part of the secret project. "The A-bomb," he said, "held up any future major wars. There are people who say we shouldn't have dropped it, but I think we did the right thing." Barry McCabe served as a member of a

SHADES OF THE PAST: Westport's original World War II Honor Roll, a wooden structure with 600 nameplates on it, which was depicted by Westport artist Stevan Dohanos on the cover of the December 15, 1943 issue of the Saturday Evening Post.

WESTPORT HISTORICAL SOCIETY

Navy Underwater Demolitions Team known as "frogmen." Even before the Japanese had formally surrendered, he was a member of a team that went into Japan to make sure it was safe for other units to land. "Were we wrong to use the atomic bomb? No one is ever going to prove it was right or wrong. Innocent civilians were killed, but that's war. I can testify that the island [Japan] was dotted with deep caves, with rails, and suicide boats, which they [the Japanese] would have been ready to use if we had invaded."[26]

Paul Kowalsky was drafted into the Army, but just before he was to report, he joined the Sea Bees and wound up in a construction battalion. At Guadalcanal, he said, "I watched a lot of ships get bombed to Hell and sunk right in the canal. I came down with malaria so many times, they couldn't control it," he recalls. "When we came back to Westport, we went to work. We just forgot about the war. We're all the same now. Nobody walks around with a big chest." John Humphrey, an Army Air Corps sergeant stationed on Tarawa in the Gilbert Islands after it was taken by U.S. Forces, served as a weatherman. "At that time — and my thoughts haven't changed that much — there was great relief that the war was over, that it ended successfully...The A-bomb cut the war short by a great amount. I've always been overwhelmed at the importance of World War II, having visited England and Japan. I wonder how the world would be if we had lost that war. Living in freedom, peace, and prosperity was made possible by those veterans."[27]

Addressing the lingering question of whether or not the United States should have used the A-bomb, Robert R. Hartsig, a retired lieutenant colonel who served three-and-a-half years in the Air Force, and was president of the Westport Veterans Council in 1995, wrote a "Commentary" in the *Westport News*,[28] entitled: "The bomb brought victory," in which he made the case for use of the bombs, but conceded, "As time passed, the dropping of the atom bomb has come to be seen as a crime against humanity, but most U.S. historians agree that Japan was committed to defending its shores to the bitter end...For all those who served in the armed forces during World War II, the decision to bomb Hiroshima and Nagasaki made the U.S. invasion of Japan unnecessary, saved thousands of lives and brought the war to an end." Historians and military men have since estimated that there would have been somewhere between 100,000 to 500,000 casualties, one-fifth of which would have been fatalities.[29]

Following the V-J Day celebration in Westport, Herman W. Steinkraus, of South Compo Road, previously described as a highly decorated World War I veteran and a nationally known industrialist and civic leader, was appointed a member of the Connecticut Labor-Management Advisory Council by Governor Raymond Baldwin. The committee was charged with accelerating the conversion of the state's economy from a wartime to a peacetime footing. Steinkraus, who had received the Distinguished Service Cross from General John J. Pershing for heroism in combat in France in the Argonne Forest, was up to this formidable task. Steinkraus, who would soon be elected president of the U.S. Chamber of Commerce in 1947 and a director of the National Association of Manufacturers in 1948, got down to work and appointed the best talent available to devise a plan for shifting into a peacetime economy. For Westport, the biggest challenges would be finding enough housing to meet the needs of returning servicemen, and the return of women who had worked during the war to their homes as housewives.

Meanwhile, in the fall of 1945 the August Matthias Post 63 of the American Legion, led by Commander Emerson F. Parker, found a way to greet all returning veterans at the railroad station, no matter when they arrived. Giant signs 3-feet wide and 8-feet high painted in red, white, and blue by Ralph Renzulli were installed on both the east and west sides of the station. They read: WELCOME HOME VETERANS, THANKS FOR A JOB WELL DONE. The Board of Selectmen, headed by Albert T. Scully, petitioned the General Assembly to provide housing for veterans and their families. The board also passed a resolution concerning the desperate housing shortage in Westport. The governor responded by urging Scully to relax the local zoning laws so that two or three families could live in single-family homes. With real estate values so high, however, homeowners could not easily make such conversions. Real estate prices that fall exceeded previous figures in the town's history. The average new house in Westport was selling for $10,000, an astronomical amount at the time. Today, the average selling price for a home in Westport is about $750,000.

Assisting in the welcoming of veterans home to Westport, Alice B. Atwood, director of the Westport Servicemen's Center, worked as a one-person clearing house for helping servicemen with family problems such as lack of housing, insurance, and jobs. As the housing shortage became critical in Westport, union workers at first resisted allowing nonunion laborers to work on new housing. When they finally relented, more than 200 Westporters with a variety of skills volunteered to assist with the Westport Housing Project. Everyone pitched in. The Teachers League made sandwiches and coffee for those who worked. This extraordinary cooperation between union members and the public caught the attention of *Collier's* magazine, which published an editorial praising the community spirit

STILL GOING STRONG: Bill Cribari, left, leads the 1999 Memorial Day Parade on the State Street Bridge. MIGGS BURROUGHS PHOTO

SERVING HIS COUNTRY: Westporter Bill Cribari, below center, during World War II in uniform at home on leave, strolls past The Riverside Barbershop in Saugatuck. At left is John Santella, owner of the shop, and father of Lou Santella, who took over the business in 1971. Cribari became a special police officer. The barbershop, which was sold in 1999, was opened in 1927. On right is John Renzulli. LOU SANTELLA PHOTO

shown by labor and the townspeople of Westport. It said, in part: "We're encouraged to hope that this spirit may spread swiftly through the American labor movement from here on."

"Housing was by far the biggest problem for returning vets," recalls Ed See, a veteran and a longtime Westport attorney. When the Army was giving away barracks, See arranged to have them brought here, despite a battle with local zoning officials. "We got the whole community behind us. Everyone pitched in and the barracks were put up on North Compo Road. It was the most satisfying community project I've ever been involved in, and I've seen a lot of them," said See. The barracks on the town-owned land were erected in the summer and fall of 1946. The project drew townwide support with the trade unions waiving their rules about non-union labor to allow any resident who wanted to participate in the construction to do so. See recalls that he got the active support of Westporter John Davis Lodge, who was then running for a seat in Congress, which he won that year. See had moved to Westport in 1941 after receiving his law degree from Yale University. Turned down for combat units because of his poor eyesight, he joined the Counterintelligence Corps instead. "They didn't care if you were blind," he laughed. "We were issued gray flannel suits and told to look for Nazi spies in New York and New Jersey." In March 1943 he was sent to Brisbane, Australia, with the Sixth Army, where he went to Officers Candidate School and was commissioned a second lieutenant. Assigned to General Douglas MacArthur's staff as the U.S. troops surrounded Manila, he became involved in planning the landing on Japan.

For Westport's returning veterans, housing, as See pointed out, was a top priority. One Westport veteran, for example, asked permission to house his family at the town farm on North Compo Road and another reported his father had to sleep temporarily in one of the local firehouses because of lack of space in the family home. First Selectmen Scully and Selectman Clarke Crossman, in the absence of Third Selectman Harold Von Schmidt, adopted a resolution stating that Westport's housing situation "is hourly becoming more acute and desperate."

In January 1947 the Westport Housing Authority announced it would consider selling preassembled housing units costing approximately $4,000. No specific site had been selected yet but it was eventually built near Vani Court. The next month, as postcards arrived at the Westport-Weston Servicemen's Council indicating that there were still 49 veterans in emergency need of housing, the Housing Authority approved temporary housing units for veterans and their families. The housing would be prefabricated Quonset huts, the Authority said, and, as it turned out, cost about $5000 by the time they were built.

For many veterans returning immediately after World War II, readjustment to civilian life was difficult. But their way was eased by the extraordinarily warm welcome from their townspeople. Today, more than half a century later, most would agree with NBC newsman Tom Brokaw's view that the men of this era represented what he called "the greatest generation any society has produced."[30]

NOTES

1. Interview conducted by WHS volunteer writer Sue Kane, 1999. In the fall of 1998, the nursery was purchased by Evan Harding's son, David. Ann Harding, Evan's daughter, is also active in the business.

2. The *Westporter-Herald*, April 9, 1942.

3. The Dragoons would be remembered by a formal military Mess Dinner at the Fairfield County Hunt Club in 1979 under the leadership of Bud Brennan, a former member of the Dragoons, along with Kenneth Powers. Its purpose was to commemorate the pre-war services of the original Gold's Dragoons. It has now become a tradition with the club, having celebrated its 20th year in May 1999.

4. Ralph G. Martin, *Henry and Clare, An Intimate Portrait of the Luces* (New York: Putnam's, 1991), pp. 218-221.

5. Willis Shelton Jones died in November, 1956. He bought the *Westporter-Herald* from his father in 1892 and operated it for 42 years until 1934. After that, he retired in St. Petersburg, Fla.

6. The newspaper, which had been founded in 1868 by John S. Jones, had thrived under the direction of the Jones family for three generations. Louis Jones, one of Willis S. Jones' sons, remained with the paper in a business capacity, as did his son, Robert L. Jones, a great-great grandson of the founder. Another of Willis Jones' sons, Willis H. Jones, Jr., a seaman second class in the U.S. Navy, was killed in an accident at the Naval Air station in Potent, Md.

7. Following is a list of the Cuseos and immediate family relatives who have served in the United States Armed Forces during World War II — CPO Aviation Michael C. Cuseo, Navy; Cpl. William Cuseo, Army; Maj. Francis Cuseo, Army Air Force; Cpl. Angelo Cuseo, Army; Coxswain Petty Officer George Cuseo, Navy; 2/C Fireman James V. Cuseo, Navy; Sgt. Nicholas Cuseo, Army; Pvt. Daniel Robert Cuseo, Army, and, he served in the Merchant Marines first; Korean War — BT2 Joseph Cuseo Jr., Navy; A 2/C Ruth Cuseo, Woman's Air Force (WAF) (brother and sister); Sgt. Anitra Cuseo Spacaratella, Woman's Army Corp; Petty Officer Mike Cuseo, Jr., Navy submarines; Vietnam War —Commander Mike Cuseo, Jr., Navy; Capt. William Cuseo, Jr., Marines; Pfc. Peter Cuseo, Army; Sgt. Park Cuseo, Marines. *Others who served*: ST2 Vincent Cuseo, Navy; Gunnery Sgt. Bruce Spacaratella, Army; Capt. Dana Joseph Spacaratella, Air Force, and he also enlisted in Army; Sgt. Joe Cuseo III, Army, and FC/2 Michael McGuire, Navy.

8. Interviews with the author, October, 1999.

9. Interview with Leo Nevas in his office in Westport, April 9, 1998.

10. Interview with Julia Bradley, July 1999.

11. The *Town Crier*, June 18, 1943.

12. The *Westporter-Herald*, June 22, 1944.

13. A. Scott Berg, *Lindbergh* (New York: Berkley Books, 1999), pp. 456-457.

14. Anne Morrow Lindbergh, *War Within and Without* (New York: Harcourt Brace, Jovanovich, 1980).

15. Interviewed by the author on January 21, 2000.

16. Rita Papazian, the *Westport News*, June 4, 1994.

17. Ibid.

18. The *Westport News*, January 6, 1971. In addition, in 1950, a group of parents established the Westport Canteen and funded the program with yearly membership dues of $3. The program was a success and Lawrence Langner donated his Country Playhouse "Player's Tavern" for the first season. An article about the Canteen appeared in *Woman's Day* magazine that year.

19. Ibid., May 4, 1994.

20. Interviewed by the author, August, 1999.

21. The *Town Crier*, June 18, 1943.

22. Dan Carson, *Westport News*, May 5, 1995.

23. From an account in the *Westporter-Herald*, August 17, 1945.

24. See Appendix I for list of World War II dead. Some 158 men and 12 women had been honorably discharged before the war ended. A brick and bronze monument listing all of the 1,380 men and women from Westport who served in the armed forces between December 7, 1941, and September 2, 1945, the official end of the war, was erected in a special ceremony on November 11, 1998 through the efforts of long-time Westporter Edward Keehan, a World War II veteran, who launched a two-year letter-writing campaign to raise funds to build a monument. Two small memorials made of granite stones with plaques honoring Korean and Vietnam veterans, flank the new World War II memorial. The Vietnam memorial lists six residents who died in battle. The Korean War memorial, which does not list names, is for all veterans who served in that war. In addition the Doughboy statue, originally dedicated to World War I veterans and located on the Post Road, was moved to the Town Common in 1986. A time capsule containing a copy of the October 18, 1987 *Westport News*, *Norwalk Hour*, and the *Bridgeport Post*, together with a color photograph of the Doughboy at its first location, was put on top of the base for anyone in the future who may move it again.

25. Principal benefactors included the Kowalsky Brothers, Paul, Edward, and Joe;

Lawrence Michaels, architect; Linda Zamensky, architectural designer; William L. Gault, L.H. Gault and Son, Inc., masonry materials; Tim Romano of Romano Construction; Joseph Kondub, Colonial Electric, lighting; and Tony and Peter Palmer, Jr. of T. Palmer Landscaping Co. Other Westport nursery and landscape companies that donated their goods and services include Geiger's Garden Center; Izzo Country Gardens; Winding Brook Turf Farm, Westerfield, Conn.; Weston Gardens, Weston, Conn.; Triple Nursery, North Salem, N.Y.; and L.L. Evergreen Nursery, South Norwalk, Conn.

26. The *Westport News*, August 23, 1995

27. The *Westport News*, August 25, 1995.

28. The *Westport News*, August 4, 1995.

29. Historian James MacGregor Burns, *The New York Times*, Sunday Week in Review, August 13, 1945.

30. Tom Brokaw, *The Greatest Generation* (New York: Random House, Inc., 1998), cover.

Poster, p. 205, Yankee Doodle Fair 1944, Westport Public Library.

CHAPTER 14

COMING OF AGE

Democracy is not a spectator sport.

— Westport League of Women Voters' motto

With the advent of a peacetime economy, commuters flocked to Westport in search of the "good life." By the end of World War II, the town was an established center for creative people — artists and advertising and communications professionals — and became the daily destination for other New York business and entertainment moguls. The informal lifestyle of the town together with all the trappings of upper middle class existence — culture, creativity, class, and charm in the town's shops, restaurants and meeting places — and privacy to boot — attracted wave after wave of these newcomers.

The pundits were hailing Westport as a bright spot on the map, and

FRIENDLY MOOD OF MAIN STREET: In the 1950s, downtown Westport was home for Mom and Pop stores, a place where customers and storekeepers recognized one another and where neither an ID nor a credit card was part of a transaction.
WESTPORT NEWS
PHOTO

it was just that. In 1940, the town's population had been a modest 8,258; by 1950, this number had exploded to 11,432 people — a growth of 38 percent. The reasons for this remarkable expansion were not hard to find: the ease of commuting, the natural beauty of the town, the school system, the recreational facilities, its remarkable number of bodies of water — Long Island Sound, ponds, and rivers; colorful Mom and Pop stores, and chic New York-type fashion shops, and, perhaps most significant of all, the variety of backgrounds and professions among the people and the community. Westport, in a phrase, was seen by some people as "Hollywood East."

It was still a small town, however. Harry Audley, a former fire chief and native-born Westporter, remembers: "Local business owners were very much connected to the town. You drove to Main Street, which then had plenty of parallel parking spaces. You went into the local A&P, for example, and got everything off the shelf and then went to the cash register and the store owner called you by your first name. You could just walk out and say, 'Put it on my bill,' and that was it. No credit, no driver's license identification, just a greeting."[1] Another longtime Westporter, A.J. (Red) Izzo, a local businessman, observed: "There was Bill's Smoke Shop, a 5-and-10-cent store, Hartman's Hardware, Colgen's Pharmacy, and more. If you wanted to see the guys, you would drop into any one of those places." [2]

The newcomers were urbane, independent-minded people who delighted, at once, in the town's New England traditions and in the fact it was home to famous artists, writers, radio and television personalities, photographers, theatrical and movie personalities, as well as top executives of some of the *Fortune* 500 companies. Westport housed them all, along with an eclectic mix of old New England Yankee farmers and shopkeepers, and generations-old ethnic working families, all of whom now staked a claim in Westport's unique history. Despite this new diversity, Westport retained its small-town milieu. But that is no longer the case. Audley's wife, Pat, attributes much of the change of atmosphere to the continuous movement of New Yorkers to Westport. "Things have changed," she lamented. "What we're seeing today is a lot of gated homes, stone walls with fences on the top, the enclosure mentality, not the neighborly type. Still, the town has accepted everyone and Westport is still a great place to live." The town, in effect, was made-to-order for many people who wanted to live in a diverse community with people of all backgrounds. The town's Board of Trade, in a promotional brochure in the postwar era, boasted that Westport was "Utopia on the Saugatuck," "Eden on the Saugatuck," and "the ultimate in Suburbia."

Major organizations in town wasted no time in getting back to normal. The postwar period was "a well-ordered one" for the Westport Woman's Club, for example. Mrs. Helen Warnock, whose presidency (1944-1946) spanned the transition period from war to peace, served in the General Assembly of the state legislature for two terms (1945-1949). At this time a new club slogan emerged: "We, the women of this organization, dedicate ourselves to truth, service, and cooperation. We will enter no activity that cannot fulfill this pledge." The club's colors were established as blue and white, and the lilac became the club flower. In 1949, the Woman's Town Improvement Association received a Certificate of Special Achievement from the National Council of State Garden Clubs. From 1957 to 1959, "a tiny breach was made temporarily in the fortress walls," in the words of the club's history, when about 12 men were officially listed as "associate members."

Probably the club's most important project during this era was the acquisition of a new clubhouse. In 1944, the Bedford Fund purchased the three-story, 11-room house at 87 Imperial Avenue, a three-story frame structure constructed in 1881 as a headquarters for the Westport Woman's Club. In 1950, the Sunday school meeting house of the Saugatuck Congregational Church on East State Street was acquired through the Bedford Fund and was moved in two sections to Imperial Avenue where it was reassembled as an auditorium. The Woman's Club sponsored the Westport Players dramas, revived in 1945 as the Westport Theatre Guild. The Club marked its golden anniversary in 1957, the same year in which it received national recognition with an award from *McCall's* magazine for "general excellent service to the community." The Westport *Town Crier & Herald* published a special inset supplement: "Westport's Helping Hands," extolling the Club's history and

CONTRIBUTING COUPLE: Bob and Connie Anstett were both active in community life from the moment they arrived in Westport in 1948. He served as Probate Judge from 1971 to 1986. Here they are shown at a ceremony applauding Anstett's successor, Earl Capuano, in 1987.

WESTPORT NEWS PHOTO

its good deeds, such as fighting for better railroad parking and a town dump, "greening" the Post Road, and launching a food closet at the Clubhouse for distribution to local needy families. In 1976, the Club placed its history and the 1976 membership list in a time capsule to be opened in the year 2076. In the past 15 years, the Club has substantially increased the number of scholarship grants to deserving students, and it has attracted a large number of professional women to its ranks. It continues to provide free space for the Braille Association of Connecticut and to rent space to the Westport Young Woman's League.[3]

One couple who exemplified the new Westporters was Bob and Connie Anstett, who arrived in Westport in 1948. When they were invited to the Woman's Club, Connie remembers, "I was recruited to dish out the spaghetti. In no time, we felt like we'd lived here forever." In 1953 Bob Anstett and John Boyd started a law practice in Westport. In 1955, Anstett was appointed civil defense director. A Republican, he subsequently served the town as Town Prosecutor, member of the Representative Town Meeting, chairman of the Board of Education, and Probate Judge for 16 years. Discussing the involvement of so many residents in town activities, Connie Anstett said: "I was always amazed at the number of commuters who got so actively involved in town affairs and gave so much of their time and talent." Bob Anstett added: "Out of the Young Republican group grew this spirit of working for good government by putting up good candidates and having a good time while working to get them elected." [4]

All that was needed to complete the multifaceted picture that was Westport was an international outlook through a conspicuous individual active in an international organization. Enter, Ruth Steinkraus-Cohen. The daughter of Herman Steinkraus, Ruth Steinkraus-Cohen — just out of Vassar College — was intrigued by the United Nations from its inception in 1945. A warm, vivacious woman and a gifted musician, she first founded a chapter of the UN Association in Fairfield County in 1945, speaking at rallies, clubs, and schools. In 1956, she became founder and continuing chairman of the International Hospitality Committee of Fairfield County. In that role, she and her committee would eventually host more than 52,000 people from all over the world on a year-round basis between 1956 and 1999. The first major event was held on October 27, 1956, when more than 40 high-level UN diplomats and their 72 guests from 19 countries arrived for a weekend with local families. As a result of her energy and enterprise, she founded the annual "jUNe Day" in Westport, which sets aside the last Saturday in June for local families to host UN families. UN delegates and their families were scheduled to visit Westport three times in 2000 — on jUNe Day, on October 24, the 25th anniversary of the founding of the UN, and on First Night, December 31.

AMBASSADOR TO THE UNITED NATIONS: Ruth Steinkraus-Cohen, indefatigable founder and chairman of the International Hospitality Committee of Fairfield County, has brought more than 50,000 international visitors to Westport in the past half century. She established "jUNe" Day, which sets aside the last Saturday in June to host the UN diplomats and their families here.
WESTPORT NEWS PHOTO

Ms. Steinkraus-Cohen also became a social worker and a supporter of the arts in Westport. Through her close affiliation with Eleanor Roosevelt, the former first lady visited Westport on several occasions, including October 24, 1952, to celebrate the United Nation's seventh birthday in the fall of 1958 when she shared her impressions of a trip to Russia at the height of the Cold War. Other Westporters involved with the UN were Rita Davidson Kaunitz, a paid staff member and a regional planning expert from 1949 to 1968; and Sally Swing Shelley, an information officer for the United Nations Educational Scientific and Cultural Organization (UNESCO). Westport's involvement with the United Nations greatly enhanced its image, as did its welcome of people of all backgrounds the world over.

Superman by Curt Swan
WESTPORT HISTORICAL SOCIETY

About the same time, sculptor James Earl Fraser was commissioned by the Lincoln Monument Committee to create a work in Jersey City, New Jersey. Other emerging Westport artists of that era were Lowell Bacon and Leon Gordon. Among the most famous cartoonists were Bud Sagendorf (Popeye), Bill Yates, (Professor Phumble), Mel Casson (Sparky), Curt Swan (Superman), Jack Tippit, Stan Drake (The Heart of Juliet Jones and Blondie), Harold Gray (Little Orphan Annie), Dick Wingert (Hubert), Chad Grothkopf (Howdy Doody), Frank Bolle (Winkle Winnie), Ham Fisher (Jo

Palooka), Hardy Gramatky (Little Toot), Robert Lawson (Ferdinand the Bull), Hank Ketchum (Dennis the Menace), and John Norment, who also wrote pieces for the *New Yorker* magazine.

Meanwhile, by 1949 there were stirrings in town that the voters had strayed a long way from the grass roots democracy they had set up in 1835. The general feeling was that the Town Meeting (TM) had become a place where only special interest groups came to vote for what they wanted. The TM no longer seemed to represent all of the townspeople. Westport petitioned the state legislature to change from a town meeting to a Representative Town Meeting (RTM) form of government under which delegates would be elected from various town districts to a legislative body. The idea was first broached in 1949 by nonpartisan groups, including the League of Women Voters (LWV), who believed that an elected body of representatives would ensure representation from residents in every section of town. The public could still attend meetings, but only the representatives could vote.

On February 26, 1949, Westporters cast two ballots: Did they think the Town Meeting form of government should be changed? And, if they voted "yes," they were asked to select either a town manager and a nine-member council structure or an RTM. One representative would be selected for every 250 electors and the town was divided into six districts, and expanded to eight in 1977 with 40 representatives. It is interesting to note that the Republican Town Committee backed the RTM, while the Democrats took no position.

The townspeople voted "yes" to change their current government structure to a nonpartisan RTM by a 760-490 margin. That decision was no casual one. Once the town agreed to a nonpartisan RTM, a Charter Revision Study Committee wrote an Enabling Act, which was presented at a public hearing in Westport on March 28, 1949. It was then sent on to the Legislature, which passed the Special Act to establish a nonpartisan RTM. Governor Chester Bowles said at the time: "I am pleased to see the residents of Westport have shown so much interest in modernization and improving their town government." Westport's residents then approved the state legislation on July 16, 1949, by a vote of 299 to 173. The first RTM was elected to office on November 8, 1949, with 26 members elected out of 206 candidates. Harry Sherwood was elected as the first moderator (see Appendix J).

After the RTM had been installed, a group of local Negroes attended

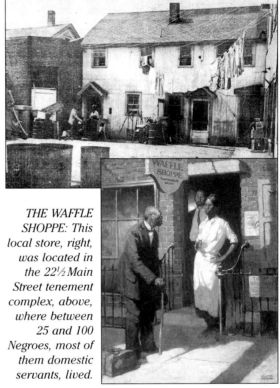

an RTM meeting in December 1949 on the housing crisis.[5] A resolution was offered proposing the building of subsidized housing. After much acrimonious discussion, a vote was taken with only one vote against the resolution and two members abstaining. Those opposed declared the housing "un-American" and "Socialistic." The Negro delegates, tenants of a ramshackle building at 22½ Main Street, asked if they would be eligible for occupancy in the proposed new housing project. The response was yes providing the

THE WAFFLE SHOPPE: This local store, right, was located in the 22½ Main Street tenement complex, above, where between 25 and 100 Negroes, most of them domestic servants, lived.

PAINTING BY J. CLINTON SHEPHERD/ COURTESY OF THE WESTPORT SCHOOLS PERMANENT ART COLLECTION/G.W. ADAMS, FILE PHOTO

requirements of veterans and of others with "more pressing" needs than those of the Negroes were taken care of first. Housing Authority Chairman Charles A. Cutler pointed out that two Negro families on the list of 42 were being considered for housing aid.

The Negro contingent then submitted a petition asking the state government to help them obtain decent, low-rent housing in Westport. The petition was signed by Doris G. Sheel, Lewis Thompson, William Turner, Mrs. Roscoe Richardson, Eva L. McDonald, William Dew, James Martin, Walter Johnson, Kenneth Durham, Johnnie May Turnipseed, Mary E. Harris, Mary G. Cadett, James L. Rogers, Charlotte Sellers, Arthur Hall, Ethel Rentz, Mr. And (sic) Mrs. Daniel Newton, and Mr. And (sic) Mrs. Paul Martin. Four of the petitioners were World War II veterans.

This unusual development drew a public warning from Connecticut Governor Chester Bowles, who strongly recommended that the town leaders adhere to the law. In a letter to town officials, he emphasized that all public housing decisions had to be made solely on the basis of need, noting that "President Truman had made very clear in a formal statement that racial discrimination would not be tolerated in General Housing projects."

Meanwhile, Town Prosecutor Vincent X. Montanaro asked that the town study conditions at 22½ Main Street where at least 25 Negroes lived in crowded quarters "with a view towards eliminating these premises." The *Town Crier* had revealed the cramped, unsafe conditions at this address 10 years earlier in 1939. A half dozen tenants expressed an interest in better living quarters but were worried over what would happen to them if the apartments were condemned. They said they would gladly move if decent housing in Westport was made available at a price they could afford.

While the existence of the slum housing was known to townspeople, it was not readily seen by most Westporters because the apartments were hidden from the Main Street shoppers through an alleyway south of the Townley Restaurant. Peter Guglierli, the property owner of record, told town officials that the number of tenants in the apartments varied because the tenants, to whom he rented rooms, more often than not took in paying guests. This paying guest system, Town Prosecutor Montanaro said, created conditions that frequently brought defendants to the Town Court on morals charges. Montanaro recommended that the selectmen request that the town health officer, the fire chief, and the building inspector conduct independent investigations with a view toward eliminating the premises as a housing facility.

The issue spilled over into January of 1950 at another RTM meeting when those representing private building interests made a last-ditch stand against low-rent housing. Although the pro-housing veterans failed to show up at the debate, First Selectman W. Clarke Crossman and Selectman Howard D. Norris were there and voted for the housing project. Selectman Albert T. Scully opposed it. Meanwhile, Alois J. Forger, newly elected chairman of the Westport Housing Authority, said his organization would proceed with plans for a 40-unit housing project, for which the state had earmarked more than $400,000.

A few months later, the problem was solved in an unexpected way. In May 1950, fire destroyed half of the apartments at 22½ Main Street. More than twenty persons were made homeless. Just as many continued to live in the smoke-filled, fire-scorched remains. While there are no records remaining of the tenants of that building, author and *Westport News* columnist Dan Woog made his own investigation in 1993 and he found a retired fireman, Dan Bradley, who said he had fought the blaze that burnt down the building and that it was reportedly started by someone who dropped a firebomb through the window.[6] However, there were no records of the cause of the fire and the apartments were never rebuilt. The remaining families at 22½ Main Street were evicted, and the alley was closed as part of the program to erect a second-story addition to the Townley Restaurant. On May 25, 1950, after years of struggling with this problem, the *Westporter-Herald* finally gave a blunt description of the whole affair: "22½ Main Street Is Rubbed Out." The news article began: "This spot, for years a pimple on the face of Westport's progress, is being rubbed out and in a few weeks the home of Westport's Negro population will have disappeared completely."

Harry Audley, a former Westport fire chief and a longtime Westporter who graduated from Staples in 1949, recalls that there was a little church hidden among the apartments at 22½ Main Street, with a minister by the name of Willie Sellers who would go around town seeking donations of meats, vegetables and other foods from local merchants. It all ended, Audley recalls, with the big fire. No one really ever knew exactly how many people lived in the squalid huts behind the alley. One woman, who preferred anonymity, told the *Westporter-Herald*: "I guess Westport has finally succeeded in getting rid of us. I hate to leave this town. But maybe it's for the best. There's no use in staying where you are not wanted." Shortly afterward, according to an account in the *Town Crier*: "The remaining shacks were torn down, the residents dispersed to parts unknown, and there the matter died."[7]

Audley also recalls one of the worst tragedies in Westport's history on May 2, 1946, when a wrecked truck on the Post Road near Sylvan Avenue blew up, touching off a spectacular fire that killed Fire Chief Frank L. Dennert, 55; a former fire chief, Francis P. Dunningan, 53; and two other firemen; and injured eight other people nearby. First to the scene was ambulance driver Arthur Audley, an uncle of Harry Audley's, and his daughter, Edna. Both Audleys helped the burned driver, and others injured, into their ambulance and other vehicles that arrived on the scene. An immediate investigation by Police Chief John A. Dolan revealed that a tire on the truck had blown causing the truck to smash into a drum filled with vulcanizing cement that exploded. The tragedy touched off support from all the townspeople: 27 blood donors volunteered to repay the Norwalk Hospital plasma that had been used in the accident; a baseball game between the Norwalk Auto Wreckers and the Westport Advertisers was held to raise proceeds for the Fireman's Fund; the Red Cross contributed to the Firemen's Fund. The *Westporter-Herald* had published an "EXTRA" on the morning after the fire, giving the paper away because, it stated, "Westport had a right to know what had happened without waiting for the afternoon papers" which did not

Babe Ruth Signs Balls For Four Fire Victims

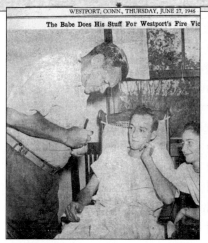

WESTPORT, CONN., THURSDAY, JUNE 27, 1946

The Babe Does His Stuff For Westport's Fire Vic

THE BABE WAS HERE: Above, head-line in the Westporter *following Babe Ruth's visit to Westport firemen in the hospital in May 1946. Ruth, above left, autographs a baseball for Westport Fireman Jimmy Powers in Norwalk Hospital as Powers' fiancée, Virginia Clossen, looks on. Powers was one of four fireman badly burned in a truck explosion in Westport on May 2, 1946. Ruth was in town at that time to play golf as a guest of a Westport doctor.*

HARRY AUDLEY PHOTO

arrive before 2 P.M., and solicited contributions from readers to the Fund.[8]

Four firemen seriously burned in the explosion, Dominic Zeoli, George and James Powers, and John Saviano, enjoyed a once-in-a-lifetime experience on Sunday June 23, when they were visited by the last person they ever expected to see: Babe Ruth, the King of Swat. Ruth was in Westport to play golf at Longshore as the guest of Dr. V.E. Caselnova, of River Lane. Ruth obliged First Selectman Albert T. Scully's request for him to visit the men in the hospital. The newspaper account of that visit in *The Westporter* on June 17, 1946, read: "A small cavalcade left Westport and was met at the town line by the Norwalk police who made an escort to the hospital. Like magic, the word spread through the hospital and every nurse and intern 'that could leave duty for a minute jammed into the mob that trailed behind the over-weight Ruth. The entrance to the ward where all four men were waiting was dramatic. They had known for about half an hour that Ruth was coming and impatiently they had been waiting. Then came the Babe, booming his 'Hi-ya fellers.' To each one he was introduced and to each he presented an autographed baseball as he kept up his bantering talk.

"Perhaps the most excited," the article continued, "was Jimmy Powers who, in his high school days and later, was rated one of the best athletes in town. To him it was like a visitation of royalty. As the Babe made his way to him, George was chewing his fingernails and holding tight to the hand of his fiancée, Virginia Clossen. His efforts to talk were futile.... Even Zeoli told Fire Chief Harold Shippey that he would be back at work a fortnight earlier than he had planned, all because of the visit of the home run king." The front page story in the June 27, 1946 issue of *The Westporter* was accompanied by photos of Ruth signing a ball for Powers and standing with Zeoli. The headline: 'THE BABE DOES HIS STUFF FOR WESTPORT'S FIRE VICTIMS."

*PLAZA OVER TROUBLED WATERS:
The Saugatuck River came right up
to the back doors of all the stores on
the west side of Main Street before
Parker-Harding Plaza was built by
filling in the river. In the early days
of the town, merchants had dumped
waste into the river from their shops.
The parking area was named after
its co-sponsors, Selectman Emerson
Parker, and Evan Harding, owner of
Daybreak Nurseries. The parking lot
opened on June 27, 1955.*

PETER BARLOW PHOTO

Housing was not the only pressing need in Westport after the war.
Downtown parking had become impossible. Finally, on July 20, 1950, members of the Westport Traffic Committee urged adoption of the Parker-Harding plan, named after its co-sponsors Emerson Parker and Evan Harding, to fill in the river area behind the stores on the west side of Main Street. After years of planning and construction, the parking lot opened on June 27, 1955, forever changing the face of downtown Westport. RTM moderator Herbert Baldwin's recommendation that the RTM name the project "Parker-Harding Esplanade" was adopted, though changed to "Parker-Harding Plaza."

The League of Women Voters first organized in 1949 when a group of 41 women gathered at the home of Mrs. Wolcott D. Street on Myrtle Avenue. The national organization had been founded in 1920 after passage of the Nineteenth Amendment, which guaranteed women the right to vote. In order to gain official status in Westport, members of the League were required to write a handbook about the town. In the course of doing that research, the women discovered that Westport had no official charter of its own. It had been operating only under state statutes.

In 1949, League President Helen Mayer called a gathering of Westport citizens, and subsequently ignited the process for gaining a charter. A Charter Committee chaired by Ed See went to work. The new charter, for which the League had fought, was approved by the RTM in a 25-5 vote in January 1957. In a public referendum held in July 1957, the vote was 2,359 people voting in favor and 1,869 against. The charter basically gave the first selectman appointive power for most town officials, including the town clerk, tax collector, controller, and assessor. It also strengthened the powers of the RTM, which could now decrease appropriations, and investigate whatever area of town life it chose. One of the many ad hoc groups that led the reform movement was the Westport Planning Association, established by Leonard Rovins. It helped restructure town government, particularly its tax structure.

The League of Women Voters has continued to be an active presence in Westport, using its status to advocate positions on issues such as education policies, open space, and changes in town government, to ensure fairness and openness.[9] The League has traditionally been a training ground for public service. Many past League members have gone on to higher office such as first selectman (Diane Goss Farrell, Martha Hauhuth, Jacqueline Heneage), second selectman (Betty Lou Cummings, Tammy Pincavage), state representative (Julie Belaga, Jo Fuchs), and commissioners on town boards and commissions. Equally important, the League's Voter Service has become known as a source of impartial and valuable information at election time. Lisa Shufro, co-president of the LWV in 1999, said the League's motto is: "Democracy is not a spectator sport."

In the spring of 1971, the Westport chapter voted to open membership to men — the first in the nation to do so. However, in 1972, at the Annual Convention of the LWV in Atlanta, Georgia, members voted down a proposal to give men full membership in the organization, despite an impassioned plea from Westport's Julie Belaga, president of the Westport LWV and one of the organizers of the "Men Suffrage 1972" campaign. Challenging feminist Gloria Steinem, who opposed equality for men at the meeting, Ms. Belaga rushed to the microphone and said: "You have just finished urging us to judge people as *human* and not as male or female. Aren't you talking out of both sides of your mouth at once?" Said Ms. Steinem: "If you must admit men, let them do the typing."[10]

The 1950s was a decade of controversies. Just as Westport was getting comfortably adjusted to a peacetime life, the Korean War broke out. The North Koreans attacked the South Koreans on June 25, 1950. President Truman said it was necessary to go to war to contain Communism. The citizens of the United States bought that rationale — and so did most Westporters. Five short years after the dramatic end of World War II, residents here were once again talking about war. On August 31, 1950, it was pointed out by Westport's Civil Defense coordinator, Roger Gleason, that state officials were aware of the possible bombing of Connecticut in the event of the outbreak of war. Governor Chester Bowles then announced rules of procedure that every citizen should know and follow in case of an emergency.

Meanwhile, in Westport, the agencies involved in preparation for war began gearing up. First, the office of the *Westporter-Herald* was named as local registration headquarters for Draft Board 16, which was based in Bridgeport. In July, Donald G. Murphy, chairman of the local Red Cross Blood program, asked anyone with "O" type blood to register immediately because the Army had an urgent need of that type for casualties on the Korean war front. At first it appeared that only two or three Westport men would be inducted in the first Selective Service draft, which was expected to get under way by September 1950. Every young man had to register for the draft within five days after reaching his eighteenth birthday. Those who failed to register within the required time were placed in 1-A category and were drafted without recourse to appeal. Headquarters was in Bridgeport, which had a quota of 57 men.

There was no question that the Korean War became a cause of national anxiety. According to a nationwide Gallup poll, in 1953 Americans in general rated their worries as follows: Korean War, 40 percent; the economy, 15 percent; unemployment, 10 percent; and Communism, 8 percent. From 1950 to the armistice in 1953, a total of 52,000 men from Connecticut served in the Korean War. Approximately 100 men and women from Westport served in some capacity during this undeclared war.[11] There were no Westporters killed in the Korean War, according to official records.

The full realization of how seriously Westporters took the Korean War was reflected in the fact that on July 25, 1951, town officials announced that the Westport-Weston territory had been divided into three major areas that could house a maximum of 4,400 refugees in case of atomic attack on nearby target cities. Officials stipulated that the refugees would be given medical and radiological examination and a simple shipping tag registration. Then they would be distributed among the welfare centers. Westporters' fear of aerial attack, so vividly aroused in World War II, had clearly returned.

The townspeople became so sensitive to the Korean War by 1952 that reports of "flying saucers" were gaining frequency in Fairfield County. People were concerned. Who knows, some people thought, the flying objects might be enemy planes headed in from the Atlantic by way of Long Island Sound. Military authorities required that the local spotters' post in Westport be manned around the clock until the invaders had been "located or destroyed." As it turned out, the local Ground Observer Corps was not fooled. The spotters identified the unknown aircraft as simply jets making a terrific noise. The infrequency of jet planes flying over this area in the dark

PILLARS OF THE COMMUNITY: Former Governor John Davis Lodge, left, in his Naval uniform, talks with First Selectman Herb Baldwin before a Memorial Day parade in the 1950s.
WESTPORT NEWS PHOTO

had led to the widespread speculation that they were "flying saucers."

At the same time that all of this preparation for war was going on, the townspeople were also aware of the needs of their children. The Little League, for example, was organized in Westport in 1952 with the backing and support of business-men and civic leaders. Originally they formed and outfitted eight teams; today the League involved hundreds of boys and girls.

A movement of another kind was afoot. In 1950, Westport Republican Town Committee Chairman Helen Warnock nomi-nated Republican John Davis Lodge of Westport for governor at the GOP convention in New Haven. He was elected to serve a four-year term — only the second time a resident of this town was elected to the highest office in the state. From 1931 to 1939, Wilbur L. Cross, a Democrat, who had worked as the first principal in the newly opened Staples High School in 1885 as a young Yale graduate, had served as governor of Connecticut. Lodge, broth-er to the illustrious politician and Boston Brahmin Henry Cabot Lodge, had served as congressman from the Fourth Congressional District (1946-1950) after Claire Boothe Luce announced she would not seek reelection. Before 1946, John Davis Lodge had been a movie actor, starring in movies with Shirley Temple and Marlene Dietrich. During the war, he served as captain in the U.S. Navy, participating in several beach landings in the Pacific. He was awarded the Croix de Guerre and General Charles DeGaulle personally decorated him with the Legion of Honor. John and Francesca Braggiotti Lodge had two daughters, Beatrice and Lily.

In defeating incumbent Governor Chester Bowles, Lodge was given a plurality of 16,237 votes in one of the biggest off-year voter turnouts in the state's history. Lodge garnered 436,325 votes to Bowles' 420,088. In 1954, Lodge was narrowly defeated by Democrat Abraham A. Ribicoff. After losing the 1954 election, Lodge was appointed ambassador to Spain, later to Argentina, and finally to Switzerland. He died on October 29, 1985 at the age of 82.

While John Davis Lodge was making headlines in 1950, a local church made national news by simply moving across the street. Seeking a better location, members of the Saugatuck Congregational Church watched in awe as the 118-year-old, 200-ton building was moved 600 feet diagonally across the Post Road on August 28, 1950 to its new home on the eight-acre Jesup property that is also the site of the parsonage. The church had been erected in 1832 and the parsonage, originally the Jesup home, in 1807. The extraordinary project attracted state and national media as more than 5,000 people watched the history-making procedure. For nine hours beginning at 5 A.M. the Post Road was completely blocked while local and state police rerouted traffic around the quarter mile section between Imperial Avenue and Compo Road. Fastened with steel rods, it was hoisted on 55 logs and at a speed of 60 feet an hour was rolled across the street.

The historical event captured the imagination of millions as a result of a *Life* magazine story in the September 11, 1950, issue headlined "ROLLING CHURCH" with a full-page photo of the church being moved. The magazine reported that sightseers from all over "fashionable Fairfield Country" came to watch, and church members sold food to help pay the $10,000 moving bill. In May 1991, the 159-year-old, 40-foot-tall steeple and belfry — taken down in February 1991 for restoration — was returned to its proper place. The church has had a distinguished history as a community resource. The Saugatuck Congregational Church was not the only church to make news in 1950. Not long after the Saugatuck Church move had been com-

pleted, a major hurricane hit Westport on November 30, 1950, killing two people and causing $300,000 worth of damage, including toppling the steeple of the Green's Farms Congregational Church, causing it to fall into the church parlor. The steeple was hoisted back into place after spending two months on the front lawn.

One Westporter called the steeple raising "a Westport happening." It was the second time in almost 100 years that the steeple had been toppled over.

Several churches were

ON A ROLL: Life *Magazine displayed a full-page photo, left, of Westport's Saugatuck Congregational Church in its September 11, 1950 issue. In an extraordinary event, viewed by some 5,000 people in awe, the church was slowly but carefully moved 600 feet diagonally across the Post Road to its current location. Aerial view, above, shows route of church's move.*

WESTPORT NEWS PHOTO, ABOVE
HOWARD MODAVIS PHOTO, BELOW

being formed in this era. The first Unitarian Church in Westport was built on Lyons Plains Road just a mile from the Merritt Parkway, with Dr. Karl Moses Christian Chworosky as minister. The building was designed by Victor Lundy in 1958 as an interpretation of a ship's keel and inspired by the Old Ship Church in Massachusetts. The sanctuary was completed and dedicated in the fall of 1964, with the pulpit donated by Norman Cousins and dedicated to Albert Schweitzer. In 1999, the church marked its 50th anniversary with the Reverend Frank S. Hall, senior minister in charge. Other churches founded or rebuilt in the 1950s were the First Church of Christ Scientist (1949), Saint Luke's Roman Catholic Church (1957), St. Francis Roman Catholic Church in Weston (1958), and the new St. Paul Lutheran Church on Easton Road (1961).

Perhaps one of the most critical challenges the town faced in the 1950s was the garbage crisis in 1957. First Selectman W. Clarke Crossman had closed the town dump at Taylor Place after the Saugatuck Landowners Neighborhood Association had successfully brought an injunction. Judge Vince R. Parmelee called the dumpsite "unethical" and an affront to the dignity of the court. The garbage disposal issue had been touched off earlier on August 8, 1952, when an editorial in the *Town Crier* said: "Many residents in the area are up in arms against the continued operation of the town dump behind Jesup Green, and, if your olfactory organ is working on even half a cylinder, you will agree that they have cause for argument."

By August 1, 1957, the garbage crisis was nearing a solution when the Woman's Club agreed to allow dumping on its site situated on the bank of the Saugatuck River behind the club at Taylor Place. By September, the dump was declared clean enough to hold a tea party. Indeed, a public invitation went out to Westporters to attend a gala reception and tea party at the club's working landfill early in October. The tea party became a national happening, attracting the news media from "Life Goes to a Party," NBC's "Monitor" radio show, and reporters from most of the New York newspapers among the 500 people who turned out for the festivities. The highlight of the event came when Westporter Amy Vanderbilt, wearing stylish attire complete with white gloves, sipped tea from a tin can. Vanderbilt, acknowledged arbiter of social decorum, sat at a table laid with linen, silver, and candelabra. Over the years, the event has become known simply as Amy Vanderbilt's tea party at the town dump.

In the fall of that same year, 1957, Herbert E. Baldwin, a Westport native, was elected first selectman. Baldwin's steady hands on the wheels of local government would last for a decade, one of the most eventful in the town's history. This tall, erect, white-thatched, 67-year-old apple farmer was a Hollywood casting director's dream. With his native Yankee instincts and his reputation as a man of integrity, he was a natural in local politics. In an unpublished manuscript telling his life's story in a memoir to his three children, dated "Christmas 1984,"[12] Baldwin said his political life began when some of his friends who were unhappy about their land assessments asked him to run for the Board of Relief, later named the Board of Tax Review. After a successful tour of duty, his name was put up for judge of the local Town Court. "I hardly knew how to respond. However, my friend who proposed my name, Sara B. Crawford, assured me of the Republican Party's appointment committee's confidence that I could and would ably fill this office. I agreed to accept and was duly appointed."

In 1951, he was elected as moderator of the Representative Town Meeting. In that post, he learned a great deal about the machinery of town government. He continued in his apple orchard business until 1957 when "all of a sudden I lost my main market for my apple crops." Providentially, in 1957, a new town charter had just made the first selectman's job fulltime with a salary of $12,000, which then was considered a living wage. A few of his friends urged him to run for that office.

But the nomination was not his for the asking. "I had a contest in securing the nomination from the Republican Town Committee," he stated in his memoirs. "This committee wanted to put down certain appointive conditions, which I could not accept." The Republican Town Committee turned him down and, instead, nominated Emerson Parker. Without the Republican Town Committee endorsement, the only way Baldwin could get nominated for elective office was to seek a primary runoff among the Republican voters. This he did — and won. In Westport, on election night November 6, 1957, there were some anxious moments as results filtered in showing a see-saw race between Baldwin and Albert T. Scully, a former Democratic Party first selectman (1942, 1944 and 1948), now running as the Taxpayer Party's candidate. (Two years later, on March 29, 1959, the Taxpayers Party was officially recognized in town.)

The final tally showed Baldwin the winner over Scully by 41 votes. Baldwin's running mate was Dr. Elliott J. Roberts, second selectman. Baldwin also defeated the Democratic ticket of Frederic P. Kimball, a member of the Board of Finance, for first selectman, and Samuel DeMattio, of Saugatuck, his running mate. Urena Clarke, an Independent and the first woman to run for first selectman, ran a distant fourth. A total of 7,444 persons voted out of a total registration of 9,677 — an astounding 77 percent turnout.

Allen A. Raymond was Baldwin's campaign manager. A tall, poised and erudite man who later would serve as the fourth moderator of the RTM and chairman of the Board of Education, Raymond described his recollection of that historic night. "I was very young and this was my first election," he says. "The returns were not looking very good and I was depressed because it looked like we had lost and I thought, 'This fine gray-haired, distinguished man, how could anybody vote against him?' I went back to the gym at Bedford, where the votes were being counted, and tears came to my eyes. Herb's wife, May Baldwin, came up to me and said, 'Here, have some smelling salts.' I had never had smelling salts before and it felt pretty good. It turned out that Herb did win and it was about one o'clock in the morning and some of Herb's campaign committee thought, 'Hey, maybe it would be a good idea if we swore Herb in.' We were then at Herb's house, so we jumped into our cars, went back to Bedford, and found Town Clerk Lois Clark, and said, 'Lois, swear him in.' The next morning he went straight to Town Hall and took office." [13]

During his years as first selectman, Baldwin worked with a group of men who became known as "the Kitchen Cabinet." This small group of advisors included Allen Raymond, Gene Sheridan, John Boyd, Luis A. J. Villalon, Dick Broadman, Dr. Guy Robbins, and Cliff Mills. At these meetings, recalls Raymond, they never talked about whether they were conservative or liberal, Republican or Democrat. "Sure, we wanted Republicans to win because Herb and his Kitchen Cabinet were all Republicans. After the election, however, we forgot party labels. There were times, in fact, when we talked about how nice it would be if local elections eschewed the party label." Raymond described the group as "idealists in Herb Baldwin's image. Westport came first." Raymond recalls when John Boyd, together with his then law partner, Bob Anstett, helped develop a strategy to deal with particularly difficult legal issues as the town grew. "Those were hot sessions, but things got done. I remember when Guy Robbins, as chairman of the P&Z, would advocate ways to control the Town's explosive growth. He was an articulate, dedicated and feisty advocate for a better Westport at a time when growth was a danger," says Raymond. Baldwin's political opponents criticized him for relying so heavily on his Kitchen Cabinet, calling the arrangement "political cronyism." But Baldwin had only the highest praise for his advisors, who, he said, were selflessly interested in the town's welfare.

Raymond described what it was like to help Baldwin run the town:

It was a very exciting time because this was after the war and the town was growing like crazy. We had floods all over town because we didn't have good drainage. We had serious planning and zoning problems. And we had growth problems, big time. But it was a wonderful challenge; at one point we were building almost a school a year. The most exciting event during Baldwin's reign was when a friend, Gay Land, told me that Longshore Country Club might be for sale. I told our Kitchen Cabinet that it might be a property the town should buy, and Herb said we should go for it, it was a great deal. It became a bipartisan project, and Julian Brodie, a Democrat, was appointed by Herb to negotiate the deal with Julius Ballard, the owner. They got very close to a price, but Ballard was resisting the final price. It was then that Julian Brodie, with a stroke of genius, said, "I'll tell you what we'll do, Julius, we'll give you a lifetime gold pass to Longshore." And Julius said, "Sold."

Brodie offered his own version of what happened: "The negotiations took four-and-a-half months and the talks were difficult. After innumerable meetings and endless Oriental rug trading, we finally got the price down to one I liked and thought the town would too: $1,925,000," Brodie, who was a commuter, said. "One Friday night I raced to the train with my homemade option [for the town to buy] signed and reposing warmly in my pocket. I felt nine feet tall. Next morning I met with the town fathers. We were all jubilant."[14] Subsequently, the RTM, in a 34-0 vote on February 14, 1960, approved the proposed purchase of the 191-acre Longshore facility as some 700 spectators gave the RTM a hearty ovation.

The acquisition was so unusual for a town that the *New York Times*, waiting until the club actually opened to the residents, devoted the top of page 1 in its July 25, 1960 edition to the story

OLD LIGHTHOUSE: Built near the swimming pool long before the town bought the Longshore Club, below, in 1960, it was taken down in the mid-1960s.

PETER BARLOW PHOTO
KASSIE FOSS ILLUSTRATION

MAN FOR ALL REASONS: The Reverend Theodore Hoskins, who described former First Selectman Herbert Baldwin on his 90th birthday in 1984, as "a prince of a man," is shown here pointing to the refurbished steeple on his Saugatuck Congregational church in the late 1980s. Hoskins, a man with an abiding social conscience, started the homeless shelter here and initiated numerous projects to help those in need.
WESTPORT NEWS PHOTO

with two photographs of the Club under the headline: "Westport Residents Enjoy Community's Own Luxurious Country Club." The lead paragraph of the story read: "WESTPORT, Conn., July 24 — Imagine a luxurious country club overlooking Long Island Sound with dues of $10 a year for a family. Well, this community has one."

The Baldwin administration and Julian Brodie are credited for making the purchase of Longshore possible. At the time, there were kudos from all quarters, including the local press. But one of the least likely — and most flattering — comments came from the trade magazine, *Editor and Publisher*, which closely followed the newspaper industry across America. An editorial published September 10, 1960, praised Westport: "It took daring and courage.... It took leadership and confident fellowship. It took understanding of trends, conditions and needs. It took a quality of thinking that is satisfied only by follow-up in action. Westport is proving that the town and its citizens have these qualities." Herb Baldwin remained in Town Hall for a decade.

On their 75th wedding anniversary, Herb and May Baldwin were given a party that recognized his lifetime service to the town. A reception was given for them by their friends and family at the Saugatuck Congregational Church. Baldwin, who was born on February 26, 1894 in Norwalk, had married the former May Smith, who was born in New York City and raised in Norwalk. The wedding took place on May 10, 1919, just after Baldwin returned from the service after World War I as an Ensign in the U.S. Navy. He wore his uniform for the wedding ceremony. May Baldwin went on to become an active member of the Westport Woman's Club and its Garden Department. On Herb Baldwin's 90th birthday, he was praised by the Reverend Theodore Hoskins, pastor of the Saugatuck Congregational Church: "He is really a prince of a man in the best sense of that word; in political leadership, style of life and character of relations with everyone."[15] Baldwin died on July 23, 1990 at the age of 96. Hoskins told those in attendance at the memorial service that his predecessor, the Reverend Gibson Daniels, had referred to Baldwin, a member of the church since 1927 and elected a deacon in 1929, as a "prince." Said Hoskins: "Maybe he was able to stand so tall because his feet were so firmly entrenched in the soil, in the town and in his family."[16]

In the late 1940s and 1950s, new businesses in Westport mushroomed: Torno Lumber, Kowalsky Brothers, the Red Barn, the Arrow Restaurant, Minute Man Travel Agency, Oscar's Delicatessen, Max's Art Supplies, Minute Man Cleaners, and Swezey of Westport. In 1955, real estate developer B.V. Brooks, Sr. almost doubled the size of the Compo Shopping Center. It was the largest retail development in Westport's history at the time. Westport was growing, indeed, and writers and moviemakers continued to take note of that fact. The town once again was put in the national spotlight with the making of a movie in the fall of 1955 based, in part, on the Westport scene. The center of attraction was movie star Gregory Peck who came to town in a gray flannel suit to film location shots at Longshore Club Park for 20th Century Fox's "The Man in the Gray Flannel Suit," based on a book by Sloane Wilson of the same title published by Simon and Schuster.

On the subject of movie stars, in 1954 the sultry movie star Gene Tierney, raised in Westport, was visited during a jet-set romance on a summer weekend by playboy Prince Aly Kahn. "She was very much a Westport girl, having grown up in Green's Farms. Westporters took pride in her glamorous career

GREEN'S FARMS GIRL: Actress Gene Tierney, raised in Westport, hosted Prince Aly Kahn here in a jet-set romance in 1954. She is remembered best for her role in Laura, *for which she received an Academy Award nomination.*
PHOTO COURTESY OF
TOM DELONG

that made her high-cheekbone, almond-eyed beauty a household word here. She was often seen downtown without looking Hollywood," wrote veteran journalist Harold Hornstein in the *Westport News.* Hornstein had been tipped off that the actress was seen with the Prince at the West-Tuck restaurant at the railroad station, where Mario's is now located. Her Cadillac and chauffeur were parked outside of the restaurant. Hornstein, who was then news editor of the *Town Crier,* lost no time in popping the key question: Were they contemplating marriage? "Well, we don't talk about that," replied the actress. "I never discuss anything personal," said the prince. He had been married to actress Rita Hayworth in 1949 and divorced two years later. When the prince left on the train, he was seen giving Tierney a kiss on the cheek. Tierney sat in her car for a while. Hornstein walked up to her again and asked her how her weekend had been. "Oh, wonderful," she said with tears in her eyes. Shortly after that she broke up with Aly and was overcome with emotional problems, succumbing for a time in a mental institution. Best remembered, perhaps, for her leading role in *Laura,* for which she was nominated for an Academy Award, she died on November 6, 1991, at the age of 70.[17]

In 1958, Mitchells of Westport began as Ed Mitchells. Committed to building a business that would serve their community, Ed and Norma Mitchell opened a modest clothing store on the Post Road in Compo Acres. By treating customers as friends and participating in community service activities, Ed Mitchells quickly gained a loyal following in Westport. In 1963, the store moved to the Westport National Bank building on Colonial Green. In the mid-1960s Ed and Norma's two sons, Jack and Bill, both joined the business bringing together two generations of Mitchells into the business at its present location at 670 Post Road East.

Through the 1990s, the business continued to grow through an expansion in 1993, as well as through other members of the Mitchell family joining the business. In 1990, Jack's oldest son Russell and wife Linda joined the business as chief financial officer /director of marketing and women's buyer/merchandise manager, respectively. In 1991, Jack's son Bob joined as vice president of men's merchandising and Todd came on board as vice president of client sales and initiatives in 1994.

When the business expanded in 1993 by enlarging the women's department, Ed and Norma changed the name of the business from Ed Mitchells to Mitchells of Westport so that the name reflected not only their efforts, but what the business had become — a multi-generational community-based family business. More expansion continued in the mid- and late-1990s. The Mitchells expanded the business outside of Westport by acquiring Richards, a family-owned men's clothing store in Greenwich. Bill's oldest son Scott joined the team in 1998 as assistant manager in the women's

Ed and Norma Mitchell
WESTPORT NEWS PHOTO

department, and Jack's remaining son, Andrew, came on board as vice president of marketing in 1999. Remarkably, even with all of the expansion, the store today still retains its family and community feeling — mostly because eight members of the Mitchell family representing three generations of Westporters now work in the business and are involved in various local organizations. The Mitchell family is known as one of the town's most community-minded, philanthropic families. They have been honored with numerous awards, including the

YMCA Faces of Achievement award (to Ed, Bill, and Jack Mitchell) and the Anti-Defamation League Community Service award. Mitchells was recognized nationally in 1997 in the October 15, 1997 issue of *Daily News Record*, an industry publication, as one of the "Top 10" men's and women's family-owned specialty stores. The magazine praised the store for having "the family touch for commuters and the Connecticut gentry."

Although he has retired to Florida, Ed Mitchell looked back on his Westport experience with great satisfaction. "It's a great place," he said. "If I had to choose any place in the world to be home — and I have done a lot of traveling —Westport is it. It has been very good to us. I feel humbled by the honors we have been given." He spends part of the year in Florida and, at age 95, remains in touch with the business through his family. "I am gratified that it worked out the way it has. It's wonderful to see the business carried on by the Mitchell family."[18]

Also in 1958, Lars-Eric Lindblad, one of the world's most famous explorers and conservationists, established his worldwide Lindblad Travel business here. He opened up many exotic parts of the world for tourism, especially Antarctica, China, the Galapagos Islands, and Africa. His company's headquarters was located at One Sylvan Road North, a stately white mansion judged by local officials as one of the most beautiful buildings in Westport. Lindblad, a man of enormous energy and eternal optimism, was active in several Westport organizations, the most prominent of which was the Westport Arts Center. *Travel and Leisure* magazine's twentieth anniversary edition in October 1991 named Lindblad as one of the "20 Greatest Travelers of All Time." The magazine put him in the company of such historic figures as Marco Polo, Christopher Columbus, Leif Ericsson, and Neil Armstrong. Lindblad died suddenly on July 8, 1994 in his native Stockholm, Sweden at the age of 67.[19]

There were new challenges for Westport women, too. In 1956, the Westport Young Woman's League was founded by 62 pioneering women. Until then, they had been part of the Junior Department of the Westport Woman's Club. The women organized themselves and met at the YMCA. Liz Land was the first president. The bylaws stated that women between the ages of 18 and 40 would be admitted. This limit was later raised to 45 years old with active membership permitted to age 50. Like the Woman's Club, from which it sprang, the League is devoted to philanthropic causes, especially needy children. In 1988, it published a cookbook, *Dining In*, and it held a fundraising house tour called "A Taste of Westport." It also runs Fresh Air fundraisers, has forged ties with the business community, and raises money for the retarded, as well as for Staples scholarships and a host of other charities and causes. In addition, it sponsors the Creative Arts Festival, initiated in 1974, and the Minute Man Race. In 1998 and 1999, it raised more than $200,000 annually. Since its inception, it has donated more than $2 million to community organizations.

One of the perennial issues debated down through the years by the League of Women Voters, and many other organizations, has been town zoning. In 1955, in an effort to protect land from too much development, the Planning and Zoning Commission upgraded all suitable land "AAA." Every area in town suitable for two-acre building was put into that class when the P&Z lifted five large tracts from AA (one-acre) to AAA (two acre) zones. The new zoning encompassed part of Green's Farms, the Longshore Club, a large section of the Fairfield Hunt Club, and part of the western Bayberry Lane region. The planners in those days envisioned a town of 36,000 people who would need more parks, a civic center, more boating slips, more playing fields, and more roads.[20] Their foresight in rezoning was rewarded when the population leveled off at about 25,000 at the end of the twentieth century. Writing in the *Town Crier* in 1958, Editor Lucia Donnelly put this milestone action by the P&Z into proper perspective: "Westport took a giant step forward in shaping the Town's future when, in 1955, it upgraded much of the residential areas into two-acre zoning — the first step in a series which will culminate with the completion of a Master Plan for the town."

Westport's growth also mandated the construction of new schools in the Fifties and early Sixties. In June 1954, a public hearing was scheduled to discuss Board of Education Chairman Bruno Arcudi's suggestion that a new high school be built. There was no serious opposition because almost everyone felt it was necessary. For more than two decades, the Westport school system had consisted of three elementary schools, one junior, and one senior high. The "population explosion" of the 1950s, with its problems of overcrowding and double sessions, created the demand for more schools. Coleytown Elementary was built in 1953 at a cost of $1 million. Then came Burr Farms Elementary in 1957. By 1958, when the new Staples High School opened on North Avenue, the cost had risen further to $4 million. The old Staples was converted to Bedford Junior High School, and the original Bedford Junior High, built in 1926, was converted into an elementary school and renamed Kings Highway Elementary in 1958. Hillspoint Elementary was built in 1961-62, and Coleytown Junior, now Middle School, was built in 1965.[21]

With its strong ties to the arts, which became special targets of

McCarthyism in the 1950s, Westport was hardly immune from the anti-Communist hysteria. First, reports began to circulate that some teachers would be investigated because of their political backgrounds. This report allegedly came from men in the August Matthias Post No. 63 of the American Legion, although both Superintendent of Schools G. E. Rast and C. Steve Vangor, commander of the local Legion post, denied the charge. The denial came after charges had been

ONLINE: The jetty at Compo Beach has been fishermen's favorite locale for decades. Here, a few brave souls on a cold, rainy day tried their luck, keeping a comfortable distance from one another.
WESTPORT NEWS PHOTO

made by George V. Burtsche, former commander of the local post and a member of the committee appointed to promote an "Americanization" program in the schools. These charges had been published in daily papers in Fairfield County and New York and had been broadcast on several radio stations.[22] The anti-Communist crusade had become so virulent nationwide that some people used the term "Red" about anyone whose views they opposed. An editorial titled "Sowing Distrust," in the *Town Crier* on December 16, 1948, warned: "A pernicious disease is gnawing relentlessly at the heart of our community, a disease not at all peculiar to Westport.... Its virus is the offhand manner in which so many Westporters call their neighbors 'Reds,' or, with a knowing smile, tell one another that this neighbor or that is 'a little to the left, if you know what I mean.' We have heard leaders of town politics called 'Red.' By their sometimes thoughtless, sometimes vicious use of the term, persons who apply it are unwittingly themselves aiding the real 'Red' cause, for what better way is there to spread disunity than to sow distrust of one neighbor for another in a town like Westport?" The anti-Communist movement, ignited by Wisconsin Republican Senator Joseph R. McCarthy in the 1950s, gained momentum and, by the time the 1960s arrived, it was known as "the Red Scare." In Westport, in 1961, the New World Affairs Center, a non-profit, non-partisan organization for peace and disarmament was opened on Taylor Place, with Adelaide Nichols Baker as one of its leaders. The event attracted pickets with signs bearing statements such as "Does Westport Condone Communism?" and leaflets from an anti-Communist committee led by a Bridgeport businessman.[23]

In the early 1950s, the U.S. Senate, reacting to political pressure, banned books that were allegedly pro-Communist. In the summer of 1953, Westport Librarian Eleanor Street calmed the fears of many Westport writers and others when she affirmed that absolutely no books had been taken off the library shelves. The ban had originated from the U.S. State Department, and included certain politically controversial books distributed by the U. S. Information Services overseas. The *Town Crier* confirmed Street's statement.

Nonetheless, the Red Scare picked up momentum here, as it did nationwide. In 1952, the Fairfield County Chapter of the National Council of Arts, Sciences and Professions, announced that it was sponsoring the appearance here of I. F. Stone, a big-name journalist closely identified with the Communist Front organization. Stone was to speak on the McCarran Act, which he described as "the latest stage in thought control." The event was canceled when it became known that the House Un-American Activities Committee had cited the Council as a Communist Front organization. Even at the time, most political observers saw this decision as an overreaction inasmuch as speakers of various persuasions — even alleged Nazi-sympathizers — had both spoken and marched in Westport.

Most people, of course, paid little attention to the political turmoil around them and savored the pleasure of Westport living. On May 29, 1957, 23 charter members of the Saugatuck River Sail and Power Squadron, Inc. founded a club for Westport yachtsmen and boating enthusiasts. Headed by Dick Beck, the club set its goals: "Establish a high standard of skill in the handling and navigation of yachts, power and sail, in order to encourage the study of scientific navigation, cooperating with federal agencies charged with enforcing the laws, and stimulate interest in activities that would support the Navy, Coast Guard, and Merchant Marines." Shortly thereafter, the Saugatuck Harbor Yacht Club was officially founded on November 18, 1959. The Club's history actually can, in a sense, be traced back to 1690 when William and Mary, the reigning monarchs of England, issued a Royal Grant allowing the tidal basin to be privately owned. The area known as the Great Salt Marsh, on the current western border of Westport, was part of the "Ludlow Tract" named after Roger Ludlow who had owned it. In 1893, the land was transferred to Henry C. Eno, a forebear of William Eno, the transportation expert who built the "Eno Mansion" in Westport. The Great Marsh changed hands a number of times until the U.L. Land Company and Frances and J.A. Probst bought it and turned it into the Saugatuck Harbor Yacht Club.[24]

The 1950s were years of explosive growth for Fairfield County, and despite Westport's prevailing desire to preserve the town's village atmos-phere, outside forces could no longer be contained. To the consternation of most townspeople, an expressway was proposed to relieve the congestion on the Post Road. It would be located in the heart of Saugatuck. Despite fierce opposition from the town — the RTM, the Board of Selectmen, the Citizens' Association of Connecticut all opposed it vehemently — the state prevailed. After years of delay caused by plans and counterplans, the town proposed laying the highway south of the Post Road parallel to the railroad tracks. Some 42 homeowners in Saugatuck, as well as the Saugatuck Methodist Church, were displaced and the New England Thruway became a reality. Especially irksome to the town had been the fact that one of their own, Governor Lodge, had promoted the highway.

The 129-mile Connecticut Turnpike, as it was also called, was con-structed at a cost of $464 million. It opened on January 1, 1958. Two hours after Interstate 95 opened, the Post Road, usually glutted in the evening rush, was a smooth-running flow between Westport and Fairfield. Beginning at Greenwich and ending at Killingly, the new toll road, now called John Davis Lodge Thruway, was designed to link Connecticut with the Massachusetts Turnpike. It traversed 28 towns and cities with 90 inter-changes and eight toll stations, passing through Stamford, Norwalk, Fairfield, Bridgeport, Stratford, New Haven and Norwich and the important intervening towns. There were eight interchanges between Norwalk and Bridgeport with a toll station located on the Norwalk line. It was possible to drive from Westport as far as Stratford without paying 25 cents. The speed limit was 60 miles per hour.

A sidelight to the date of opening: originally, Governor Ribicoff had announced it would open on December 31, 1958. However, an indefatigable letter writer named Hugo F. Scatena, who was head proofreader of the *Town Crier*, and who was known as "the walking dictionary," had previously appealed to the governor not to open it on New Year's Eve because of the danger of drunken driving. Ribicoff acquiesced to the man's suggestion, saying in a letter to Mr. Scatena: "Thanks a lot for your note, I am pleased that the opening date of the Thruway meets with your approval."

The public fight over the turnpike was just one of many such struggles in the Fifties. Arguably the most highly publicized squabble of all focused on a U.S. Army proposal to build a Nike missile site on 6.2 acres of town-owned land on North Avenue and additional land owned by private landowners. At the end of 1954, RTM Moderator Herbert Baldwin asked the

RTM to look into a possible Nike installation on North Avenue and Bayberry Lane. The Citizens Planning Association, of which Baldwin had long been a member, had already recorded its strong opposition to the proposal, which it saw as a threat to the community.[25]

The controversy became so heated that CBS-TV sent a camera crew to Westport to film a stormy meeting at the Woman's Club forum on the issue for Eric Sevareid's Sunday afternoon "American Week" television program. Clearly, the town wanted to find a way to keep the Army out. However, after an Army general told the RTM that the government would not take "no" for an answer, the RTM voted 21-4 to drop all official opposition. The Army finally took possession in early 1955, and on March 7, 1957, the Nike site was ready for operation. Despite all of the protests beforehand, neither the site nor the troops stationed here had much effect on the community. The final judgment on the controversy came in the form of a satirical novel *Rally 'Round the Flag Boys!* by Westport author Max Shulman, which was a takeoff on the story of the Nike site. There followed a movie by the same title, coincidentally, starring Westport's own Paul Newman and Joanne Woodward. The character played by Newman was modeled on Ralph Sheffer, who had represented the RTM in the negotiations. The final outcome of the site was that it was turned back to the town for educational purposes.

FAVORITE SPOT: During the 1950s, this well-known restaurant located on Long Lots Road and the Post Road was one of many local restaurants Westporters frequented. It has since changed names and owners several times.
FROM COLLECTION OF BILL SCHEFFLER

After all that had happened to improve Westport, it was not really surprising that in 1959 the town received perhaps the greatest honor in its history: It was recognized as an "All America City" for "progress achieved through intelligent citizen action" during 1958. The National Municipal League and *Look* magazine, co-sponsors of the competition, announced the coveted award.[26] The town, rightfully proud of this achievement, widely celebrated its newest accolade. *Look*'s publisher, Vernon Myers, described Westport as "out of the blueprint stage of citizen action."

A crowd of Westporters watched the town hoist its banner proclaiming it an All America City atop the municipal flagpole in Parker-Harding Plaza during a brief ceremony in February 1959. The town was also flooded with posters, bumper strips, flags, and other evidences of celebration. And the *Town Crier* published a special edition on February 26, 1959, telling the full story of how Westport won the coveted award. The six areas of competition for all towns were: governmental structure, rational land use, tax reform, education, refuse disposal and a sound police organization. Praise came from the *Town Crier* and could also could be heard on the brand new local radio station WMMM, which opened in Westport in 1959. Kudos also came aplenty to Westport town officials during those heady days, not the least of which were from the following: President Dwight D. Eisenhower, Connecticut Senator Thomas J. Dodd, Governor Abraham A. Ribicoff, and former Governor John D. Lodge. The migration into Westport in the decade from 1948 to 1958 had increased the town's population from 11,300 to 17,000. With its reputation and profile considerably enhanced, Westport had become a prominent place on the national horizon.

NOTES

1. Interview with Harry and Pat Audley, September 8, 1998.
2. Statement from A.J. Izzo, November 1999.
3. *A History of the Woman's Club*, compiled by C. X. Panish, April 1972, p. 38.
4. Joanna Foster, *Carousel*, June 1990, p. 8.
5. The *Westport Town Crier*, December 15, 1949.
6. Dan Woog, "Woog's World," the *Westport News*, February 26, 1993.
7. The *Town Crier*, May 19, 1949.
8. The *Westporter-Herald*, May 9, May 16, 1946.
9. In 1999, the League of Women Voters celebrated its fiftieth anniversary, co-chaired by Tammy Pincavage and Lorraine Boyton, with a number of activities throughout the year. The membership in 1999 had grown to more than 170, including 22 men.
10. The *Westport News*, May 10, 1972.
11. Estimate from Edward Keehan, a Westport veteran.
12. Manuscript of Herbert Baldwin's life story made available to the Westport Historical Society by Martha Baldwin Ordeman, 1998.
13. Transcript of Allen Raymond's talk, 1998.
14. Julian P. Brodie, *Suburbia Today*, June 1962, p. 10.
15. The *Westport News*, March 2, 1984.
16. The *Westport News*, July 25, 1990
17. The *Westport News*, November 13, 1991.

18. The sources are Pam Heyden, advertising, of Mitchells of Westport and telephone interview with Ed Mitchell on January 20, 2000.

19. The *Westport News*, July 12, 1994.

20. The *Westporter-Herald*, February 17, 1955.

21. Joyce Losen, assistant to the superintendent of schools, Westport Board of Education, November 1999.

22. *Westporter-Herald*, December 16, 1948.

23. The *Town Crier*, April 23, 1961.

24. Bob Graves, *Saugatuck Harbor Yacht Club, A Brief History, 1959-1999*. A club flag was created in 1961 with the help of Mrs. Probst, wife of the Club's founder. In 1967, the Club had 110 boats and by 1998 there were 171 club members. In 1991, the clubhouse was renovated, and in 1994 "Spousal Equality" amendments to the club's bylaws were passed providing equal treatment for both men and women in the club. By 1999, the club got its own Web site and celebrated its 40th anniversary.

25. *Westporter-Herald*, December 16, 1954.

26. *Westport News*, January 22, 1959.

Bumper sticker, p. 233, Westport Town Crier.

CHAPTER 15

RISING EXPECTATIONS

Westport is changing – it's at the crossroads.

— Sidney Kramer, owner,
The Remarkable Book Shop, and
founder, Save Westport Now

The 1960s opened with an extraordinary optimism — indeed, exhilaration — as the nation's youngest elected president, John Fitzgerald Kennedy, began his administration. America became a nation of rapidly rising expectations and Westporters reflected that mood. During the presidential campaign, Westport Democrats had been solidly behind the charismatic senator from Massachusetts.

On November 5, 1960 the Democratic standard bearer drew an enthusiastic crowd of 75,000, including hundreds of Westporters, at a rally in nearby Bridgeport. Jerome A. Kaiser, who managed the Kennedy campaign in Westport, appointed Ruth Solway to arrange for the Westport motorcade to Bridgeport. She organized a fleet of 300 cars that left Westport, all of them carrying placards saying, "Vote for Kennedy" that her 14-year-old daughter, Linda, had prepared. Solway recalls the day vividly: "This was a very special day in my life," she said. She remembers the cars lined up in the Baldwin parking lot. When they arrived in Bridgeport, she found herself standing right beside Kennedy at one point. "He was good-looking and friendly," she added. She had been involved in politics for a long time and this was "a thrill for me to be on the same ticket as Senator Kennedy, since I was running for Justice of the Peace in Westport. His name was on the top and mine at the bottom."[1] In Westport, she won; he lost.

A few days before Election Day, the *Town Crier* had published a story headlined, "Kennedy Motorcade Planned by Area's Dems."[2] Westporter Jerry Davidoff, a Democratic candidate for state representative in the General Assembly in Hartford, received a public endorsement from the senator, which was also front-page news in the *Town Crier*. Two days later, Kennedy triumphed in Connecticut by 90,000 votes — 656,873 to 566,783, and barely won the national election. Richard Nixon won Westport, by a 2-1 margin, 6,842 to 3,825.[3] In fact, Nixon's plurality helped Westport Republican candidates John Boyd, a former town court judge and GOP town chairman, and Howard Dreyfous, Boyd's running mate, who were elected as state representatives, defeating Democrats Frederic Kimball and Davidoff.

STEINKRAUS WITH JFK: Herman W. Steinkraus, left, of South Compo Road, chairman of the board of the United Nations Association, with President John F. Kennedy in 1962. He was a member of a hand-picked delegation honored by the president. It included, second from left, Prof. Arthur Holcombe, head of the history department at Harvard University; Norman Cousins, editor of The Saturday Review; *Walter Reuther, head of the AFL-CIO; Oscar De Lima, president of the United Nations Association; Sol Linowitz, businessman/ambassador. Steinkraus also served as president of the U.S. Chamber of Commerce and director of the National Association of Manufacturers after the war.* PHOTO COURTESY OF RUTH STEINKRAUS-COHEN

The Kennedy administration's early burst of social conscience and emphasis on the arts was reflected in Westport. It was during this era that the United Way, founded in 1959, had its first full year of operation in 1960, reminding the community that local families were in need amidst all of the affluence around them. It was founded by, among others, the late Elizabeth Roberts, a generous, compassionate person who worked in the office in the YMCA building and whose name is still invoked today in the course of United Way board meetings and discussions about the goals of the organization. She and Dorothy Tarrant, head of the Community Council, were perceived as the heart of the postwar volunteer movement in this community. These two organizations and a number of others were merged in the 1980s. Dick Brooks, a Westport cartoonist, and the originator of "The Jackson Twins," served as the organization's first president. Its early leaders included highly respected town officials such as former First Selectman Herbert Baldwin. Its fund drives have increased every year until 1998-99 when more than 4,100 families contributed to the campaign carried out by more than 200 campaign volunteers. It now helps fund 60 vital health and human services programs serving all demographic segments of the community. Combined with donations that Westporters give at their workplace, the total amount of money collected in 1999 was about $1 million.

As affluent as Westport may be, it is a town — like many thousands across the nation — with people in need. There are still a significant number of people and families with a variety of social problems.[4] Among the most prevalent is the growing alienation that many young and elderly people feel in Westport. Further, the number of men and women in the homeless shelters has been on the rise; calls to the Women's Crisis Center hotline have increased five-fold since 1985, due in part to the national publicity about domestic violence; there is a long waiting list for child care facilities, reflecting the growing number of two-income families; and the number of elderly requiring Meals on Wheels is increasing as the number of elderly increases. Says Executive Director Bernice Corday: "The thing that distinguishes Westport from other communities is the way people respond to challenges. Having been here for 16 years, I cannot convey strongly enough the caliber of people I have had the pleasure of working with and the intelligence and heart they bring to responding."[5]

Speaking of challenges, The Mid-Fairfield County Youth Museum Association was founded in June 1958. Its name was changed in 1974 to the Nature Center for Environmental Studies, and it has served as a focal point for environmental education in southern Fairfield County. The center concentrates on wildlife preservation and rehabilitation, and water quality research. It attracts more than 70,000 visitors a year, including Westport school children who regularly visit the site, to a 62-acre Wildlife Sanctuary

ART IN MINIATURE FORM: Westport artists have contributed stamps to the U. S. Postal Service. Above, stamps created by Stevan Dohanos, top left, Leonard Everett Fisher, bottom left, Edward Vebell, right. WESTPORT HISTORICAL SOCIETY PHOTO/LEO CIRINO COLLECTION

and 22,000-square-foot Natural Science Museum. The Nature Center acquired the land over a long period of time; the vast majority of it deeded to the Center by private individuals. In all, a staff of 10 full-time people and 7 part-timers with a $1 million budget, runs one of the best organizations of its type in the state, under Executive Director John Horkel. The Center has run after-school programs and a pre-school program for more than 30 years and, in recent years, has offered scholarships to inner city families who otherwise would not be able to afford to send their children to preschool centers.

In 1963, Arthur Summerfield, the new U.S. Postmaster General, contacted Arnold Copeland, a graphic designer and past president of the "Westport Artists," to meet with him in Washington to form a committee of three graphic arts people to choose and supervise the work of illustrators who would be doing forthcoming stamps under a new policy for U.S. stamps. The philatelic artists were called "The Citizen's Stamp Advisory Committee." Copeland was the first titular head of the design group and went on to design 29 stamps. Much later, Stevan Dohanos took over the post. He, too, designed and supervised many stamp issues. "Postage stamps present art in miniature form," said Dohanos. "Ideas of great importance, man's highest achievements, the widest spectrums of our culture, nature's wonders, architecture, national parks, historic landmarks, are all presented in this small space," he said. His six-cent stamp of the American flag with the White House underneath is reportedly the most popular stamp ever made. Stamps were assigned to scores of other Westport illustrators, including Ward Brackett, Miggs Burroughs, Naiad Einsel, Walter Einsel, Leonard Everett Fisher, Bernard Fuchs, Robert Lambdin, Howard Munce, Paul Rabut, Walter Reed, Charles Reed, Carl Sacks, Jim Sharpe, Dolli Tingle, and Edward Vebell. Until a few years ago, the Westport Post Office had a display case in the lobby of stamps done by local artists. Unfortunately, one night it was ripped off the wall and has never been recovered.

There was a monumental scare at the outset of the Sixties in Westport: The town was momentarily shaken by an extraordinary invasion of the Police Department. An armed attack on any police headquarters is rare, even in the nation's big cities. But in Westport it had never happened — until July 4, 1961, when an hour before dawn a young man barged into the headquarters building and started firing a semi-automatic pistol at two policemen behind the front desk. One officer, Patrolman Donald Bennette, was wounded before the man fled to the parking lot. Other officers followed him into the parking lot and the gunman shot a second officer, Patrolman Andrew Chapo, before being wounded by police himself. In all, 11 bullet holes were found at the police station, inside and out. The policemen recuperated from their wounds, but the gunman, identified by police as Brendan McLaughlin, an advertising executive who worked in New York City, died from his wounds a few weeks later in Norwalk Hospital. An investigation showed that McLaughlin, as an ex-Marine, had shot and killed his father, Eugene B. McLaughlin, of Gorham Island Road, about 2 A.M. during a family argument. The two police officers recovered from their wounds. The lobby of Police Headquarters remained the same until it was renovated in 1988 with more security precautions taken for the police.[6]

John J. Kemish, a personable and highly competent public servant, was elected first selectman of Westport in 1967 following Herb Baldwin's announcement that he would not run again. Kemish defeated Democrat Gerard Wheeler. Westport was at a crossroads. It was about to face one of the most defining moments in the town's history. Just before Kemish's election, the residents of Westport were made aware of the fact that the United Illuminating Company of Bridgeport was planning to build a 14-story nuclear power plant on Cockenoe Island, less than one mile off Compo Beach. The headline in a Bridgeport newspaper in the summer of 1967 took most Westporters by surprise: "UI PLANS A-PLANT OFF WESTPORT."[7] Even though there was not yet a stigma attached to nuclear power — it was, in fact, perceived as a clean and inexpensive source of energy — opposition to the plan came swiftly and loudly, led by the crusading editor of the *Westport News,* Jo (Fox) Brosious.

Kemish had won second and third terms over Mark Marcus, the Democratic standard-bearer, in 1969 and 1971. The town had hired Kemish in 1958 as its first professional controller under the new Town Charter and he was Baldwin's logical successor. As controller he won high praise for improving the town's credit rating from A to AAA. Kemish would soon

THE BRIDGEPORT POST

WEATHER FORECAST · NORWALK EDITION

VOL. LXXXIV, NO. 183 · BRIDGEPORT, CONN., MONDAY, AUGUST 7, 1967.

UI PLANS A-PLANT OFF WESTPORT

UNION BEGINS | Reds Down 5 Copters | Veil of Mystery Lifted From Island | UTILITY BARES

BREAKING NEWS: The headline in an issue of the Bridgeport Post *August, 1967 shocked most Westporters: The town, led by the local newspaper and civic-minded residents fought fiercely under the banner of the slogan, Save Cockenoe Island.* BRIDGEPORT PUBLIC LIBRARY

become one of the key figures in the Cockenoe campaign.

Brosious, a talented editor with a zest for good old-fashioned crusading journalism, called for a letter-writing campaign to petition state and federal authorities to stop what she described as an infringement on the town's unspoiled, undeveloped offshore island, which was open space used mainly for camping, clamming, mooring, and picnicking. She was also adept at bringing out housewives in this campaign and, at one point, recruited what was commonly called her "petticoat" army. Brosious, later known as Jo Fox, recalls the battle plan of her campaign: "Save Cockenoe was an all-out battle. It was war. The proponents of saving the island were divided into two fronts: anti-nuclear power and pro-space preservation. In order to win, the *News* focused on the latter because millions of dollars had been spent trying to convince the national populace that nuclear power was clean and cheap. UI, which had purchased Cockenoe for the purpose of building an electric generating plant, had geared itself for the anti-nuke 'nuts,' but we cleverly dodged that bullet by emphasizing the importance of open space." [8] The *News* had run a coupon for people to indicate whether or not they were in favor of saving Cockenoe as open space. Hundreds of letters poured in, the majority in favor of purchasing Cockenoe. The campaign to save the island was relentless. The talented husband and wife duo, Naiad and Walter Einsel, designed a stunning SAVE COCKENOE NOW poster which has become a collectible in Westport. In August 1967 the RTM voted unanimously to proceed with all possible steps to save the island. Former Democratic Governor Abraham A. Ribicoff was quoted as warning against being "profligate" with our environment.

During the next year-and-a-half, the *News* also published full-page photo spreads of activities such as picnics that took place on the island. Opponents of the plant then copied those photos, and two editorials, and mailed a packet seeking support to every member of the State Legislature and all the major state media. A film showing the heavy recreational use of the island, especially by young people, was created for presentation at a legislative hearing on two Cockenoe-related bills that would come before the General Assembly in Hartford.

Regular strategy meetings were held at Brosious' house on Sunday mornings. Out of these meetings came the ideas for two bills: establish the Town of Westport as having the higher power of eminent domain in the case of the UI Company and Cockenoe; give all 169 towns in the state the higher power of eminent domain over *all* utilities. Both bills were introduced by State Representative Louis Stroffolino (R) and first-term State Representative Edwin Green (D), who had been elected with the support of the *News*. Meanwhile, the *News'* competing newspaper, the *Town Crier*, edited by Luis A.Villalon, an influential member of former First Selectman Herb Baldwin's "Kitchen Cabinet," argued that the UI plant would so enhance the town's Grand List that local taxes would be sharply reduced.

The publicity generated by the *Westport News* resulted in a turnout of hundreds of Westporters in Hartford on March 10, 1969, for the hearing on the Cockenoe bills. A caravan of buses carried many of the townspeople, while others car-pooled. The proposed legislation threatened the unlimited power of eminent domain of utilities and put such fear into the utility lobby that many of its members — gas, telephone, water companies — eventually turned against the UI purchase and urged UI to sell. The *New York Times* published an editorial giving resounding support to Westport's campaign to preserve its natural resources. No sooner had the hearing in Hartford concluded than John Boyd, town attorney in the Kemish administration, received a phone call from United Illuminating with an offer to sell if Westport would drop the legislation. According to the final pact, Cockenoe Island was sold to the town of Westport for $200,000 — or the equivalent of $800,000 in the year 2000 — with state and federal funds covering 75 percent of the acquisition costs. The historic decision came on Thursday, April 17, 1969, when the RTM met to consider an appropriation of $200,000 request-

CRUSADING EDITOR: Joe Fox Brosious, the editor of the Westport News, *galvanized the community through stories and editorials in her paper to stop the construction of a 14-story nuclear power plant on Cockenoe Island, less than one mile off Compo Beach. She blasted the United Illuminating Company's proposal as an infringement on the town's unspoiled, undeveloped offshore island. She is shown here on Cockenoe Island in 1967. She drew support from all segments of the community and from the* New York Times, *which published an editorial supporting the town's campaign to preserve this natural resource.*
GEORGE SILK/ LIFE MAGAZINE © TIME, INC.

CAMPAIGN POSTER: This poster, designed by Naiad and Walter Einsel, left, could be seen all over town during the campaign to thwart the proposed nuclear power plant. It became a collectible over the years.

WESTPORT NEWS PHOTO

ed by Kemish to purchase Cockenoe. Kemish and Third Selectman Wheeler, a Democrat, spoke in favor. Second Selectman Wildes W. Veazie, a loyal colleague of Baldwin's, broached the possibility of referring the appropriation for the acquisition of Cockenoe to a referendum. RTM member Donald J. Lunghino blasted the idea immediately, pointing to the fact that the RTM was completely representative and responsive to the electorate and was not in need of referendum confirmation. The RTM then voted unanimously to buy the land. It was a resounding victory for Westport.

In a 1999 interview, Kemish congratulated the "visionary, aesthetically minded" supporters of the campaign to preserve Cockenoe, particularly Jo Fox and the *Westport News*. On April 3, 1969, the *News* published an editorial thanking those people who played key roles. They included State Representatives Green and Stroffolino; the Westport negotiation team, headed by Richard Broadman and including Town Attorney Boyd, First Selectman Kemish, Second Selectman Wildes Veazie, and Conservation Commissioner Stanley Atwood; and those who presented the case on the floor of the Hartford Legislature. RTM member Hamilton Brosious, husband of the *News*' editor, gave the lead testimony, with Westport Attorney Alan Senie joining in. By April 18, the Westport RTM voted unanimously to purchase the island as RTMer Donald Lunghino passionately argued that the body was "completely representative" of Westport voters. The Cockenoe story had a fitting ending. In its December 24, 1969 issue, after the sale had been approved by the Public Utilities Commission, the *News* ran an editorial with this headline: "ISLE BE HOME FOR CHRISTMAS." Kemish presented the United Illuminating Company's representative, Arthur D. McGovern, with a check in the amount of $212,740.08, which included the $200,000 purchase price, $10,242 in interest calculated from the initial agreement on April 1, and $2,498 as a tax rebate for the previous six months. The town wound up actually paying about $50,000 for the island, since the state and federal governments under the open space acquisition program would return 75 percent of the costs. *Life* magazine ran a photo spread on the epic struggle, featuring a picture of Jo Brosious standing on Compo Beach with Cockenoe Island in the background. The magazine heralded the town's acquisition of Cockenoe as one of the most significant conservation victories in the nation in its "Fourth of July Special" issue of 1970.

In other retrospective comments on Cockenoe in 1999, Kemish gave perhaps the most perceptive assessment of what the struggle had been all about.[9] "The real story," he said, "was between those who had a vision of beauty and environmental values as opposed to a great many who had

UI Will Sell Cockenoe I.

VICTORY! The Westport News *headline in April, 1969, was the culmination of the bitter battle that involved the state legislature, the voters of Westport, and the power company. Representative Edwin Green, right, shows his pleasure from the historic decision on Thursday, April 17, 1969, when the Representative Town Meeting passed an appropriation of $200,000 for the acquisition of Cockenoe. By April 18, the* Westport RTM *voted unanimously to purchase the island. In its December 24, 1969 issue, after the sale had been approved by the Public Utilities Commission, the* News *ran this headline:* "ISLE BE HOME FOR CHRISTMAS."*

WESTPORT NEWS PHOTO

their eyes on adding five billion dollars to the Grand List and cutting the tax rate by half or more." Kemish also pointed out that, at that time, Three Mile Island had not yet imploded, nor had Chernobyl's nuclear power plant exploded. Due to its enormous effect on the future of Westport since that time, Cockenoe remains a vivid memory.

Thirty years later, in September 1997, Westport's local leaders, past and present, turned out for Town Hall ceremonies, marking the Cockenoe victory. Jacqueline Heneage and Martha Hauhuth, both former first selectmen, reminisced about Westport's past and they recognized Westporters who had served the town. RTM members from the Cockenoe era were given awards, and other public office holders and community groups— including the yacht clubs and the boating community — active in the fight were also recognized. Jo Fox received a special award from the Connecticut General Assembly and from the Westport Historical Society. When she stood up, the crowd erupted with applause for several minutes and was on its feet in her honor. After a sing-a-long by Dorothy Bryce, a Westporter and veteran Broadway entertainer, everyone walked across the street to the Westport Historical Society for a party and to view an exhibit on the *Westport News'* campaign to save Cockenoe.[10] The next day, a series of events took place on Compo Beach. During that celebration, the centerpiece was a large cake made by Westporter Dale Lamberty, founder of the Great Cakes Bakery. It featured a relief map of Cockenoe Island in perfect detail.

In addition to leading the fight to save Cockenoe, Kemish chalked up some impressive accomplishments that went a long way in preserving and

TRANSPORTATION INNOVATION: The Minnybus came to Westport in the mid-1970s to alleviate traffic and help commuters, shown here with briefcases in hand. The buses were launched by the new Transit District.
WESTPORT NEWS PHOTO

enhancing the town's natural assets during his three terms in office: He established the first significant beautification program for the town by appointing a Beautification Committee headed by Claire Ford and widely publicized by Winifred Balboni. The committee planted trees and was able to restrict signs on the Post Road with the support of the Planning and Zoning Commission. Kemish also succeeded in eliminating ugly telephone poles at very little cost in the downtown area with the cooperation of the Southern New England Telephone Company and Northeast Utilities; he was credited with the acquisition of the 38-acre Wakeman farm as open space; he led the town's effort to acquire the Nike site on Bayberry Lane for the Westport-Weston Health District and the Rolnick Planet Observatory; and he was responsible for the acquisition of the North Avenue Nike Site, providing additional land adjacent to the Staples High School property; finally, he played a role in the creation of the Transit District and the subsequent introduction of the Minnybus.

The Transit District was one of the most far-reaching changes in modern Westport, overcoming a great deal of negative reaction at the outset from those who wanted to maintain the status quo in Westport. The concept of a Minnybus system for Westporters, especially the elderly and the young, was first brought to public attention by Paul R. Green, a former RTM member, in 1967. Green recalls that, as an RTM member in District 1, he had heard from his constituents, "many of whom were not as affluent as other Westporters," especially the elderly, that they could not get around to shop or use the town's recreational facilities. Innocently, I told them at the time, "the answer would be to get a bus." In the summer of 1968, the RTM by a margin of 23-7 voted to consider establishing a transit district. In November 1968 the voters of Westport approved the concept by a 2-1 margin in a referendum on Election Day, a step required under state statutes because the transit system would be financed by state and federal funding. For the next four years, however, the issue continued to be debated while studies were made of the types of buses needed for a transit service, the proposed routes of the buses, and how it would be financed.

In 1973 RTM Moderator Edwin Kahn's ad hoc transit advisory committee, chaired by RTM member Roy M. Dickinson, recommended once again to the body that it approve the district. The committee consisted of Dickinson, Martin Levin, Donald Levy, Frances Cowden, Marion Cardell, and Rita Steinberger. Gladys Mansir, chairman of the Commission for the Elderly, made a compelling case, stating that the bus system was "vital" to the needs of Westport's senior citizens. In the course of a heated debate, Dickinson pointed out that a one-cent increase in the local gasoline tax would pay the cost. "One cent won't even be noticed," said the legislator who stressed that such a transportation system would benefit commuters, the elderly, and youngsters too young to drive. The key to ridership, he argued, would be to make it the vogue. He noted that one town with a similar system had painted its buses purple.[11] Responding to a suggestion that school buses be used as a trial run on Saturday, Dickinson said: "I don't think too many people would want to climb up on a yellow school bus and bounce down to town." After a heated session about this major change in lifestyle in Westport, the RTM voted 21-14 in favor. It also voted to appoint Paul R. Green as its first director. A year later, on Saturday, August 10, 1974, the buses began to roll, beginning with eight 16-passenger Minnybuses.

Soon after, the Maxytaxi service was successfully introduced, serving as a means to provide transportation to businesses for picking up passengers as well as business documents, and other retail goods. This was supplanted by the Maxybus, a 33-passenger vehicle to service commuters for the first time from the Green's Farms station. Since then, Westport's minibus routes have changed over time. Further, in 1991 a Superior Court judge awarded more than $1 million in damages to Michael and Anthony Gilbertie, owners of the defunct Westport Taxi Service who successfully claimed that the district used unfair practices to drive them out of business. The judgment was appealed by the Transit District to the state Supreme Court, which upheld the previous court ruling but reduced the final in 1996 to be $854,000. In 1999, the brothers, who had been unable to collect the award, unsuccessfully turned to the RTM before filing a suit against the town and the Westport Transit District. The case remained unresolved at the outset of 2000. Paul Green observed in 1999: "I like to think that the bus system is helping reduce traffic congestion, particularly at train times. As congestion grows, the bus will become more important in the future."[12]

The Transit District was not the only significant town organization created in 1973. That same year Westport's Historic District Commission was established under state charter. It was given legal authority to protect existing Historic Districts and to assist in the creation of future Historic

Districts in Westport. It is composed of five commissioners and three alternates appointed to five-year terms by the first selectman. Anyone owning an historic building must obtain the commission's approval before making any exterior changes or permanent alterations to their property; such changes must be consistent with state and federal guidelines and in keeping with the historic character of the district.

KING IN WEST-PORT: The Reverend Dr. Martin Luther King, Jr. spoke at Temple Israel in 1964, hosted by Rabbi Byron Rubenstein. King asked for support in the fight for civil rights. Shortly after that, Rubenstein would be arrested along with King in a nonviolent march in the South.

TEMPLE ISRAEL PHOTO, ABOVE
WESTPORT PUBLIC LIBRARY
PHOTO, BELOW

Westport's conscience was tested in the 1960s in the way it handled the generations-old issue of race relations. The issue of racial equality was literally brought home to Westport when the Reverend Dr. Martin Luther King, Jr. preached at Temple Israel on Friday evening, May 22, 1964. King had been invited here by Jerome Kaiser. In 1968, his widow, Roslyn Kaiser recalled that King arrived at her home in the late afternoon of a warm day. "We sat on the porch and talked with Dr. King and two of his aides...[He] told us he never traveled alone. One had to be impressed with his sincerity, warmth, intelligence, and genuine personal concern for those about him — our children, for instance. He seemed very young to bear such a burden of leadership." [13]

King spoke on the topic "Remaining Awake Through a Great Revolution." He compared the people of his time to Washington Irving's Rip Van Winkle who, in Irving's story, slept 20 years through an American Revolution. "The most striking thing," King told a packed audience, "is not that he slept 20 years, but that he slept through a revolution. The greatest liability of history is that people fail to see a revolution taking place in our world today. We must support the social movement of the Negro." During his visit, King accepted a gift of three woodcarvings from Westport artist Roe Halper representing various aspects of the civil rights struggle. His wife, Coretta Scott King, hung them on the front hallway of their home.[14]

A decade later, in January 1974 at a Sunday evening meeting at the Grace Baptist Church in Norwalk on West Avenue, King's supporters gathered to commemorate his death by an assassin's bullet on April 4, 1968 in Memphis, Tennessee. The highlight of the ceremony was a talk by Temple Israel's rabbi, Byron Rubenstein, in which he spoke about being arrested in a non-violent march along with King in June 1964. "It was in jail that I came to know the greatness of Dr. King," said Rabbi Rubenstein. "While in jail, I never heard a word of hate or bitterness from that man, only worship of faith, joy, and determination."[15]

With the assassinations of King and Robert F. Kennedy in 1968, a country already gravely wounded by the assassination of President Kennedy and the Vietnam War exploded with demonstrations of discontent, anger and disillusionment. Westporters, like others across the nation, began holding rallies, beginning with a "Mobilization Day for Peace" led by Herbert Cohen, a Westport attorney seeking the Democratic nomination for Congress, and Emanuel Margolis, a Westport attorney who represented the Connecticut Civil Liberties Union.

The racial divide was made abundantly clear on the evening of May 13, 1968, when a huge turnout of more than 1,000 Westporters gathered to attend a meeting of all the boards and commissions to decide whether or not to open up Westport's Summer School and Beach School programs to a group of 25 to 40 black and Hispanic children for a six-week period.[16] The kids would be sponsored by an established agency, the Action for Bridgeport Community Development (ABCD) of Bridgeport. Following a rancorous debate, Westport made history that night when both the recreation and education boards unanimously approved the integrated summer program.

Westport attorney Alan Nevas said he remembered when they were debating the camp. Sponsors of the camp wanted to let the kids use Compo Beach during the summer, but many people just did not want black kids from Bridgeport coming to Westport. "That was the bottom line," said Nevas. Lou Nistico, owner of the Arrow Restaurant with his brothers, was the chairman of the Recreation Commission at the time. "He stood up and I remember him saying, 'What is the problem? What are you afraid of? What do you think? That the color is going to wash off these kids in the Sound?'"[17] Nevas, who became a Federal District Court judge, was among a handful of Westporters who went down South in 1964 to represent, pro bono, Negro nonviolent protestors who had been arrested for demonstrating. Westport attorneys George Constantikes and Lawrence Weisman also went to Mississippi in 1964 to offer their legal services. Weisman explained why he got involved. He had been to a meeting in Harlem listening to some black kids speak, he said. "One speaker urged everyone to do something. He said, 'What are you going to tell your children when they ask you where you were in the summer of '64?' That got to me. My wife, Mary Lou, was pregnant at the time, but I knew I had to go." [18] Artist/illustrator Tracy Sugarman, Nevas and Rubenstein spoke to a group of more than 100 teenagers from Staples High School that summer, inspiring them to raise money by soliciting funds from people on local beaches and in recreation centers.

In May 1967 an integrated Intercommunity Camp of Norwalk, Westport and Bridgeport blossomed here. Children from these towns were brought together for a few hours a day to play and meet one another in Westport. Looking back on the beginning of this camp, June Sugarman, who organized a celebration benefit called the "Ten Summers Tall Birthday Party" in Westport on June 12, 1977, described the reunion as "a coming together of the hundreds of families who have been touched by the camp, the ones I call believers." It was seen as a living memorial to Martin Luther King; and it became an accepted part of the community. The idea was conceived by Rich Bradley, a Staples High School teacher. June Sugarman continued: "It's [the camp] a microcosm of what we would like to see in the world. Freedom of choice, freedom to be what you are and it all happens naturally. A lot of people believe in that."[19] CBS-TV newscaster and Westport resident Harry Reasoner, among others, held a party to raise funds for the camp. Realizing swimming was an important element in a summer program, volunteers found Westport families who opened their pools on a regularly scheduled basis to the campers and staff. Although some residents with pools declined, enough responded to make it worthwhile.

Tracy Sugarman is, perhaps, the most conspicuous among the old-time liberals in Westport. In an interview in 1999, he said he was satisfied that, except for an occasional incident, there no longer was any overt anti-Semitism in Westport. But race, he said, is another issue. Looking back on his visits during the civil rights movement to Ruleville, Mississippi in 1964 and 1965, he says today:

> In my heart, I fear that we may be going backwards. Racism
> has been part of our society from our very beginnings. No, I
> don't think people are consciously racists. Neither do I
> think the kids are racists. My wife [the late June Sugarman]
> and I put two kids through our school system. But, in truth,
> they did miss something — the opportunity to get to know
> and understand others of different backgrounds, different
> skin colors, different histories.... Most people don't see
> black folks around here. Is Westport a microcosm of
> America's suburbs? Yes, it is what every American suburb

wishes it was. It's got wealth, the beaches, and it's got Paul Newman. But it does not have diversity. Our kids will have to find that somewhere else. Is this subconscious racism? Most people I think would rather take two steps to the side and keep on walking. That's the natural instinct. Not to get involved. Plus there is the rise of black separation because integration often is not comfortable or totally successful. But we have moved light years ahead from the "closet society" of the South and the often-institutionalized racism of the North. There really is no turning back. It is so complicated.

Sugarman, a 78-year-old artist/writer who was among the fighting men who landed on France's Utah Beach on D-Day,[20] adds: "I've had two invasions in my life. One was Normandy and one was in Mississippi and both of them opened doors and possibilities for our whole society." In his book, *Stranger at the Gates,* he describes his experiences in Mississippi in 1963 and 1964.

TELLING IT LIKE IT IS: Westport artist/illustrator/writer Tracy Sugarman talks to a group of Staples High School students in the summer of 1964 about his experience helping Negroes to register to vote in Ruleville, Mississippi.
WESTPORT NEWS PHOTO

In addition to those Westporters who participated in the civil rights movement, the year 1964 was significant in another way in Westport. It marked the first anniversary of President Kennedy's assassination. An 8-foot bronze plaque designed by the late Joseph Salerno, a Westport architect, and unveiled by First Selectman Herb Baldwin, was mounted on an exterior wall of the Staples administration building. Speakers at the ceremony included Westport attorney George Constantikes, then an RTM member and chairman of the memorial committee. The president of the Staples Student Association, Julian "Tony" Koslow, accepted the memorial on behalf of the student body and described the late president as "a symbol of youth and its finest hopes and aspirations, a man whose dream of a future America was to remain unfulfilled at the time of his tragic death. But his words on the plaque are words which have become a part of the American tradition."

Of all the programs designed to foster better race relations, by far the most controversial was the urban-suburban program called Project

Concern. Funded by state and federal grants, Project Concern had started in Hartford in 1966, with a relatively small number of inner-city children bused to schools in surrounding suburbs. In the spring of 1970, the concept of busing a limited number of Bridgeport children to Westport had the backing of several religious groups, including the Green's Farms Congregational Church, the Saugatuck Congregational Church, Temple Israel, and the Unitarian Church. Soon, however, critics of the plan surfaced. Westport author John Tarrant, in his book, *The End of Exurbia*, neatly summed up the problem: "Bridgeport's about 20 miles from Westport. In terms of money, society, attitude, and style of life, the distance might be measured in light years."[21]

In an emotion-charged atmosphere that brought some to the verge of tears and others to the edge of rage, the Board of Education met in mid-April in 1970, to discuss Project Concern. Although it was not on the agenda, busing was the ostensible issue that brought an estimated 1,000 residents to Staples High School that night. Boos and occasional heckling of board members filled the night air as some 42 citizens argued the pros and cons of the program. Within a few days, the *Westport News* on April 20, 1970 published a letter to the editor signed by five black Westport couples:

> Those of us who live in Westport do so because we have faith in it. Despite occasional racial incidents, we have felt our white fellow townsmen were basically decent. Those of us who attended the Board of Education meeting are wondering what kind of town this is after all. What was all that bigotry disguised in euphemistic phrases about concern for the black man in the voice of Westport? Were those rude, vicious, hate-filled BEST people the real Westport? Are most of the thirty thousand people here filled with fear of the thought of 25 black children from another town going to school with their children? We think of our friends and neighbors and find it difficult to believe that the "haters" are in the majority.... We are at a crossroads: Westport can become just another suburban town vainly trying to pretend that the rest of the world isn't out there or it can be an example of brotherhood.

An organization calling itself the Bipartisan Education Study Team (BEST), sprang up almost overnight to send out questionnaires to the community. Some 90 percent of the respondents, BEST reported, expressed opposition to Project Concern. And, in forming an unlikely coalition, conservatives from Westport joined with some black leaders in Bridgeport in opposition to the plan, obviously for different reasons.

As various groups mobilized against or in favor of the plan, Board of Education members gained some insight into a Project Concern program already in place in Westport. Monsignor Patrick Donnelly and Sister Theresa Kelleher, principal of the Assumption School in Westport, invited the board members to view the program in action at their school. It had been in effect since September 1970 when 25 youngsters from Bridgeport, grades 1 through 5, began attending Assumption. Thus, the board was able to show that a traditionally conservative, influential body demonstrated its commitment to Project Concern.

The battle finally came to a head on December 7, 1970, when the education board voted 3-2 to accept the proposal to bus a limited number of Bridgeport students, on a voluntary basis, into Westport schools. Less than 48 hours later, thousands of letters went out to Westport residents under the letterhead of the Recall Committee of Westport, urging that the chairman of the education board, Joan Schine, be subject to a recall election because, as the letter stated, "against the interests and desires of the people of Westport, she has opened the schools to the children of Bridgeport."

Opposition to Project Concern was vocal and well organized. The Bipartisan Education Study Team (BEST), the Recall Committee, the Conservative Citizen's Club of Westport, and Westport Citizens for Neighborhood Schools all weighed in. In response, a bipartisan group calling itself Democracy on Trial (DOT), co-chaired by Allen Raymond, a Republican, and Jim O'Connell, a highly respected, liberal Democrat, quickly emerged. Their first townwide letter began with this brief paragraph: "You have just been called to jury duty. On trial, in the recall election coming up, is democracy in Westport." Another influential Schine supporter was Richard Leonard, Westport Education Association president: "I am saddened by this mishandling of a tool of democracy. But I am confident that if the election does take place, Westport will not vote to recall." Leonard, a resident of Westport for 15 years at the time, was father of four children in Westport schools and the elected spokesman for the Westport Education Association, the teachers union.

Despite petitions for recall and despite appeals to the state Supreme Court, despite months of debate, in the end the 3-2 vote held and in 1971, some 25 students from Bridgeport entered Burr Farms School, with other Bridgeport students who had enrolled in the Coleytown and Bedford Elementary schools. When Schine bowed out at the close of 1971, she explained: "For six years, second only to my family, the schools have been the central focus of my life, my time, my thought and my energies. I have no regrets that this has been so." Some two decades later, in 1991, Schine would receive the 1991 Woman of Valor Award for her long record of community service with children. The award came from the Educational Equity Concepts, a non-profit group in Manhattan that promotes equality of opportunity for all children. A memento she still cherishes from that time is a personal note from Lou Nistico, who had remained a staunch supporter from the onset. He wrote: "Dear Joan: You are a lighthouse shining through a dense fog. You stand tall, kind, intelligent, dignified, compassionate, honest. For this I kiss you on both cheeks. With great respect and admiration. (signed) Lou Nistico."

Project Concern drew support from the Westport-Weston Ministerial Association, the League of Women Voters, the Community Council of Westport-Weston, the Coleytown Elementary School PTA, and Temple Israel. Local families rallied enthusiastically by helping the Bridgeport students stay after school for all kinds of activities: scouts, Little League, gymnastics, swimming, ballet, and music lessons. They paid the tuitions and hosted their visitors overnight. Later, a "late bus" back to Bridgeport was added to accommodate those participating in these after-school activities. Attorney Leo Nevas joined with a number of other community leaders to establish another new group, Westporters for Equality in Education, to support implementation of Project Concern.

But the busing experiment would last only ten years. It began to peter out in June 1982 when the Bridgeport school system reduced the number of students bused from 53 to 21 students because, according to Juan Lopez, then Bridgeport director of developmental programs, the state had been funding the busing but withdrew that financial support. The city, he said, could not afford the $28,000 cost for two additional buses that would be needed to transport all 53 students. Westport Schools Superintendent Claire Gold tried to find monies to continue the project, but in vain.[22] And so the 1971-1981 program, which had been judged a success by educators, ran out of money and quietly died.

As a footnote to this seminal event, of all the black families who signed the letter to the editor of the *Westport News* on April 22, 1970, Venora Witherspoon Ellis has been in Westport the longest, having moved here in

1942. A college graduate, she grew up in Yazoo, Mississippi. "We were segregated and there was not that much interaction between the races," she said. "The only prejudice that affected me growing up was that we did not have equal education opportunities, books, buses, or school equipment." She first encountered race prejudice, she said, "when I came to Westport. I went to a dentist and I asked him if he would take me. When I called he said, 'I detect that you are colored.' And I said, 'Yes, I am.' He said, 'I will take you on Thursday when I don't have any other

VENORA AND LEROY ELLIS: *There were practically no blacks in Westport when they arrived in Westport in the late 1940s. "I came to Westport," she says, "because I wanted to make sure my kids got a good education."*
PHOTO COURTESY OF VENORA ELLIS

patients.' And I said, 'No. That's okay. My husband is fighting the war in the South Pacific for this country. Never mind.' So I rode around and I found another dentist on the Post Road. Another example when I first came here in the early 1940s was an ad in the paper from an employment agency. It said: 'Nanny Wanted. Only light-skinned apply.'"

Having majored in home economics, Ellis had spent summers in Westport while she was at Tougaloo College because most of her teachers were from the New England states. "I worked for Chester Bowles one summer. He was head of the Office of Price Administration at the time, and he later became governor. Then I moved to Westport because I had a scholarship at Teachers' College at Columbia and Mrs. Bowles had friends here with whom I could stay." In 1942, she had married Lawrence Brady, a college classmate who, in her words, was also "half-and-half." She finished her course work but did not graduate because she became pregnant. Divorced in 1949, she married Leroy Ellis in 1952. The couple has two grown daughters, both of whom graduated from Staples High School and went on to earn college degrees.

"I came to Westport," she said, "because I wanted to make sure my kids got a good education. I was a dressmaker for 10 years, then I became a house couturier making draperies, bedspreads, slipcovers, and house dressings. I did it for 42 years and retired in 1982." She added: "Had it not been for my Jewish friends, their understanding and concern, I probably would have moved on." There were only 13 black families here when she got involved with the Intercommunity Camp. Is Westport open to blacks today? "Yes, of course it is. It was not that way in the 1940s and 1950s. Are whites afraid of blacks? Yes, because many of them have never been exposed to blacks. They have never seen them other than as a servant, a gardener. Will it change? I don't think so, soon. Is this a diverse town? No. But most people here think it is Utopia."[23]

Dr. Albert Beasley, a black resident of Westport who is still a practicing pediatrician at the age of 78, has been an active member of the community ever since he moved here in 1953. The grandson of a Harvard-educated Boston attorney who helped found the NAACP, Beasley came from a family that settled in Boston and then in New York City. His father was a doctor who went to Harvard and his mother was a graduate of Radcliffe. "My parents were always up front about wanting me to go into a free society," he said in an interview in 1999. His father had practiced medicine in a town called Millis, Massachusetts. "As a doctor, my father was accepted because he was the only physician in the area. When I grew to school age, it was obvious this small community was not too receptive for me to grow up in and be educated. So my father started a practice in New York. They wanted a good liberal education for me. They found a very progressive school called the Walden School." Beasley went to the University of Wisconsin. After his freshman year he returned to New York and married Jean Tallman whom he had met while in high school. He graduated from New York University Medical School. After his residency at Children's Memorial Hospital in Chicago, he went into the Air Force during the Korean War. "It was my first true experience of overt prejudice," he said, "even though the Air Force was integrated. I was based in Houston and there was a lot that was difficult to live through." His wife, Jean, also a pediatrician, finished her residency at The New York Hospital-Cornell Medical Center while he was in the Air Force. When he returned they moved to Westport with their first child, Scott, who was born in Chicago. Their second child, a daughter, Jean, was born five months after their move to Westport.

Why did they move to Westport? "Well, my world had been the Walden School. I guess I had been looking to continue that feeling of freedom and I wanted to offer my kids that same freedom." Harry Bragg, a black man who had been his father's attorney, owned a summer place in Westport in 1953. The Beasleys rented a house on 11 acres from him for $90 a month. "We started to look to set up our practice in Bridgeport, but after a while we decided to start right here. After a while people accepted us and we built up our practice," Beasley explained. Beasley recalls that when he moved here, there were fewer than five black families in town. Then the couple bought some land from a fellow physician, Dr. Mal Beinfield. "Mal came to me and said he had this property on Bayberry Lane that he and Nat Greenberg had purchased. Then we decided to build a house and we went to various bank-lending institutions. We had trouble getting a mortgage. Banks used as an excuse that they did not like contemporary dwellings. Until one day, Oliver Clapp, who was a friend and a resident of Weston, said we should try Westport Bank and Trust. I said, we were told they lend to hardly anyone. 'Well,' he said, 'Let's go see the president of the bank, Einar Anderson.' So off we went. Anderson greeted us. 'How are you today, Oliver?' He looked at me and said, 'How much money do you want?' I told him. He said, 'You need $20,000 to build a $28,000 home. There's no problem with that. Let us know when you want it.'" Beasley continued: "During all the years I lived in this community, I have felt that, yes, I am a Negro or black, but the term 'African American' does not describe me or my children or most of the black or Negro population in this country. To me it's another term sort of like Italian American or Jewish American. I am a black American. I like to be considered as an individual." Beasley's wife, Jean, died in 1973. In 1979, he married Janet Grybski Schneyer, a native of Berlin, Germany, and a survivor of a concentration camp in Czechoslovakia.[24]

Many Westporters believe the reason there are so few black families here is economics. Most black families, it is argued, simply cannot afford to move here. Those who are here, some say, have been made to feel at home and participate in many of the community's mainstream activities. Some examples: Rai Cockfield, an IBM executive, has played an important role on the Fairfield County Quality Education and Diversity Council, and serves as a board member of the United Way of Westport-Weston. Martin Hamer, a former General Electric and IBM executive and a writer and author, has been instrumental in working towards integration in Westport schools, and has been a columnist for a local newspaper; Steven E. Daniels is president of the United Way of Westport-Weston. Winston Allen and Cheryl Scott-Daniels have served as presidents of the Westport Sunrise Rotary Club. And there are many other blacks and other minorities who have played important roles in Westport's cultural, business, and educational life. Nonetheless, despite the best efforts of black and white families in town, in terms of percentages, Westport's educational system has made little progress since 1970 in terms of integration. On the 25th anniversary year of Project Concern, in the fall of 1995, according to town school office records, fewer than 1 percent of Westport students were black; 3 percent were of Asian extraction; 2.7 percent Hispanic; and 94 percent were white.[25]

In the 1970s, the major issue in education shifted from race relations to money. In the early summer of 1973 a referendum on cutting the education budget by $800,000 or 6.1 percent was approved by 60 percent of the voters, who were worried about spiraling town expenses and their taxes. Merald Lue, organizer of the Westport Tax Watchers, said he was "overwhelmed by the groundswell." The Tax Watchers were backed by former First Selectman Herb Baldwin. Another referendum in 1978 on a $11.8 million high school modernization and renovation project resulted in a victory for those opposed to cutting $9 million earmarked for building a field house and pool. The early 1970s also marked the establishment of the Green's Farms Academy, a private preparatory school in 1972, and the formation of the Westport Girls Softball League in 1974, with a handful of girls turning out. A decade later, there were eight teams with 100 players; by 1994, there were 40 teams with more than 400 girls playing.

Zoning and the town's growth was the source of yet another controversy in the volatile Sixties. Dr. Guy F. Robbins, chairman of the Planning and Zoning Commission, stated publicly in 1962 that Westport should not be a town just for the rich and should therefore broaden the tax base. Various zoning plans were proposed to control growth, while at the same time allowing commercial development to continue in spite of critics who were concerned about the "hodge-podge" development of the Post Road in particular. Among the regulations adopted at that time were Design Development Districts (DDD), allowing restricted commercial development in residential sites of four acres or more; Multiple Family Dwellings (MFDs), which permitted construction of houses for more than one family; and a Restricted Office Retail District (RORD), which expanded business space, as well as regulations allowing apartments, which passed, then were repealed.

DWARFED: This huge, four-story office building erected in the late 1970s far overshadowed the quaint retail store in front of it at the corner of Riverside Avenue and the Post Road.

MIGGS BURROUGHS PHOTO

In the wake of these and other regulatory changes in zoning, the ensuing years saw a record number of lawsuits filed against the P&Z. Planning in Westport came under fire, while pressure for the town to grow and develop also continued under the P&Z. State Representative Julie Belaga (R-136), who chaired the P&Z commission from 1971 to 1975, commented that the massive four-story Wright Street building is a good example of what the regulations allowed before they were changed. The building dwarfs a charming little wooden building in front of it at the intersection of Riverside Avenue and the Post Road, reminding longtime townspeople of what Westport once looked like. Because of its imposing structure, the building was commonly called "the Wright Street monstrosity" by some townspeople who did not like it. Others argued that it blended nicely into the hillside. However, even the buildings' public relations director said in 1979 when the building was first renting space to commercial tenants that he was concerned with "the attitude of the Westport community that the building is an eyesore." Subsequently commercial buildings were restricted to two stories in height, coverage was reduced and setbacks increased.

Patricia Coplen, P&Z chairman from 1975 to 1979, noted that previous commissions had updated the Town's Plan of Development. In writing regulations to implement the town plan, she said, the commission should recognize the importance of following the town plan. Ann Gill, another former P&Z chairman, said the town failed to anticipate pressure to expand as people and companies moved out of New York City. "Until the plans for the Wright Street building were submitted," Gill said, "the town was mostly unaware of this movement." The P&Z had also moved to reduce commercial potential on the Post Road by legislating housing alternatives such as the Mobile Home Park District (MHPD) and the Planned Residential District (PRD).[26] The war between the residents and the commercial builders seemed never-ending.

In 1981 a nonprofit group, Save Westport Now, was founded by Sidney Kramer. The group asked the P&Z to impose a moratorium on commercial development in Westport until a new town plan could be written. Save Westport Now endorsed P&Z candidates and put up some of its own. Connie Greenfield, an active Democrat in town running on the Save Westport Now line as well as the Democratic line, won a seat on the P&Z, and became an influential chairman of that body. The group's aim, Kramer said, was to protect the town from increased traffic, increased sewage and harm to the environment. "I wish to see Westport preserved. It has been an important part of my life," Kramer said. He and his family moved to Westport from New York City in 1950. He is an attorney specializing in copyright matters, and an accountant, publisher, and literary agent (Mews Books Ltd.) in Westport.[27]

Despite the bitter feuds about regulations, many of which wound up in court battles, business in Westport prospered. In 1961, Sam Sloat Coins and Sportsmen of Westport were founded; in 1964, another new business was opened in Westport with the publication of the first issue of the *Westport News* on March 5, 1964. It was launched because of a split in the Republican Party. The *Town Crier*, the existing newspaper, was perceived as the voice of the Republicans in power, during the Baldwin years. The *News* was formed so that the opposition Republicans, many of them members of the Taxpayers Party, would have a voice in future elections. In April 1964 Jo (Fox) Brosious, who had helped launch the paper, was named editor. The *News* would outlast the *Town Crier*, which ceased publication in 1970. When asked about the formation of the *News*, Publisher B.V. ("Dexter") Brooks explained:

> Why is Westport different from other towns? Let me relate a story that dates back to the mid-1960s. We were at an annual meeting of the New England Press Association where there was a display of member newspapers. That week's *Westport News* was 84 pages. One of the members hefted the 84-page issue and said to me, "How big is Westport, anyway?" I replied that the population is slightly under 25,000. He was amazed, saying, "How can you fill an 84-page paper with news from such a small town?" I said, "You don't know Westport." The statistics show that shoppers coming here from other places push Westport's retail sales per capita to the highest in the state. The number and quality of restaurants here is renowned far and wide. The house selling prices and the income levels here are among the highest in the state. But the statistics don't tell the whole story. At the heart of the difference here, in my opinion, is the dynamics, the widespread activism that engulfs Westport. We kid that the shortest time span in the world is the time between when the light turns green and the guy behind you blows his horn. Westport boasts the world's shortest time for organizing a group "pro" and a group "con" on any local issue.[28]

Also in 1964 the Willows Medical Center, commonly known as Fort Apache Village because of its unusual, western-looking architecture, was completed; Nursing and Home Care, a non-profit visiting nurse agency — now part of a network that includes Family Center Services, Inc. and Mid-Fairfield Hospice, Inc. — was founded; and, Coastwise Marine opened for business. In 1965 the Three Bears Restaurant opened; in 1967 Mario's Place at the railroad station, under the management of partners Mario Sacco and Frank DeMace, first opened its restaurant/bar; and in 1970 after a long dispute Stauffer Chemical broke ground at Nyala Farms, the

IN THE NAME OF PROGRESS: Stauffer Chemical broke ground at Nyala Farms, the 52-acre dairy farm on Green's Farms Road in 1970 after a long dispute.
ANDREA FINE PHOTO

52-acre dairy farm on Green's Farms Road; in 1971, the Downtown Merchants Association (DMA) was founded by local businessmen to strengthen business, raise money for beautification and maintenance of downtown Westport, and for new trees, Christmas lights, planters, and trash containers. "The goal of the DMA," said Bob Hertzel, president, "is to keep downtown Westport as the vibrant heart of a great community." [29] In 1971 the Marketing Corporation of America, headed by James McManus, opened its doors on Riverside Avenue and the same year another local newspaper, *Fairpress*, was founded and edited by Jo (Fox) Brosious. The paper would serve six communities, including Westport, and would be purchased by the Westchester-Rockland Newspaper Group of the Gannett News Group in December 1975. *Fairpress* ceased publication in 1993, but the same year the *Minuteman,* a weekly newspaper, emerged as another alternative to the *Westport News.*

And then there was Vietnam — perhaps the most divisive issue of all in the Sixties. Opposition to the war began early in Westport. In 1964, a public forum was sponsored by a number of groups, including the Unitarian Church, the Ethical Culture Society, the Fairfield County Chapter of the Sane Nuclear Policy Organization, American Friends Service Committee, Women's Strike for Peace, Westport-Weston Chapter of the American Association for the United Nations, and the Women's International League for Peace and Freedom. Politically, the war was neither a Democratic nor Republican issue; leading members of both major parties began to speak out against the war. It touched off participation in the political process: The Republican Women of Westport organization was founded, for example, and some of its members spoke out publicly on the war issue.

In May of 1966 a number of Westporters, among them the World Affairs Center activists, held weekly peace vigils in front of Town Hall, which at that time, was housed in a quaint cobblestone building on Post Road East beyond the Main Street intersection. Rain or shine, protestors stood silently for one hour every noon, including weekends, until the end of the war. Sometimes a counter-protestor shouted from across the street. Emotions were so high during the war that a local taxicab driver once jumped out of his car, grabbed one of the American flags held by an elderly lady standing in the vigil, and growled: "You can't carry *my* flag!" The *Westport News* ran a photo on May 15, 1969, of a group of protestors and an unidentified man carrying a poster that read, "REDS, FASCIST, ANTI-AMERICANS." Of the 104,000 men and women from Connecticut who served in the Vietnam War between 1962 and 1973, fewer than 100 from Westport were called up and drafted. But that did not diminish the protests here.

While the *Westport News* regularly ran the names and addresses of servicemen in Vietnam and churches and other organizations mailed packages, a Westport youth, Timothy Breen, a fulltime student, challenged the Selective Service's right to reclassify him 1-A as punishment for surrendering his draft card to a minister at an anti-Vietnam War protest rally in Boston in 1967. The case slowly made its way to the U.S. Supreme Court, where Westport Attorney Emanuel Margolis argued Breen's case. Margolis was sworn in, along with his seven-year-old son, Josh Margolis, who also raised his right hand, at his side. Margolis won the case, with Justice Hugo Black writing the opinion. Looking back on this experience, Margolis commented: "An extremely small minority of lawyers ever gets to argue a case before the United States Supreme Court. I was fortunate enough, not only to argue such a case, but also to win a reversal for our client by a unanimous decision. With the help of the CCLU [Connecticut Civil Liberties Union] and Attorney Lawrence Weisman, we took this case on a pro bono basis through all the appeals." The front page of the *New York Times* on January 27, 1970, carried the headline: HIGH COURT CURBS USE OF THE DRAFT TO PUNISH CRITICS. Two days later, the *Stamford Advocate* commented in an editorial: "No matter how irritating and frustrating to a country's leaders these youthful demonstrations may be, this is still a free country and draft boards shouldn't be permitted to take the law into their own hands." Added Margolis: "In the light of the Breen decision, the Selective Service System discontinued its shameful practice of reclassifying registrants as punishment for turning in their draft cards."[30]

Vietnam hit home for many Westporters when, on December 15,

1967, 21-year-old Staff Sergeant Michael Paquin became the first Westport serviceman to die in Vietnam, succumbing from wounds he suffered when hit by an enemy grenade as he was getting out of his truck. He was one of six Westport men killed in the war in Southeast Asia. Paquin had just returned from 26 days of combat duty near the Cambodian border when he was struck down. Before entering the service, he had graduated from Central Catholic High School in Norwalk, even though his family lived here. He had enlisted in the Army in 1964 , had spent three years in Germany and, after receiving his discharge after a few months at home, he had re-enlisted and volunteered for duty in Vietnam. Before leaving the United States, he became engaged and had planned to be married April 6, 1968. In all, six Westporters were killed in action in the Vietnam War.

A group of about 15 Westport women made news in January 1968 when they rode to Washington by bus to demonstrate their opposition to the war on the first day of the congressional session.[31] The next month, Lance Corporal Timothy M. Barmmer, 20, son of Mr. and Mrs. Russell G. Barmmer, became the first Staples High School graduate to die in combat in the Vietnam War. The other four Westport men who were killed in Vietnam were Stephen A. Shortall, Francis A. Walsh, Jr., Frederick M. Rader III, and Bruce Meeker.

With time, nationwide, the Vietnam War protests grew in size and volume. In September 1969, the anti-Vietnam activists here started gathering signatures on a petition urging the RTM to pass a resolution asking the President and Congress "to take immediate action to withdraw from the war."[32] By the time the RTM considered the resolution at its October meeting, more than 1,000 signatures had been gathered mostly through the efforts of the petition originator, Harry Wunsch, a Westporter and a member of the national Business Executives Movement for Vietnam Peace. Only 20 signatures were necessary to get the item on the agenda. Actress Joanne Woodward, who was active with "Another Mother for Peace," went to the RTM meeting to support the peace resolution. After many impassioned speeches, the RTM voted 17-15 to plead for withdrawal from the war.[33] The precedent-setting action resulted in a front page story in the *New York Times*, on October 9, 1969, headlined: "WESTPORT CALLS FOR WAR PULL-OUT, TOWN MEETING BACKS PLEAS TO NIXON BY 17-15 VOTE."

Two Westporters, Anne Wexler and Paul Newman, were picked to attend the Democratic National Convention in Chicago in August 1968, both supporting Democratic Minnesota Senator Eugene McCarthy, a peace candidate. Wexler and Newman later teamed up with local Democratic leader

Miles Pennybacker to throw their support behind the senate candidacy of Joe Duffey, a Yale graduate and a Congregational minister, the national chairman of the Americans for Democratic Action (ADA), in an unsuccessful senate challenge from the left in November 1969. At a fundraiser in Westport, a crowd of 250 people turned out to donate money for Duffey's U.S. Senate campaign in 1970, lured perhaps by the appearance of Newman and other stars.[34]

Wexler became Duffey's campaign manager and, in 1974, his wife. Duffey lost the election, but his wife became a Democratic consultant in Washington and has since served as undersecretary of commerce in President Jimmy Carter's administration, then assistant to the president, White House Office of Public Liaison. After that she became a Washington, D.C. public policy consultant. Her husband served as assistant secretary of state for education and cultural affairs and as chairman of the National Endowment for the Humanities in the Carter administration, and then was named by President Bill Clinton to serve as head of the United States Information Agency since 1992.

Returning to 1968, Westport reflected the turbulence of the national scene. In March Yale University's chaplain, William Sloane Coffin, Jr., a Presbyterian minister and one of many liberal activists invited to speak in Westport, got a standing ovation from an overflow audience at Coleytown Junior High School. As a crusading clergyman, he appealed to patriots to allow their country "to be human." In October 1969 some 2,000 people gathered in front of the YMCA to attend a peace rally. Carrying American flags, some embellished with doves of peace, protestors wearing black armbands and "Enough" (war) buttons, waved peace signs and chanted, "Peace Now!" and "Hell no, we won't go!"

That same year, more than 1,200 students from Staples High School and the town's three junior highs marched peacefully from the high school to the steps of the Y, joining college students and faculties throughout the nation in an event known officially as "Vietnam Moratorium Day." And so the protests continued in Westport, some with guest singing stars like Judy Collins, others with large numbers of residents ranging in age from 16 to 65. The protests kept up until the long sought-after peace agreement between North and South Vietnam was finally signed on January 23, 1973. Said First Selectman John Kemish in a newspaper article in 1973: "When I first heard the president's announcement, my feeling was almost one of disbelief; it's been so long, and so difficult, and so divisive."

STUDENTS PROTEST VIETNAM: Some 1,200 students from Staples High School and the town's three junior high schools peacefully protest the Vietnam War in 1969 in front of the YMCA on "Vietnam Moratorium Day."   COURTESY OF STAPLES HIGH SCHOOL

Reflecting the general unrest in the 1960s was the increase in drug and alcohol abuse across the nation. Westport was unfairly smeared with the same brush that stereotyped all suburbs. In January 1964 Westport was portrayed on a 15-minute segment of NBC's "Today" show coast-to-coast as a town where young people allegedly drank heavily. The incident turned out to be a one-day story. Nonetheless, local officials on guard against the trend towards drug use, took preventative action. Police Chief Samuel Luciano, Schools Superintendent A. Gordon Peterkin and Health Director Dr. Jack Shiller all appealed to Westport citizens to turn over to authorities all information, or even suspicions, of someone known to them who was involved in the use or sale of narcotics. But the townspeople were in denial.

By 1969, however, a headline in the *Westport News* told parents: "EPIDEMIC DRUG USE WORRIES ALL CIVIC LEADERS." The article said: "Nobody today doubts that Westport has a drug problem, not school officials, not town officials, not medical and psychological professionals, not police. And some have said that drug use is 'epidemic' here and across the nation. Our affluent suburban town, in fact, is the subject of a four-part CBS radio series, 'Children of the Dream,' which publicizes the startling fact that children even younger than teenagers are involved with drugs here. Project Renaissance, a self-help drug treatment program, opened its doors [to help teenagers] last September." [35]

Police began to arrest Staples students for possession and/or pushing of drugs, thus displacing vague anxieties with concrete fears. Reacting with typical Westport vigor, the townspeople swung into action. Schools Superintendent Peterkin organized a meeting of citizens in search of new ideas about how to combat the drug scourge. Perhaps the most exciting proposal came from Dr. Paul Kaunitz, a local psychiatrist, and backed by Fermino Spenser, a Peace Corps veteran and principal of Staples. They envisioned a corps of teenagers, like a local Peace Corps, working in Bridgeport and Norwalk and learning to give a little to someone else, thereby gaining some self-respect and fulfillment. It never got off the drawing board.

By the end of 1969, the police reported that drug-related crimes had doubled in Westport. There had been a 100-percent rise in narcotics and drug incidents — from 43 in 1967-68 to 86 in 1968-69. In 1973 the Alcohol and Drug Dependency Council, which provides outpatient substance abuse treatment, interventions, information and referral services, and prevention and education programs, opened its doors.[36]

A few years later, in 1976, the growing use of alcohol by increasingly younger Westport teenagers was the focus of a conference on The Quality of Life for Westport Children. Sponsored by five community agencies, the discussion touched on curfews, drugs, drinking, smoking and communication problems in the junior high schools.[37] Parents in Westport, already deeply worried about their children, grew even more concerned on October 31, 1979, when the *Westport News* reported that eight teenagers had overdosed on angel dust. Some became severely ill but none died. Staples teachers prominently displayed on their lounge bulletin board alongside this episode another photo from the same issue of the *Westport News* of 10th grader Lucy Wolgast helping a Brownie Troop. And some teacher had added a handwritten caption, "They're not all bad!"

Coincidentally, three days after this near calamity, Westport residents Paul Newman and Joanne Woodward narrated a one-hour documentary on Channel 5 entitled, "Angel Death," which graphically described the dangers of PCP (phencyclidine hydrochloride). Partially as a result of the drug menace, Westport psychologist David Singer founded Mohonk House, a home for teenagers who were orphaned, came from divorced families, or who were unable to live with their own families. While seen as controversial in some quarters, it helped some Westport teenagers cope with emotional problems. In 1980, Westport Community Action Now (WECAN) was founded to prevent alcohol and drug abuse. It was a time of concern parents — for all Westporters.

Amidst the controversies of the 1960s, the neighborly spirit of Westport continued to flourish. In 1963, the New Neighbors of Westport — a social group of more than 400 families — was founded and the first summer school was opened under Westport Continuing Education; in 1964, the Green's Farms Pre-School was established by Kate Moore, Nursing and Home Care was created, and the Westport Music Center was founded. Also in 1964, the United Methodist Church, originally

MARINA: The new boat marina at Longshore was dedicated in 1968 to E.R. Strait, minister of the Green's Farms Congregational Church.
WESTPORT NEWS PHOTO

dedicated on July 20, 1851, purchased land for a new church on Weston Road. It was dedicated on September 29, 1968. That same year, the new boat marina at Longshore was dedicated to E.R. Strait, minister of the Green's Farms Congregational Church.

The ever-present issue of open space in Westport also emerged as a vital issue during the 1970s and 1980s. While efforts were underway to preserve open space, there was no legal protection of the tidal marshes along the shores. Barlow Cutler-Wotten, elected in 1963 as president of the League of Women Voters, made it her business to attend all Planning and Zoning Commission hearings. When an application was filed to construct a geriatric hospital at the corner of Wilton Road and King's Highway North (a large salt marsh was part of the application), she turned to Attorney Leonard A. Schine for help. She and Virginia Karchere became car counters, morning and night, and reported their findings to Schine. When he went before the P&Z, he used that data to win his case. The P&Z denied the application, and the salt marsh remained untouched. In 1987 it was given to the Aspetuck Land Trust and remains an integral part of Westport's open space.

OPEN SPACE? Farmer Isaac Wakeman looks out at the playing fields that have been built on what was once 38 acres of rich farmland that he worked since he was a youngster. He would have preferred for the town to leave it untouched. They named the area Wakeman Fields in his honor. DAVID MCLAIN PHOTO

In another major step to preserve open space, in 1970 the town acquired the 38-acre parcel of farming property located on Cross Highway just off North Avenue from Isaac Wakeman for $200,000, except for 2.2 acres on which he and his wife, Pearl, lived. The Wakeman family had owned the farm since 1900. Born on December 29, 1911, "Ike" Wakeman came from a long line of Wakemans who first came to America in 1630.[38] Wakeman later said he thought he had sold the land with the understanding that it would remain as "open space." But officials at that time recalled that the town paid a fair price — $200,000 — with no restrictions on the land. A huge fight erupted in the early 1990s when Wakeman and many others vigorously opposed the town's plan to build playing fields on the land. Wakeman made much of the fact that he had a "handshake" agreement with Ed Mitchell in 1970 to maintain the land as open space. Mitchell was then chairman of the Board of Finance. During the controversy in the 1990s, Wakeman's claim of an agreement on "open space" was denied by Mitchell and by John Kemish, the first selectman in 1970. For two years the fight for playing fields was a long, agonizing political process during which the definition of "open space" became a topic of considerable controversy. Townspeople lined up on both sides of the issue: Neighbors of the Wakeman farm who opposed any change in the area argued publicly against the ball field lobby, which was headed by Ed Weil, president of the Westport Soccer Association and by Bill Mitchell. In the end, the plan was approved — but on the specific condition that it be landscaped and made to blend in with the general country environment. This particular controversy proved to be an outstanding example of the democratic process in action. In a gesture of goodwill, in 1994 First Selectman Joe Arcudi named the grounds Wakeman Farms Athletic Fields.

RIDING HIGH: Veteran Westport farmer-businessman Alan Parsell steers his tractor, a 1947 John Deere Model M, which he sold to attorney Stan Atwood, behind Parsell, in 1985. Photo was taken in 1986 on Riverside Avenue in the lineup for the Memorial Day parade.
WESTPORT NEWS PHOTO

The sale of the Wakeman farm, of course, was only part of the disappearance of virtually all farming in Westport in the past 30 years. Rippe's Farmstand on the Post Road in Westport, which for 40 years was a regular stop for thousands of fruit and vegetable shoppers, closed in 1977. It was one of the last in Westport, to be replaced by the upscale Harvest Commons condominiums, the first in Westport. Long before that, however, one by one the orchards, the vegetable farms, and the dairies closed. The price of equipment and labor costs had jumped, there were fewer acres for farmers to grow produce, and supermarket prices undercut farmers. Westport farmers said their taxes drove them out of business. James Belta owns and works one of the last remaining pieces of farmland in Westport. Fred Comfort, whose wife and mother-in-law were trustees of the Rippe's estate, said that those people who have come here in the last half century simply did not understand farming, nor did they have any stake in keeping farming going. On the other hand, the farmers got a pretty good price for their land, which became quite valuable.

One of the town's best-known and most outspoken farmers, Alan U. Parsell, loved farming and the hard work that went with it. In an interview in 1970, he recalled the time when work, not play, was "Westport's way." Parsell was a crusty, stubborn man seen as the ultimate Yankee farmer. "When I was growing up," he said, "all children were expected to work as soon as they were able. Today's children are taught to enjoy their leisure time watching and playing games. We didn't put up with that sort of nonsense. Fathers and mothers set good working examples for their children. Not that my mother went out to work, mind you. She kept the flower garden, churned the cream for butter and raised the children, telling them that 'Satan can always find some work for idle hands to do.'" [39] At age six, Parsell started work, carrying the milk pail every morning to his father, Increase Alan Parsell, who would wait for it in the cow barn of the old Parsell farm on Maple Avenue. He married Evelyn Couch in 1922, and went on to serve the town on the Board of Education, including as chairman, from the late 1930s until the early 1950s. He was also a leading member of the RTM for 22 years until he retired in 1975. A few years earlier, he had sold his business, Parsell's Garden Mart, to Frank Geiger, his landscape designer. Parsell died at the age of 90 in December 1992. Allen Raymond, who was moderator of the RTM when

GORHAM ISLAND: This beautiful house on the the 6.5-acre site off Parker-Harding Plaza that extends into the Saugatuck River was once a landmark in Westport. In 1983, after a fight to save the house failed, a developer knocked it down and and constructed a 40,000-square-foot office building in its place.
KATHERINE ROSS
PAINTING

REMARKABLE COUPLE: Sidney and Esther Kramer pose in front of their beloved pink-colored book store that was so much a part of Main Street from 1962 to 1997, when it was sold to Talbots Petite. Ebenezer Coley built the structure in 1775 and it was used as a ship's store.
KRAMER PHOTO

ARTIST'S RENDERING: This painting of the Remarkable Book Shop is among those artworks on display at the Westport Library .
HOWARD MUNCE ARTWORK

Parsell was there, said of the farmer: "He was a walking, talking historian who wore the cloak of penny-pincher. That was a subterfuge. He was warmhearted and immensely human." The Alan U. Parsell Public Works Transfer Station on the Sherwood Island Connector was named in his honor.

Farming was not the only sign of old Westport to have faded. A beautiful, pre-Civil War colonial residence, once a stately Victorian home built on Main Street in 1860 by Elijah Downes, and later owned by the Taylor family, was moved in the early 1960s to Gorham Island and then torn down. The "island," a 6.5-acre site off Parker-Harding Plaza, extends into the Saugatuck River. One of the most cherished landmarks in Westport, the house was a familiar sight to Westporters. A stone cottage designed by Frazier Peters and built in 1933 was also on the island.

The end of a three-year battle to save the house came on February 16, 1983 when Paul Lehman, administrative assistant to the First Selectman William Seiden (who had been elected in 1981) announced that Gorham Island Associates signed an agreement enabling it to build a 40,000-square-foot office building. The principals involved were Robert Silver, the developer; the Planning and Zoning Commission, and Sidney Kramer, who was included in the settlement because his wife, Esther, owned the Remarkable Book Shop, which was within 10 feet of the proposed development. The name Remarkable stemmed from Kramer spelled backward.

Commenting on Westport today, Kramer said:

We are at a "What's-to-become-of-Westport" crossroads.
But then I look back years and I recall that we have always
been at a "what's-to-become" crossroads. When my wife and
I arrived in Westport, the town's population was 12,000,

land cost $200 an acre and there was plenty of choice. We could buy a spool of thread on Main Street, a tank of gas, a newspaper, a book, lunch at a drug store counter, our meat and fresh produce at a general store who delivered our package to our home with a "thank you for your business" enclosed with the bill. Doctors came to our bedside when we were ill. Best of all and most gratifying we soon had a nodding acquaintance, a smile, a greeting, and a wave of the hand from almost strangers. A walk down Main Street became a remarkable social event. The PTA and the Boy Scouts put us to work.... We oldtimers are handing over a hard-fought functioning community with limited commercial development, lovely residential qualities, a good school system and a wonderful, privileged place by the sea to live and bring up children under excellent young management. I think that years from now Westport will still be a lovely place to live in and today's newcomers, battle-scarred and venerable by then, can stand in the middle of the Post Road and say, ruefully "Westport is changing — it's at the crossroads." The time to worry is when there are no crossroads.[40]

Change, after all, is the essence of a living town. Still, people are sentimental about many of the historic buildings that are no longer here. Author Eve Potts spoke for all of these when she wrote, "We mourn the landmarks, as we do long-gone friends."[41]

One of the people who helped change Westport's image in the 1970s was Martha Stewart, a one-time model and Wall Street stockbroker. She moved to Westport with her family into an abandoned farmhouse on Turkey Hill Road. By 1977 she had renovated the old barn to the point where

LIFESTYLE LEADER: Martha Stewart, one of the celebrities who helped change Westport's image in the 1970s, was a former model who moved into a farmhouse on Turkey Hill Road. In 1999, Stewart's company, Martha Stewart Living Omnimedia, went public on the stock market, making her one of the world's richest women. She was named by Newsweek *magazine in its January 20, 2000 issue, as one of the nation's top 25 business managers.*
WESTPORT NEWS PHOTO

297

it was featured in an article in *House and Garden* magazine. Stewart later founded a gourmet food shop, Market Basket, which led to her creating a catering company, later named Martha Stewart, Inc. In October 1999, Stewart's company, Martha Stewart Living Omnimedia, held an initial stock offering, making her one of the world's wealthiest women. Ms. Stewart was named by *Newsweek* magazine in its January 20, 2000 issue, as one of the nation's top 25 business managers, based on a survey of the magazine's staff of 149 writers and editors in 25 bureaus around the world. Headlined "Martha's World," the article said Ms. Stewart, 58, "has created a sprawling media and merchandising empire that leaves larger rivals salivating with envy as they rush to replicate her formula." The magazine added: "[Stewart] is trying to build an empire that will teach the masses how to organize weddings, parties, and the perfect home — then sell the converts all the gear they need to do so."[42]

On November 7, 1973, Jacqueline Heneage, who had been active in town affairs — including a stint as president of the League of Women Voters — won the first selectman's office for the Democrats for the first time since 1948 by defeating incumbent Republican John Kemish. She was also the first woman ever to be elected first selectman in the town's history. Heneage would serve from 1973 to 1981, including the first four-year term in the town's history, from 1977 to 1981, twice defeating Republican Vincent Rotondo, who was director of the Public Works Department. The charter changed the first selectman's term of office from two years to four in 1976, the year of the town's bicentennial celebration. A large committee, headed by Shirley Land, undertook to make the bicentennial year memorable.

Perhaps the town's most remembered symbol of that celebration is the Westport Bicentennial Quilt, which depicted 200 years of Westport's history. It was designed by artist Naiad Einsel with Micki McCabe, a quilting consultant, and 33 Westport women who worked all year sewing it. The quilt contains 20 squares and is 78 inches wide and 105 inches long. Each square depicts some part of old Westport: churches, old bridges, the Compo cannon, the Minute Man, a basket of onions from old Saugatuck. A reproduction of one of the quilt squares of the Westport Fire Department served as the cover of the Bicentennial Calendar, designed by Howard Munce and 14 Westport artists. The quilt today hangs in Town Hall.

The Bicentennial bus tour of the town's historical highlights brought thousands of people to Westport from all parts of the region after it was featured in the *New York Times* travel section. Residents and visitors saw 55 historic points of interests on the tour that started and ended at Jesup Green. Bob and Eve Potts, co-chairman of the tour, received visitors from all over the state, New York City, and Westchester County. Many foreign visitors took the Maxybus, which was equipped with a one-hour narrated tape by nine actors from Westport and Weston. Six of Westport's 10 schools took bus-loads of students; the Weston Real Estate board had an outing for seniors, and various church and Boy and Girl Scouts groups chartered the bus.

The actual celebration took place on the four-day July 4 weekend in 1976, a time when Main Street became a one-way thoroughfare. Billed as "Colonial Assembly," the event engaged many of the townspeople. Three years later, in 1979, Town Hall was the site of the first Heritage Tree, given by the Westport Historical Society, with 70 decorations donated by town artists. Also in 1981 another significant "first" took place when the Westport Apple Festival at Staples was founded by Westport-booster Betty Lou Cummings. That was the same year in which the town's Emergency Medical Service (EMS) was organized.

Looking back on her election to the town's highest office, Heneage said that when she was elected in 1973, she felt that the town had, for too long, taken an overly cautious attitude. Namely that having spent so much money on building schools in the early 1960s, it could not spend money on other needs. Yet, she added, Westport was fiscally strong and had many demands both social and operational, which were not being addressed.[43] Although the town had grown to a population of more than 29,000, Town Hall still operated like a small village, she added. Planning and Zoning was under pressure to create apartments, at least for the elderly, and had prob-lems with huge growth demands in the commercial zones. "There was a lot to do. I helped galvanize Westport citizens and town officials into getting things done. I was a Yankee who hated to spend money and inflation kept getting worse, but I knew that if many of our physical needs could be met, economies in operations would follow."

Heneage staffed the town's first personnel department and estab-lished recruiting and human resources procedures. Being a Democrat, she was not fearful of obtaining state and federal grants. She therefore hired a grantswoman who obtained nearly $2 million, which was used for the Bedford Elementary School/Town Hall conversion, open space acquisition, the youth center, elderly housing, the police department, and beautification projects.

Heneage said she planned ahead and extended long-term projects like flood control, sewers and road improvements more realistically over time. Because there was still plenty of land to develop, P&Z issues were problematic. Her position, constantly expressed to the elected P&Z, was that Westport was and should remain primarily a residential town. She felt the town had more than enough commercial zoning which needed to be amended to reduce building sizes, increase setbacks and eliminate Design Development Districts, which threatened all residential zones. The P&Z accomplished much of this, as well as permitting condos on the Post Road. Did all those projects go smoothly? Of course not, she says. Did most of them generate controversy? Of course. But homework, persistence and wonderful support from her fellow selectman, Ted Diamond, other town officials, and Westport citizens, made it worthwhile and a lot of fun, she adds. After eight years — and having been elected three times to the helm at Town Hall — Heneage decided that eight years at Westport's helm was enough.

During Heneage's tenure, Westport's school population declined sharply. It became necessary to close and find new uses for many of the town's schools. Hillspoint became a child development center; at Burr Farms a prefabricated construction was removed; Bedford El became the Town Hall and Community Theatre; Green's Farms was turned into the Westport Arts Center; and Saugatuck became affordable housing for seniors. Other changes included the Youth Center (now housing the homeless) located on the site of the old public works garage; the building of the public works garage and transfer station on the Sherwood Island connector; extension of sewers on Post Road East and in many residential areas; and the move of the central fire station from the center of town near the YMCA to the Coppola Post Road property.

Heneage's propensity for thriftiness was widely known and appreciated in Westport. Author/historian Mollie Donovan, who has served as co-curator of the Westport Schools Permanent Art Collection with Eve Potts for 20 years and is now its historian, offers this example: "One day while renovations were in progress converting Bedford Elementary School to Westport Town Hall, I looked up at the wonderful brass letters spelling out BEDFORD ELEMENTARY SCHOOL and wondered if we could recycle them to spell WESTPORT TOWN HALL. I figured out that we had all the letters except five. When we told Jackie, she had the missing letters (W,P,T,T,W,) cast and recycled the rest to spell out WESTPORT TOWN HALL. After doing this, we still had 12 unused letters. We asked Jean Woodham, nationally known sculptor and Westporter, if she could do something with them. Her sculpture, entitled *The Bedford Juggler* stands between the auditorium doors in the Town Hall lobby."[44] The conversion of Bedford Elementary School to the Town Hall that stands today was completed in 1979.

Perhaps more than any other symbol of Westport's long-standing commitment to the arts, construction of the Levitt Pavilion and its first season's opening in 1973 gave Westporters a good feeling about their town that it had, after all, kept its promise to maintain Westport's image, though not as robust as in the

MUSIC TO OUR EARS: The Levitt Pavilion opened in 1973, adding to Westport's cultural heritage. Fronting on the Saugatuck River, it is located one block from the center of town. The major contributor was Mortimer Levitt, founder of the Custom Shirt Shop, for whom the pavilion was named.   RAY PORTER PHOTO

past, as an artist's colony. Fronting on the Saugatuck River, adjacent to the town parkland, and just one block from the center of town, the site offered easy access to town parking facilities and major traffic arteries. The first $60,000 for construction of the pavilion was raised by the Kiwanis Club, the Westport Young Woman's League, and the Westport-Weston Arts Council, with the cooperation of the Downtown Merchants Association. The major contributors were Mortimer Levitt, founder of the Custom Shirt Shop, and his wife, Mimi, for whom the pavilion was named.

The reclamation of the landfill site removed an ugly eyesore and replaced it with a well-planned highly utilized green space. The Levitt governing board members included representatives from the schools, Recreation Commission, YMCA, summer school program, the RTM, Youth Adult Council, and the architects of the pavilion. Barbara Schadt, president in 1999, credited the pavilion to the commitment of Winnie Scott, the first executive director of the Arts Council, who dreamed of a year-round arts center, and to Parks and Recreation Chairman Lou Nistico. Architect Bruce Campbell Graham donated his services in designing and supervising construction of the pavilion.

Also in 1973, through public and private interest, a campaign named the Greening of the Post Road was launched.[45] Frank Geiger of Parsell's Garden Mart was in charge of the planting; Eloise Ray served as landscape architect; and Mrs. Milton L. Rusk, president of the Garden Department of the Westport Woman's Club, coordinated the planting of more than 70 trees

*LITTLE MISS WESTPORT, CIRCA 1970:
Leanne (Jisonna) Small, the daughter of
Lawrence and Barbara Jisonna, was the
winner of a contest held at the Green's
Farms Congregational Church, which
sponsored the event. The three-year-old,
who competed against 20 other girls,
today works for the Greenwood
Publishing Group. The photo appeared
on the front page of the* Westport News
in the spring of 1970.
WESTPORT NEWS PHOTO

along the Post Road's main artery. The Woman's Club received a national award for this effort.

Another important development in the 1970s was the negotiations over the property owned by Baron Walter Langer von Langendorff. The Austrian-born baron, also known by his Americanized name, Dr. Walter Langer, had purchased the 32-acre site on East State Street for $1.5 million in 1967. He and his wife, Gabriele, had made their home in Westport since 1945, living in a mansion directly across from the property that would eventually be bought by the town. Through a spokesman he indicated that he planned to make the property — which was zoned for business — available to the town for use as a civic center in order to protect the area against further commercialization. The Baron was to pursue the civic project, which he originally conceived in 1968, with several administrations at Town Hall.

The Baron's mansion was torn down before the town acquired the land. Watching the wrecker's ball smash into the Grecian facade of Compo House, moved many to tears, including Westport historian Eve Potts who stopped her car with her children in it at the site in 1971. "The children asked me why I was crying and I said it was because they were tearing down that beautiful old home," she said. The beautiful eighteenth century colonial home, Compo House, was once the center of Westport's social life. Richard Henry Winslow, the business tycoon, had built it as a home for his bride, Mary Fitch Winslow and, as noted earlier, the Winslows entertained many prominent personalities, including former U.S. President Millard F. Fillmore.

By 1979 after long negotiations with the Heneage administration, the Baron was angered by the town's proposal that he sell the 32 acres for the small sum of $2.38 million.[46] Saying he was in ill health, he broke off negotiations. Next, Heneage sought federal and state funds to help purchase the property. By now, rumors had begun to circulate that Langer planned to build a perfume museum and a chemical research laboratory for producing fragrances, and that one building would be used as a museum of dolls dressed in replicas of those worn by America's First Ladies. In June 1979, however, the RTM, after nearly five hours of debate, voted 25-9 to appropriate $3.48 million to buy the property. But it postponed giving Heneage condemnation authority should the Baron refuse to sell his land. The issue of what would happen to the 32-acre tract was thrown into flux with the Baron's death on September 14, 1983.

In July 1987, the RTM passed a resolution by a 26-8 vote to condemn the land. The townspeople, in a referendum in December 1987, voted by 54 percent to 46 percent to acquire the land by condemnation. The town, moving ahead with condemnation proceedings under eminent domain, ultimately paid $9.42 million for the property. The question now was: What to name the park? In a contest, more than 200 suggestions for names of the park poured into the offices of the *Westport News,* which served as a conduit for Town Hall. The overwhelming choice and winning suggestion was submitted by Joan Dickinson: Winslow Park, named after Richard Henry Winslow. As a matter of record, the *Westport News'* Town Hall reporter, John Capsis, a Westport history buff, claimed he was the first person to suggest naming it Winslow Park. His column two years before the naming contest on July 31, 1991 carried the headline: "BARON'S PROPERTY SHOULD BE NAMED WINSLOW PARK."[47] And so it was.

One of the town's most cherished institutions is the Westport Historical

HISTORY HAVEN: Wheeler House, above right, at 25 Avery Place is the home of the Westport Historical Society, organized in 1889. Listed on the National Register of Historic Places, the house was built in 1795.   ANDREA FINE PHOTO

PROOF OF THE PAST: The octagonal cobble-stone Bradley-Wheeler barn behind Wheeler House, opened in 1996, was dedicated to former Historical Society President Joan Dickinson, and to Joanne Woodward. It includes a photo display showing the history of Westport, as well as tools and other items from past eras. It also features a scale model diorama depicting "Westport as It Was, Circa 1900."
ANDREA FINE PHOTO

Society, organized in 1889 as the Saugatuck Historical Society of Westport and reactivated in its present name in 1958. Wheeler House at 25 Avery Place was purchased on February 23, 1981 from Christ and Holy Trinity Church. The Reverend Dana Forrest Kennedy was rector at the time. The Wheeler House, as it is also called, is listed on the National Register of Historic Places. The house dates to 1795 and was built by Captain Ebenezer Coley for his son, Michael. The house changed hands many times until 1891 when it was left to Julia A. Wheeler. It became known simply as the Wheeler House. Willed to Christ and Holy Trinity Church, it was offered for sale to the Westport Historical Society by the church. Fundraising was led by Joanne Woodward and Paul Newman as Honorary Chairmen. The building was restored to its Victorian beauty through the Wheeler House Fund Raising Committee. Members who raised funds for the purchase of Wheeler House included Connie Anstett, Stanley P. Atwood, John W. Boyd, Joan Dickinson, Mollie Donovan, Barbara Elmer, Jo Fuchs, Ginger Gault, Peggy Henkel, Joyce Mueller, Eve Potts, Eleanor Street, and Fran Thomas. They raised more than $375,000.

An 11-year effort to restore the octagonal stone Bradley-Wheeler barn behind Wheeler House culminated with a grand opening in July 1996. Pete Wolgast, Westport Historical Society president, was master of ceremonies and Roy Dickinson cut the ribbon to open the barn, which was dedicated to his late wife, Joan Dickinson, and to Joanne Woodward. It includes a photo display depicting the history of Westport from the time of the Pequot Indians to the present. The exhibit was put together by a team of volunteers, including Eve Potts, Barbara Van Orden, Margaret O'Donoghue, and designers Walter and Naiad Einsel. Robert Gault served as the restoration architect, and Leo Cirino was chairman of the Barn Restoration Committee. The restored cobblestone Bradley-Wheeler barn with its mysterious 12-foot-deep cellar and trap door displays the implements of Westport's history — farming tools, clam rakes, a market boat's block and tackle, and products of the town's early mills. A highlight of the barn museum is a scale model exhibit, or diorama, a gift of Barbara and Ray Howard, depicting "Westport as It Was, Circa 1900."

The Historical Society was not the only organization seeking funds in Westport in the 1980s. Senator Edward M. Kennedy (D-Mass.) came to town with his entourage as a presidential candidate in 1980 for an appearance at a Westport fundraiser to bring some undecided Democrats into his camp and get delegates' support for his bid at the Democratic National Convention in August against incumbent President Jimmy Carter. A crowd of 200 attended the fundraiser hosted by Allan and Doris Cramer of Yankee Hill Road, netting more than $10,000 for the Kennedy campaign, with another $5,000 pledged. The large turnout indicated substantial support for him here, although his bid ultimately failed.

The election of 1981 in Westport brought victory to the Republican slate of William Seiden and Barbara Butler over the Democratic team of Martha S. Hauhuth for first selectman and Ralph Sheffer, who came out of retirement, to run for second selectman. Seiden prevailed on the basis of his promise to preserve the past and protect the town's open space.

HONORED: Lou and Marge Santella, top, for decades active in the Italian community in Saugatuck, were grand marshals in the Festival Italiano Parade in 1998.

SANTELLA FAMILY PHOTO, ABOVE
MIGGS BURROUGHS PHOTO, BELOW

Toward this end, Seiden helped bring back one of Westport's most treasured traditions known as Festival Italiano, which had been inspired by the feast of St. Anthony, first celebrated by the Saugatuck Italian community in the late 1800s. The festival attracted large crowds of people, especially for the display of fireworks on the last night. The original festival was sponsored by a local organization, the Sons of Italy, and later was carried on by another group, St. Anthony's Society, until the building of the New England Thruway in 1951 tore Saugatuck apart and dispersed most of the Italian community. In 1983, a younger Italian generation formed a new Sons of Italy and revived many of the old traditions. In 1984, the festival's revival was attended by more than 100,000 people who enjoyed the three-day weekend. Lou Santella, a Saugatuck barber and a longtime community leader, said the event sponsored by the Sons of Italy might have faded quickly had not John LaBarca, the WMMM radio personality, promoted the renewal of the festival at the urging of Seiden's administrative assistant, Paul Lehman. The father and son team of Peter A. and Peter T. Romano also played key roles, along with Santella and his brother, Chip. They asked Bill Vornkahl III to serve as chairman of the parade, since he also runs the

ARNIE'S PLACE: Arnold Kaye with Diablo, left, and Zorro. The video arcade owner fought bitterly with First Selectman Bill Seiden. Kaye chained himself to a steel post in Town Hall, was arrested, but the case against him was thrown out by a judge who found "bias" among local zoning officials.
WESTPORT NEWS PHOTO

Memorial Day parades for the town.

Pete Romano, a leading member of the Sons of Italy, said: "It's the greatest community effort in Westport. We get 80,000 to 120,000 people through here in four days, and the number of people who pitch in to make it happen is incredible."[48] The festival raises about $70,000 annually, which is donated to charity.

Lou and Marge Santella remember Saugatuck as it once was. "Saugatuck was a special place," Lou said. "It was truly a neighborhood. It was more of a village, an Italian enclave, and prior to that it was Irish. I remember as far back as the '30s, near the end of the Depression, families helped each other survive. There was a lot of sharing. People brought each other vegetables from their garden when someone in the family was sick. It was a community and still is. It's called the Italian Festival but it's really much more than that; it's a celebration of the whole community. I think the festival has become the largest single function in the history of this town. That's how the Italian Festival got started."[49]

Bill Seiden's head-to-head style of administering town affairs resulted in a series of confrontations — most of them with local businessman Arnold Kaye — that led to public disillusionment. Their bitter feud began in 1981 when Kaye was repeatedly turned down on his plan to build a video arcade on the Post Road, called "Arnie's Place," for the town's youngsters. Decisions having to do with applications for permits to build in Westport are the responsibility of the Planning and Zoning Commission. Nonetheless, Seiden continued to oppose Kaye and, in January 1982, the first selectman disclosed that he felt "intimidated" by Kaye. He said he was opposed to the controversial electronic game room because it would attract teen-age drug pushers to Westport. Finally, Seiden complained that Kaye had been "harassing" his staff at Town Hall and Seiden decided he would no longer talk to Kaye. Kaye ultimately built his game room and it was a wonderful success. Contrary to Seiden's fears, the arcade was a safe haven for youngsters, and parents felt comfortable leaving their children there on their own because of Kaye's caring staff and excellent security.

Nonetheless, Kaye continued to get under Seiden's skin. The personal enmity between the two men came to a dramatic climax when, on January 22, 1982, Kaye chained himself to a steel post in Town Hall and refused to leave. Police released Kaye on a promise to appear in court. On March 31, 1982, Judge Harold H. Dean of Darien, in Norwalk Court, dismissed the case telling Kaye that it appeared that the zoning officials were "biased" against his application. The movement by Kaye to recall Seiden failed to get the required 1,600 signatures, and the matter ended there.

In November 1982, Seiden appointed the Homeless People's Committee, consisting of a group coordinated by Second Selectman Barbara Butler who determined there was a need to make free meals available for homeless people regardless of ability to pay. "There is a real need for such a program in Westport," said David Kennedy, town human services director. "In Westport there is a hidden side of poverty. It's not huge, but it's not miniscule either. It's a part of our town." Indeed, it came as a shock to some Westporters that as many as 46 people came forward to take advantage of the soup kitchen. Residents were also made aware that there were elderly in town unable to climb stairs in their own homes, non-working widows on inadequate pensions, spouses and dependents of people in alcoholic and psychiatric treatment programs, abused women, working poor, and people who were just plain lonely, according to a Needs Assessment Report compiled by Operation Bootstrap, established by the Saugatuck Congregational Church for the homeless. Some Westporters objected to the soup kitchen, on the grounds that it would draw hordes of outsiders to the town.

In 1983 the soup kitchen attracted the attention of Westporter and TV personality Phil Donahue, who invited town Human Services Director David Kennedy and the Reverend Theodore Hoskins of the Saugatuck Congregational Church to appear on his talk show as an example of affluent towns with a social conscience. With camera lights and more than a dozen reporters covering the event, some 14 people enjoyed minestrone soup and bread as Westport's soup kitchen formally opened.[50] Others on the scene were Hoskins, several members of the Homeless Peoples Committee, including James Bacharach, chairman of the kitchen steering committee, and Barbara Butler, Seiden's running mate and second selectman who would serve as director of human services in future administrations. Hoskins held annual Thanksgiving feasts at his church, initiated housing for the homeless, and played a key role in the town's Interfaith Housing Association, headed by the Reverend Peter Powell, executive director. Hoskins would leave Westport in 1994 to join the Maine Seacoast Mission,

where he holds worship and social services off the coast of Maine as he travels on his boat, *Sunbeam*.

Another milestone in the town's history that occurred on Bill Seiden's watch was the new public library. In early June 1984 the president of the Westport Public Library's trustees, Allen Raymond, announced plans to build a new library on a site adjacent to Jesup Green. From the outset there was considerable discussion about how to raise the money needed for the new library and where it should be located. In October 1984, however, the Westport Taxpayers Association opposed the project and gathered enough signatures for a referendum. The WTA also objected to the proposed site, a former landfill that it called "the dump site," and to the possible traffic problems that the new library would bring. After the new site was approved in a referendum, plans for the $4.5 million project went forward. The plaza at the entranceway was slated to be named after longtime Westport resident Arnold Bernhard, who donated $300,000 to the building campaign,

UP, UP AND SOLD: Ralph Sheffer, second from right, former RTM moderator and chief fundraiser for the new Westport Public Library, painting the rising thermometer in front of the old building on the Post Road. He was assisted by Carol Diamond, left, and a Fire Department aide. Sheffer raised more than $4 million in the fund drive and an additional $2.8 million by selling the old library — quite a feat, since many local observers did not think it would fetch more than $1.1 million. RALPH SHEFFER PHOTO

which was run by Ralph Sheffer, fundraising chairman. Despite opposition to the site on Jesup Green, the 300,000-square-foot, $4.6-million Jesup Library, as it was called, was built and opened on Labor Day 1986.

Bernhard and Lucille Lortel, founder and artistic director of the White Barn Theatre, and James McManus, president of MCA, provided funds that helped the library to meet its goal. Bernhard, cited by *Forbes* magazine in the fall 1983 issue as one of the wealthiest men in America, was the owner of Arnold Bernhard and Co., Inc., securities and investment advisors in New York City. He reportedly owned more than 80 percent of Value Line, the largest investment advisory service in the country. For Ralph Sheffer, this "last hurrah" was a great success. He had stepped out of public service in 1969 as the well-respected moderator of the RTM after serving 10 one-year terms as moderator and as a member for 16 years.[51] Sheffer almost single-handedly sold the old library — which was 78 years old — on the Post Road for $2.8 million in 1986. He won numerous awards, including an official citation for "Outstanding Record of Public Service to the Town of Westport" from the Connecticut General Assembly in 1988. The Betty R. Sheffer Foundation is named for his late wife. The Foundation donates funds to the arts, to education and community health care, and to projects that help preserve the town's history.

NEW LIBRARY: Opening ceremony for the new Westport Public Library overlooking Jesup Green and the Saugatuck River, September 6, 1986. Left to right, Ralph Sheffer, Arnold Bernhard, library President Allen Raymond (holding drawing of the original library, by Bernard Barton), and Mrs. Carlton Gette, who was presented the drawing on behalf of her mother, Kathryn Dunningan, the third person to hold a library card when it first opened in 1907. Sheffer was the major fundraiser for the library ("He was simply fantastic," said Raymond), while Bernhard, founder of Value Line, was one of the significant benefactors, for whom the parking plaza was named.

WESTPORT NEWS PHOTO

Toward the close of the Seiden administration in 1985, the first selectman appointed Barbara Roth to be chairman of a committee planning a year-long celebration for Westport's 150th birthday in 1985. Great excitement lay ahead for the townspeople.

NOTES

1. Interview with Ruth Solway in Westport, August 13, 1999.

2. *The Town Crier*, November 3, 1960.

3. The *Bridgeport Post,* November 9, 1960.

4. "The Index of Social Health for Westport-Weston," based on the research of Dr. Marc Miringoff at the Fordham Institute for Innovation in Social Policy. The index is the first of its kind for any local community in the nation.

5. Interview with Bernice Corday, February, 2000.

6. Captain David Heinmiller, *History of the Westport Police Department*, 1993, p. 13.

7. The *Bridgeport Post*, August 7, 1967.

8. Prepared statement by Jo Fox, August 1999.

9. Memorandum from John Kemish, August 1999.

10. The *Westport News*, September 17, 1997.

11. Ibid., June 8, 1973.

12. Statement from Paul R. Green, September 22, 1999.

13. The *Town Crier,* April 11, 1968.

14. Ibid., June 25, 1964.

15. Ibid., April 25, 1968.

16. The program was funded by the town.

17. Interviewed by Jo Fox, July 2, 1999.

18. From an interview with Larry Weisman, September 1999.

19. Gloria Cole, *Fairpress,* May 19, 1977.

20. Conversation with Tracy Sugarman, September 1999.

21. John H. Tarrant, *The End of Exurbia* (New York: Stein and Day, 1976), p. 99.

22. The *Westport News*, June 11, 1982.

23. Interview with Venora Ellis, 1998, in Westport.

24. Interview with Dr. Albert Beasley, October 1999.

25. The *Westport News*, October 20, 1995.

26. Ibid., January 3, 1980.

27. Sidney Kramer interviewed by the author, September 14, 1999.

28. Letter from B.V. Brooks dated February 16, 1998.

29. Statement submitted to the author from Bob Hertzel, September 1999.

30. Statement from Emanuel Margolis, October 1999.

31. The *Westport News*, January 11, 1968.

32. Ibid., September 11, 1969.

33. Ibid., October 2, 1969.

34. Ibid., November 13, 1969.

35. The *Westport News*, May 22, 1969.

36. Ibid., November 20, 1969.

37. Ibid., May 28, 1976.

38. The *Westport News*, September 14, 1983.

39. Ibid., December 4, 1992.

40. Statement from Sidney Kramer, October 1999.

41. Eve Potts, *Westport...A Special Place,* Westport Historical Society, 1985.

42. *Newseek,* January 20, 1999.

43. Statement submitted to the author from Jacqueline Heneage, August 23, 1999.

44. E-mail message to the author from Mollie Donovan, September 15, 1999.

45. The *Westport News*, April 25, 1973.

46. Ibid., April 13, 1979.

47. John Capsis, *Westport News*, July 31, 1991.

48. The *Westport News*, July 9, 1999.

49. Ibid., November 10, 1982. Lou and Marge Santella served as the grand marshals of the 16th annual Festival Italiano in 1998.

50. Ibid., February 2, 1983.

51. The *Town Crier*, September 3, 1969.

Photo, p. 263, Main Street, Westport News

CHAPTER 16

THE PARADOX OF PROGRESS

Westport voters tend to be more passionate about issues than other communities, and they are more willing to engage each other in lively debate. Westport citizens have the sophistication to concern themselves not just with local issues, but with state, national, and international issues as well.

— Representative Christopher Shays,
Republican, Fourth Congressional District,
Connecticut

In the spring of 1985, Westporters once again came together for an occasion that showed just how much they cared about their town. Their deep and abiding commitment to their town's rich heritage was clearly evident during a series of spectacular events that celebrated Westport's 150th birthday. The fanfare began with the sound of church bells ringing at 5 P.M. on Friday night, April 26 marking the town's birthday and the state's 350th anniversary.

A kick-off event for the year-long tribute, chaired by Barbara Roth, a civic leader, was held at Town Hall where Westporters witnessed formal presentations of two books that would become part of the town's folklore in the years to come. Jack and Dorothy Tarrant presented their book, *A Community of Artists,* to First Selectman William Seiden.[1] The Westport Historical Society also published a hardcover historical photographic book, *Westport... a Special Place*, written and compiled by Eve Potts and designed by Howard Munce — its first such undertaking. The opening of the sesquicentennial exhibition, also called "A Community of Artists," took place in the Arts Council gallery. In addition, the *Westport News* published a 150th anniversary issue containing a complete history of all phases of life in Westport.

There was plenty of reading matter to mark the occasion, but what stands out in the minds of most Westporters who attended these events was the reenactment of the day that Westport's founder, Daniel Nash, Jr., left the town, then called Saugatuck, for the state capital seeking independence for himself and his fellow townsmen. Sunday, April 28 marked exactly 150 years to the day that Nash left for Hartford to present his petition to the state legislature. Accordingly, on this day in 1985, in the same place, at the same time, in the Saugatuck Church meeting house, modern-day Westporters sat in excited anticipation of what would happen when the reenactment got underway.

Joan Dickinson, president of the Westport Historical Society, graciously welcomed the overflow crowd. She was followed by Town Historian Dorothea Malm and Historical Society Vice President and author Eve Potts, who presented certificates to 20 families who were directly related to the original petition signers. Republican Julie Belaga, Westport's state representative from the 136th District, one of the town's most popular politicians, delivered a rousing speech praising the town, and she also brought greetings from Democratic Governor William O'Neill. Finally, after all of the official welcome and congratulations, the curtain on the stage went up. The play, written and directed by Ed Bryce, portrayed a scene in April 1835 in Daniel Nash, Jr.'s house on the day he departed for Hartford with the town's petition for independence. Ed Bryce played Nash; Dorothy Bryce played Nash's wife, Rebecca; Edward Nash, a Nash son, was played by Phil Bryce; and Andrew Nash, another Nash son, was played by Scott Bryce. When the curtain came down, the crowd clapped and cheered in appreciation of the actors who had brought to life one of the most significant days in the town's history.

On Monday, May 27, 1985 crowds began to gather along the streets to watch the Memorial Day Parade. A brand-new green, blue, white, and gold silkscreen flag with the outline of the Minuteman kneeling on one knee in the foreground — the first official Westport Town flag — flapped proudly in the breeze atop Town Hall. The colors symbolized the historic characteristics of Westport: the blue depicted the Saugatuck River as the lifeline of commerce of early Westport, the green represented the abundant farmland from which the community grew and prospered, and the gold symbolized the warmth and vitality of the people, according to the flag's designer, Miggs Burroughs. The townspeople had every reason to be in a festive mood: In addition to being a national holiday it was just one day shy of the town's official founding on May 28, 1835. A feeling of belonging to something special was palpable. Most everyone realized that this historic day was, indeed, one to remember.

HISTORIC OCCASION: Westport's new Town flag, designed by Miggs Burroughs, left, was unveiled on Memorial Day 1985. Funding was made available by comedian Rodney Dangerfield, a Westport resident, center, who is meeting with First Selectman Bill Seiden, right, in the home of Barbara Roth, chairman of the year-long Sesquicentennial Birthday Celebration in 1985. The flag shows the Minuteman kneeling with musket in hand.
NORWALK HOUR PHOTO

Among those at the head of the long parade on this sesquicentennial occasion were Grand Marshall Harry O'Connor, one of the first paid firemen in the town and a World War II Navy veteran, and three of the town's most heralded veterans, Robert Hartsig, Leonard Rovins, and John Davis Lodge. Hartsig had been a lieutenant colonel in the U.S. Air Force; Rovins was a retired U.S. Army colonel; and Lodge a retired U.S. Navy captain. More than 40 town organizations participated in this landmark event, cheering from the sidelines as the marchers passed by. Little children held more than 1,000 small town flags in their tightly clasped hands —a gift to the town from Westporter Rodney Dangerfield, who donated funds for the flags. Bill Vornkahl III, a Korean War veteran, served as chairman of the Memorial Day parade, a role he had played since 1971.

Next on the celebration calendar was the July 4-7 holiday weekend in 1985 with a town-wide event on a grand scale. On July 4, all traffic and parking were suspended on Main Street and Parker-Harding Plaza from 5 P.M. to 11 P.M. A block party took up the entire downtown area from The Remarkable Book Shop to the Westport Public Library. Every organization in town was represented, and many provided balloons, buttons, flags, souvenirs, sweatshirts, games and pony rides, and a treasure hunt. On the

Town Common, life in colonial times was reenacted, and a mock battle between the British and colonial troops was staged. Many dancers, musical groups, and singers appeared at Compo Beach to liven up picnickers.

The only discordant note to this celebratory extravaganza was a hoax perpetrated by an employee of the Inn at Longshore who had purportedly persuaded the rock music duo of Hall and Oates to perform at the celebration. Nearly 5,000 people, including 3,500 ticket holders who had paid $20 a ticket, showed up. But as the time for the entertainment approached, there was no sign of the "mystery" entertainers. A loud chorus of boos greeted First Selectman Bill Seiden's announcement that the entertainers were a no-show because their equipment had not arrived.

Eve Potts, a member of the committee that organized the celebration, recalls that when she first heard of Hall and Oates, "None of us had a clue as to who this band was — but I offered to check with my son, Mark, who was then with the *Washington Post.* He was enthusiastic about the idea. Excited, he said he and his friends would be here, no question. He said, 'Do you know how big these guys are? You'll have a sellout. Prepare for a big crowd.' So we did. We decided not to allow any traffic into Longshore. Everyone had to park downtown and would be bussed to the park. They were required to show their tickets to board the bus. On the day of the event, Mark came down in the morning to help set up chairs. As soon as we set foot on Hendrick's Point, he said, 'Mom, nothing is going to happen here today.' He explained that setting up for this kind of a concert took a full day."[2] Mark Potts was right. Nonetheless, while some were disappointed, a vast majority of the crowd enjoyed the get-together and many stayed at the Inn for dinner.

The next day, Seiden said that the whole town had apparently been victims of a hoax. The Longshore employee disappeared without a trace after the no-show and ticket holders got their money back.[3] But, Westport being Westport, the incident caused a stir in the world of show business and was reported in *People* magazine.

CONTINUITY: *Former state Representative Jo Fuchs Luscombe celebrates victory for Ken Bernhard, her successor representing the state's 136th district in Westport.* WESTPORT NEWS PHOTO

Adding to the stirring atmosphere in Westport in 1985 was the election of Democrat Martha S. Hauhuth as first selectman in November. Although she had been beaten by Seiden four years before, she waged a strenuous, upbeat campaign in 1985 and won handily. She and her running mate, the outspoken and politically adroit Randolph "Wally" Meyer, captured 5,171 votes to 3,393 for Seiden and his running mate, the effervescent Jo Fuchs. Seiden stepped down as third selectman, due to personal commitments and business responsibilities. So Hauhuth named Fuchs, a Republican, to replace him. Fuchs had served the town as chairman of the Zoning Board of Appeals, as president of the Republican Women's Club, and had

BRIDGE STREET BRIDGE CONTROVERSY: Blocking the state's plan to build an iron swing bridge on Route 136 in Saugatuck, First Selectman Martha Hauhuth persuaded the state Department of Transportation to repair and keep the old, landmark bridge which had been built in the 1880s. A temporary bridge, left, was removed, leaving the trusty old bridge, right, intact. PROTESTERS, right: Top row, from left, Jacqueline Heneage, Andy Ackerman, Hauhuth, and Sylvia Kamerow. Front row, left to right: Bobbi Liepolt, Jordan Liepolt, and Lorna Christophersen.
WESTPORT NEWS PHOTOS

twice been elected a Justice of the Peace. She would later step aside as third selectman to successfully run for state representative for the seat from the 136th district vacated by Julie Belaga, who ran for governor as the Republican nominee in 1986.

Hauhuth's years in office (1985-1989) were lively, marked by change and several controversies:[4]

- *The Baron's Property*. Four first selectmen before Hauhuth had tried to purchase the property now known as Winslow Park. She succeeded.

- *The Weigh Station* on I-95. In 1986, Governor O'Neill, under intense pressure to do something about the increased number of truck accidents on the Turnpike, announced the construction of a temporary truck weigh station on I-95 near Exit 18. Even though Hauhuth took the state to court over his decision, the weigh station was built and operated for several years before it was closed down in Westport.

- *The Bridge Street Bridge*. The state wanted to replace the Route 136 iron swing bridge with what Hauhuth called "a new cookie cutter 'McBridge'" in Saugatuck. She said this would have destroyed the landmark bridge [the last of its kind in the state], increased traffic on Imperial Avenue, South Compo and Bridge Street and ruined the scale and character of Saugatuck village and its surrounding neighborhoods. With the help of

315

State Representatives Alex Knopf and Jo Fuchs, Hauhuth convinced the state Department of Transportation (DOT) to repair and keep the old bridge, which had been constructed in the 1880s. Once traffic was diverted to a temporary bridge, the bridge was dismantled and trucked over to the Exit 17 cloverleaf where every piece was individually scraped, cleaned and repainted.

The DOT had originally told the town of Westport that if it wanted to keep the old bridge, the state would repair it but after that the town would be responsible for repair and maintenance of the bridge and 1½ miles of highway on each side of the bridge. Hauhuth was prepared to go ahead on this basis. The RTM, led by Moderator Doug Wood, however, was not willing to accept this responsibility and liability for the town. Hauhuth and Town Attorney Keith Dunnigan said that the RTM had no role in the matter. RTM members then contributed funds from their own pockets to hire an eminent legal professor from the University of Connecticut who said the RTM had to approve the takeover of the bridge and roadway if the town was to proceed as Hauhuth proposed. This stalemated the takeover of the bridge.

After some time, Hauhuth convinced the state DOT to repair the old bridge and to back off from its position of making the town responsible for the road and bridge. The story of how Hauhuth convinced the DOT to back off has never been made public — and for good reason. "I'm not sure what did it," Hauhuth says candidly. "I told the state how important it was to me, personally, and to our community. Then one day Pat Scully of my office [in Town Hall] came in with a letter from a deputy commissioner of the DOT saying they had approved my request. It's a mystery to me to this day." However, since the battle over the bridge took place after the weigh station siege, she said it was possible that the governor's office may have interceded for political reasons to win back the support he had lost by jamming the weigh station down Westport's throat. But that is just a theory, Hauhuth says. She said she never inquired further

PLAYGROUND PROTEST: Local residents, right, carry a sign that reads "SAVE COMPO BEACH" and "NOT THIS SPOT" but when the playground, designed by architect Robert Leathers, was finally built, left, beach residents and townspeople alike all enjoyed it.   WESTPORT NEWS PHOTOS

because she got what she and the town wanted.

Years later, when Hauhuth was driving downtown with her husband, Bob, and she went to make a right turn on Imperial Avenue, she heard the bells of the bridge clanging, so she and her husband got out of their car to watch the bridge open. "A group of people gathered and it was delightful. There were people waving from a sailboat in the water. It was a wonderful, marvelous small-town summer scene. As Bob and I were watching, somebody behind us said, 'The town did the right thing in keeping this bridge. It's wonderful.' That made me feel as good as anything I did as first selectman."

- *The Compo Playground.* A playground for children, designed by the noted architect Robert Leathers, and built at Compo Beach, turned into one of Westport's most controversial issues of the 1980s. It even brought a death threat to Hauhuth, the only one she ever received. Beach neighbors, fearing traffic and distressed at a structure being built on scarce beachfront, went to court and got an injunction to stop it. Hauhuth supported the parents who wanted the playground, and went to court to dispute the injunction. While the judge was making his decision, she drove back to Compo to wait. As soon as the injunction was lifted, the hammers came out and everyone worked together to build one of Westport's "happiest attractions," as Hauhuth describes it.

The second half of the 1980s was marked by commercial expansion and change, with downtown Westport booming. Retail space downtown was going for $50 a square foot — the highest in Fairfield County. One real estate agent boasted that Westport's downtown was being compared to Rodeo Drive in Beverly Hills. In the fall of 1986, bulldozers worked quickly to destroy one of Westport's landmarks, the nearly 50-year-old Mobil service station at 90 Main Street. It was replaced by an attractive New England-style building containing a retail store, The Limited, and a group of condominiums above it. A few months later, in February 1987, Arthur Tauck of Tauck Tours bought the old Fairfield Furniture store, a building, as previously noted, that had over the years served alternately as the town's meeting hall, high school, newspaper office, and bank. Tauck converted the building into a nationally acclaimed inn and restaurant known as National Hall. It staged a grand opening in 1993 and was subsequently listed on the Register of Historic Places. The block on which it stands was rezoned as a Historic Design District (HDD) by the town, as a result of which the Westport Chamber of Commerce subsequently gave him an award for his vision and service to the community.

TREASURE DISCOVERED: This giant mural done by Westport artist Edmund M. Ashe, Jr. was revealed when sections of drywall that had been in place for 50 years was removed by workmen renovating the former Klein's store to make way for Banana Republic at 44 Main Street in 1999. SETH GOLTZER PHOTO

KLEIN'S SUPPLANTED: Klein's, a longstanding presence on Main Street, rented its ground floor space to the Banana Republic in 1999. Here, Pete McGovern, who writes a column, "Sense of Rumor," for the Minuteman, *is seen in front of the old store, which remained in business but with an entrance off Elm Street.* ANDREA FINE PHOTO

In 1986, Henry Klein, at age 85, was the owner of Klein's and the grand old man of Main Street. "I'm a lucky man. I have my work. I live near my family. We enjoy each other. I like my employees. We're like a big family here,"[5] he said. However, in another ten years, even Klein's gave in to the inevitability of time and change. In January 1999, Klein's son, Stanley, retired. Klein's leased the ground floor to the Banana Republic, and moved its business to the second floor, considerably downsized. Klein's is now operated by Stanley Klein's son-in-law, Bob Hertzel, president of the store. He also serves as president of the Downtown Merchants Association. When Banana Republic began to renovate its new store at 44 Main Street, a 190-square-foot multi-color tempera and oil cartoon mural done by Edmund M. Ashe, Jr. (1908-1986) was discovered when workmen removed sections of drywall that had been in place for 50 years. The whimsical, cartoon-like mural is painted on a one-inch-thick slab of plaster and represents patrons in a speakeasy. It depicted a group of men drinking at a bar in a saloon and, according to longtime Westport artist Howard Munce, at least three of the characters in the scene were recognizable to him. The mural was done in the late 1930s or early 1940s. Its whereabouts had remained a mystery until Klein's renovation in 1999. The mural was originally painted as a wall decoration for the Triangle Tavern, a speakeasy-type bar on Main Street. Banana Republic was praised for its decision to restore the 28-foot-long mural as a focal point behind its front register. Said Sheila O'Neill, executive director of the Historical Society: "Our role was to be instrumental in alerting all of the people in the corporation [Banana Republic] to the importance of this, because none of them knew anything about Westport other than the fact they wanted to open a store here." [6]

The 1980s also brought to light an inspirational Westport man whose courage and perseverance have become legend. John Huminski, born with cerebral palsy, founded a nonprofit organization in 1986 named "I Can Do It Too." It sponsors swimming, running, and weightlifting competitions with both disabled and able-bodied athletes. Huminski, now in his late 40s, has been wheelchair bound since his early 20s, but he did not let that hamper his ambition to be an athlete. He mentors students at Norwalk High School, where he went to school himself; he works with disabled and able-bodied children through his organization, and he regularly works out with weights serving as an example for children in need of self-esteem. Huminski was described in a newspaper article as "a lesson in courage."[7] He completed the Marine Corps Marathon in Washington, D.C. for six consecutive years, and has competed in world athletic games in Holland. He has participated in road races, swimming meets, and weightlifting competitions and also enjoys parasailing, kayaking, basketball,

QUIET HERO: John Huminski, born with cerebral palsy, overcame his handicap and founded a nonprofit organization in 1986 called "I Can Do It Too," which sponsors athletic events for physically handicapped people. Huminksi is congratulated by Connecticut Governor William O'Neill, right.
COURTESY OF RUTH HICKOX

soccer, and is a certified scuba diver. From 1972 to 1990 Huminski was a part-time teacher in the Westport school system, working with learning-disabled and handicapped children. Says Ruth Hickox, a friend from nearby Weston who serves as his secretary and who has known him since the 1970s: "He always seems like a happy guy with a bad problem. He's a warrior. He goes up against circumstances that come along and plows right through them. His ability to surmount all odds makes him a giant among giants."[8]

Westport's profile continued to rise in the late 1980s and early 1990s. In 1992, home buying here received national attention when a crew from CBS's "This Morning" did a live television broadcast from the town's Planning and Zoning Department. The Westport broadcast was part of a five-segment consumer series titled the "CBS This Morning Home Buyer's Guide" done by the program's consumer correspondent, Hattie Kauffman. Clearly, Westport was no longer a small town, but a number of local shops continued to try to maintain that small-town feeling. Among them was the Compo Barbershop owned and run by Tom Ghianuly. Old photos of Westport scenes are prominently displayed on the shop's walls. Those scenes and hairstyles have changed considerably since he opened his shop in 1959.

Westport in the late 1980s and early 1990s was not all prosperity and progress. Indeed, as in every other locale in America, substance abuse was seriously eroding the quality of life for many families. In the spring of 1987, the Westport Committee on Alcohol and Drug Abuse submitted a report showing that drug use was widespread and had no generational boundaries: astonishingly, it even existed among pre-teens and the elderly here. According to Police Chief Ron Malone, substances most often abused in the 1980s were alcohol, marijuana, and cocaine.

By the 1990s, the town's Police Department had grown to 70 fulltime officers. It established a Youth Bureau and units specializing in burglaries, narcotics, bad checks and frauds, and general investigations. It started a Drug Abuse Resistance Education (DARE) program, equipped a Marine Division, formed a K-9 patrol, and a Support Division with officers assigned to public safety, railroad parking, and Emergency Medical Services (EMS), the latter being one of the most publicly praised organizations in the town. The department was also faced with occasional incidents of arresting outsiders who happened to be meeting in Westport to exchange drugs—something that could happen in any town in America.[9]

Drugs and alcohol were not the only crimes on the rise. Perhaps the most insidious were vandalism and race and hate crimes. In 1986 four teenage vandals were arrested after they went on a rampage, smashing automobiles and spraying anti-Semitic slurs and swastikas at the medical complex at 162 Kings Highway North. The four were linked to at least 14 other incidents of vandalism. This incident proved to be the last straw. Some 32 community leaders, parents, clergymen and teachers responded to an invitation from First Selectman Hauhuth to discuss vandalism.

In 1993 other anti-Semitic incidents occurred. An anti-Semitic slur, a white supremacist slogan, and a swastika were printed on the mailbox of a Russian Jewish couple living in Westport. More hate graffiti surfaced when a swastika and racist slogans, as well as a threat against African Americans, were found by Westporter Larry Aasen, written on the lifeguard building at Compo Beach. He saw the graffiti while on a Saturday stroll and he called the police. However, when Aasen, a member of the RTM, returned the next day, the writing had not been touched. So he painted over the graffiti himself. "I was so shocked to see this; I felt shame and anger," he was quoted as telling a *Westport News* reporter.[10] Swastikas and anti-African American slurs were written also in a Taylor Place office bathroom in downtown

Westport. The discovery was made by local Attorney Raymond Ross, who also notified police. Following that, an outbreak of vandalism with Nazi symbols was reported in the midst of Passover celebrations. Swastikas were painted on cars at O'Keeffe's Cadillac on the Post Road. The incidents, though infrequent, continued.

In May 1999 some 150 Bedford Middle School parents attended an emergency meeting after hateful letters and graffiti were found at the school. Several children stayed home from school after hearing reports that "Kill all Jews," swastikas and "KKK" were found in small writing on walls and inside stalls in the boys' bathroom. As a result, a townwide forum, "Community Concerns: Tolerance and Crisis Response," was held to address the issue in 1999. Said Rabbi Robert Orkand of these displays of prejudice: "This tells us that despite the unprecedented freedom under which Jews of the United States live, there are still those who wish us harm. While I am not an alarmist who sees anti-Semitism everywhere, I am also not naive enough to think that it does not remain a very real threat. If in fact young people are responsible for many of the acts of anti-Semitism we have witnessed, one must ask what has happened in the lives of these young people that causes them to lash out at others in hateful and hurtful ways."[11]

Rabbi Orkand has reached out for prominent speakers at Temple Israel, many of whom draw an overflow crowd of Westporters of all faiths. In 1996, for example, Nobel Laureate and writer Elie Wiesel told a soldout crowd of some 1,200 residents that, as a result of the assassination of his longtime friend, Prime Minister Yitzhak Rabin, he was deeply concerned about a growing "fanaticism" that had developed between Arabs and Jews. He said Jews must acknowledge that fanaticism exists not only in the Arab world but within the Jewish community, as well, noting that it was a Jew who killed Rabin. Wiesel, recipient of the Presidential Medal of Freedom, praised President Bill Clinton who, he said, "was so personally touched and heartbroken at Rabin's death." He said that Westport Jews — and those in communities all over the country — "must somehow feel a connection to Israel."

WIESEL'S WARNING: Noble Laureate Elie Wiesel, right, a Holocaust survivor and world-known author, came to Westport in 1996 as a guest of Temple Israel Rabbi Robert Orkand, left. He called on American Jews to support Israel and to ease the tension between Arabs and Jews.

TEMPLE ISRAEL PHOTO

Two years later, Orkand was honored in November 1999 when he delivered the invocation in Congress and Representative Christopher Shays (R-4), in whose district

321

Westport is located, praised the rabbi by noting that his "energy and compassion are testimony to his dedication to all that he believes and cherishes." He added: "Rabbi Orkand is a man of God and a true healer." Orkand responded by commenting: "It was an awesome honor for me to stand at the seat of our government. No matter how jaded or pessimistic we become, to stand at this podium [in Congress] from which presidents have spoken is inspiring."[12]

There were other forms of prejudice, too. In the past decade and a half, as more and more people came out of the closet, bias against gays and lesbians was in the news in Westport. A story in the *Westport News* reported on an organization called Parents & Friends of Lesbians and Gays (P-FLAG) of Southern Fairfield County, formed to fight prejudice. The Fairfield County group is a chapter of the national organization that has been dealing with this particular bias for many years. Other incidents have occurred in recent years, and the pattern is always the same: alarm and shock is expressed at the time. And the community goes on with its life.

While most Westporters adhere to an unwritten, unspoken rule of courtesy and civility, there have been occasional complaints of too many cars speeding, horn honking on the road, citizens being outspoken to the point of personal attacks at public meetings, and writing nasty letters in the newspapers. And, like thousands of other towns across America, Westport has been trying to cope with an increasing amount of litigation. The *Westport News* made the point when, in an obvious exaggeration of the problem, it described Westport in 1990 as "the place lawyers call Sue-City." The story pointed out that people in town were more litigious than ever; they turn to the court to battle issues they would have settled informally 20 years ago.

LEADING LAWYER: Leonard Rovins, a resident for nearly 50 years, describes Westporters as "litigious and confrontational." Yet, he says, a large number of residents volunteer their time to help make Westport "a great town."
WESTPORT NEWS PHOTO

Leonard Rovins, an attorney who was head of the first Recreation Commission in Westport and a former Board of Education member, has been an attorney and Westport resident for nearly 50 years. He said in a statement: "Westporters historically are litigious and confrontational, projecting a 'NIMBY' or Not In My Back Yard attitude. They insist on protecting their property interests and oppose any encroachments perceived or real. On the other hand, their devotion to Westport and its future prompts an exciting number to volunteer time and effort to active participation in various governmental, charitable, and community activities which help make Westport a great town."[13]

One of the most widely publicized lawsuits in recent years was the case of attorney and delicatessen owner Julius Gold against Paul Newman in what popularly became known as "The Salad Wars." Gold filed a breach of contract suit against Newman, claiming Newman had promised him a share of the profits from the salad dressing Newman sold. The trial opened on May 31, 1988, amid extensive hoopla. It was a media circus. TV cameras and press photographers recorded the scene in front of the tall brick courthouse on Main Street in Bridgeport as hordes of reporters besieged the principals. Gold testified that he had been instrumental in developing and marketing a salad dressing originally concocted by the actor at his Coleytown Road home in Westport. In return for his professional advice and expertise, which extended over a three-year period, Gold stated that he had been promised a one-twelfth stock interest in Salad King, Inc., a company formed to market the dressing. The jury of three men and three women deliberated for five hours over two days before deciding that Gold's role in the inception of Newman's Own salad dressing was not significant enough to award him damages.

As for the issue of Westporters being too outspoken, Westport writer Nat Hentoff comments: "There are always controversies, political and otherwise, that can't be predictably categorized as coming from the left or the right — but each is always personally and deeply felt. And usually unresolved. Westport, like many other towns where individuals can try to redress their grievances more openly than in big cities, is never dull."[14]

Placing these problems in proper perspective, drugs, prejudice, and lawsuits are sad facts of life throughout America today. Westport is no exception. Very much aware of the troubling trends, however, Westporters do not attempt to turn away. The town has scores of public and private agencies at work, including support groups, trying to identify those people and those families who are in need. Moreover, the vast majority of Westporters spend their time, money and energy on positive activities, many of which reflect their spirit of volunteerism and philanthropy. Some examples in recent years are:

• The Library Riverwalk and Gardens, a brick pathway from the library to the Levitt Pavilion. The idea began with Hyla O'Connor, well-known cook-

PATH TO REMEMBER: Betty Lou Cummings, sparkplug of The Library Riverwalk and Gardens, was the prime mover in the drive to sell bricks with the names of donors engraved on them. The Riverwalk consists of some 11,000 bricks and, together with other enhancements, has beautified the Jesup Green area and the entrance to the Westport Public LIbrary.
WESTPORT NEWS PHOTO

book author and longtime Westport resident, who died in 1988. She and Pat Coplen envisioned a walkway and a park bordering the river behind the library that exists today. Betty Lou Cummings, Westport's second selectman in the administration of First Selectman Joseph P. Arcudi (1993-1997) and affectionately known as Westport's First Cheerleader, was the prime mover in the drive to sell bricks with names of the donors engraved on them. The Riverwalk and Gardens consists of 11,000 bricks, about half of which are engraved with individual names of the donors; 78 pink granite squares, 57 benches, 3 picnic tables, 21 pole lights, trees, shrubs and bushes. Phase I was completed in 1992. Phase II, extending the walk from the library to the Post Road, was completed in 1999 in a special ceremony. It featured a sculpture, *A Bridge in Time,* by Westport artist Bobbie Friedman, using the bearings from the old Post Road Bridge, and new gardens donated by the Westport Garden Club. Ned Dimes, chairman of the Board of Finance from 1978 to 1997, was the keynote speaker. Mollie Donovan, of the Arts Advisory Committee, presented the sculpture.

Also of note was the renovation and expansion of the library. Philanthropist Joel Smilow, former president of Playtex, donated $1 million for the new library expansion in 1996, giving a jump start to the campaign that raised an additional $2 million. And, perhaps the most creative innovation at the library was the tile wall, 6 feet x 26 feet in size, known as the "River of Names." The project was spearheaded by Betty Lou Cummings and Dorothy E. Curran, library trustee. The handmade tiles were designed by Marion Grebow, an artist who turned her sculpting and painting talents to custom tile design. The mural contains 80 historical tiles, four thematic corner tiles, and 1,843 donor tiles — a total of 1,927 bas-relief tiles of varying size depicting significant events in the town's history.

In addition, another noteworthy event was the placing of a time capsule in the cornerstone of the new library. It was filled with artifacts and essays describing life in Westport today. The capsule, dubbed "The Great Time Machine," will remain encased near the library building's cornerstone until November 2097 when it will be opened by library and town officials, giving them a glimpse of life in the late twentieth century.

- The meeting of Westports of the World (WOW) on Compo Beach. WOW is an organization of some 28 towns named Westport from nations around the world, which meet at an annual convention. Founded in 1985, the purpose of the organization is to promote friendship among the towns named Westport. In July of 1991, delegates of WOW met in Westport, Connecticut, with Lois Schine and Lou Santella as co-chairmen and Betty Lou Cummings and Eve Potts serving as Westport coordinators. Representatives from Indiana, California, Missouri, Maine, Massachusetts, New York, Connecticut, South Dakota, Washington, Ireland, New Zealand, Nova Scotia, and Ontario, Canada, were treated to a long weekend series of events.

Join the fun!
July 11-14, 1991

WESTPORTS OF THE WORLD: Some 18 towns named Westport came here in 1991, with Lou Santella and Lois Schine serving as co-chairmen of the host committee, and Eve Potts and Betty Lou Cummings as coordinators.

- The Great Race: A tradition begun during the national centennial celebration in 1976, was suspended for a time but made its comeback in 1991 when the Sunrise Rotary Club sponsored the competition. Kayaks, canoes, boats, sunfish, catamarans, windsurfs, sailing dinghies, and a class of craft that defies description — the Funtastical boats — were launched into the Saugatuck River at Jesup Green. On Jesup Green there were craft booths and rides for children. Jim Long, the Westport postmaster, set up a postal booth for the cancellation of a special Great Race stamp designed by famous Westport artists. A skydiver, former Westport policeman Howard Burling, landed between the Green and the river to the amazement of the crowd. Through the Great Race, the Westport Sunrise Rotary Club has raised more than $100,000 which it has contributed to many local and international charities. The Sunrise Rotary Club, a Friday breakfast club, was formed in 1989 as a spinoff from the Westport Rotary Club, which holds Tuesday luncheon meetings. Pete Wolgast, president of the Sunrise Rotary Club, says the club

FUN FLOAT: Youngsters enjoy their ride in a boat entered in the "Funtastical" category of the annual Great Race sponsored by the Sunrise Rotary Club. WESTPORT NEWS PHOTO

has about 75 members. The club recognizes an outstanding Staples High School student of the month, among its various activities.

- The Parade of Champions. In a "first," in December 1993, a parade was staged to honor the Staples High School boys' soccer and girls' swimming teams who that year won state championships.[15] The boys' soccer team broke a state record when the team captured its 11th Class LL Connecticut Championship. Also honored were members of the Staples Players who that year won the New England Theatre Conference's Moss Hart Award for their production of *Cabaret*. Another form of recognition for all Staples students occurred in 1993 with the launching of the successful "Be an Angel, Buy a Seat" fundraising drive for the Staples Auditorium restoration program led by Pat Dever. In 1995, Parade of Champions II honored the state champion girls' basketball and girls' swimming teams. Also that year, Westport celebrated the 50th birthday of the United Nations by flying 185 flags representing member nations on the downtown bridge.

- An important innovation bringing healthy competition in the local print media occurred in November of 1993 when the first issue of the *Minuteman*, a weekly newspaper appeared, with Lise Connell, former editor of the *Westport News*, as its founding editor and Mark Owades as publisher. While it is an entrepreneurial private enterprise, it can be seen as a form of public service in the best traditions of journalism.

- The annual First Night. Organized in the spring of 1994, it has been held in each successive year. The national New Year's Eve program started in Boston in 1976 as a way to bring suburban communities together, while providing the public with an alternative, family-oriented, alcohol-free way of ushering in the New Year. The event, organized by Executive Director Rita Smircich, includes a wide variety of entertainment in a number of venues, as well as fireworks at midnight.

- The annual Town Beautification Day and Clean-Up Westport Day, which got a big boost in 1995 under the leadership of a Beautification Committee chaired by Don Torrey.

- Improvements at Longshore: Westport's new ice skating rink opened at Longshore Club Park November 29, 1996. It was built by the Police Athletic League with funds from a $100,000 private grant. In 1997, Longshore was improved when the town installed a new pool, a building for residents, and seven new Har-Tru tennis courts replacing the old clay courts. The next year, a skateboard park was created at Compo, opening up a new sport for many Westport youths.

- The Sister City program with the city of Yangzhou, China. In 1995, a delegation from Yangzhou visited Westport to establish a Sister City relationship with Westport, to promote Sino-American understanding. Mayor Shi Guoxing of Yangzhou and First Selectman Joseph P. Arcudi signed a Sister City agreement. Westport's first official visit to Yangzhou took place in the fall of 1996 with a delegation that included Second Selectman Betty Lou Cummings and Judy Landa, chairman of the Westport/Yangzhou Sister Cities Council.

MAKING HISTORY: At Town Hall, Westport First Selectman Joe Arcudi, right, signs historic agreement with Yangzhou Mayor Shi Guoxing, center. At left is Deng Quing, vice director, Yangzhou Foreign Affairs Office.
WESTPORT NEWS PHOTO

During this visit, Landa signed an agreement with Yangzhou to continue the town's cultural and educational exchanges, and Cummings signed another agreement with Chinese officials to accept a pavilion as a gift from Westport's Sister City. The offer of the pavilion became controversial when some Westporters, objecting to China's human rights abuses, expressed dismay that Westport would accept a gift from a city in China. Among those who vigorously opposed the gift was Nat Hentoff, a syndicated *Washington Post* columnist and a weekend resident of Westport. He attacked the plan at a P&Z hearing in town and wrote a column about the Westport battle that was read nationwide. The topic became moot when nothing further was done. Opponents consider it a dead issue. Nonetheless, contact between the Sister Cities has flourished. Delegations from Westport's public school system and the teacher exchange have continued. Another exchange has been the Summer Student Exchange sponsored by the Westport/Yangzhou Sister Cities Council. Musically gifted students from China performed at the Levitt Pavilion in August 1999 to an audience of approximately 400. The Westport/Yangzhou Sister Cities Council formed an umbrella agency in 1997, the Westport Sister Cities Association, with Bob Jacobs as president.

- The Kids' Wall. At the outset of 2000, a unique project was approved by town officials, thanks to the perseverance of First Selectman Diane Goss

Farrell. A 6-foot x 44-foot wall, composed of 64 separate panels, each one created by one of the 64 art classes in the Westport Middle Schools, is seen by artists as a historic addition to Westport's landscape. It is the most ambitious piece of public art in Westport's history, located at the children's pool at Longshore. The wall was conceived by Katherine Ross, painter, teacher and an active member in Cultural Arts and Art Smart programs for Westport children. It is designed and coordinated by Ross and graphic artist Miggs Burroughs, a member of the board of the Levitt Pavilion and the YMCA. Covered with colorful ceramic tiles, it is a mosaic of art, environment and community honoring and beautifying a public space with students' artwork. The artists say it is intended to celebrate the spirit and creativity of the children and to instill in them a permanent sense of pride and participation in the town.

WALL TO WALL ART: Kathy Ross, originator of the Kids' Wall, surrounded by the mosaic panels, created by over 1,300 middle school students, that make up the 6' x 44' long mural installed at the Longshore pool.
MIGGS BURROUGHS PHOTO

In addition, social service programs have been maintained and improved as Westport closed out the twentieth century with a number of creative new projects:

PROMINENT VOLUNTEER: Tammy Pincavage, former second selectman in the administration of Doug Wood, also served as president of the Westport Young Woman's League, president of the PTA Council, president of the Westport Woman's Club, and president of the Connecticut PTA. She was appointed by the RTM and the Board of Education to serve as vice chairman of the Westport School Building Committee.
WESTPORT NEWS PHOTO

- Project Return, a place where seven young women can go to have a home away from home, is one of the best known. The project was launched in 1985 when the decrepit frame building on North Compo Road was rehabilitated by a team of local volunteers and craftsmen. A nonprofit undertaking, it was conceived by a number of social-minded people, including Assistant Superintendent of Schools Kate McGraw. Project Return pays the town a token rent of $1 a year. In 1995, the first annual Bird House Sale was held as a fundraiser. The bird houses are designed and built by volunteers and auctioned off. Thus far, this project has raised some $150,000. Says Totney Benson, who with her husband Rick, has supervised the project: "I've been blown away by the success we have had from area artists. The generosity of the artists' contributions to it is just amazing."

- On April 18, 1997, the historic Toquet Hall on the Post Road was leased by the town for a Teen Coffeehouse, a gathering place for Staples High School and Green's Farms Academy students. Its opening marked the successful three-year effort by a variety of community leaders. Tammy Pincavage, second selectman during the Wood administration (1989-1993) and chairman of the Teen Center Steering Committee, pushed for a place where the town's teenagers could entertain themselves and spend their free time together. Betty Lou Cummings culminated the effort to find a place for teenagers with the opening of Toquet Hall during the Arcudi administration.

- While not directly impacting Westporters, Paul Newman, in association with Yale-New Haven Hospital, built a one-of-a-kind Connecticut summer camp by the colorful name of The Hole in the Wall Gang camp (taken from his classic movie, *Butch Cassidy and the Sun Dance Kid*), for children with cancer and other life-threatening diseases. It is located on a 300-acre site complete with its own lake in Ashford and Eastford, Connecticut. Half of the estimated $8 million construction came from Newman's Own, the profits of which are donated to charity, according to A.E. Hotchner, Westport author and Newman's business partner in the food company. In 1992 a book of selections by children who attended this camp was published entitled, *I Will Sing Life,* that carries an introduction by the actor.[16] Newman said publicly on CNN's "Larry King Live" on February 27, 1998 that this project was the most important thing he ever did.

- In July 1995, Westport hosted 80 Special Olympics athletes and coaches from Cameroon. The Westport Rotary Club sponsored the Special Olympics Host Town Committee. In 1996, the Olympic Torch passed through Westport for the 1996 games in Atlanta. Within the town itself, a new organization called RESPECT (Recreational Special Education Teams) was founded by Toni Rubin who, with her husband, Steve, also served on the town's Host Committee for the Special Olympics World Games held in New Haven. RESPECT was created in 1995 to provide recreational activities for preschool to middle-school children with special needs. The YMCA donated pool time, and the

DI LUCA + MAKRIS DESIGN
LANE DUPONT ILLUSTRATION

329

ACHIEVER: Arthur Tauck, community-minded owner of Tauck Tours, completely rebuilt National Hall and turned it into one of the town's leading attractions. Tauck has been recognized by the YMCA, the Chamber of Commerce, and other groups for his contributions to Westport.

WESTPORT NEWS PHOTO

Westport Soccer Association scheduled field time for the youngsters.

• The YMCA's Faces of Achievement award for outstanding volunteers in Westport has been given to 18 people since the award was first given in 1996. They are Rick Benson, Totney Benson, Miggs Burroughs, Betty Lou Cummings, Christine DiGuido, Leslie Michelle Fuchs, The Gault Family, David Giunta, Heather Hightower, Glenn Hightower, Lindsey Kaufman, Robert Knoebel, Kevin Lally, Jo Fuchs Luscombe, Ed Mitchell, Bill Mitchell, Jack Mitchell, Marcellino Petroccio, Gabriel Phillips, Joanie Reznik, Peter Romano, Sr., Peter Romano, Jr., Joel E. Smilow and Arthur Tauck, Jr. Jim Nantz, the premier CBS sports commentator, has donated his time to serve as emcee of the event for several years. Like other national sports broadcasters and writers such as Win Elliot, Sal Marciano and Frank Deford, Nantz chose Westport for his home.

No assessment of Westport in the 1990s would be complete without a glance at education, which as always had a dominant role in Fairfield County. People, more than anything else, have made the greatest difference in the education of youngsters in Westport. One of the most outstanding among them, Al Pia, a revered and beloved drama teacher, retired in 1998 at the age of 70 after 30 years at Staples. He performed miracles as drama coach of the Staples Players. Perhaps his most outstanding production, *Cabaret*, won the New England Theater Conference Moss Hart Award, one of the most prestigious awards for theater. Under his guidance, Staples Players won a total of six New England Theater Conference Awards with *War and Peace* (1969), *Soldier, Soldier* (1970), *Black Elk Stands* (1978), *Cabaret* (1982 and 1993), and *The Sound of Music* (1990). Among his proteges were David Marshall Grant, Scott Bryce, Kevin Conroy, Teresa Eldh, and Cindy Gibb. Before Pia, under the direction of Craig Matheson in the 1960s, the Players had also won numerous awards. In 2000, under the direction of Judy Luster, they were invited to represent the United States at the Edinburgh Theatre Festival.

Staples' efforts in the theater, as in other aspects of school life, cost money, and, while Westport boasts an education system that is among the best in the nation, some Westporters over the years have objected to the

*CHAIN OF COMMAND: At the Staples High School gradua-
tion ceremonies in 1994, Elizabeth Irvine, right, receives
diploma from her mother, Board of Education Chairman
Joan Irvine, center, as Staples Principal Gloria Rakovic,
left, and Superintendent of Schools Paul Kelleher, far left,
look on.* WESTPORT NEWS PHOTO

*SAFETY FIRST: Westport school children get some helpful
tips from Westport Police Department Youth
Officer Arnie DeCarolis at the beginning of a typical school year.* WESTPORT NEWS PHOTO

cost of this education. Some have called for referenda to keep the education budget from getting out of control. In the period from 1985 to 1999, referenda were held but, for the most part, the community supported the Board of Education:[17]

- In May 1986, the Board of Education 1986-87 budget of $24,625,876 was approved by the RTM after a petition by the Westport Taxpayers Association had proposed a $1.3 million cut, or slightly more than 5 percent. First Selectman Marty Hauhuth called the proposed cut "punitive." As it turned out, the anti-referendum forces swept to victory, as Westporters voted "no" to reducing the education budget.

- In 1991, the Westport Taxpayers Association collected 1,596 signatures needed to force a townwide referendum on the town's education budget of $34,311,830 for 1991-92, which represented a 4.2 percent increase. The WTA proposed a $703,493 cut, keeping the increases to only 2 percent. The referendum failed.

- In 1992 the WTA was more successful, nixing the Board of Education's $3.9 million expansion plan. And in 1993, yet again there was a drive for a referendum, which failed this time, as it failed in 1991.

- In 1996 the WTA forced another referendum to cut $1 million from the budget, but it failed by a margin of 2-1. So the story on education seems to be a most predictable one, with challenges to the budget cropping up every now and then, but with the residents responding, for the most part, by strongly supporting the necessary spending for the town's educational system.

Yet another problem that Westport educators have had to face in the last decade and a half of the century is school integration. The landmark *Sheff vs. O'Neill* court decision condemning de facto school segregation in Connecticut, filed in Hartford, spurred the state legislature in June 1993 to pass, and Governor Lowell P. Weicker, Jr., to sign what was called An Act Improving Educational Quality and Diversity.[18] The act divided the state into 11 planning regions and required communities in each of them, among other things, to enhance student diversity and awareness of diversity. No specific plan was proposed, but the act called for each local Board of Education to appoint a committee to assess the needs of the community served by the district and to develop a proposal for how the community could contribute to regional plans. In November 1993 the Westport Board of Education appointed the Westport Advisory Committee for Enhanced Quality and Diversity in Public Schools. The committee, chaired by attorney Eugene F. Cederbaum, was made up of 34 civic and business leaders, teachers, parents, students, and other concerned citizens.

Among those applauding the act was former Superintendent of Schools Claire Gold. A longtime advocate of diversity in schools, Gold left the local school system in 1988 and took up the school desegregation issue to which she is passionately devoted. In a 1996 interview in her office at Cooperative Educational Services (CES) in Fairfield, where she was serving as a consultant specializing in school integration, Gold said, "You can talk for just so long and then you have to do something [about school desegregation]."[19] That same year Gold was named "Connecticut Educator of the Year" by the Connecticut Council of Teachers of English for her work on behalf of minority students and the cause of school integration.

Before making its recommendation, the Westport Diversity Committee conducted a community-wide survey, which asked for citizen input on the important question. While a majority of respondents believed that it was important for Westport students to learn to get along in a culturally, ethnically, racially, and economically diverse world, the committee's report stated, "Only about one-third agreed that exposing students to people of other cultures, different economic groups, races and ethnic groups will meaningfully improve the overall quality of education in Westport." The committee's final recommendations reflected the divergent views of its citizens. First, it called for the establishment of a townwide task force on diversity that would address such issues as multicultural awareness training. The Board of Education, after holding a public hearing and meeting with the RTM as required by the law, approved the report and forwarded it to the regional forum. Next, a regional plan was formulated and submitted for approval. But, as it turned out, 8 of the 11 regional planning groups in the state rejected their regional plan and the issue went back to square one—the courts.

Another diversity program entered Westport and accomplished much of the diversity training issues endorsed by the diversity committee. Entitled "A World of Difference," the program's aim was to combat prejudice and discrimination and promote an appreciation of diversity. It was originally created by the Anti-Defamation League in 1985, and it was adopted by school systems, towns, and cities throughout the country. Spearheading the effort was Harold Levine, a Westporter and former advertising executive who also started the Westport Educational Foundation, a nonprofit group that supports the Westport public school system.

June 1999 marked the end of the first year of yet another diversity project, the Choice Program, which, by all reports, has worked well for the initial Bridgeport students, recently joined by 29 more, who have been attending classes here. The program, coordinated first by Green's Farms School Principal Angela Wormser-Reid and now by Deputy Schools Superintendent John Brady, was developed in response to *Sheff vs. O'Neill*. Its aim is to provide an opportunity for children from urban areas to attend better-equipped schools in more affluent suburban areas. Those suburban districts, including Westport, are required to accept as many students as they can accommodate in existing classrooms.

Crowding in the schools presented another challenge in the Nineties. In the spring of 1996 education officials announced that the former Green's Farms School would be reclaimed from the Westport Arts Center, which, since 1984, had been located in the old Green's Farms School building, along with the Senior Center. The artists objected but failed in their request that the Board of Education build a school somewhere else, and so vacated the building in 1997 to make way for the beginning of a reclaimed elementary school after the town agreed to pay the Arts Center $625,000 for their improvements to the building. Some tried to perceive the contest as pitting the education community against the artistic community. But nothing could be further from the truth. In fact, there were many residents who vigorously supported both the arts and education.

One such person is Ann Sheffer, who bridges the worlds of the arts and education, philanthropy and politics. Sheffer, whose roots in the community go back to the 1930s, resigned in 1998 from the Westport Arts Center board to serve as a mediator between the town and the Arts Center in an epic power struggle over which agency should occupy the former Green's Farms School building, first opened in 1927. As a member of the RTM, she

HILLARY SUPPORTERS: Ann Sheffer, left, Hillary Clinton, and Ann's husband, Bill Scheffler at a Fairfield County fundraiser. The First Lady came to Westport in the fall of 1999. Ann Sheffer serves on the President's Committee on the Arts and Humanities, of which Hillary Clinton is honorary chairman.

STEPHEN SCHWARTZ PHOTO/CAMERA ARTS

helped gain the necessary votes among her peers on the RTM to approve a $625,000 buyout of the Westport Arts Center. Sheffer describes herself as an "integrator," a person who brings diverse people and interests together. "I tend to know people in different fields — my mother's [Betty R. Sheffer] friends, my contemporaries, young people...lots of times I know someone who is doing something and who needs something someone else has to offer."[20] In Westport, she serves on a long list of boards, including the Betty R. Sheffer Foundation. Nationally, she has worked with Hillary Rodham Clinton on the President's Committee on the Arts and Humanities, of which Sheffer is a member and Hillary Clinton is honorary chairman. In 1991, Sheffer volunteered to host a fundraiser at her home for a little known governor of Arkansas by the name of Bill Clinton. In 1992, Sheffer ran for state senate against Republican incumbent Judith Freedman (R-26). Sheffer lost, but she carried Westport by 55 to 45 percent. She chairs the Westport Millennium Coordinating Committee in 2000, bringing together all of these public service themes in town with the publication of a Westport Community Gift Catalog that suggests specific ways townspeople can contribute to the "town that doesn't have everything... yet." Together with her husband, Westport attorney Bill Scheffler, she spends a great deal of time on projects celebrating the history and culture of Westport.

The townspeople in Westport take politics as seriously as they do education. In 1986, the town felt great pride when Julie Belaga won the Republican nomination for governor. She had served from 1976-1985 as state representative from the 136th district to the General Assembly in Hartford, where she became assistant minority leader and then a deputy majority leader. That same year, the *Hartford Courant* named her one of the top 10 legislators of the year. Although Connecticut had not elected a Republican governor since Thomas J. Meskill in 1970, Belaga was eager to try a run at the governorship. And Westport had not had a governor in Hartford since John Davis Lodge was elected in 1952. During her time in the General Assembly, Belaga had successfully introduced measures to keep Long Island Sound protected from contamination. But she tired of the routine and of the perception many Westporters had of her job. "Some people in Westport — mostly ex-New Yorkers — actually asked me, 'How can you continue to commute from Westport to Albany and back every day?'" After winning the GOP nomination for governor, she ran a vigorous campaign but was soundly beaten by the incumbent Democratic governor, William A. O'Neill. If there was a silver lining, Belaga did carry her hometown, gaining 67 percent of the vote.[21]

PUBLIC SERVANT: Julie Belaga, left, one of the town's most widely admired political figures, ran for governor of Connecticut in 1986 as the Republican nominee. She campaigned throughout the state, including at the railroad stations, above. She had previously served as state representative from the 136th district for 10 years. Following her defeat in the gubernatorial race, she taught at the Kennedy School of Government, served in the Bush administration as regional administrator of the Environmental Protection Agency, and then as a member of the Import-Export Bank. Her husband, Mike, a retired business executive, served as chairman of the Republican Town Committee.   WESTPORT NEWS PHOTO

Shortly after the election, Belaga became a Fellow at the Institute of Politics at the John F. Kennedy Graduate School of Government, as well as a television commentator at WTNH-TV, the ABC affiliate in New Haven, while she continued teaching at Harvard. Yet, she remained restless to return to the political arena. Soon after George Bush was elected President in 1988, she was named a regional administrator of the federal Environmental Protection Agency located in Boston. When the Clinton administration took office in 1993, Senator Christopher J. Dodd, a Democrat, recommended her for a seat on the Import-Export Bank. It was a presidential appointment for which she received Senate confirmation.

In 1989, the next major election for first selectman pitted Republican Douglas Wood against the incumbent, Marty Hauhuth. Wood, who served on the RTM for a decade, including a term as moderator, was a former IBM executive with an impressive resume. He campaigned on a theme of fiscal integrity and sound government. Along with his campaign manager, fellow RTMer Pete Wolgast, he chose Tammy Pincavage as his second selectman running mate. Pincavage was president of the Westport Young Woman's League and president of the townwide PTA Council. Later she became president of the Westport Woman's Club and president of the Connecticut PTA.

While voters had no major gripes about Hauhuth, her tenure had been marked by unusual turmoil, especially the weigh station, bridge, and playground. Wood also pointed out during the campaign that the budgets and taxes had increased fairly rapidly during Hauhuth's administration. The electorate, seeing Wood as a viable alternative, handed him an impressive victory: 5,250 votes to Hauhuth's 3,957. True to the voters' perception, Wood's tenure was a relatively quiet but productive time in the town's history.

In 1990, Wood's first year, the nation and the state were suffering from an economic recession with banks in particular hit hard, and a collapse in real estate values. Despite these difficult conditions, Wood stated: "Tough times call for tough measures. We're in the midst of a nationwide taxpayer revolt." He noted that the previous year's town budget had led to a 10.8 percent tax increase. By 1992, Wood reported, Westport had righted itself and was once again financially strong. The state of the town is "very, very good," he said. From a financial standpoint, it was excellent, he declared. There was no tax increase at all in 1993, for the first time in memory. In his fourth year in office, his objective, he said, in the previous three years had been to keep taxes low in order to keep Westport attractive and available to all of its citizens.

Wood made a surprise announcement on May 17, 1993, saying he would not run for reelection, thereby becoming the first Westport first selectman in history not to seek reelection after having held office for just one term. Wood said signing on for four more years would mean he would

TOWN LEADERS: Six former Westport first selectmen are brought together for a historic photo. From left, Douglas Wood, 1989-93; William Seiden, 1981-85; Jacqueline Heneage, 1973-1981; Joseph Arcudi, 1993-1997; Martha Hauhuth,1985-1989; and John Kemish, 1967-1973.
DOUG HEALEY PHOTO, PRODUCED BY JOHN CAPSIS
TOWN HALL ILLUSTRATION, KASSIE FOSS

be 67 when he stepped down, and there were many things in life that he wanted to do. Wood's four years were filled with numerous accomplishments, few of which made big headlines, but all of which added up to considerable progress for Westport. For example, he achieved a no-tax increase objective in 1993 following a zero-growth first selectman's budget in 1991 and 1992; implemented backyard pickup of recyclables on time and without incident; brought state-of-the-art data-processing procedures to Town Hall; restored the tide gates at Sherwood Mill Pond in nine months at a fraction of the prior bid price; and established a successful composting facility at the former Nike site on North Avenue.

In addition, he instituted the first merit pay system for nonunion employees; enabled construction of the first Little League ball field in two decades, tax-free through a gift to the town by the Jeffrey White family; obtained funding for two playing fields that were later built at Wakeman Farm; initiated the Mid-Fairfield County Selective Enforcement Unit, the first permanent cooperative police effort with the neighboring towns of Weston, Wilton and Norwalk; resolved the issue of the cost of Winslow Park with a court-ordered judgment of $9.4 million — far below pessimistic estimates of $15 to $20 million.

Further, under the Wood administration, the town obtained approvals and funding for engineering design work for expansion of the Compo Marina, paved the controversial Imperial Avenue parking lot tax free; added 152 parking spaces for commuters at the Green's Farms and Saugatuck railroad stations; revived the long-dormant flood control stream improvement projects; initiated an architect-designed master plan for refurbishing Longshore Club Park; reached a quick, amicable resolution for the long-festering lawsuit over ownership of the library; achieved a 3 percent reduction in staff through normal attrition and with no reduction in services; and collected $3.6 million in back taxes from 1990-1993 vs. $1.7 million for the comparable period during the prior administration. Perhaps the most meaningful contribution Wood made to the town from 1989 to 1993 was to represent the town, both inside and outside of its borders, in a thoroughly professional way. A tall, soft-spoken but firm leader, he put his business acumen and corporate experience to good use, dealing with public and private organizations in an even-handed manner.

Wood's announcement that he would not run again came several months after Joe Arcudi, deputy moderator of the Representative Town Meeting and a founder and coach in Westport's Little League for decades, had announced he would run for the Republican nomination — whether or not Doug Wood ran again. Arcudi, the Saugatuck-born candidate who owned restaurants in Westport and Milford, made his announcement on the steps of the former Saugatuck Elementary School — the school built in 1930 that he attended as a child — on a frigid day in February, 1993. Arcudi had been an RTM member for 24 years — longer than anyone in Westport history. Arcudi's campaign from February to November contacted virtually every family in Westport by phone, mail or in person and established an effective grass-roots door-to-door organization that turned out the vote. He did just that. On November 2, 1993, he and his running mate, Betty Lou Cummings, won a stunning victory over Democrat Nick Thiemann, a longtime town attorney, and his running mate, Ellie Lowenstein. They won by 6,179 votes to 3,037, the largest plurality in town history, with a solid 60 percent of the voters turning out.

Westporters were also very much involved in politics on the state level. In 1995, Eugene Gavin, a Republican who had served on Westport's board of finance and as state representative from the 133rd district, was named by Governor John Rowland commissioner of the state Department of Revenue Services. Gavin had made an unsuccessful run for state comptroller against Democrat Nancy S. Wyman in 1994. A Certified Public Accountant who holds M.B.A. and law degrees, Gavin had been working as director of state and local taxes for the consulting firm of Coopers & Lybrand. He went into his new post determined to change the image of the state agency. When he took office in 1995, he launched a "Call the Commish" hotline and was swamped with hundreds of calls, many of which he answered himself. Gavin has made it a point to try and make his department more "customer-friendly" and, towards that goal, he launched a program that included tax amnesty for those taxpayers who were in arrears. If delinquent taxpayers failed to take advantage of this program, they were faced with the prospect of possibly seeing their name among the state's top 100 tax delinquents on the Internet, a move that was viewed with pessimism by other state tax agencies but which turned out to be highly successful. Said Gavin: "There are two things certain in life: death and taxes. I want to make sure the people aren't scared to death of their taxes," he said. He believes he has met this goal and that other states and the federal Internal Revenue Service "are beginning to get Connecticut's message. That's a good thing." [22]

In 1996, First Selectman Joe Arcudi's supporters seemed confident their candidate would win reelection in 1997. He had worked hard and had personally been responsive to the public, days, nights, and weekends. Under his tenure the former Saugatuck School, built in 1930, had been converted into The Saugatuck for moderate-income senior housing — a project started by the Wood administration. He completed the construction of two athletic fields, also begun in the previous administration; and he improved electrical service and kept the town budget down. Still, the wildcard in this race was hard to predict. Arcudi denied a charge of sexual harassment by a female town employee and the case was settled by the town's insurers, but it remained an unspoken issue in the minds of many voters and dogged him throughout his term. Whispers about political patronage and cronyism in his administration were also not helpful.

There was another concern in the air as the 1997 townwide election approached: Spiraling costs and the distinct possibility of a hefty tax increase on the horizon. While some of the aforementioned public-spirited changes in Westport in the 1990s considerably improved the town, by 1996, a Citizens Long-Range Planning Task Force, headed by Lou Gagliano, released a 41-page report that reinforced some sobering news: If all of the town's capital building plans were implemented, the average home-owner would see taxes rise by 80 percent by 2006. The report was based, in part, on the findings of two Board of Finance members, John Laurino and Don Warren. The RTM also expressed concern about long-term expenses, when its pro-active moderator, Gordon Joseloff, appointed an RTM Special Long-Range Planning Committee in the summer of 1996 to make ongoing recommendations to the full RTM on subjects ranging from land acquisition to school population forecasts.

Even as officials expressed concern about capital building expenses, the effort to add to the town's dwindling open space continued. On March 14, 1997, with Paul Newman and Joanne Woodward and about 25 others watching, the Board of Finance recommended appropriating $3.7 million to purchase 30 acres of open land in the Coleytown area known as the "Poses Property." As part of the purchase, the board also endorsed the town's plan to accept a gift of 7.5 acres of land adjoining the property belonging to Newman and Woodward. Under terms of the approval, two acres would be used as a buffer for the Newman land. Thus, of the 37.5 acres involved, 9.5 would be restricted and always be open space. Meanwhile, there were other developments in the town. In January 1999 yet another local institution, Brooks Community Newspapers, publisher of the *Westport News,* was sold by B.V. Brooks to Thomson Newspapers. The *News* remained in business with BCN President Kevin J. Lally, a roll-up-your-sleeves, civic-minded business executive, succeeding Brooks as publisher. At the same time, there were some changes in the banking field. The Hudson Union Bank purchased

DIMES' DOMAIN: Board of Finance Chairman Edwin "Ned" Dimes, at home in 1998 with his wife, Toni, and their four dogs, from left, Zephyrus, Pearl, Maybelline, and Cecil, (on floor). Painting in rear by Earl Goodenow.

PHOTO COURTESY OF EDWIN DIMES

the old Westport Bank and Trust.

Meanwhile, the Democrats were not about to roll over when it came to challenging the incumbent Republican first selectman. Democratic Town Chairman Martha Aasen and Campaign Manager Dora Stuttman mobilized the Democrats behind Board of Finance member Diane Goss Farrell, a bright, articulate, high-energy candidate who had been raised in Westport and who had represented the younger generation of Democrats in town. A woman who knew her way around the community's social circles, she was a strong candidate for first selectman and the Democrats were eager for her to run against Arcudi because of the sharp contrasts in styles and personalities. Whereas Arcudi was hard-nosed and, at times, blunt in his language and political decision-making, Farrell appeared to be more approachable and seemed to have an upbeat manner that quickly put people at ease.

As an aside, it should be noted that during the campaign, Ned Dimes, the longtime chairman of the Board of Finance, announced he would retire from that board. Many veteran town political observers saw him as Westport's number one powerbroker. The steady-as-you-go Republican chairman of the board of finance, who held a tight reign on the town's expenditures, would be missed. Dimes' retirement brought bipartisan thanks and congratulations to a man who had served on the finance board for 18 years, 15 of them as chairman. As a Republican he could not politically support Farrell, a Democrat, in the campaign. Nonetheless, it was widely known that Farrell, during her term on the finance board, modeled herself after Dimes as a fiscal conservative and was considered his protege by political insiders familiar with finance board meetings.

As election eve 1997 approached, the contest appeared to be a toss-up. Arcudi and Farrell both campaigned vigorously, punched and counter-punched in a series of debates, and rallied their respective parties behind them. The result, however, was a stunning surprise: Farrell buried Arcudi in a landslide — winning 6,160 votes to Arcudi's 4,124, with town employee candidate John A. Klutchnik bringing up the rear with 131. Town Clerk Joan Hyde

PRESIDENT VISITS WESTPORT: President Bill Clinton greets crowd outside of National Hall on March 10, 1998, on the first of three fundraising visits to Westport in 15 months. He was introduced to a luncheon of Democratic faithful by Robert Rose, senior managing director of Bear Sterns. Rose and his wife, Yvette, served as hosts of the luncheon. Rose, inset, is a longtime Clinton fundraiser and political ally.
PHOTO BY STEPHEN SCHWARTZ/CAMERA ARTS

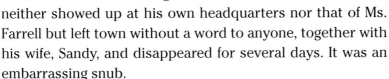

said the turnout was 43.6 percent of all registered voters. Breaking with tradition on election night, Arcudi neither showed up at his own headquarters nor that of Ms. Farrell but left town without a word to anyone, together with his wife, Sandy, and disappeared for several days. It was an embarrassing snub.

For the first time in recent memory, in 1997 the townspeople voted the Democratic party in charge of all the town boards and commissions, except for the Board of Assessment Appeals. For the first time since its creation in 1919, the Board of Finance had a Democratic majority. This outcome was all the more remarkable in light of the fact that in 1997 the registered voters were divided as follows: 6,532 Republicans, 4,379 Democrats, and 4,061 Unaffiliated. The Democratic sweep appeared to be a continuance of a general trend toward voting Democratic in Westport. The year before, in 1996, President Bill Clinton carried Westport by a margin of 5,785 to Bob Dole's 5,125.

Diane Farrell was not the only Democrat with a high profile in town in 1997. Vice President Al Gore came to town on October 9, 1997, in search of campaign financial support at the invitation of Westport couple Yvette and Robert Rose. Rose, a senior managing director of Bear Stearns, was a longtime Clinton fundraiser and ally. Between 30 and 40 people visited with Gore at the Inn at National Hall. President Clinton himself came to Westport on a cold March 10, 1998, for a Democratic National Committee fundraiser at the Inn at National Hall at $10,000-a-plate for 40 invited guests. Rose introduced the President and told him he was only the third sitting President to visit Westport after George Washington and Franklin Delano Roosevelt. Clinton responded, smiling: "It has been a long road since I first came to Westport [in 1991] as a candidate. I can't imagine why only George Washington and Franklin Roosevelt have been here. The others [Presidents] must not have known what they were missing."[23]

On June 8, 1998, Clinton returned to Westport for yet another fundraiser but at only $5,000-a-plate, held in Martha Stewart's television studio. The event, also at the invitation of Bob Rose, raised about $500,000 with $150,000 ticketed to the gubernatorial campaign of U.S. Representative Barbara Kennelly (D-1), who would go on to lose to incumbent Republican Governor John Rowland in November. The Clintons continued to come to Westport. On October 7, 1998, Hillary Clinton visited Westport for the Women's Leadership Forum of the Democratic National Committee, at the home of Fran Goldstein and Sandra Wagenfeld who, with her daughter Valerie, hosted some 700 guests. Greeting Hillary Clinton enthusiastically on the speaker's podium, among others, was First Selectman Diane Goss Farrell.

Hillary Clinton returned to Westport a little less than a year later on September 21, 1999, to raise funds for her New York senatorial campaign. The $1,000-per-person reception at the Beachside Avenue home of film executive Harvey Weinstein was co-hosted by Joanne Woodward, Paul Newman, and Martha Stewart. Despite a heavy rain, the event drew a large crowd, enabling Weinstein to announce to a surprised First Lady and other guests that the evening had raised $275,000. On June 28, 1999, Bill Clinton made a third appearance here, this time with a small group of 50 people at the Judy Point Lane estate of Goldstein and Wagenfeld. It was a $10,000-a-plate luncheon, and many Westporters outside of the compound looked on, disappointed that they could not even get a look at the President. State troopers had barricaded the Exit 18 entrance on I-95. The President's Marine helicopter landed at Sherwood Island. Clinton was joined in his limousine by Farrell, who could be seen waving through the tinted windows of the limo. Afterward, she told friends that she had discussed applying to colleges with the President, since his daughter was at Stanford University and Farrell had a daughter at prep school preparing for college.

Farrell spent her first two years in Town Hall wrestling with major challenges: the worrisome prospect that townwide capital expenditures could double taxes in the not-too-distant future. She announced that in the nation's strong economy she offered what she called a "breakeven" budget that contained no significant increases. In May 1999, a record budget was announced — $96,894,949 to run the town of Westport for the 1999-2000 fiscal year, up 6.9 percent over the previous year's budget. The education budget — over which the first selectman has no direct control — represented an increase of 11.86 percent, while the Town Hall side of the budget would rise only 0.12 percent. Showing her desire to protect public funds, she eschewed an RTM subcommittee recommendation to raise her salary by 13 percent, but later said she would accept a 3-percent raise, which would apply on average across the board to all Town Hall employees — including the departments and agencies reporting to her. The first selectman's salary in 1999 was $87,550.

Meanwhile, a major victory in the drive to preserve open space took place on January 29, 1999, when the town officially acquired the 22.6-acre Baron's South property on the corner of Post Road and Compo Road South, just across from Winslow Park. The RTM had approved the $7 million purchase by a 31-4 vote on October 20, 1998. The closing took place at Town Hall when First Selectman Diane Farrell and Town Attorney Ira Bloom handed over the $7 million payment to the Baron's heirs. Even before the town closed on the purchase, debate raged over what to do with the property. Some wanted it to remain as open space; others wanted to locate a community center, a senior center, or an arts center there. The most controversial proposal came from the YMCA, which suggested relocating to Baron's South from its overcrowded facility on the corner of Post Road East and Main Street — its home for more than seven decades. Farrell appointed a special committee headed by Harold Levine, which recommended that the town not permit any construction "at the present time" on either Baron's South or the more level terrain of Winslow Park. Farrell said she thought the report was thorough. As promised at the time of the purchase, she then asked the RTM for a "sense of the meeting" resolution on the plan that she would eventually have to implement. She initially recommended that the property not be used for the YMCA building because, she said, it would take up nearly one-third of the space available and she said that "future Town of Westport municipal development opportunities would include but are not limited to: the relocation of the police station, the relocation of the Parks and Recreation maintenance facility currently at Longshore, athletic fields, the brush/leaf transfer area and community gardens." She also recommended that a portion of the Baron's South property be sold to defray the purchase price.

With no clear support from the RTM, Farrell announced that she would contact and begin work with a nonprofit municipal-space-planning organization for a thorough review of the entire Westport downtown area. She said in a letter to RTM members that it was "warranted and may in fact help solve the Y's as well a some of the town's other downtown challenges, including parking and better utilization of the Jesup Green area." [24] Aware that there is little space left in town for development, Farrell appeared to be searching for a consensus from the community about what the residents want for

DEVELOPMENT OUTLOOK:
Chamber of Commerce President Lois Schine concedes that there is little land left in town for commercial development, but wants to use existing space to its fullest.
STEVE ZAVATSKI PHOTO

Westport in the future. Even Chamber of Commerce President Lois Schine admitted: "Under current zoning laws, commercially zoned property is pretty much filled up, leaving not much space for expansion. Therefore, for the foreseeable future, the focus of the Chamber will be on maximizing utilization to the fullest."[25]

Following on the heels of the Baron's South purchase, the town added another .83-acre parcel on April 6, 1999, when the RTM voted 27-5 to approve $1.2 million to buy the Allen's Clam and Lobster House property on Hillspoint Road fronting the Sherwood Mill Pond. Farrell managed to recover some of the funding through private donations that included gifts of $50,000 each from Paul Newman and film mogul Harvey Weinstein. Another prominent Westporter, culinary guru Martha Stewart, contributed $10,000.[26] Even with the generous contributions from Stewart, Newman, and Weinstein, however, the first selectman temporarily fell short of her goal of privately raising half the purchase price by appealing to those wishing to perform a service to the community. Meanwhile, a committee headed by Roy Dickinson and appointed by Farrell determined that the restaurant should remain in place for another five years. As an interim solution, the town agreed to lease the restaurant for five years. Farrell continued to seek private funding.

Farrell also announced the formation of a new Charter Revision Committee, to which she appointed former Town Clerk Joan Hyde and former First Selectman Marty Hauhuth as co-chairmen. Hyde had retired as Town Clerk in early 1998 after 47 years of service to the town. She served 12 terms under nine different first selectmen. The last time the charter was revised was during Bill Seiden's administration (1981-1985). The charter is the principal town document that establishes the outline of town government. Farrell's most admirable trait, most observers agree, is her ability to listen. Her "brown bag" lunches on Wednesdays have given residents a sense that local government is open to them, that it is made up of people, and is not just some entity controlling their lives. While she has maintained good will and public support from many quarters, her style of appointing committees rather than making decisions herself, has been questioned by some Republicans. The townspeople were watching her closely as her third year in office unfolded. However, one thing remained clear: Ms. Farrell was

BROWN BAGGING IT: First Selectman Diane Goss Farrell, far end of table in Town Hall, takes the pulse of the people as she presides over a typical Wednesday "brown bag lunch." The luncheons attract many townspeople who want to ask her questions or tell her about their concerns. It has been praised by almost everyone who attends as a successful means of two-way communications.

MIGGS BURROUGHS PHOTO

still popular with the voters at the outset of the millennium. Even though she was not on the ticket because her term does not expire until 2001, the November 1999 election returns in Westport showed that her coattails had at least a two-year life. The voters kept the Democrats in power, enabling them to continue to control the boards and commissions.

Also in 1999 Westport's Board of Education grappled with the challenge of building new schools and repairing others as a result of a projected enrollment increase in the immediate future. The Westport School Building Committee, with Jo Fuchs Luscombe as chairman and Tammy Pincavage as vice chairman, continued its work overseeing a number of projects, including the new $38 million North Avenue Middle School, the reopening and expansion of the Green's Farms School, which cost the town $16 million; and the $19 million renovation and rehabilitation of the Coleytown Middle School. The renovation and expansion of Staples and the conversion of Bedford Middle School to an elementary school were still in the planning stage.

These and many other educational challenges were handed to incoming Schools Superintendent Dr. Elliott Landon, who succeeded Dr. Paul Kelleher, a controversial educator with a national reputation for excellence who, nonetheless, managed to alienate many Westporters with his dogmatic top-down management style. He left on a note of sharp discord, unaccountably blasting those who had criticized him at the Staples graduation ceremonies in 1998. Other newsworthy events in 1999 included the unsuccessful effort by Westport gadfly David Royce to persuade the RTM to vote for his proposal to ban guns in Westport. His gun control request came in the aftermath of the shooting tragedy at the Columbine High School in Colorado.

In December more than 200 Westporters who had served on the RTM since its inception in 1949 gathered together to celebrate its 50th birthday with a party and meeting at Town Hall. As Allen Raymond, a former moderator, said: "The nice thing is it's a bunch of Republicans and Democrats working together." With RTM member Ann Sheffer and others arranging for the event and printing a special program containing the history of the town's legislative body, the members voted Moderator Gordon Joseloff and Deputy Moderator William Raines to another two-year term. Joseloff called the RTM "the most important body of government in our town." At the meeting, a number of accomplishments were mentioned as a result of Alice Shelton's research, including the fact that Mary Jenkins had been the RTM's only woman moderator (1977-1986). The Gilbertie family had five members — the most members who served the RTM, starting with John Gilbertie, Sr. who was a member of the original RTM in 1949.

In Westport, as in the world in general, the twentieth century proved to be the most dynamic in history, a time of rapid change, of technological breakthroughs, of dramatic improvement in living standards, and of a communications revolution that made the world smaller, countries more interdependent, and cities and towns across America daring and bold in their hopes and dreams. Westport celebrated the turn of the new century, as it had in 1901, with fireworks and a celebration that involved more than 8,000 participants and 400 volunteers. One highlight of the alcohol-free "First Night" event was the unveiling of a Millennium Quilt, sponsored by the Westport Millennium Committee, which stitched together wishes for the future from hundreds of residents. It hangs in the lobby of Town Hall, across from the Bicentennial Quilt which celebrates Westport's history, thus epitomizing the theme of the millennium celebrations here and across the country: "Honor the Past and Imagine the Future."

What does the future hold in store for Westport? Generally, there is optimism with the arrival of the new millennium. Watts Wacker, a Westporter and a futurist, has an upbeat view of Westport's future. He recently wrote in his online newsletter: "Westport [in 2099] will be the crown jewel of the New York 'Mythopolis' by virtue of the critical mass of its creative expression in the performing, physical, literary, intellectual and commercial arts — including a number still undreamed of."[27] Quite an exciting forecast for a small town that has risen through the centuries to prominence in America.

NOTES

1. The book, *A Community of Artists*, designed by Howard Munce, was the idea of Joyce Thompson, then president of the Westport-Weston Arts Council.
2. Eve Potts is the source.
3. The *Westport News*, August 9, 1985.
4. Statement provided by Martha S. Hauhuth, July, 1999.
5. The *Westport News,* April 30, 1986; August 26, 1987.
6. Dieter Stanko, Connecticut, Section 14, the *New York Times,* December 19, 1999, p. 2.
7. The *Minuteman*, December 8, 1994.
8. Statement from Ruth Hickox, December 1999.
9. The *Westport News*, May 13, 1992.
10. The *Westport News*, February 24, 1993.
11. Statement from Rabbi Robert Orkand, December 1999.
12. The *Westport News*, December 3, 1999.
13. Statement from Leonard Rovins, December 1999. Rovins has been Westport's labor negotiator under eight consecutive first selectmen.
14. Statement to the author from Nat Hentoff, September, 1999.
15. In an interview with Paul Lane, former Staples High School football coach, in January 2000, he said the prowess of Staples High School athletes down through the years has been one of the school's most outstanding achievements. "Over the last 30 years, if you were a coach at Staples, you were in a very competitive league. Staples has had its share of championships." Lane, who coached football from 1954 to 1967, noted that his undefeated and untied 1975 team, led by Captain Len Hartman, won the state championship. Another great football team, he says, was the 1963 club, which went into the state championship with an 8-0 record but lost. The team with "the greatest backfield," he says, was the 1964 team with a 7-2 record. The backfield consisted of John Bolger, left halfback, who played football at West Point; Buzz Levitt, right halfback, who played football at Wake Forest; Bill During, fullback, who played football at Syracuse; and Jack Forehand, who did not play at Georgia. *The Norwalk Hour,* says Lane, called this backfield "the best ever" in Staples' history. Interestingly, Lane coached two sons at quarterback, Skip Lane '79, who went on to play professional football with the New York Jets, the Kansas City Chiefs, and the Washington Redskins; and Pete Lane '81, who played quarterback for University of Connecticut. In all, Lane says he has coached more than 18,000 youngsters in football, track, and basketball.
16. Ibid., the *Westport News*, February 5, 1993.
17. Office of the Town Clerk, Controller's Office.
18. The *Westport News*, March 5, 1993.
19. Ibid., November 8, 1996.
20. Interviews by the author, 1998-1999.
21. Woody Klein, the *New York Times*, Connecticut Weekly, May 12, 1996, p. 1.
22. Author's interview with Gene Gavin, January 21, 2000.
23. Text of President Clinton's speech at the luncheon made available by Westporter

Robert Rose, the host of the event.

24. Letter dated November 4, 1999 to all members of the RTM, "Re: Plans for the Baron's South Property."

25. Statement from Lois Schine, September 29, 1999.

26. Martha Stewart created an international stir in October 1999 when her company, Martha Stewart Living Omnimedia, held one of the most successful initial stock offerings in history. Her estimated worth reportedly was $1.2 billion.

27. Watts Wacker, Westport futurist, *Firstmatter*, Internet, September 20, 1999.

Photo, p. 311, Fine Arts Theatre closing, 1999. Miggs Burroughs.

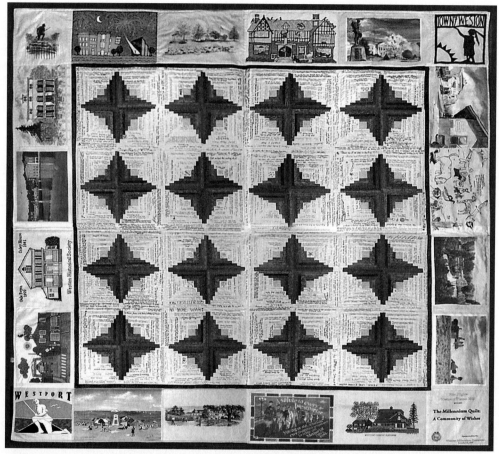

FIRST NIGHT WESTPORT/WESTON 2000 MILLENNIUM QUILT: "A Community of Wishes" Chairmen: Totney B. Benson, Carol Cohen, Kassie Foss. Participating artists: (Clockwise, from top left corner:) Al Willmott, Minuteman statue; Westport Library & Levitt Pavilion, Miggs Burroughs; Weston Town Hall, Lynn Sellon; Westport/Weston YMCA, Carol Young; Westport Town Hall, Tracy Sugarman; Weston sign, Totney Benson; Westport train station, Kathy Ross; Westport Parks, Sarah Kennedy; Cobb's Mill Inn, Weston, Kathy Jakobsen; Compo Beach Cannons, Andrea Fine; Dedication square, Totney Benson; Westport Country Playhouse, Barbara Bangser; Westport Memorial Day parade, Howard Munce; Longshore Inn & golf course, Al Willmott; Compo Beach, Maryanne Charmoz; Westport flag, Totney Benson/Miggs Burroughs; Saugatuck, Naiad Einsel; Weston Historical Society, Gale Beyea; National Hall and Saugatuck River, Andrea Fine; Westport Historical Society, Kassie Foss. Dedicated December 31,1999. Sponsored by the Westport Millennium Committee, Ann Sheffer chairman.

APPENDIXES

APPENDIX A
Westport at a Glance

- **Size**: 22.4 square miles with 122.22 total road miles.

- **Type of town**: residential/retail/service. Virtually no manufacturing.

- **Population demographics:** 25,100 – 13,148 males, 11,952 females. Make-up: 93 percent white; 1 percent black; 3 percent Asian Pacific; 3 percent Hispanic; .01 percent Native American.

- **Median age**: 39.3 years. The largest age categories are 40-44 (2,363), 45-49 (2,357), 50-54 (2,204). Among senior citizens, the age categories are: 65-69 (1,156), 70-74 (1,120), 75-79 (827), 80-84 (507), 85 and older (410).

- **Labor force**: 16,670 people. Unemployment is 1.6 percent; 1.3 percent of families are below the poverty level; 61 people are on welfare.

- **Households**: 9,891 with an average of 2.54 persons per household.

- **Homes**: Average sales price of homes sold, January-September, 1999: $814,022; 47 homes sold for over $1 million.

- **Average family income:** $91,000.

- **Number of automobiles:** 23,551 — 47 percent sports utility vehicles, 17 percent luxury cars, 36 percent sedans and station wagons.

- **Municipal Bond Rating:** Aaa

- **Annual Town Budget:** $96.9 million for 1999-2000; $3,954.58 per capita on townwide services.

- **Environment rating:** #1 in Connecticut (as of January, 1998).

- **Media:** Two local newspapers, two magazines.

- **Yearly precipitation:** 47.5 inches.

- **Public Library:** Circulation: 578,379 items, including books, the second busiest in the state in terms of circulation per capita, with an average of 1,200 visitors per day.

- **Commerce:** More than 3,000 business establishments, 2.5 million square feet of office space and 1.5 million square feet of retail space. 12 banks, 660 retail outlets, 93 establishments selling or serving liquor and more than 100 restaurants. Of the town's business establishments, 46 percent are in service; 26 percent in trade; 12 percent in finance; insurance and real estate; 7 percent in light manufacturing, 3.9 percent in transportation and utilities, 3 percent in construction and mining, 1.1 percent in government, 0.9 percent in agriculture.

- **School System:** 4 elementary schools, 2 middle schools, one high school; 4,678 pupils including pre-kindergarten, with an average per-pupil expenditure of $11,232, among the highest in the state. Latest available figures list Westport as #2 behind Greenwich in 1997-98 with per pupil average of $10,475. Adult Education year-round program, several nursery schools and day care centers. Two private schools: Landmark Academy, which offers a preschool for ages 3 to 5, and Green's Farms Academy, a co-ed day school for K-12.

- **Average Scholastic Aptitude Scores:** (1999) 552: verbal, 561: math. A combined score of 1,113. More than 93 percent continue their education.

- **Total Town Worth:** $8 billion (includes all real estate, motor vehicles, personal property, commercial, industrial, public utilities).

Sources: Planning and Zoning Commission; Board of Education; Controller's Office; Westport Chamber of Commerce; Westport/Weston Health District; State of Connecticut Office of Policy and Management; the Connecticut Policy and Expenditures Council; Westport Town-Line; The *New York Times;* The *Westport News;* The *Minuteman; Connecticut* magazine; Fairfield County Community Foundaton; State of Connecticut Department of Transportation; State of Connecticut Department of Economic and Community Development; Southwestern Regional Planning Association; U.S. Department of Commerce; Moody's Investors Service.

Photo, p. 349, Compo Beach pavilion, Andrea Fine.

APPENDIX B
Bankside Farmers' Agreement with Town of Fairfield

Impramus: It is agreed that Thomas Newton, Henry Gray and John Green shall have liberty to sit down and inhabit at Machamux: and shall have for each of them laid out as in property to themselves and their heirs forever, twenty acres in upland, to be laid out indifferently by the appointment of said town, in a convenient place, where it may not be too obnoxious to the depasturing and feeding of the cattle of said town. And that if they improve the said land, to make a sufficient mound or fence, or mounds and fences, to secure their said town and land from the trespass of the cattle of the inhabitants of said town. And their fence shall be viewed by said town, or their deputies, whether or no, and shall be therein subject to such orders as the town shall make about other farms of the town.

ITEM: That there shall be sufficient passage and way of ways for the cattle of said Fairfield to pass to the sea-shore; and all the way to feed and depasture to and again in those parts; and that neither the inhabitants of the said town nor their cattle may be prevented that way.

ITEM: That there may be sufficient quantity of meadow land laid out by the inhabitants of said town, or their deputies, to the parties above said, for their comfortable subsistence in that place. And that the parties above shall only keep their own sheep in and upon their said land and commons adjoining, and not take cattle to foragement and depasture in the commons of said town.

ITEM: That the aforesaid parties and their heirs be subject to all taxes and rates of the said town wherein they have a common benefit together with said town, and are subject to the officers of said town, save only watch in and warding.

ITEM: That there may be liberty to said parties to take in two more inhabitants by full consent and approbation of the town of Fairfield: and that they be approved as aforesaid, there may be like quantity of upland and meadow set out to them by the town upon the terms aforesaid.

ITEM: It is agreed that if said town and the parties are not agreed between themselves about the meadows and upland, the court to be the indifferent judges.

The above said is a true copy of the original paper that I found in the file of the Court acts left with me as Clerk by Mr. Ludlow. The frontispiece of the original writing I have not copied it being so defaced and worn through age that I cannot take a copy thereof but I find it was an agreement between the Town of Fairfield and the above said parties (and) the Court, it being the tenth day of November 1648.
Willm Hill Clerk

Series 1, Vol. 1, Doc. 52
Conn. State Library
Connecticut Archives
Manuscript Index

APPENDIX C

Westport Postmasters

Post Office Established on July 7, 1835

Ira Baldwin:	July 7, 1835
William Platt:	March 11, 1837
Hezekish Nichols	May 26, 1841
George L. Coble	May 10, 1884
John W. Taylor	July 5, 1849
Solomon C. Taylor	July 2, 1853
George L. Coble	July 16, 1853
Edward M. Lees	April 27, 1861
John S. Jones	Jan. 22, 1865
Henry P. Burr	April 29, 1869
William E. Nash	June 7, 1877
Henry P. Burr	Aug. 7, 1882
George F. Thorpe	Aug. 9, 1886
John R. Palmer	Sept. 27, 1890
Joseph G. Hyatt	Oct. 25, 1891
Samuel B. Kluch	Feb. 13, 1896
Charles Harris	Jan. 18, 1900
William J. Woods	Dec. 16, 1915
William Krause	Dec. 17, 1924
John J. Murphy	June 12, 1933
Edward McElwee	Dec. 18, 1936
Edward J. Butner	Feb. 25, 1954
John P. Grant	Dec. 9, 1972
John Wocanowicz	1986-1991
James Long	1991-

Saugatuck Postmasters*

Post Office Established on July 1, 1807

Stephen Barlow	July 1, 1807
Stephen Morehouse	N/A
Ira Baldwin	Nov. 26, 1833

*P.O. Discontinued July 7, 1835.
Name changed to Westport. Saugatuck P.O.
P.O. Re-established Oct. 28, 1852

Harvey Allen	Oct. 28, 1852
Edwin L. Stevenson	April 17, 1863
J.E. Hubbell	April 29, 1869
Francis Driscol	Feb. 14, 1890
Hiram Jelliffe	March 12, 1898
Gould D. Jelliffe	Aug. 6, 1898
Arthur B. Jelliffe	Dec. 9, 1902
Joseph Morton	June 17, 1910
Robert T. Oatis	Oct. 23, 1913
Florence Remlin	June 1, 1919
Frank J. Serena	April 29, 1920
Joseph V. Serena	Dec. 16, 1925
Irving Putney	March 18, 1927
Frank H. Northrup	Aug. 4, 1928**

**P.O. Discontinued June 30, 1929.
Made a station of Westport.

APPENDIX D
Petition of Daniel Nash to the Connecticut
General Assembly

To the Hon. General Assembly of the State of Connecticut to be Held at Hartford in said State on the first Wednesday of May 1835. The petition of Daniel Nash, San Taylor, Seth Taylor and Taylor Hurlbutt and Henry Sherwood all of Norwalk in the County of Fairfield. John Q. Wilson, Lewis Raymond, Nathaniel L. Hill, David Richmond and William H. Jesup all of Fairfield in said county and Mathis Coley, Morehouse Coley and John Goodsell of Weston in said county and others whose names are hereinto subscribed living in the towns aforesaid respectfully herewith. That there is a population of about 1600 souls living on the west side of the town of Fairfield aforesaid and the East Side of said Norwalk and on the south side of the society of Norfield in the town of Weston aforesaid and within the following boundaries viz. Commencing at the Northwest corner bound of the town of Fairfield on Sturges Highway so called and running southerly in the center of said highway to a point half a mile south of Cross Highway so called thence westerly to a Stone bridge in the highway south and near the dwelling house of Bradford Davis. Thence southerly in the center of said highway last mentioned turns westerly and thence south easterly to the west fence of the old burying grounds in Greens farms thence following said creek to Gallops Bridge so called. Thence in a due south course to Long Island, again commencing at the first mentioned boundry and running Westerly in said Weston, crossing Aspatuck and Saugatuck rivers, passing north of the dwelling house of Paul Sherwood to the diving line between the towns of Weston and Norwalk at a stone bridge in the highway a little south of the dwelling house of the late Daniel Dikeman deceased thence northerly in said highway on the line between said Weston and Norwalk to the northeast corner boundry of said Norwalk, thence following the dividing line between Norwalk and Wilton to a stone boundary in the highway north westerly of he dwelling house of the late James Fillow deceased and near an oak tree long known as a town boundry between said Norwalk and Wilton. Thence southerly to the center of road at the four corners so called near the blacksmiths shop lately occupied by Darius Olmstead now deceased. Thence to the center of said highway, passing David M. Fillows dwelling house, southerly to the barn, commonly known and called Muncys barn, thence southerly to a stone bridge over Saugatuck brook so called a little west of Joseph Scribners on the Old Country Road so called. Thence southerly to the center of the highway heading around Duck Pond so called and following the center of said highway until it reaches the head of said Pond and thence in a due south course to Long Island Sound. That territory within said boundaries embraces a part of Fairfield, Weston and Norwalk aforesaid and the inhabitants living within it are subjected to great inconveniences of living on the borders of the aforementioned towns, and a majority of them must travel more than six miles to do the ordinary town business, to attend town and electors meetings, to examine records and to have deeds recorded. The inhabitants living at the seaport within the limits aforesaid, in most of their public improvements, living at the seaport within the limits aforesaid, have interests diverse from those of the seaports in Fairfield and Norwalk and such improvements however valuable are often defeated by those other portions of the towns who have the control and possible different interests. It is also believed that small towns are managed with much less expenses than larger ones. It is well known that the towns of Fairfield, Norwalk and Weston are each large in territory and population and your petitioners who compose nearly all the electors living within said limits cannot doubt that it will be greatly to their interest to be separated and becoming a town by themselves. They therefore pray your honors to inquire into the allegations aforesaid and on finding the same to be true, to grant our petitions request and pass on act incorporating a town within the limits aforesaid with all such rights and privileges as are usually bestowed upon towns in this state, or grant to your petitioners such other and further relief as your honors shall deem right and proper and your petitioners as in duty bound will ever pray. Dated at Fairfield on this 28th day of April, 1835.

It was signed by Daniel Nash and 145 other townspeople in the following order: David Sanford, Nathan Gregory, William Bradley, William S. Comstock, James Gilbert, Hiram Hoyt, Plaid W. Fairchild, David Richardson, George Blackman, Stephen Morehouse, E.B. Williams, Edwin Hurlbutt, Daniel Andrews, Lewis Raymond, Andrew Comstack, Nathaniel L. Hill, Lewis N. Nash, S.P. Hunneyman, Sam Downes, Samuel Wood, Jesse B. Scribner, William Richards, Thomas H. Richards, David Coley, Philo Smith, Oliver Burr, Ozias M. Bennett, John B. Bennett, Peter Winton, Jesse Linn, Benjamin Allen, Thomas Bennett, Daniel S. Perry, David B. Bennett, Wakeman Couch, John Q. Wilson, Francis L. Hedenberg, James Bennett, Maltbie Allen, John Hilton, Joseph Disbrow, Edwin B. Bennett, Burr Keeler, Allen Hilton, Dennis Nash, Charles Wright, Dan Taylor, Edwin Taylor, George Seely, Davis Taylor, George N. Hurlbutt, Edwin Wheeler, William Nash, Hezekiah Wakeman, John W. Taylor, Philo W. Jones, Oscar Weed, G.P. Williams, George Sanford, William Platt, Henry Platt, Aaron Adams, John B. Adams, Obediah Wright, Seth Taylor, Taylor Hurlbutt, Charles Nash, David Lord, George Nash, Lewis Smith, John Sturges, Keeler Nash, William Burwell, William Hanford, Andrew C. Nash, Joseph L. Marvin, Isaac Adams, David S. Hubbell, David M. Marvin, Platt Pearsall, Gould Jelliff, Sylvester Stevens, John Baker, Coley Bartram, Henry Sherwood, Samuel Finch, Alva Finch, Alfred Taylor, Paul L. Taylor, David Taylor, David Fillow, Lewis Patrick, Moses Gregory, Stephen Hanford, Nathan O. Gregory, Zalmon Sanford, John Allen, Henry H. Nash, Edward H. Nash, Solomon G. Taylor, George Folet, James Fillow, Joseph Scribner, George Scribner, Edwin Taylor, John Platt, Josiah Raymond, Gilbert Taylor, Gilbert H. Taylor, Lewis Goodsell, Nathan Smith, John Taylor, William E. Dikeman, Ebenezer Bennett, Gould N. Banks, Uriah Taylor, John Allen, Daniel Platt, Richard Pike, Charles Jesup, William H. Jesup, Seymour Taylor, Elnathan Wheeler, Dennis H. Peck, Isaac Bennett, Stephen B. Wakeman, Burr Meeker, Daniel Taylor, Samuel S. Smith, Joseph Meeker, Jr., Andrew B. Godfrey, Daniel Murray, Gershom B. Guyer, John Allen, Robert Raymond, Israel Brotherton, Walter Gray, Henry Gray, Seymour Taylor, Walter Coley, Zalmon Adams, John Goodsell, Morehouse Coley, William Coley, Silas Meeker.

APPENDIX E
Charter of the Town of Westport

At a General Assembly of the State of Connecticut holden at Hartford in said State on the first Wednesday of May in the year of our Lord One Thousand Eight Hundred and Thirty Five.

Upon petition of Daniel Nash and others, inhabitants of that part lies within the limits hereafter described, stating that they live non the borders of the towns aforesaid and a majority of them more than six miles from the place where Town and Electors meetings are always held and the Town Records are always kept and suffer great inconvenience in consequence thereof. That the rival sea ports in said Norwalk and Fairfield on which is within said limits have conflicting interests and the growth and prosperity of such as lie far from the centre are thereby greatly retarded, praying to be incorporated as per petition on file dated the 28th day of April 1835.

Resolved by this Assembly that the parts of the several towns of Fairfield, Norwalk and Weston in Fairfield County lying within the following limits, namely; commencing at the Northwest corner of the town of Fairfield on Sturgesí Highway so called, and running Southerly in the centre of Said highway to a point half a mile south of the cross highway so called thence westerly to a stone bridge in the highway South and near the dwelling houses of Bradford Jarrod; thence Southerly in the centre of said highway last mentioned past the Dwelling house of Lockwood Baker to where said highway turns westerly and thence southeasterly to the west fence of the old burying ground in Greens Farms, thence following the course of said fence to compo creek so called thence following the east side of said Creek to Gallops-gap bridge so called the east end thereof thence in a due south course to Long Island Sound, again commencing at the first mentioned bound and running westerly in said Weston across Aspatuck and Saugatuck rivers passing north of the dwelling house of Ruel Sherwood to the dividing line between the towns of Weston and Norwalk at a stone bridge in the highway a little south of the Dwelling house of the late Daniel Dikeman decíd. the northerly in said highway on the line between Weston and Norwalk to the Northeast corner boundary of said Norwalk thence following the dividing line between Norwalk and Wilton to a stone bound in said dividing line in the highway Northwesterly of the dwelling house of the late James Fillow Deceased and near an Oak tree long known as a town bound between said Norwalk and Wilton thence southerly to the centre of the road at the four corners so called near the blacksmithís shop lately occupied by Darius Olmsted deceased thence in the centre of said highway passing David M. Fillowís Dwelling house southerly to the barn commonly known by the name of Murrayís barn, southerly to a stone bridge over Saugatuck brook so called a little west of Joseph Scribners on the Old County road so called thence southerly to the centre to the highway leading round Duck Pond so called and following the centre of said highway until it passes the head of said Pond and thence in a due South course to Long Island Sound. South on Long Island South embracing the island situated south of said territory in Long Island Sound and in this State with all the inhabitants residing therein be and the same is hereby incorporated into a distinct Town by the name of Westport. And the Inhabitants aforesaid and their successors forever residing within said limits shall have and enjoy all the powers, privileges and immunities which are enjoyed by other towns in this state with the privilege of sending to the General Assembly of this State one Representative.

And it further Resolved that said new Town shall pay such proportion of all debts now due and accrued against each of the towns from which it is taken and of such debts and claims as either of said towns shall hereafter be liable to pay by reason of any claim now existing except claims or contracts for building any new Town House which house is not now complete or for money borrowed for that pur0pose as the list of 1834 of the part taken from any such indebted town bears to the whole list of such town for the same year.

And the poor of said town of Fairfield, Norwalk and Weston who were born within the limits hereby incorporated and who have not gained a settlement elsewhere and who have gained a settlement within said limits shall be deemed inhabitants of said Town of Westport and shall be maintained accordingly whether said poor are now maintained by said towns or not, and said town of Westport shall be liable to maintain such poor of the towns from which it is taken and are or may be absent therefrom, provided such persons or person at the time of their departure belong to either of those parts of said Towns thereby incorporated or resided therein. That the collectors of the town and state taxes of the respective towns Fairfield, Norwalk and Weston aforesaid are hereby authorized to collect their respective taxes already laid in the same manner as though this resolve have not passed but if the taxes thus collected by either of the towns last mentioned exceed the whole amount of such debts and claims against said towns as the town hereby incorporated is bound by this act to pay its proportion of, then such town shall pay over to said Westport such proportion of the balance left as the list of the part hereby taken from such towns on which such tax is laid bears to the whole list of such towns the same year. And be it further Resolved, That the first meeting of said town of Westport shall be held on the third Tuesday of June 1835 at the Presbyterian Meeting house in said Westport and Thomas F. Rowland, Esq. And in case of his failure, James C. Loomis, Esq. Shall be Moderator of said Meeting and shall warn said meeting by setting up a notification of the same on the oak tree near Meeting house and at such other places as either of said persons may deem proper at least six days before said first meeting. And said town of Westport shall at said first meeting have all the power incident to other towns in this state and full right to act accordingly to elect town officers and the officers so elected at such meet9ng shall hold forth their offices until others are chosen and sworn in their stead.

State of Connecticut at the office of the Secretary of State,
Hartford, May 28th, 1835.

I hereby certify that the foregoing is a true Copy of record in said office. In testimony whereof I have hereunto set my hand and seal of this state on the 28th of May A.D. 1835.

Roy L.R. Hinman,
Secretary

APPENDIX F
Westport Selectmen (1835 - 2001)

1835-1837
Thomas Rowland
Taylor Hurlbutt
John Gray, 2d

1838
Jabez Adams
Thomas Rowland
John Gray, 2d

1839
John Gray, 2d
Isaac Bennett
Alfred Taylor

1840-41
Jabez Adams
Thomas Rowland
Hezekiah M. Coley

1842
David Coley
John Gray, 2d
Street H. Keeler

1843
Hezekiah M. Coley
Isaac Bennett
Street H. Keeler

1844
Hezekiah M. Coley
Isaac Bennett
Burr Jennings, Jr.

1845-1848
Isaac Bennett
Gordon Jelliff
Daniel Burr

1849
Hezekiah M. Coley
Alva Gray
Alfred Taylor

1850-1851
Alva Gray
Hezekiah M. Coley
David Coley, 2nd

1852
Daniel Burr
Burr Meeker
Burr Keeler

1853
Alva Gray

1854-1855
William J. Finch
Aaron B. Adams
Lyman Banks

1856
William J. Finch
Lyman Banks
William Burwell

1857
William J. Finch
Bradley Godsell
John N. Betts

1858
William J. Finch
Bradley Godsell
Alfred Taylor

1859-1861
William J. Finch
Alfred Taylor
Talcott Wakeman

1862- 1863
William J. Finch
Edward J. Taylor
Lonson Coley

1864
William J. Finch
Franklin Sherwood
Orrin W. Hotchkiss

1865
William J. Finch
Edward Taylor
Aaron B. Hull

1866-1869
William J. Finch
Edwin J. Taylor
William T. Wood

1870-1971
William J. Finch
Edwin J. Taylor
Frederick Morehouse

1872
William J. Finch
Eaward J. Taylor
Burr Meeker

1874
Silas B. Sherwood
James Smibert
Gersham B. Bradley

1875
Charles Kemper
Silas B. Sherwood
Gershom B. Bradley

1876-1878
Charles Kemper
Silas B. Sherwood
Frederick Morehouse

1879
Gersham B. Bradley
John H. Jennings
Charles H. Kemper

1880
George S. Adams
John H. Jennings
Silas B. Sherwood

1881
Silas B. Sherwood
Henry H. Gilbert
John H. Jennings

1882
Gersham B. Bradley
John H. Jennings
Eliphalet Gray

1883
Charles H. Kemper
Eliphalet Gray
John B. Morris

1884
Charles II. Kemper
Eliphalet Gray
Rufus Wakeman

1885
Charles H. Kemper
Henry Gilbert
Rufus Wakeman

357

1886
Charles H. Kemper
Henry Gilbert
Rufus Wakeman

1887
Rufus Wakeman
Daniel Bradley, Jr.
Silas B. Sherwood

1888
Silas B. Sherwood
Orland J. Allen
Rufus Wakeman

1889-1890
John W. Hurlbutt
Daniel Bradley, Jr.
Rufus Wakeman

1891
Samuel Wheeler
Rufus Wakeman
Daniel Bradley, Jr.

1892
Samuel B. Wheeler
William H. Taylor
George P. Jennings

1893-1895
Robert Coley
Charles Buckley
Daniel Bradley, Jr.

1896-1902
Lewis P. Wakeman
Robert Coley
Oscar Smith

1902
Oscar Smith
Lewis P. Wakeman
Samuel B. Wheeler

1903-1904
Edward C. Birge
John K. Gault
Samuel B. Wheeler

1905
Lewis P. Wakeman
John K. Gault
Samuel Wheeler

1906
Edward C. Birge
John K. Gault
F.W. Taylor

1907
Fred Kemper
Edwin A. Beers
George S. Jennings

1908
Lewis P. Wakeman
Robert Coley
Merrick H. Cooley

1909-1910
Lewis P. Wakeman
Robert Coley
Samuel Banks

1911
Robert Coley
John K. Gault
Samuel Banks

1912
Robert Coley
John K. Gault
Lewis P. Wakeman

1913
Austin Wakeman
Robert Mills
Robert H. Coley

1914
Austin Wakeman
Nathanial Gault
Robert Mills

1915-1917
Austin Wakeman
Welford Lewis
Robert Mills

1917-1919
Austin Wakeman
Welford Lewis
Eli Mead

1920
Austin Wakeman
Welford Lewis
William Wood, Jr.

1921
Austin Wakeman
Welford G. Lewis
Robert Mills

1922
Austin Wakeman
Welford Lewis
Thomas Glynn

1923
E.C. Nash
Harry Ayers
Welford Lewis

1924
K.W. Mansfield
Welford Lewis
Walter Duffy

1926-1929
King W. Mansfield
Welford Lewis
John P. McCormack

1930-1931
K.W. Mansfield
Charles Wakeman
John P. McCormack

1932-1933
K.W. Mansfield
Charles Wakeman
Milton D. Harrington

1935
K.W. Mansfield
Alois J. Forger
Milton D. Harrington

1937
K.W. Mansfield
Alois J. Forger
Willard R. Williams

1939
K.W. Mansfield
Alois J. Forger
Harold Von Schmidt

1941
K.W. Mansfield
John P. Brennan
Harold Von Schmidt

1943
Albert T. Scully
Harold Von Schmidt
K.W. Mansfield

1944-1946
Albert T. Scully
Harold Von Schmidt
W. Clarke Crossman

1946-1948
Emerson F. Parker
W. Clarke Crossman
Daniel B. Driscoll

1948-1949
Albert B. Scully
W. Clarke Crossman
Daniel B. Driscoll

1949-1952
W. Clarke Crossman
C. William Janson
Albert B. Scully

1952
W. Clarke Crossman
C. William Janson
Hedwig Sloan

1953
W. Clarke Crossman
C. William Janson
Charles F. Spear

1955
W. Clarke Crossman
Emerson F. Parker
Jeanette Egan

1957
Herbert E. Baldwin
Elliott J. Roberts
Allbert T. Scully

1959-1961
Herbert E. Baldwin
Elliott J. Roberts
Albert T. Scully

1963
Herbert E. Baldwin
Elliott J. Roberts
Emerson F. Parker

1965
Herbert E. Baldwin
Elliott J. Roberts
Gerald E. Wheeler

1967
John J. Kemish
Wildes W. Veazie, Jr.
Gerald E. Wheeler

1969
John J. Kemish
Thomas Delmar Lyne
Mark J. Marcus

1971
John J. Kemish
Howard L. Kany
Mark J. Marcus

1973 -1975
Jacqueline Heneage
Theodore Diamond
John J. Kemish

1975-1977
Jacqueline Heneage
Theodore Diamond
Vincent J. Rotondo

1977-1981
Jacqueline Heneage
Theodore Diamond
Vincent J. Rotondo

1981-1985
William Seiden
Barbara Butler
Martha S. Hauhuth

1985-1989
Martha S. Hauhuth
Randolph W. Meyer
William Seiden
[Barbara Butler]

1989-1993
Douglas R. Wood
Tamarra R. Pincavage
Martha S. Hauhuth

1993-1997
Joseph P. Arcudi
Betty Lou Cummings
Nicholas W. Thiemann

1997-2001
Diane G. Farrell
Carl Leaman
Joseph P. Arcudi

APPENDIX G
Town Clerks (1835 - 2000)

1835	Edwin Wheeler	1897-1911	Joseph G. Hyatt
1835-1838	Lewis Raymund	1912-1914	W.J. Wood, Sr.
1839-1873	John W. Taylor	1915-1934	E.C. Birge
1873-1879	Edward J. Taylor	1934-1944	William A. Krause
1880-1881	Henry P. Burr	1944-1959	Lois R. Clark
1882-1885	William J. Finch	1959-1963	Dorothy Janson
1886-1887	Henry P. Burr	1963-1998	Joan M. Hyde
1888-1897	William J. Finch	1998-	Patricia H. Strauss

APPENDIX H
Westport Historical Society Presidents

1889-9   Horace Staples
(Note: The name changed to Saugatuck Historical Society
in 1890; voted to admit women to membership in 1894).

1897-98   Rev. George Weed Barhydt

1898-99   Rev. James Edward Coley

1899-01   William H. Saxton

1901-03   Rev. George Weed Barhydt

1903-06   Thomas C. Stearns

1906-07   Rev. Ellis B. Dean

1907-08   William H. Burr

1908-10   Col. John N. Partridge

1910-12   John F. Godillot

1912-14   William L. Taylor and Acting
              President Merrick H. Cooley

1914-16   Rev. Kenneth Mackenzie

1916-   Sylvester M. Foster
(Note: The next record is of an organizational meeting
on December 14, 1957 as the Westport-Weston
Historical Society, recipient of a $59 bank account.)

1957-58   Harry R. Sherwood

1958-59   Joseph Adams

1959-61   George H. Waltz (died 9-30-61)

1961-62   James Daugherty, President pro tem
              (named Honorary President in 1963)

1962-66   John R. Cuneo

(Note: name changed to Westport Historical Society).

1966-67   John Sherwood

1967-69   Julia Dorothy Bradley

1969-73   Robert Gault

1973-77   Peggy Henkel

1977-83   Bobby Elmer

1983-85   Joan Dickinson

1985-87   Beverly MacGregor

1989-91   Helen Luedke

1991-93   Barbara Shriver

1993-95   Cheryl Bliss

1995-97   A.K. (Pete) Wolgast

1997-99   Roy M. Dickinson

1999-   Darlene Letersky

Executive Director: Sheila O'Neill

APPENDIX I
World War II Westporters Died in Service

Ball, Donald
Cherub, Michael P.
Cuseo, James
DeMaria, Charles
Dougherty, William E., Jr.
Dustman, Roger F.
Elder, David Page
Finnegan, Thomas R.
Gair, George W., Jr.
Gallo, Antonio
George, L. Livingston
Gerlach, Frank J.
Gish, Carl K., Jr.
Giannitti, Frank, Jr.
Harrison, Charles D.
Hoy, Dion A.
Jones, Willis H., Jr.
Karstensen, Merton E.
Keith, John M.
Laidlaw, Thomas
Lauterbach, Sebastian P., Jr.
Lindquist, R. Vernon

Lown, William D.
Malins, Victor P.
McKenna, E. Sheridan
Meyers, William T.
Miller, Douglas E.
Nash, Lloyd W.
Potvin, Samuel G.
Reilly, William S.
Rohr, Gustav
Rohr, Jospeh L.
Skau, George E.
Slade, George L.
Smith, Douglas E.
Suduv, James
Taylor, George
Tremonte, Liberty
Vani, Michael J.
Wassell, Charles P.
Wassell, Frank L., Jr.
Wassell, Harry B., II
Westing, Ann

APPENDIX J
Representative Town Meeting Moderators
(1949 - 2000)

Harry R. Sherwood	1949-50
Bernard S. Peck	1950-51
Herbert E. Baldwin	1951-57
Allen A. Raymond	1957-59
Ralph Sheffer	1959-69
Edwin H. Kahn	1969-73
Donald J. Lunghino	1973-77
Mary M. Jenkins	1977-86
Douglas R. Wood	1986-89
Anthony J. Lowe	1989-95
Gordon Joseloff	1995-

SPONSORS

This book was made possible
by the generous support
of the following individuals and organizations:

THE BETTY R. SHEFFER FOUNDATION

THE WESTPORT WOMAN'S CLUB

L. H. GAULT & SON, INC.

TAUCK TOURS

SONS OF ITALY

MARTHA STEWART LIVING TELEVISION

THE WESTPORT YOUNG WOMEN'S LEAGUE

STEW LEONARD'S

WESTPORT NEWS

BARBARA AND PAUL VAN ORDEN

BETSY AND ROY DICKINSON

ANN SHEFFER AND BILL SCHEFFLER

JANET AND PETE WOLGAST

WITH MATCHING CORPORATE GIFTS FROM:

EXXONMOBIL

PFIZER

PHILIP MORRIS

GENERAL ELECTRIC

FEDERATED DEPARTMENT STORES

INDEX

Photo, p. 363, George Silk

About the Author

WOODY KLEIN, an award winning author and journalist, has been a columnist for the *Westport News* for three decades. He served as editor of that newspaper from 1992 to 1997. In 1998 Mr. Klein, a Westport resident for 33 years, was commissioned by the Westport Historical Society to write this book. He earned a B.A. from Dartmouth College and an M.S. from the Graduate School of Journalism, Columbia University. After college, he served as a U.S. Army Public Information Officer during the Korean War. He began his career as a reporter on the Mount Vernon (N.Y.) *Daily Argus*, became a reporter for the *Washington Post*, and then an investigative reporter and columnist for the *New York World-Telegram & Sun*. In 1965 he was appointed as New York Mayor John V. Lindsay's first press secretary. In 1968 he joined IBM and served as editor of *Think* Magazine until he retired in 1992. Mr. Klein has written two books, *Let in the Sun*, and *Lindsay's Promise*. He contributes to numerous publications and he has been an adjunct professor of journalism at Fairfield University, the University of Bridgeport, and Iona College, New Rochelle, N.Y. He has served as a member of the Westport Representative Town Meeting and is on the board of the United Way of Westport-Weston.

About the Designer

MIGGS BURROUGHS, a lifelong resident of Westport, has been creating award-winning graphic design since 1972, including a U.S. Commemorative Postage Stamp, several covers for *Time* Magazine, as well as hundreds of logos, posters and brochures. In 1985 he was chosen to design the Westport town flag, and continues to do work for many community organizations. He has taught graphic design at Fairfield University and at UCONN, and has been the producer/host of MIGGS B ON TV, a Cablevision program, since 1984. A 1998 YMCA Faces of Achievement honoree, he serves on the Board of both the YMCA and the Levitt Pavilion. Miggs is also the recipient of the 1999 Distinguished Arts Advocate Award from the Connecticut Commission on the Arts, and the 1999 Paul Harris Fellowship award from the Westport Rotary. A 1967 graduate of Carnegie Institute of Technology's School of Drama, Miggs is listed in *Who's Who in the East*.